Law and Society

An Introduction

Law and Society
An Introduction

John Harrison Watts • Cliff Roberson

CRC Press
Taylor & Francis Group
Boca Raton London New York

CRC Press is an imprint of the
Taylor & Francis Group, an **informa** business

CRC Press
Taylor & Francis Group
6000 Broken Sound Parkway NW, Suite 300
Boca Raton, FL 33487-2742

© 2014 by Taylor & Francis Group, LLC
CRC Press is an imprint of Taylor & Francis Group, an Informa business

No claim to original U.S. Government works

Printed on acid-free paper
Version Date: 20130923

International Standard Book Number-13: 978-1-4665-8329-0 (Hardback)

Library of Congress Cataloging-in-Publication Data

Watts, John Harrison, author.
    Law and society : an introduction / John Harrison Watts, Cliff Roberson.
        p. cm.
    Includes bibliographical references and index.
    ISBN 978-1-4665-8329-0 (hardback)
    1. Sociological jurisprudence. 2. Law--Philosophy. I. Roberson, Cliff, 1937- author. II. Title.

K370.W38 2014
340'.115--dc23   2013037631

Visit the Taylor & Francis Web site at
http://www.taylorandfrancis.com

and the CRC Press Web site at
http://www.crcpress.com

Contents

Preface   xv
About the Authors   xvii

1   An Overview of Law and Society   1

     Chapter Objectives   1
     Introduction   1
     Law and Society   2
     Definitions of Law   4
         Functions of the Legal System   7
         Dysfunctions of the Legal System   9
         Law and Morality   11
     Classifications of Legal Rules   12
     Approaches to Law and Society   18
         Consensus Paradigm   18
         Conflict Paradigm   19
     Rule of Law   20
     Summary   22
     Endnotes   27

2   Legal Systems   31

     Chapter Objectives   31
     Common-Law Systems   31
     Civil-Law Systems   35
     Islamic   38
     Socialist   38
     American Indian Law   39
     Theories of Law   40
         Natural Law   41
         Legal Positivism   43
     European Pioneer Theorists   43
         Baron de Montesquieu (Charles Louis de Secondat
         1689–1755)   43
         Herbert Spencer (1820–1903)   44
         Sir Henry Sumner Maine (1822–1888)   44

Interrelationship between Society and Law   45
   Karl Marx (1818–1883)   45
   Max Weber (1864–1920)   46
   Emile Durkheim (1858–1917)   47
   Sociological Jurisprudence Movement   48
      Roscoe Pound   49
      Benjamin Nathan Cardozo (1870–1938)   50
   Legal Realism   51
      Oliver Wendell Holmes   51
      Karl Llewellyn (1893–1962)   52
      Jerome Frank (1889–1957)   52
      Max Gluckman (1911–1975)   52
Modern Legal Theorists   53
   John Rawls   53
   Richard Posner   53
   Laura Nader   54
   Donald Black   54
   Edward Levi   55
Critical Legal Studies   55
Feminist Legal Theories   56
Critical Race Theory   57
Summary   58
Endnotes   61

3   Social Research Methods   **63**

Chapter Objectives   63
Introduction   63
Fundamentals of Research   64
Methods of Inquiry   65
   The Experimental Method   67
   The Classic Experimental Design   68
      The Solomon Four-Group Design 69
      The Posttest-Only Control-Group Design   70
   Quasi-Experimental Designs   70
      Nonrandomized Control Group Pretest-Posttest Design   70
      Time-Series Designs   71
      Equivalent Time-Samples Design   72
   The Observation Method   72
   Types of Participant Observation   73
   Simulation Research   75
   The Survey Method   76
      Personal Interviews   77

Telephone Interviews   78
Mail Surveys   78
Historical and Archival Research   80
The Case Study   82
Policy and Evaluation Research   84
Differentiating Between Social and Criminal Justice   87
Key Terms   90
Endnotes   90

4   Legal Structures   93

Chapter Objectives   93
Introduction   93
Courts   94
Court Jurisdiction   94
Court Organization   95
The State Court System   95
Courts of Limited and Specific Jurisdiction   96
State Court of Appeals   96
Federal Court System   97
U.S. District Courts   97
U.S. Courts of Appeals   98
Supreme Court of the United States   98
Court Unification Movements   99
Classifications of Law   100
Common Law and Civil Law Systems   100
Sources of Law: Constitutional, Statutory, and Case Law   101
Constitutional Law   101
Statutory Law   102
Case Law   103
Scope of the Law   103
Administrative Law   103
Civil and Criminal Law   104
Functions: Substantive and Procedural Law   106
Participants   106
Litigants   107
Counsel   107
Judges   108
Juries   109
Grand Juries   110
The Court Administrator   110
Flow of Litigation in Civil Proceedings   111
Flow of Criminal Proceedings   114

Lawmaking   117
   U.S. Congress   118
State Legislatures   121
How a Bill Becomes a Law   122
   Introduction of a Bill   122
   Assignment to Committee   122
   First, Second, and Third Readings   123
   Senate   123
   Conference Committees   123
   Executive Actions   124
Administrative Agencies and Rulemaking   124
   Lobbyists   124
   Governance of Lobbyists   125
Law Enforcers   126
   Local Law Enforcement   127
   State Law Enforcement   127
   Federal Law Enforcement   127
Punishment   128
   Sentencing Guidelines   128
   Correctional Institutions   129
   Community-Based Corrections   130
Summary   131
Endnotes   135

5   Social Control   137

Chapter Objectives   137
Behavior and Social Controls   137
Informal Social Controls   139
   Enforcement of Norms   140
   Social Norms and Deviance   142
   Moral Learning   142
Formal Controls   144
   Criminal Law   146
   Texas Penal Code, Section 49.02   147
   Victimless Crimes   148
   White-Collar Crimes   150
   Civil Commitment   150
   Administrative Law   151
   Tort Law   151
   Contract Law   152
Controlling Dissent   152
   Individual Rights versus Law and Order   152

Civil Disobedience   152
Freedoms of Speech, Association, and Press   154
Language Morphology Issues   154
Summary   155
Endnotes   156

6   Lawmaking as a Form of Social Control   159

Chapter Objectives   159
Introduction   159
Nature of Lawmaking   164
  Group-Influence Model   165
  Functionalist View   165
  Conflict Perspective   166
Legislative Lawmaking   166
  Legislative Committee Work   168
  Role Orientation   169
  Term Limits   170
  Congressional Investigation   173
Administrative Lawmaking   177
  Proclamations and Executive Orders   181
Judicial Lawmaking   187
  The Use of Writs   188
  Lawmaking by Precedents   189
Interest Groups   193
  Source of Funds   195
Endnotes   196

7   Dispute Resolution   199

Chapter Objectives   199
Introduction   199
  Hidden Harmony Myth   201
  Dispute Categories   201
Dispute Resolution Methods   201
  Hierarchy of Types   203
Litigation as a Means of Resolving Disputes   203
Alternative Dispute Resolution   204
  Court-Annexed Arbitration   205
  Mediation   206
  Arbitration   206
  Selecting an Arbitrator   209
Conflict Resolution and Delinquency   210
International Arbitration and Mediation   211

Endnotes   212

8 Social Change and Law   215

Chapter Objectives   215
Introduction   215
Nature of Social Change and Law   216
Courts as Mechanism for Social Change   217
  Magnitude of Court Decisions   222
  Legitimacy of Law to Create Social Change   223
  Public Opinion   224
  Limitations of Law to Create Social Change   224
Impact of Social Change on Law   225
  The Civil Rights Movement   226
  The Antiwar Movement   226
  The Women's Movement   228
  Rights for Sexual Minorities   229
Endnotes   230

9 Lawyers   231

Chapter Objectives   231
Introduction   231
The Legal Profession   232
The Legal Profession in the United States   233
  Evolution of the Legal Profession in the United States   233
  Legal Education   234
The Legal Profession Today   237
  Courthouse Work Groups   237
  Malpractice   238
  Private Practice   239
Lawyer Advertising   239
  Should Attorneys Be Allowed to Advertise?   239
  Advertisement Restrictions   241
  Solicitation of Clients   243
  Fields of Practice   243
  The Internet   243
Professional Responsibility   244
  Lawyer's Duties to the Client   244
  Client's Rights   246
  Duties to Others   247
  Conflicts of Interest   249
  Trial Publicity   249
  Prohibited Conduct by Attorneys   250

Future of the Law   250
Summary   251
Endnotes   255

10   Private Life and the Law   **257**

Chapter Objectives   257
Introduction   257
Right to Privacy   258
Privacy Act of 1974   259
    Freedom of Information Act   261
    The Right of Publicity   264
    The Federal Electronic Communications Privacy Act
    (ECPA)   265
    Computer Fraud and Abuse Act   265
Abortion   278
Pornography   281
    Pornography and the Internet   281
Endnotes   283

11   Crime and Justice Issues   **285**

Chapter Objectives   285
Introduction   285
Exclusionary Rule   286
Plea Bargaining   291
Hate Crimes   292
Stalking   297
    Interstate Stalking Punishment and Prevention Act of 1996   298
        Punishment   299
    State Anti-Stalking Legislation   299
Capital Punishment   301
    The Death Penalty in America   302
Imprisonment   303
    Private Prisons   304
Endnotes   305

12   Labor Issues and the Law   **307**

Chapter Objectives   307
Introduction   307
Governmental Labor Policies   308
National Labor Relations Act   309
Present State of Labor Unions   311

Federal Preemption   311
Exclusivity   311
Employers and Employee Rights   313
Bargaining Subjects   313
Right-to-Work Laws and Unions   315
Concerted Action   316
Union Affairs   317
Fair Labor Standards Act   318
Discrimination   319
Equal Employment Opportunity Commission   320
Pregnancy   320
Age Discrimination   321
Reverse Discrimination   321
Workers' Compensation   322
Endnotes   323

Index   **325**

Preface

This text on the study of law and society is more than a look at how law controls or influences our society. It is designed to open the students' eyes to the fascinating topics involving law and society. Our approach is to present a text that may be used in a one-semester course on law and society or a sociology of law course. While each chapter builds on the previous chapters, the text is designed so that the chapters may be studied in a different order, depending on the design of the course.

The text is written in a manner that may be understood by college students and thus enable instructors to focus on selected issues and topics during class time. Too often in the law and society area, textbooks can be understood only by instructors, and thus valuable class time must be used to explain the meaning of the concepts covered in the text. To overcome this problem, we followed the example of Ernest Hemingway and used familiar, concrete words and short sentences whenever possible. This approach should allow valuable class time to be used to encourage critical thinking on the part of the students.

A few acknowledgments are appropriate: Carolyn Spence, our editor, for her encouragement and guidance; and our colleagues at Washburn University, Professors Ted Heim, Michael Birzer, and of course the department chair, Gary Bayens. A hug of appreciation to Prudy Taylor Board, the project editor at Taylor & Francis, and Doug Burke, the copy editor, for an admirable job in producing a text from the manuscript.

About the Authors

Harrison Watts, PhD, is an associate professor in the Criminal Justice and Legal Studies Department at Washburn University, Topeka, Kansas. Dr. Watts's research interests are legal issues surrounding criminal law. He is the author of numerous book chapters, journal articles, and instructors' resource manuals to accompany textbooks.

Cliff Roberson, LLM, PhD, is an emeritus professor of Criminal Justice at Washburn University, Topeka, Kansas. Dr. Roberson recently retired as the managing editor of the international journal, Police Practices and Research (PPR). PPR is a refereed journal and is distributed in 48 countries. Previously, he served for four years as the editor in chief of the Professional Issues in Criminal Justice Journal. He has authored or co-authored more than 50 books and texts on legal subjects.

An Overview of Law and Society

1

Chapter Objectives

After reading this chapter you should be able to

- Describe the issues involved with the law and its interchange with society
- Provide a workable definition of law
- Explain how law influences our daily lives
- List and explain the three approaches to issues in law and society discussed in the chapter
- Discuss the roles sociologists should take when addressing law and society issues
- Define the concept of rule of law

Introduction

In today's society, law permeates all forms of our social behavior. The law is everywhere, with us and around us. To get to class, traffic law dictated the manner in which we drove or where we walked across the street. Law even governs our right to sit in class and our obligations to pay tuition. It is a vast, though sometimes invisible, presence. Chapter 1 introduces readers to the issues involved between law and society. The problems with definitions of law are discussed along with classifications of law. Three approaches to law and society issues are discussed, along with the ramifications associated with each approach. The final section of the chapter looks at the concept of the "rule of law."

The study of law and society has never been more interesting and important as it is today. In studying law and society, we should remember that the law is an enormous and complicated process. Any attempts to simplify it are usually a failure. The law is also parochial in nature. For example, mathematics is more or less the same subject in Rome, Italy, as it is in New York, New York. The legal system operating in Rome, however, is vastly different from the legal system operating in New York. While two plus two should always equal four, the law is constantly changing. Presently, the pace of social change is unsurpassed in history. The pace of legal change is also unmatched in history. Yet, often the law does not keep pace with social change. As will be noted in the text, changes to laws frequently lag behind social change. In the text, we present the major theories and points of view without advocating any particular slant. Our goal is to expose the readers to the major theoretical perspectives without advocating a particular position, ideology, or theoretical position.

Chapter 3 examines the contributions of sociological research and its impact on the law. There are differences of opinion over what roles sociologists should take when conducting research in law and society issues. The traditional approach is that sociologists should conduct their research in a value-neutral and empirical fashion and then report the findings in a similar manner. Others contend that sociologists should do more than merely describe and explain social events. They contend that sociologists should assert their rights to criticize and advance ways of rectifying or redressing law and society problems.

A PARADOX

The more civilized individuals become, the greater is the individual's need for law, and the more law he or she creates. Law is but a response to social needs.[1]

Do you agree with the paradox? Assuming that the paradox is correct, how do you explain it?

Law and Society

Law and society is the field of study that encompasses the many relationships between, and the effects of law on, the social sciences and humanities. What do we mean when we use the term *law and society*? Secondly, how does the concept of law and society differ from the field of sociology of law? It may be easier to consider the second question first.

It is sometimes difficult to distinguish between the fields of law and society and the sociology of law. There is no bright line separating the two disciplines. For the purposes of this text, we have accepted Javier Trevino's concept of the distinction between the two.[2] According to him, sociology of law analyzes the relationship between law and society from a sociological perspective, while law and society examines the relationship from a broader point of view that includes the social sciences as well as the humanities. Under that concept, sociology of law is a subset of law and society. Trevino states:

> I define sociology of law, or legal sociology, as an academic specialty within the general discipline of sociology that attempts to theoretically make sense of, and explain, the relationship between law and society, the social organization of the legal institution (order or system), the social interactions of all who come in contact with the legal institution and its representatives…, and give meaning that people give to their legal reality.

Trevino compares his definition of sociology of law with Friedman's definition of law and society. Friedman describes law and society as a movement that involves the efforts of legal sociologists and other scholars who study judicial behavior, historians who explore the role of nineteenth century lawyers, psychologists who seek to determine why juries behave the way they do, and so on. For the purposes of this text, we will consider law and society as the field of study that encompasses the many relationships between, and the effects of law on, the social sciences and humanities. However, many researchers consider that the two terms, *law and society* and *sociology of law*, are interchangeable. For example, Dragan Milovanovic's definition of the sociology of law is very similar to Trevino's definition of law and society.[3]

The disciplines of law and sociology are both concerned with norms, which are rules that prescribe the appropriate behavior for people in given situations. Both are also concerned with the nature of legitimate authority and conflict resolution. Other concerns of both disciplines include issues of human rights, mechanisms of social controls, the relationship between individuals and political organizations, and formal contract commitments.[4] While there are many overlapping concerns, as we will note later, there are also substantial differences between law and sociology.

In the study of law and society, we should keep in mind that the law is an authoritative and reactive problem-solving system that is designed to meet specific social needs. The search for truth has different meanings to the lawyer and the social scientist. Lawyers and social scientists are, also, reinforced by different professional cultures. Legal thinking is also different from "scientific" thinking. As noted by Vilhelm Aubert, reasons for this difference in thinking include:

- Law is more inclined toward what happened in a specific case, while the social sciences focus on the general.
- Law does not attempt to establish dramatic connections between means and the ends, e.g., the impact of the verdict on the defendant's future conduct.
- The truth in law is normative and not probabilistic, i.e., a law is valid or invalid, or something happened or it did not happen. There is no middle ground.

- The law is generally oriented toward the past or the present and is rarely concerned about the future.
- Legal consequences may be valid even if they did not occur. For example, in a given fact situation involving an alleged theft, the element "ownership of property" is valid even if that element is absent from the fact situation, and thus a required element of the crime is missing.
- Law is generally a win or lose process with little room for compromise, e.g., the client either wins or loses the case. This does not mean that there are not compromises in litigation, but only if the case goes to a judicial conclusion. There is no middle ground.[5]

The lawyer is an advocate. He or she is concerned about the resolution of the problems of his or her client. Lawyers are also guided by precedents. In contrast, the social scientist attempts to attack problems with an open mind and makes decisions only after all the evidence has been examined.

Lawyers and behavioral scientists do not talk the same language, according to Edwin Schur. Lawyers tend to make decisions in the here and now, while the social scientist has an apparently unlimited willingness to suspend final judgment on an issue.[6] Legal professionals use a strange language that includes specialized vocabulary and an arcane style, a language that is foreign to the social scientist.

In the next section, we will look at the difficult task of defining law. The concept of *society* is easier to define. It has several common definitions. One common definition, and the one we will use for the purposes of this text, is that a society is a group of people usually having geographical boundaries and sharing certain characteristics such as language or culture. Another definition is that it is a body of persons associated for a common purpose, e.g., an association, club, or fraternity. The third definition is that it pertains to the wealthier portion of a community. For our purposes, we will not use the latter two definitions when we refer to *society*.

Definitions of Law

Law is extremely important in our society. Explaining exactly what is meant by the word *law* is difficult. Definitions vary widely. Lawrence Friedman states that *law* is an everyday word, part of our basic vocabulary. It is, however, a word of many meanings, "as slippery as glass, as elusive as a soap bubble." Law, like the legal system and the legal process, is not a concrete object. It is a concept, an abstraction, and a social construct.[7]

John Austin claimed that law may be defined without any reference to its content. According to him, law is simply the command of the sovereign, backed by appropriate sanctions. He defined the sovereign as that individual or body to whom the people have a habit of obedience.[8] Austin's definition has clarity, but there are many kinds of law to which the model of command cannot be applied without distortion, e.g., the law of contracts. Too often, our definitions of law, like Austin's, concentrate on criminal law and the police. But law is more than criminal justice. It also includes our civil obligations, duties, etc. The latter obligations are more numerous than those imposed by the criminal statutes.

Roscoe Pound, a principal figure in sociological literature, stated that law was a specialized form of social control that exerts pressure on an individual "in order to constrain him or her to do his or her part in upholding civilized society and to deter him or her from antisocial conduct, that is, conduct at variance with the postulates of social order."[9]

Max Weber suggests that law is an order characterized by legitimacy. He states that "an order will be called law if it is externally guaranteed by the probability that coercion (physical or psychological), to bring about conformity or avenge the violation, will be applied by a staff of people holding themselves especially ready for that purpose."[10] He argues that law has three distinct features that distinguish it from customs and conventions. The three distinct features are

- The pressures to comply with the law are external.
- The external pressures involve coercion or force.
- Those who implement the coercive threats are individuals whose official roles are to enforce the law.

Even though customs are rules of conduct, they are not laws because they do not have the above three functions, and they are generally observed without deliberation and "without thinking." Weber labels customary rules of conduct as usages and points out that there is no sense of duty to follow them. He considers "conventions" as rules of conduct that involve a sense of duty and obligation. Pressures, including expressions of disapproval, are exerted on individuals who do not conform to conventions. Conventions, unlike the law, lack specialized personnel to implement coercive power to enforce. Critics of Weber contend that he places too much importance on coercion and ignores other considerations that induce individuals to obey the law.[11]

R. M. Dworkin looked at the "concept of law." He claimed that law exists in at least three different senses, each of which is problematic. First, there is "law" as a distinct and complex type of social institution. Under this sense, we may consider that "law" is either one of the proudest achievements of man, or that "law" is an instrument through which the powerful oppress the weak, or that "law" is more primitive in some societies than in others. Second, there is "law" as a body of rules that are distinct from other types of rules in society. Third, there is "law" as a particular source of rights, duties, and obligations in relations with other individuals.[12]

Donald Black states that law is a governmental control system. According to him, law is "normative life of a state and its citizens, such as legislation, litigation, and adjudication."[13] Black contends that there are several styles of law that are observable in every society. Each style of law corresponds to a style of social control.

Black lists four styles of social control that are represented in law: penal, compensatory, therapeutic, and conciliatory. The penal style views the deviant as a violator of a prohibition and therefore subjected to condemnation and punishment. The compensatory style sees a person as bound by a contractual obligation and therefore owes restitution to the victim. In both the penal and compensatory style, there is an accuser and a defendant, i.e., a winner and a loser. In the therapeutic style, the offender's conduct is described as abnormal and needing help. The conciliatory style sees the deviant as representative of one side of a social conflict, and there is a need to resolve the conflict without consideration of who is right or wrong. Both the therapeutic and conciliatory styles are designed to help people in trouble and to ameliorate an unpleasant social situation.

Black contends that the quality of law varies in time and space, that it varies across the centuries, decades and years, months and days, even the hours of a day. He also contends that it varies across societies, regions, communities, neighborhoods, families, and relationships of every kind. Black states that it varies with who complains about whom, who the legal official is, and who the other parties are. It varies with all aspects of the social environment.

Former Supreme Court Justice Benjamin Cardozo defines law as "a principle or rule of conduct so established as to justify a prediction with reasonable certainty that it will be enforced by the courts if its authority is challenged."[14] Oliver Wendell Holmes defines law as "the prophecies of what the courts will do in fact, and nothing more pretentious."[15]

It is easy to agree with E. Adamson Hoebel, who once noted that the search for the definition of law is as difficult as the search for the Holy Grail, and trying to define it precisely can be frustrating.[16] It may be easier to consider not a definition, but a framework or perspective for looking at and understanding the law. The framework includes considering the law

- as a body of rules and
- as a process.

Cardozo, in his previously noted definition, considers the law as a body of principles or rules of conduct. Relying on the body of rules as the definition of law implies that if you can recite the rules, you understand the law. As we progress in the text, you will note that understanding the legal issues involves more than a mere recital of the rules. Accordingly, the focus of the text is on the "legal system," which is an expanded domain and includes law.

In addition to indicating the problem with finding a single definition of law, the foregoing definitions show that there are alternative ways of looking at law. They also indicate the universality of its applicability. Considering law as both a body of rules and as a process or system allows the reader to take a considerably broader vision of law. This viewpoint requires the individual to think not only of the rules (laws), but also of lawmakers, lawbreakers, lawyers, victims, police, and all others involved in the legal system. It also allows for consideration of the values that influence individuals and the interaction among the actors in the legal system.

Functions of the Legal System

The role of the legal system is primarily social control. Everything else is secondary. It has structure, e.g., courts, lawyers, lawmakers, and police. It has substance, e.g., rules, norms, and behavior patterns of people. It also has culture. The legal culture is the climate of social thought and social force that determines how law is used, avoided, or abused.[17] In Chapter 2, the major legal systems in the world are discussed.

We do not mean to imply that a formal legal system is required in all societies. For example, some of the early traditional societies relied exclusively on "customs" as the source of rules of appropriate behavior and resolved disputes by mediation and conciliation by village elders. Many societies today rely both on a legal system and on "customs" monitored and enforced by the village elders. In some societies, the majority of disputes are resolved by village elders. In the United States, we rely very heavily on the formal legal system to resolve our disputes. Accordingly, we are a very litigious society.

Conflict or dispute resolution is one process by which the legal system implements its social control aspects. The dispute or conflict may be two people arguing over ownership of an automobile, a married couple over child custody in a divorce proceeding, or classes of individuals in disagreement of "the right to demonstrate." Often the phrase "dispute resolution" is used when we are talking about small-scale local disagreements between individuals and businesses. Conflict resolution is generally used when referring to macro disagreements between groups or classes of individuals.

The legal system is also an instrument of social engineering, e.g., restricting the right of tobacco companies from advertising in order to reduce the number of individuals who smoke. U.S. citizens are required to pay federal taxes. A part of the taxes are then given to the needy in the form of food stamps, medical care, and other types of assistance. The concept of social engineering does not mean that the legal system is constantly at work reforming society. Generally, the legal system functions to maintain a status quo rather than to force a change.

The law enforces property rights, creates a monetary system, and enforces contracts in its function of maintaining a framework of order and thus provides social control. This does not mean that the legal system is always maintaining the status quo. There are times when the legal system does enforce change. For the most part, the change must be regular, orderly, and in a patterned way. In most cases, for change to take place, there must be an official modification of the rules (either by Congress or court decision), and then the modification is enforced by enforcers in the legal system. In many cases, the system also acts as a safety valve; it prevents too much change and slows down change that goes too fast. The legal system is also a method for distributing goods and services. It rations scarce commodities. It uses taxes to redistribute wealth by progressive taxing and then providing public funds to those less fortunate.

Milovanovic provides a similar view as to the functions of a legal system. He states that law has repressive, facilitative, and ideological dimensions.[18] According to him, any given system of law will probably have aspects of all three within it, although one may be dominant. The repressive function refers to the coercive nature of the law. Law can be more or less repressive, as the repressive function is variable. *Repressive* refers to the degree of mobilization of physical force in furtherance of social control. There is a theoretical argument regarding the degree of repression needed within the legal system. One view (Freudian or Hobbesian perspective) contends that because of strong hedonistic, self-centered (egoistic), or biological impulses, individuals left in a state of nature would act out their impulses without regard to the rights of others if it were not for the repressive functions of the law.

A different perspective contends that while some repressive functions of the law are necessary, an excessive amount is generated to maintain a political economic system advantageous to those in power. According to the Marxist position, the propertied class uses the repressive functions of law to maintain control at the expense of the laboring class.

The facilitative functions refer to the degree to which the law aids in ensuring predictability and certainty in behavioral expectations. According to this perspective, in a rapidly changing society, people need reference points. We need to know what can happen when we fail to make a car payment. Can the finance company have us committed to jail? The facilitative functions of law provide reference points for both the finance company and for us. Both can predict what will happen if we go to court over the failure to make the car payment.

The third function of law is as an ideological perspective. Milovanovic contends that ideology as a belief system is always present in a legal system. According to him, the law systematically embodies the values of some people and disregards some values of others. Ideological and repressive functions of the legal system often appear together, with the repressive functions enforcing the ideological perspective.

Dysfunctions of the Legal System

There are certain dysfunctions of the legal system that should be considered. For example, in many cases, justice is denied, and in some cases, innocent people are convicted. Often the wealthy use the law to their advantage. Reasons given for these dysfunctions include the legal system's conservative tendencies, the rigidity inherent in its formal structure, the restrictive aspects associated with its social control functions, and the fact that certain types of discrimination are inherent in the law.

Hans Morgenthau suggested that the legal system perpetuates the status quo, with the courts being the chief instruments of the system acting as agents of the status quo.[19] By maintaining the status quo, the law has a definite tendency toward conservatism. Once rights and duties are established by the legal system, revisions are generally avoided in the interest of protecting predictability and continuity. Social changes in society generally precede legal changes. Accordingly, in times of crisis, the law is subject to breaking down, thus providing an opportunity for discontinuous adjustments. A good example of social changes preceding legal changes occurred in the case of Baby M.[20] In that case, a married couple paid a young woman to bear a child, using the husband's sperm. When the baby was born, the womb mother refused to give up the baby, claiming that she was its mother. The court held that the contractual agreement could not be enforced. The court then treated the case as a simple custody dispute case and awarded custody to the father. Since then, many states have enacted statutes regulating surrogacy contracts. Some states have enacted legislation banning them.

Legal rules are generally drafted with general, abstract, and universal terms that produce rigidity inherent in its framework. Accordingly, legal rules operate as straitjackets in certain situations.

Another dysfunction of the legal system concerns the restrictive aspects of normative controls. Norms are shared convictions regarding appropriate or inappropriate patterns of behavior for members of a group. Norms serve to combat social disorganization. In some cases, the legal system can overstep its boundaries and overregulate certain behaviors and thus become repressive. According to Roscoe Pound, in the nineteenth century, the public administration in the United States was hampered by an overrestrictive use of the legal system.[21]

Certain types of discrimination are dysfunctions of the legal system. The system's rules generally apply to everyone, but the effect of these rules may fall unevenly on some individuals. As Anatole France[21a] once stated: "The law in its majestic equality ... forbids the rich as well as the poor from sleeping under bridges, begging in the streets, and stealing bread." If the traffic fine for speeding 10 miles over the posted limit is $80.00, what financial effect would payment of this fine have on you? Would it have the same effect on a multi-millionaire? The law is often applied unequally. For example, Donald Black states that the more wealth that people have, the more litigious they are, and the more success they have with their litigation as well.[22] He also contends that an automobile accident causing an accidental injury to a wealthy person is more likely to be defined and litigated as a case of negligence than a similar injury to a person of lesser status. The criminal law case of the famous football player O.J. Simpson is a good example. Many consider that O.J. was acquitted not because he was innocent, but because he had an expensive legal team. If you were under indictment for murder, would you prefer a court-appointed attorney or the finest legal team that money can buy?

CULTURAL INSANITY

Blaine Gamble was charged with robbing the First National Bank of Herminie, Pennsylvania. Gamble, allegedly dressed as an elderly woman, entered the bank and robbed the tellers at gunpoint. At a pre-trial motion before U.S. District Court Judge William Standish, Gamble requested that a black psychologist or psychiatrist with expertise on cultural insanity examine him. He contended that he was a victim of posttraumatic stress disorder caused by "unwarranted exposure, victimization and repetitive confrontation with white racism." He stated he had had scraps with the police and that when he was a teenager, his mother had showed him a magazine cover depicting a murder victim. He claimed that he was innocent by reasons of cultural insanity caused by longtime exposure to racism.[23]

Should he be allowed to submit this evidence to the jury?

The law is subjected to outside pressures. These pressures come from special-interest groups, each advocating their special interest or belief. Regardless of whether you support "gun control" or are against it, you must recognize that the National Rifle Association is one of the strongest special-interest groups in the United States. A similar interest group "protects" the rights of our school teachers. One teacher's association had so much influence with senators and congresspersons that a former secretary of education labeled the association as a "terrorist organization."

Should we, as a civilized society, use the death penalty? Is abortion a woman's freedom of choice, or is it murder? Should gay couples be allowed to marry? These controversial issues indicate that the law is subject to outside pressures.

Law and Morality

What should be the relationship between law and morality? The First Amendment to the U.S. Constitution provides that Congress shall make no law respecting an establishment of religion or prohibiting the free exercise thereof. There are numerous examples, however, of the law supporting one view of morality over other views when values clash, e.g., forbidding prayers in public schools or a woman's right to abortion. It is often stated that the bodies of law in the various states in the United States are among the most moralistic laws in the world.

FIRST AMENDMENT RIGHTS AND THE PULPIT

A 1954 amendment to the Internal Revenue Service Tax Code prohibits all tax-exempt organizations, including churches, from directly or indirectly endorsing candidates for political office. This restriction prevents clergy from advocating a certain political candidate when they are in their pulpits. In the 2008 election, a small group of clergy held a Pulpit Freedom day. Thirty-three clergy took an active part in the event. In the 2012 presidential campaign, a similar Pulpit Freedom day was held, and over 1,000 clergy took part in it.

While clergy are citizens and have the right to express their political opinions, does the flaunting of their political muscle subject their churches to losing their tax exempt status? Many of the involved clergy contend that the 1954 amendment to the tax code was politically motivated and is unconstitutional.

Should religious leaders have the right to recommend to their congregations which political candidates they should vote for?

Was the restriction in the tax code designed to increase tax revenue, or was it designed to control certain individuals' behavior?

In a pluralistic society like ours, it would be hard for law and morality to be identical. In almost all societies, however, there is a strong relationship between law and morality. The role of morality and values of social control are discussed in Chapter 5. One scholar summarized the relationship between law and morality as follows:

- *Society has a moral order.* The many different and sometimes conflicting values of individuals and institutions may merge into dominant moral positions in a society. These dominant moral positions constitute the "core" of the moral order. The core is dynamic and as it changes, society moves in that direction.

- *The law has moral content.* The moral content of the law is also dynamic and over time as it changes, the law tends to move in the direction of the change.
- The moral content of the law and the moral order in society are seldom identical.
- A natural and necessary affinity exists between the moral content of the law and the moral order in society.
- When there is a gap between the two, movement to close the gap is likely.[24]

Classifications of Legal Rules

There are common classifications of legal rules (laws). One classification is by content, i.e., substantive or procedural. A second classification is criminal or civil. A third classification could be based on how the rule was formulated, i.e., legislative, administrative, or judge-made. Each law fits within each of the three classifications, e.g., the prohibition against wrongly taking someone's property without permission would generally be classified as substantive, criminal, and statutory law. Finally, laws may be classified as public or private laws.

All legal rules may be classified as either *substantive* or *procedural* according to their content. Substantive laws consist of rights, duties, and prohibitions. They inform us which behaviors are permitted and which are prohibited. A statute that prohibits firing a weapon from an automobile is a substantive statute, as is a statute that prohibits the unlawful killing of another human being. Procedural laws are rules concerning how the legal process is to be administered, enforced, changed, and used. The laws involving search and seizure are procedural laws. Laws that describe the formal processes required to draw up valid wills are also procedural laws.

A public law is one that is concerned with the structure of government, the duties and powers of officials, and the relationship between individuals and the government. Public law includes constitutional law, administrative law, criminal law, and laws relating to the proprietary powers of the state and its subdivisions. Private laws are substantive, and procedural laws concern the relationships between individuals. Private laws include the law of torts, contracts, property rights, wills, inheritance, marriage and dissolution of marriage, and adoption.

Civil law, as private law, is intended to govern the relationships between individuals. Violations of civil laws are considered as torts, i.e., private wrongs for which individuals may seek redress in civil courts. Criminal law looks at the definition of crime (substantive) and the prosecution of crime (procedural). Violation of a criminal law is a crime and is an offense against the peace and dignity of the society. The distinction between criminal substantive statutes and civil substantive statutes is that only the violation of a criminal statute places a person in jeopardy of a criminal sanction, e.g., confinement and/or fine. A crime is considered as a "public" offense, and in theory it is the state, not the individual, who is harmed. It is the state that takes action against the offender. Henry Hart states that a crime is conduct that will incur a formal and solemn pronouncement of the moral condemnation of the community. According to Hart, both the moral condemnation and the consequences that may follow constitute the punishment for the offense.[25]

An act may be both a criminal and civil wrong. For example, Joseph takes money by force from Robert. The act would be considered the crime of robbery, and Joseph would be subject to criminal penalties for his conduct. The act would also be the private wrong (tort) of wrongful conversion of property, and Robert could sue Joseph for monetary damages.

CONFLICTED JURY DECISIONS

The famous ex-football player, O.J. Simpson, was found not guilty of the 1994 murder of his ex-wife Nicole Brown Simpson and her friend Ronald Goldman in a criminal case prosecuted by the state of California.

In a separate case, Ronald Goldman's father, in a civil action, sued O.J. in a California State court for the wrongful death of Ronald. The jury in the 1997 civil case found O.J. liable for the wrongful death and awarded the Goldman family a large sum of money. In the criminal case, the state was required to prove beyond a reasonable doubt that O.J. committed the murder. The criminal jury concluded that the state had failed to meet its burden of proof. In the civil case, the Goldman family was required to establish by a preponderance of evidence that O.J. committed the acts that caused the wrongful death of Ronald. Probably because of this lesser burden of proof, O.J. was determined to be liable for the death of Ronald Goldman and ordered to pay monetary damages.

Laws are also classified as to their manner of enactment: constitutional, statutory, judge-made, executive orders, or administrative. Constitutional law is generally concerned with political organizations and their powers. It also sets substantive and procedural limitations on governments. Constitutional law by its very nature is a public law. A law that is created by a duly enacted statute is a statutory law. Statutory law is also known as legislative law. Statutory law may either be a public or private law. Judge-made law, also known as case law, is based on appellate court decisions. Usually case law interprets constitutional and statutory provisions. Executive orders are regulations issued by the executive branch of a government. Administrative law is that body of law created by administrative bodies.

ADMINISTRATIVE LAW EXAMPLE

TITLE 29 CODE OF FEDERAL REGULATIONS § 1904(1)(A)

If your company had ten (10) or fewer employees at all times during the last calendar year, you do not need to keep OSHA (Occupational Safety and Health Administration) injury and illness records unless OSHA or the BLS (Bureau of Labor Statistics) informs you in writing that you must keep records under § 1904.41 or § 1904.42. However, as required by § 1904.39, all employers covered by the Occupational Safety and Health Act must report to OSHA any workplace incident that results in a fatality or the hospitalization of three or more employees.

Judge-Made Law

The Supreme Court's decision in *Miranda v. Arizona*, 384 U.S. 436 (1966) addressed four different cases involving custodial interrogations. In each case, the defendant was questioned by police officers, detectives, or a prosecuting attorney in a room in which he was cut off from the outside world. In none of the cases was the defendant given a full and effective warning of his rights prior to the interrogation process. In all the cases, the questioning elicited oral admissions and, in three of them, signed statements that were admitted at trial.

In the Miranda case, he was arrested at his home and taken in custody to a police station, where he was identified by the complaining witness. He was then interrogated by two police officers for two hours, which resulted in a signed, written confession. At trial, the oral and written confessions were presented to the jury. Miranda was found guilty of kidnapping and rape and was sentenced to 20–30 years imprisonment on each count. On appeal, the supreme court of Arizona held that Miranda's constitutional rights were not violated in obtaining the confession.

The U.S. Supreme Court stated: "The prosecution may not use statements, whether exculpatory or inculpatory, stemming from custodial interrogation of the defendant unless it demonstrates the use of procedural safeguards effective to secure the privilege against self-incrimination."

Separate Is Not Equal: Another Example of Judge-Made Law

In the case of *Brown v. Board of Education*, the U.S. Supreme Court declared state laws establishing separate public schools for black and white students unconstitutional.[26] The decision overturned the 1896 decision of *Plessy v. Ferguson*, which held that state-sponsored segregation was legal. The U.S. Supreme Court held in the 1896 decision that as long as the separate facilities for the separate races were equal, segregation did not violate the Fourteenth Amendment clause that "no State shall ... deny to any person ... the equal protection of the laws."

The Brown case, decided on May 17, 1954, in a unanimous (9–0) decision, stated that "separate educational facilities are inherently unequal." Brown established the rule that racial segregation was a violation of the Equal Protection Clause of the Fourteenth Amendment of the U.S. Constitution. This decision paved the way for school integration and is considered as a major victory of the civil rights movement.

The principal legal systems may also be classified as common law, civil law, socialist, and Islamic systems. Common law is that system of law used in the United States and Great Britain, which relies on precedents set by judges to decide a case. In this classification, civil law refers to those legal systems whose developments are based not on case law, but on the basic law found in codes. The civil law systems' development was influenced by the *Corpus Juris Civilis*, which were a collection of Roman law codes. France is a civil law system. France's system is based on the civil code of France, which was first enacted in 1804. One distinction between a common law system and a civil law system is the role that precedents play in a case. For example, in a case involving a criminal homicide, in the common law system the judge would look to precedents for a definition of criminal homicide if the statute is unclear. In a civil law system, the judge would look only to the codes for the definition.

The source of socialist law is legislation, and the role of the court is to apply it. In the Islamic system, law is integral to the religion. Islam implies that the individual should submit to the will of God, and the rules of conduct are based on divine command and revelation. The distinctions between these systems and the basic concepts of each are discussed later in the text.

REGINA V. DUDLEY AND STEPHENS

Dudley and Stephens were indicted for the murder of Richard Parker on the high seas.[27] At trial in Devon on November 7, 1884, the jury found the following facts:[28]

On July 5, 1884, the prisoners, Dudley and Stephens, with one Brooks, all able-bodied English seamen, and the deceased were the crew of an English yacht. They were cast away in a storm on the high seas 1,600 miles from the Cape of Good Hope, and were compelled to put into an open boat belonging to the said yacht. There was no supply of water and no food except for two tins of turnips, and for 3 days they had nothing else to subsist on. On the fourth day, they caught a small turtle, upon which they subsisted for a few days, and this was the only food they had up to the 20th day, when the act now in question was committed. That on the 12th day the remains of the turtle were entirely consumed, and for the next 8 days they had nothing to eat. They had no fresh water, except such rain as they caught in their oilskin capes. At the time, the boat was drifting on the ocean and was probably 1,000 miles from land.

On the 18th day, when they had been without food for 7 days and without water for 5, the prisoners spoke to Brooks and suggested that someone should be sacrificed to save the rest. The boy, to whom they were understood to refer, was not consulted. Brooks dissented. Dudley proposed that lots should be cast who should be put to death to save the rest, but Brooks refused to consent, and it was not put to the boy, and in point of fact, there was no drawing of lots. On July 25, Dudley told Brooks that he had better go and have a sleep. He then made signs to Stephens that the boy had better be killed. Stephens agreed.

Dudley offered a prayer asking forgiveness for them all. Dudley then went to the boy and put a knife to his throat and killed him. All three fed upon the body for 4 days. On the fourth day, they were rescued by a passing boat. If the three men had not fed upon the body of the boy, they would probably not have survived to be picked up and rescued. The boy, being in a weaker condition, was likely to have died before them.

Were the defendants guilty of murder? How would you rule?

Argument for the Crown (prosecutor)

The law is that when a private person acting on his own judgment takes the life of a fellow creature, his act can only be justified as self-defense— self-defense against the acts of the person whose life is taken. The prisoners were not protecting themselves from any acts of Parker. If he had

had food and the prisoners had taken the food from him, they would have been guilty of theft, and if they killed him to obtain this food, they would have been guilty of murder.

Argument for the Prisoners (defense counsel)

This homicide is excusable through unavoidable necessity and upon the great universal principle of self-preservation, which prompts every man to save his own life in preference to that of another. The essence of the crime of murder is intention, and here the intention of the prisoners was only to preserve their life.

Judgment of the Court

There remains to be considered the real question in this case—whether the killing under the circumstances set forth in the verdict be or be not murder.... We are dealing with a case of private homicide not imposed upon men in the service of their Sovereign and in the defense of their country.... Though law and morality are not the same, and many things may be immoral which are not necessarily illegal, yet the absolute divorce of law from morality would be of fatal consequence; and such a divorce would follow if the temptation to murder in this case were to be held by law an absolute defense of it. It is not so. To preserve one's life is generally speaking a duty, but it may be the plainest and highest duty to sacrifice it.... It is not correct, therefore, to say that there is any absolute or unqualified necessity to preserve one's life....

In this case, the weakest, the youngest, the most unresisting, was chosen. Was it more necessary to kill him than one of the grown men? The answer must be "NO."

The court then proceeded to pass sentence of death upon the prisoners. The sentence was later commuted by the Crown to six months' imprisonment.

Questions:

1. Do you agree with the court's statement that there is no "absolute or unqualified necessity to preserve one's life"? Justify your answer.
2. Brooks did not take part in the killing, but fed on the boy. Should he also be punished? Note that he did nothing to prevent the killing.
3. In a footnote attached to the opinion of the court, the judge stated that his brother had proposed the following logic: "If the two accused men were justified in killing Parker, then if not rescued in time, two of three survivors would then be justified in killing the third, and of the two who remained, the stronger would be justified in killing the weaker, so that three men might be justifiably killed to give the

fourth a chance of surviving." If you were the defense counsel in this
case, how would you rebut that argument?

4. If all four seamen, including the victim, had agreed and a lot was
   drawn, would it still be murder to kill the individual who drew the
   unlucky lot?

5. Do you agree with the Crown's reduction of punishment to only 6
   months' confinement? What should have been the punishment in
   this case?

Approaches to Law and Society

Sociological issues regarding law and society generally are framed in one
of two conceptions of society: consensus and conflict. The two conceptions
are also referred to as "society's paradigms" and are discussed in the following sections. They are ideal types. There are elements of truth in each
paradigm.

Consensus Paradigm

The consensus approach sees society as a functionally integrated, relatively
stable social system held together by consensus of basic values. Under this
approach, the social order is considered as more or less stable, and individuals
can achieve their interests by cooperation. The consensus approach stresses
cohesion, solidarity, integration, cooperation, and the stability of society.
Society is united by a shared culture and by basic agreement on its fundamental values and norms. Social conflict is the result of struggles between
individuals and groups who do not have a sufficient understanding of their
common interests and basic interdependence. Law is seen as a neutral framework for maintaining social integration.

Roscoe Pound contended that law in a heterogenous society like the
United States can best be understood as a social compromise with an
emphasis on social order and harmony.[29] He contended that the historical development of law indicates what the law has become—a means of
providing for the common good and the satisfaction of social wants.
According to Pound, law is a form of social change directed toward
achieving social harmony. He sees the purpose of law as maintaining
and ensuring the values and needs required within the social order.
The primary purpose of the law, according to him, is to control interests and maintain harmony and social integration. The law does this not
by imposing one group's will on others, but by controlling, reconciling,

and mediating the diverse and conflicting interests of individuals and groups within society.

Harry Bredemeier sees the law as essentially a neutral agent that dispenses rewards and punishments without bias by supplementing informal social controls with formal mechanisms for generating and sustaining cooperation.[30] To him, law is a body of rules designed to maintain order and stability. Talcott Parsons argues that the primary function of the legal system is to maintain integrity and mitigate potential elements of conflict.[31]

Conflict Paradigm

The conflict paradigm takes the exact opposite approach. The conflict theorists see the law as a weapon of the ruling class to maintain a status quo. The conflict approach emphasizes the role of special-interest groups in society. Many conflict theorists agree that social institutions were originally designed to meet basic survival needs, but are now controlled by the power elite that manipulates them expressly to maintain its own privileged position of wealth and power.[32] Richard Quinney contends that law is an expression of interest and a device to control society. He states:

> Law is made by men, representing special interests, who have the power to translate their interests into public policy. Unlike the pluralistic conception of politics, law does not represent a compromise of the diverse interest in society, but supports some interests at the expense of others.[33]

William Chambliss, who embraces the conflict perspective of law, contends that the power of economic and commercial interests to influence legislation is illustrated by a historical analysis of vagrancy laws. He notes that the vagrancy laws in England were established during a period when there was a need for cheap labor by landowners and that the purpose of the vagrancy laws was to force those who were able-bodied and unemployed to work.[34] Lawrence M. Friedman examined the vagrancy laws in the state of Mississippi during the 1870s. He argues that those laws were designed to force blacks to go back to work under conditions of virtual serfdom.[35] Friedman also noted that other laws made it illegal for outsiders to "entice" workers away from their jobs—by offering better jobs that would enable black workers to "defraud" employers by quitting their work on white farms. In practice, the law worked to keep the black farmhands chained to white masters.

Rule of Law

In 1739, David Hume asked the following question:

> Here are two persons who dispute for an estate; of whom one is rich, a fool, and
> a bachelor; the other poor, a man of sense, and has a numerous family: the first
> is my enemy; the second my friend. To whom should the estate be awarded?

To Hume, the moral decision would be to award the estate based on principles of law without regard to any passions or particular motives. We have established general rules that are unchangeable by spite or favor, and by particular views of private or public interest. By following this course of action, we are adhering to the "rule of law," not the "rule of man."[36]

The concept of "rule of law" refers to the practice of a society of deciding legal disputes based on the established legal principles and rules and not on the passions or motives of individuals. For example, following the rule of law, the judge in making the decision in answer to Hume's question should decide the issue based only on principles of law and not whether one person is more worthy than the other.[37]

Eugen Ehrlich stated in 1912:

> The principle that the courts must base their decisions exclusively upon the law
> was never more important.…. The sovereignty of the state in the field of law, which
> is so significant for modern law, is based on the stability of the legal norms.[38]

Ehrlich argued that adhering to the "rule of law" in making legal decisions provides the stability to our society. Immanuel Kant noted that "the best Constitution is that in which not Men but Laws exercise" the powers of the state.[39]

Jean Jacques Rousseau contended that the power of the state to make laws originated from a social contract among members of the society. He also advocated the necessity of following the "rule of law." Rousseau opined:

> From whatever side we approach our principle, we reach the same conclusion,
> that the social compact sets up among the citizens an equality of such kind,
> that they all bind themselves to observe the same conditions and should there-
> fore all enjoy the same rights. Thus, from the very nature of the compact, every
> act of Sovereignty, i.e., every authentic act of the general will, binds or favors
> all the citizens equally; so that the Sovereign recognizes only the body of the
> nation, and draws no distinctions between those of whom it is made up.[40]

As can be noted from these quotations, the concept of government by the "rule of law" and not the "rule of man" has been discussed for several centuries. How valid is the concept today?

In December 1999, George Melloan, in discussing the central economic lessons of the 20th century, augured that the rule of law must be sustained. He stated that "nation-states have a role to play in maintaining a rule of law, insuring national security and preserving the stability of money. But ultimately it is the freedom offered each individual that creates economic wealth."[41]

The concept of the rule of law applies to the government as well as the private individual. Accordingly, the government must also abide by the law. For example, Bruce Gilley, an *Asian Wall Street Journal* correspondent, noted that Hong Kong will be both a litmus test and a challenge for China's evolving sense of the rule of law. As a litmus test, it will provide further evidence of whether Beijing is taking seriously the notion of a state subject to law. And as a challenge, it will force lawyers and jurists in China to consider the deficiencies of their own system as they watch with bemusement how their own government is forced to play by the rules in legal dealings with Macau.[42]

Michael S. Horn, an international lawyer discussing an Indonesian president who attempted to establish the concept of rule of law in his country, stated that the tasks confronting a president and his cabinet are daunting. Nowhere has the rule of law been established overnight. The rule of law requires a government's willingness to subordinate itself to law, sacrificing flexibility and other powers in favor of a promise of certainty. He noted that governments often do not like the results when they become subject to their own laws, and the temptation is great to bend the rules at times.[43]

In 1997, the British government arrested Augusto Pinochet, the former dictator of Chile, on a warrant from a Spanish magistrate who wanted him extradited to Spain, where he would face trial for murder, torture, and other "crimes against humanity." A British court quashed (invalidated) the warrant on October 28, 1998. An English appellate court reinstated the warrant.

The warrant raises an interesting question regarding the rule of law. Should Pinochet be punished for any murders or other atrocities that he was proven to have ordered or permitted during the time he was ruler of the country? If he violated the law, shouldn't he be punished like any other citizen? To allow him to go unpunished appears to establish a double standard.

Pinochet, like many former rulers in South America, surrendered his power only after receiving assurances that he would not be punished for what he and his regime had done. There is some question as to whether this is a legal condition that a ruler may attach to an agreement to step down from office. Will punishing him encourage other dictators to cling to power at all costs if they might otherwise be snatched and tried by any country that can get its hands on them? No head of state who has stepped down voluntarily has ever been criminally sanctioned by another nation, particularly (as in this case) over the objections of his own country.[44] How would you rule on the case? Would your answer be different if it was proven that he had ordered the 1976 car bombing in Washington, DC, that killed Orlando Letelier and Ronni Karpen Moffitt? How does the rule of law apply in this case?

In March 2000, the British home secretary released Pinochet and allowed him to return to his home in Chile. The secretary stated that Pinochet was too sick to be extradited to Spain to face charges of torture. Despite his release, the case may have established new international law. The fact that he was arrested, that four countries sought his extradition, and that his claim of immunity was rejected may indicate a change in the way the world deals with former dictators.[45] Does the British action in allowing him to return to Chile comply with the rule of law?

Summary

- In today's society, law permeates all forms of our social behavior. The law is everywhere with us and around us.
- Three approaches to law and society issues are discussed with the ramifications associated with each approach.
- The study of law and society has never been more interesting and important as it is today.
- The law is parochial in nature.
- The current pace of legal change is also unmatched in history. Yet, often the law does not keep pace with social change.
- There are differences of opinion over what roles sociologists should take when conducting research in law and society issues.
- The traditional approach is that sociologists should conduct their research in a value-neutral and empirical fashion and then report the findings in a similar manner.
- Others contend that sociologists should do more than merely describe and explain social events. They contend that sociologists should assert their rights to criticize and advance ways of rectifying or redressing law and society problems.
- It is sometimes difficult to distinguish between the fields of law and society and the sociology of law. There is no bright line separating the two disciplines.
- Javier Trevino's concept of the distinction between the two is that sociology of law analyzes the relationship between law and society from a sociological perspective, while law and society examines the relationship from a broader point of view that includes the social sciences as well as the humanities.
- Under that concept, sociology of law is a subset of law and society.
- Friedman describes law and society as a movement that involves the efforts of legal sociologists and other scholars who study judicial

behavior, historians who explore the role of nineteenth-century law-yers, psychologists who seek to determine why juries behave the way they do, and so on.

- The disciplines of law and sociology are both concerned with norms, which are rules that prescribe the appropriate behavior for people in given situations. Both are also concerned with the nature of legitimate authority and conflict resolution. Law is more inclined toward what happened in a specific case, rather than in general as is the situation in the social sciences.

- Law does not attempt to establish dramatic connections between means and the ends, e.g., the impact of the verdict on the defendant's future conduct.

- The truth in law is normative and nonprobabilistic, e.g., a law is valid or invalid or something happened or it did not happen. There is no middle ground.

- The law is generally oriented toward the past or present and is rarely concerned about the future.

- Legal consequences may be valid even if they did not occur. For example, in a given fact situation involving an alleged theft, the element "ownership of property" is valid even if that element is absent from the fact situation and thus a required element of the crime is missing.

- Law is generally a win or lose process with little room for compromise, e.g., the client either wins or loses the case. There is no middle ground. This does not mean that there are not compromises in litigation, but only if the case goes to a judicial conclusion.

- Explaining exactly what is mean by the word *law* is difficult. Definitions vary widely. Lawrence Friedman states that *law* is an everyday word, part of our basic vocabulary. It is, however, a word of many meanings, "as slippery as glass, as elusive as a soap bubble." Law, like legal system and legal process, is not a concrete object. It is a concept, an abstraction, and a social construct.

- John Austin claimed that law may be defined without any reference to its content. According to him, law is simply the command of the sovereign, backed by appropriate sanctions.

- Roscoe Pound, a principal figure in sociological literature, stated that law was a specialized form of social control that exerts pressure on an individual "in order to constrain him or her to do his or her part in upholding civilized society and to deter him or her from anti-social conduct, that is, conduct at variance with the postulates of social order."

- Max Weber suggests that law is an order characterized by legitimacy. He states that "an order will be called law if it is externally guaranteed by the probability that coercion (physical or psychological), to bring about conformity or avenge the violation, will be applied by a staff of people holding themselves especially ready for that purpose."

- Even though customs are rules of conduct, they are not laws because they do not have these three functions (external pressure involving coercion or force exercised by law enforcement officials), and they are generally observed without deliberation and "without thinking."

- R. M. Dworkin looked at the "concept of law." He claimed that law exists in at least three different senses, each of which is problematic. First, there is "law" as a distinct and complex type of social institution. Under this sense, we may consider that "law" is either one of the proudest achievements of man, or that "law" is an instrument through which the powerful oppress the weak, or that "law" is more primitive in some societies than in others. Second, there is "law" as a body of rules that are distinct from other types of rules in society. Third, there is "law" as a particular source of rights, duties, and obligations in relations with other individuals.

- Donald Black states that law is a governmental control system. According to him, law is "normative life of a state and its citizens, such as legislation, litigation, and adjudication."

- Black contends that there are several styles of law that are observable in every society. Each style of law corresponds to a style of social control.

- Former Supreme Court Justice Benjamin Cardozo defines law as "a principle or rule of conduct so established as to justify a prediction with reasonable certainty that it will be enforced by the courts if its authority is challenged."

- The role of the legal system is primarily social control. Everything else is secondary. It has structure, e.g., courts, lawyers, lawmakers, and police. It has substance, e.g., rules, norms, and behavior patterns of people. It also has culture. The legal culture is the climate of social thought and social force that determines how law is used, avoided, or abused.

- The legal system is also an instrument of social engineering, e.g., restricting the right of tobacco companies from advertising in order to reduce the number of individuals who smoke; requiring U.S. citizens to pay federal taxes.

- The law enforces property rights, creates a monetary system, and enforces contracts in its function of maintaining a framework of order and thus provides social control. This does not mean that the legal system is always maintaining the status quo. There are times when the legal system does enforce change.

- The law is subjected to outside pressures. The pressures come from special-interest groups, each advocating their special interest or belief.

- In a pluralistic society like ours, it would be hard for law and morality to be identical. In almost all societies, however, there is a strong relationship between law and morality.
- There are common classifications of legal rules (laws). One classification is by content, i.e., substantive or procedural. A second classification is criminal or civil. A third classification could be based on how the rule was formulated, i.e., legislative, administrative, or judge-made.
- All legal rules may be classified as either *substantive* or *procedural* according to their content. Substantive laws consist of rights, duties, and prohibitions. They inform us which behaviors are permitted and which are prohibited.
- A public law is one that is concerned with the structure of government, the duties and powers of officials, and the relationship between individuals and the government.
- Private laws are substantive and procedural laws are those that concern the relationships between individuals. Private laws include the law of torts, contracts, property rights, wills, inheritance, marriage and dissolution of marriage, and adoption.
- Laws are also classified as to their manner of enactment: constitutional, statutory, judge-made, executive orders, or administrative.
- Constitutional law is generally concerned with political organizations and their powers. It also sets substantive and procedural limitations on governments. Constitutional law by its very nature is a public law.
- A law that is created by a duly enacted statute is a statutory law. Statutory law is also known as legislative law. Statutory law may either be a public or private law.
- Judge-made law, also known as case law, is based on appellate court decisions. Usually case law interprets constitutional and statutory provisions.
- Executive orders are regulations issued by the executive branch of a government.
- Administrative law is that body of law created by administrative bodies.
- The principal legal systems may also be classified as common law, civil law, socialist, and Islamic systems. Common law is that system of law used in the United States and Great Britain, which relies on precedents set by judges to decide a case.
- France has a civil law system. France's system is based on the civil code of France, which was first enacted in 1804.
- One distinction between a common law system and a civil law system is the role that precedents play in a case.
- The source of socialist law is legislation, and the role of the court is to apply it.

- In the Islamic system, law is integral to the religion. Islam implies that the individual should submit to the will of God, and the rules of conduct are based on divine command and revelation.
- Sociological issues regarding law and society generally are framed in one of two conceptions of society: consensus and conflict. The two conceptions are also referred to as "society's paradigms."
- The concept of *rule of law* refers to the practice of a society of deciding legal disputes based on the established legal principles and rules and not on the passions or motives of individuals.

Questions in Review

1. The traditional approach of sociologists in conducting research in the area of law and society has been to carry it out in a value-neutral and empirical fashion. What role should they take in rectifying or redressing law and society problems?
2. It is difficult to distinguish between the fields of law and society and sociology of law. How would you distinguish between the two?
3. The disciplines of law and sociology are both concerned with norms, the nature of legitimate authority, and conflict resolution. How are they different?
4. Defining what is meant by *law* is difficult. It is a word of many meanings. How would you define it?
5. Both customs and conventions are rules of conduct. How do they differ?
6. Donald Black lists four styles of social control that are represented in law: penal, compensatory, therapeutic, and conciliatory. Define each style.
7. Oliver Wendell Holmes defines law as "the prophecies of what the courts will do in fact, and nothing more pretentious." What are the problems with this definition of law?
8. The role of the legal system is primarily for social control. How does it achieve that role?
9. One of the dysfunctions of the legal system is that innocent individuals are convicted of crime. How could the system rectify or reduce the occurrence of this dysfunction?
10. There is a strong relationship between law and morality. Is this relationship too strong or not strong enough?
11. The two common value conceptions of society are consensus and conflict. What are the basic tenets each?
12. The concept of rule of law refers to the practice of societies in deciding legal disputes based on law and not on passions or particular motives. Why is the rule of law important in society?

Practicum

Assume you are the manager of a resort in Southern California. One of your employees is required to "walk" the grounds at least once each hour. The walking of the grounds is very difficult for the employee because she is obese. She requests the use of the resort's golf cart to cover the area.

How would you answer her request?

Consider the following facts:

- *Case law*: Three recent federal court decisions hold that obesity is a condition (disability) under the Americans with Disabilities Act (ADA).
- *Statutory law*: The ADA requires employers to accommodate disabled individuals as far as reasonably possible so that they can perform their jobs.
- *Society*: According to a 2012 report from the Centers for Disease Control and Prevention, adult obesity has more than doubled in the United States from 1970 to 2012. Researchers predict that by the year 2030, almost half of the people will be considered as obese.[46]

Endnotes

1. Adapted from E.A. Hoebel. (1954). *The law of primitive man: A study of comparative legal dynamics* (p. 292). Cambridge, MA: Harvard University Press.
2. A.J. Trevino. (1998). Nine law and society/sociology of law textbooks and readers for the 1990s: A comparative review. *Teaching Sociology, 26,* 354–380.
3. D. Milovanovic. (1994). *A primer in the sociology of law* (2nd ed., pp. 5–6). New York, NY: Harrow and Heston.
4. L. McIntyre. (1994). *Law in sociological enterprise: A reconstruction* (pp. 10–27). Boulder, CO: Westview Press.
5. V. Aubert. (1973). Researches in the sociology of law. In M. Barkum (Ed.), *Law and the social system* (pp. 50–53). New York, NY: Lieber-Atherton.
6. E. Schur. (1968). *Law and society: A sociological view* (p. 8). New York, NY: Random House.
7. L.M. Friedman. (1998). *American law: An introduction* (Rev. ed., p. 17). New York, NY: Norton.
8. A. Flew. (1999). *A dictionary of philosophy* (2nd ed., p. 31). New York, NY: Gramercy.
9. R. Pound. (1941). *In my philosophy of law* (p. 18). St. Paul, MN: West.
10. M. Weber. (1954). *Law in economy and society* (E. Shils & M. Rheinstein, Trans., p. 27). Cambridge, MA: Harvard University Press.
11. E.A. Hoebel. (1954). *The law of primitive man: A study of comparative legal dynamics*. Cambridge, MA: Harvard University Press.
12. R.M. Dworkin. (1977). *The philosophy of law* (pp. 2–3). New York, NY: Oxford University Press.
13. D. Black. (1976). *The behavior of law* (p. 2). New York, NY: Academic Press.

14. B. Cardozo. (1924). *The growth of the law* (p. 52). New Haven, CT: Yale University.

15. O.W. Holmes. (1897, March). The path of law. *Harvard Law Review, 1897*(10), 457–461.

16. E.A. Hoebel. (1954). *The law of primitive man: A study of comparative legal dynamics.* Cambridge, MA: Harvard University Press.

17. L.M. Friedman. (1998). *American law: An introduction* (Rev. ed., p. 21). New York, NY: Norton.

18. D. Milovanovic. (1994). *A primer in the sociology of law* (2nd ed., pp. 8–9). New York, NY: Harrow and Heston.

19. H. Morgenthau. (1993). *Politics among nations* (revised by K.W. Thompson, p. 418). New York, NY: McGraw-Hill.

20. In the Matter of Baby M, 537 A.2d. 1227 (N.J. 1988).

21. R. Pound. (1914). Justice according to law. *Columbia Law Review, 14*(1), 12–13.

21a. Anatole France. (1894). *Le Lys Rouge (The Red Lily).* (Originally published in France.) Reprinted 2010, Charleston, S.C.: Nabu Press.

22. D. Black. (1976). *The behavior of law* (p. 27). New York, NY: Academic Press.

23. *Houston Chronicle.* (1999, December 24). p. 9A, col. 1.

24. L.D. Wardle. (1980). The gap between law and moral order: An examination of the legitimacy of the Supreme Court adoption decisions. *BYU Law Rev., 1980,* 811–835.

25. H.M. Hart, Jr. (1958). The aims of criminal law. *Law and Contemporary Problems, 1958*(23), 401.

26. 347 U.S. 483 (1954).

27. *Law Reports, Queen's Division*, Vol. 14. (1884–1885). pp. 273–288.

28. Note: The facts have been edited to reduce the length of the material and to make the case more readable.

29. R. Pound. (1943, October). A survey of social interests. *Harvard Law Review, 1943*(57), 1–39.

30. H.C. Bredemeier. (1961). Law as an integrative mechanism. In W.J. Evan (Ed.), *Law and society: Exploratory essays* (pp.73–90). New York, NY: Free Press.

31. T. Parsons. (1961). The law and social control. In W.J. Evan (Ed.), *Law and society: Exploratory essays* (pp. 56–72). New York, NY: Free Press.

32. M. Useem. (1984). *The inner circle: Large corporations and the rise of business political activity in the U.S. and U.K.* New York, NY: Oxford University Press.

33. R. Quinney. (1970). *The social reality of crime* (p. 35). Boston, MA: Little, Brown.

34. W.J. Chambliss. (1964). A sociological analysis of the law of vagrancy. *Social Problems, 12*(1), 67–77.

35. L.M. Friedman. (1998). *American law: An introduction* (Rev. ed., p. 299). New York, NY: Norton.

36. The question has been edited to make it easier to read. Taken from David Hume, *A treatise of human nature*, Vol. II, Book III "Of Morals," Section VI "Some Further Reflections Concerning Justice and Injustice." Reprinted in C. Morris (Ed.). (1959). *The great legal philosophers: Selected readings in jurisprudence.* Philadelphia, PA: University of Pennsylvania Press. (Original work published 1740)

37. One manuscript reviewer asked: "But, what if there was a statute saying that the 'more worthy' should receive any property in dispute?" This would raise serious questions regarding the "due process" rights involved in the statute.

38. E. Ehrlich. (1959). *Fundamental principles of the sociology of law: Part IV, Social and state sanctions of norms*. Reprinted in C. Morris (Ed.), *The great legal philosophers: Selected readings in jurisprudence*. Philadelphia, PA: University of Pennsylvania Press. (Original work published 1913)

39. I. Kant. (1791). *The Philosophy of Law: An exposition of the fundamental principles of jurisprudence as the science of right* (W. Hastie, Trans.). Edinburgh, Scotland: T.&T.

40. J.J. Rousseau. (1959). *The social contract*, Book II, Chapter IV. Reprinted in C. Morris (Ed.). *The great legal philosophers: Selected readings in jurisprudence*. Philadelphia, PA: University of Pennsylvania Press. (Original work published 1762)

41. G. Melloan. (1999, December 28). Global view: The central economic lesson of this century. *The Wall Street Journal Interactive Edition*.

42. B. Gilley. (1999, December 16). Macau and the future of China. *Dow Jones Newswires*.

43. M.S. Horn. (1999, December 15). International commentary: Indonesia needs a Magna Carta. *Wall Street Journal Interactive Edition*.

44. S. Taylor, Jr. (1998, November 9). Bad effects of feel-good laws. *Texas Lawyer*.

45. A. MacLeod. (2000, March 3). Pinochet goes free, but sets a precedent. *Christian Science Monitor*, p. 1.

46. L. Jones. (2012, October 1). Legal issues involving obesity and the ADA. *The National Law Journal, 2012*, 4.

Legal Systems

2

Chapter Objectives

After studying this chapter, you should be able to

- Explain the difference between common law and statutory law
- Discuss what constitutes common law
- Differentiate between civil law and common law systems
- Discuss the theoretical aspects of the U.S. legal system
- Identify the pioneers and contemporary legal theorists
- Explain the difference between "natural law" and "positivism"
- Discuss how judges make law

Common-Law Systems

In this chapter, the major legal systems and legal theory are explored. The theoretical aspects of our law are also examined. The chapter also includes a discussion on both pioneer and contemporary theorists.

Common law is considered as judge-made law because it developed out of decisions made in prior cases that were adopted as precedent. The name "common law" comes from the idea that English medieval law, as administered by the courts of the realm, reflected the "common" customs of the kingdom. Whereas civil-law judges resolve disputes by referring to statutory principles arrived at in advance, common-law judges focus more intently on the facts of the particular case to arrive at a fair and equitable result for the litigants.

The three major nations whose law is based on common law are the United States, Canada, and England. The common-law system was originated in England after the Norman Conquest. It is used in English-speaking countries except Scotland and South Africa.[1] Colonial expansion transferred the common-law systems to those Third World countries formerly controlled by England. In some of the countries, like those with Muslim populations and India, the adoption of the common-law system was not complete. In those countries, portions of the system exist along with the traditional forms of their own legal systems.

At the time of the Norman Conquest there was no uniform criminal law in England. Individual courts were dominated by sheriffs who enforced village rules as they saw fit. To reduce the arbitrary aspects of the law, William the Conqueror decreed that all prosecutions should be conducted in the name of the king. This practice exists today in criminal-law cases, where all criminal cases are conducted in the name of the state, people, or commonwealth.

By the 1600s, the primary law of England was based on the mandatory rules of conduct laid down by the judges. The rules became the common law of England. Prior decisions were accepted as authoritative precepts and were applied to future cases. When the English settlers came to America in the 1600s, they brought with them the English common law.

The legal system in the United States is presently a complex blend of common and statute law. When the first English colonists came to America in the 17th century, they brought English customs with them, but there was little expertise in law. Colonial charters, or agreements with England, gave the colonists the Englishmen's traditional rights that had developed as part of the common law. But there were few men trained in the law, few judges, and no schools of law. Local jurisdictions passed their own statutes to meet specific situations.

During the American Revolution, there was hostility toward the English in America. This hostility extended to the common-law system. Most of the new states enacted new statutes that defined duties and responsibilities in the legal area. The statutes, however, were basically a restatement of English common law. All states, except Louisiana, can trace their legal systems to the English common-law system. Louisiana, whose system was originally based on the French and Spanish code law concepts, officially adopted common law as the basis for their system in 1805.

One of the basic principles of common law is the doctrine of judicial review. This doctrine provides courts with the authority to review all statutory enactments, judicial decisions of lower courts, and administrative determinations within their jurisdiction. This common-law principle was formally recognized by the U.S. Supreme Court in the famous case of *Marbury v. Madison.*[2] In that case, Chief Justice John Marshall held that it was the duty of the courts to determine what the law is and that when the courts apply a rule or statute to a particular case, they must of necessity expound and interpret that rule or statute. If two laws conflict, the courts must decide on the operation and scope of each.

At the time that Chief Justice Marshall made the decision, President Thomas Jefferson objected to the concept of judicial review. In an 1820 letter, Jefferson stated: "To consider the judges as the ultimate arbiters of all constitutional questions is a dangerous doctrine ... and one which would place us under the despotism of an oligarchy." Jefferson correctly pointed out that the concept of judicial review is not contained in our federal constitution. Despite Jefferson's fears, every state's highest court in the United States has accepted the principles set forth in *Marbury v. Madison.*

MARBURY V. MADISON (1803)

The *Marbury v. Madison* case is generally considered to be the most important early U.S. Supreme Court decision and the leading authority for the concept that the Court has the power and duty to strike down acts of Congress that violate the Constitution. In the first years of our republic, the powers and role of the courts were unsettled. They are treated only briefly in the Constitution itself. It was in the Marbury case that the power of judicial review was first used.[3] Chief Justice John Marshall opined that an act of Congress conflicted with the Constitution. His critics attacked his decision as a naked assertion of power, and one that was not justified by the Constitution.

In the presidential election of 1800, Thomas Jefferson defeated the incumbent president John Adams. The election campaign was bitter. At that time, the new president did not take office until March 3, 1801. Two weeks before Jefferson was inaugurated, the Federalist-dominated Congress adopted and then President Adams signed two statutes. The first statute was the Judiciary Act of 1801, which created a number of new federal judgeships, which Adams quickly filled. The second created a government for the newly created District of Columbia. The second one also empowered the president to appoint justices of the peace for the new city.

Just before leaving office, Adams appointed William Marbury to one of the new justice of the peace positions. He was confirmed by the Senate, but the commissions were not delivered by the secretary of state to Marbury and three other appointees. When Jefferson took office, the new secretary of state was James Madison. Madison asked the outgoing secretary for the commissions. He refused to give them to Madison. Marbury and the others then turned to the Supreme Court, asking it to issue a writ ordering Madison to turn over the commissions.

When the Court met, Madison ignored the Court's order to appear. While Marshall believed that Marbury and others deserved the commissions, he believed that Madison would ignore any order to turn over the commissions from the Supreme Court. This action would humiliate the Court. Marshall's decision was a brilliant legal opinion. First, he criticized Madison (and therefore Jefferson). Next, he avoided a confrontation with Madison by not ordering Madison to do anything. Finally, he established the power of the Court to declare a law of Congress unconstitutional. Marshall concluded that withholding the commission violated Marbury's rights. He implicitly criticized Madison and Jefferson by stating that even King George III of England never fails to comply with a judgment of his court. Then he concluded that the Judiciary Act of 1789, which authorized the Supreme Court to issues certain writs, was unconstitutional, since that power was not specified in Article III, Section 2 of the Constitution and that Marbury must pursue this matter in the lower courts.

As judicial decisions accumulate on a particular kind of dispute, general rules or precedents emerge and become guidelines for judges deciding similar cases in the future. Subsequent cases, however, may reveal new and different facts and considerations, such as changing social or technological conditions.

In the common-law system, a pyramidal structure of courts exists to define and refine the law. At the base of the pyramid are trial courts. Above the trial courts, layers of appellate courts, composed entirely of judges, exist to adjudicate disputes. These disputes center on whether or not the trial judge applied the correct principles of law. The interpretations of law made by appellate courts form the precedents that govern future cases. Furthermore, the importance of a precedent for any given court depends on that court's position in the pyramidal structure; for example, a precedent set by an appellate court has greater force in trial courts than in other similar level appellate courts.

If a common-law judge feels that the facts are sufficiently different from prior cases and there is no binding precedent, then the judge is free to depart from precedent and establish a new rule of decision This new decision sets a new precedent, as it is accepted and used by different judges in other cases. In this manner, common law retains a dynamic for change. As the U.S. Supreme Court Justice Oliver Wendell Holmes wrote in his book, *The Common Law* (1881): "The life of the [common] law has not been logic; it has been experience."

THE TRIAL OF WILLIAM PENN

William Penn, a Quaker, was a colonial hero of American liberty. During the latter part of the 17th century, the Protestants persecuted the Catholics and the Catholics persecuted Protestants. Both Protestants and Catholics attacked the Quakers and Jews. It was during this period that Penn established an American sanctuary that protected freedom of conscience. Almost everywhere else, colonists stole land from the American Indians, but Penn traveled unarmed among the American Indians and negotiated peaceful purchases. He insisted that women deserved equal rights with men. He gave Pennsylvania a written constitution that limited the power of government, provided a humane penal code, and guaranteed many fundamental liberties. In 1670, William Penn held a worship service in a quiet street that was attended by a peaceful group of Quakers. Penn and another Quaker, William Mead, were arrested on a charge of disturbing the king's peace and summoned to stand trial. As the two men entered the courtroom, a bailiff ordered them to place their hats, which they had removed, back on their heads. When they complied, they were called forward and held in contempt of court for being in the courtroom with their hats on.[4]

Excerpts from the record of trial:

William Penn to Judge: I desire you would let be known by what law is it you prosecute me, and upon what law you ground my indictment.

Judge: Upon the common law.

Penn: Where is that common law?

Judge: You may not think that I am able to run up so many years, and over so many adjudged cases, which we call common law, to answer your curiosity.

Penn: This answer I am sure is very short of my question, for if it be common, it should not be so hard to produce.

Judge: The question is, whether you are guilty of this indictment?

Penn: The question is not, whether I am guilty of this indictment, but whether this indictment is legal. It is too general and imperfect an answer to state that it is the common law, unless we knew both where and what it is. For where there is no law, there is no transgression and that law which is not in being, is so far from being common, that it is no law at all.

Judge: You are impertinent, will you teach the court what the law is? It is *Lex non scripta*, that which many have studied 30 or 40 years to know, and would you have me tell you in a moment?

Penn: Certainly, if the common law be so hard to understand it is far from being common.[5]

Civil-Law Systems

From its origins in continental Europe, the civil law has spread to areas in Africa, Asia, and Latin America that were colonies of France, The Netherlands, Belgium, Spain, or Portugal. When they gained independence, most of the former colonies continued the civil-law orientation of their legal systems. Civil-law systems were also voluntarily adopted in South Korea,

Taiwan, Thailand, and Turkey. Today, civil law is used in most nations in Europe and Latin America, as well as in some countries in Asia and Africa. Japan has mostly a civil-law system with a mixture of common law in the area of criminal procedure. The common-law influence in Japan was caused by the American occupation following World War II. Until 2011, Mexico used a Spanish civil-law system. In 2011, Mexico started its transition to the common-law system.

The term *civil law* is derived from the ancient Roman term *ius civile*, meaning law, which was used to distinguish the proper or ancient law of the city of Rome from the laws applying to the people of the Roman Empire. The civil-law systems are also referred to as Romano-Germanic law. The system started in ancient Rome. The principles of Roman law were based on legislation and on the works of legal scholars who were routinely asked for their opinions by judicial officers when confronting difficult legal questions. In the 6th century, Roman Emperor Justinian ordered that all sources of law be collected and consolidated. The consolidated law became the *Corpus Juris Civilis* (Body of Civil Law), also called the Justinian Code.

The Justinian Code was essentially limited to the eastern half of the Roman Empire; the western half had already been overrun by Germanic invaders. From the 5th to the 10th century, Europe was in a cultural decline, and no significant developments occurred in civil law. In the second half of the 11th century, the Corpus Juris was rediscovered in Italy. At the same time, the study of academic law was instituted at the University of Bologna, where professors based their legal teaching on the Corpus Juris. Soon other European universities followed, and the Corpus Juris became an important part in the development of Continental Law until relatively modern times. Other references included Canon law and the customs of merchants. Based on these references, a body of written transnational law (known as *jus commune*) was developed by academic legal scholarship, with which lawyers and judges throughout continental Europe were familiar. Eventually, local statutes and numerous local customs, often of Germanic origin, were also committed to writing. In the frequent cases in which these local statutes and local customs did not furnish an answer, however, courts and lawyers tended to be guided by the transnational *jus commune*.

During the 17th and 18th centuries, the authority of the Corpus Juris began to decline as its rules were reexamined in the light of reason. Several attempts were made to develop a systematic and comprehensive codification of modern civil law. France, under the guidance of Napoleon, adopted the Code of Napoleon in 1804. With revisions, it still remains in force and has been a major influence in the legal systems of most European countries and in Latin America. The Code of Napoleon was made necessary by the diversity and confusion of laws that had developed in France and other parts of Europe during the Middle Ages and early modern period. The premise for the code was the idea that, for the first time in history, a law based purely on common sense should be created, free of all past prejudices and inequities. Under the code, all citizens were recognized as equal, and all class privileges were done away with.

France's efforts in addition to the Code Napoléon were the Commercial Code (1808), the Penal Code (1811), the Code of Civil Procedure (1807), and the Code of Criminal Procedure (1811). The influence of the Napoleonic code was somewhat diminished at the start of the 20th century by the introduction of the German Civil Code in 1900 and the Swiss Civil Code in 1912. Japan adopted the German code and Turkey, the Swiss code.

Codification of the civil law had several major consequences:

1. The codes constituted comprehensive and authoritative legal texts that superseded all earlier authorities in the teaching of law as well as in legal practice.
2. In each nation, the codes brought about a national unification of the law. The unification, along with systematization and reform, enhanced the certainty and predictability of the law.
3. In substance, the codes differed from one nation to another, thus marking a shift from the transnational *jus commune* to separate national legal systems. In recent years, there have been vigorous efforts by the nations of the European Union and elsewhere to replace certain isolated national laws with uniform legal practices.

While the codes of civil law and court procedures vary widely, in general they are distinguished from common law in several significant ways. In civil law, judicial interpretations are based primarily on this system of codified written law, rather than on the rule of precedent that is emphasized in the common law. The law of evidence, so important in common-law countries, has no counterpart in the civil law. Civil law separates public and private law. Generally, public-law disputes are determined by a hierarchy of administrative courts, which are separate from the ordinary courts that have jurisdiction over private-law disputes and criminal cases. In common-law countries, private- and public-law disputes usually are determined by the same courts.

Trial by jury, an important feature of the common-law system, is not often used in the civil law. A jury is never employed in the determination of civil procedures. In some civil-law countries, laypersons participate in the adjudication of criminal cases; generally, however, these laypersons do not sit as jurors but act as judges who, together with professional judges, decide on the innocence or guilt of the accused and on the sentence to be imposed. The civil-law systems go further in implementing the principle of freedom of contract, by specifically upholding almost all contractual promises and by enforcing penalty clauses. Freedom to dispose property by wills and trusts is more restricted in civil-law nations, where the testator's children and any surviving spouse receive a certain portion of a parent's estate regardless of the provisions of a will or trust.

Despite differences in methods, similarity is found in the ultimate results reached by both civil- and common-law systems. The present trend is toward a closer relationship between the common law and the civil law.

Islamic

The word *Islam* literally means to surrender to the will of God. The Islamic legal system, rather than being independent, is an integral part of the Islamic religion. Islamic law is derived from four principal sources: the Koran, the Sunna, judicial consensus, and analogical reasoning. The Koran is considered as the word of God as given to the Prophet. The Sunna includes the sayings, acts, and allowances of the Prophet as they are recorded in the Hadith. The judicial consensus is based on the historical consensus of legal precedents and acts as limitations on individual judges. Analogical reasoning is used by the judges for circumstances not provided for in the other sources.

The sanctions attached for violations of Islamic law are religious rather than civil. Islamic law is based on religious and philosophical principles that are alien to most of the non-Islamic world.[6] To understand Islamic law, one needs to have a basic knowledge of the Islamic religion and civilization. Accordingly, errors may result when individually analyzing elements of Islamic law.

Socialist

Many scholars point out that there are elements of civil-law tradition in the socialist legal system. Others contend that there is not a separate legal family of socialist law. There are also differences among the socialist countries.

Socialist law is based on legislation, and in Communist countries legislation is an expression of the Communist Party. The socialist system can be traced to the 1917 Bolshevik Revolution. Two years after the revolution, a statement of principles was adopted to guide the administrative of justice in the Russian Soviet Federative Socialist Republic. The statement said that the proletariat should not adopt the ready-made bourgeois state machinery, but should instead abolish it and create its own system of justice. However, Lenin and the other leaders of the 1917 revolution did not have a precise pattern for a legal system. The statement established a framework for the new society. It deprived individuals of the ownership of land, banks, insurance companies, shipping fleets, and large-scale industry; created restrictions on the employment of labor; and removed marriage and divorce from the sphere of church activities.

In 1922 and 1923, codes were developed in the Soviet Union to be used in the courts in criminal, civil, family, land, and labor matters. In principle, the legislature was to be the only source of law, but in practice it was the presidium, a smaller body elected from the membership of the legislature, that has made the laws and day-to-day changes in it. Ratification by the whole legislature was, according to the Soviet constitution, deemed necessary, but, in actuality, altering presidium action became impossible.

In theory, the orders and decisions of the Communist Party were not a source of law. But, in fact, the party provided the initiative for most legislative action, especially in economic planning. The wishes of the party were followed because the party's secretary was normally the real ruler of the nation. Joseph Stalin, for example, was party secretary for the entire time he ruled the Soviet Union.

Soviet law has always reflected the strong presence of the state in the lives of the people. The law covered virtually every activity in which the state and its citizens were engaged. There were extensive regulations concerning the ownership and management of property. Central to these regulations was the provision that the state owns and operates all the means of production. The state managed economic planning, social insurance, artistic creation, and family relationships.

A court system was established by the judiciary act of October 31, 1922. At the local level, there were people's courts with a full-time judge and two lay judges. The lay judges were selected for a few days of service from a panel of local citizens. Appeals from the people's courts went to provincial courts, which also had original jurisdiction in certain security, criminal, and civil cases. At the top of the legal system was the supreme court of the Soviet Union. It heard cases on appeal from the provincial courts, but it was also responsible for disciplining the lower courts, issuing rulings to interpret the legal codes, and trying cases of a significant nature to the state. There was no separation of powers between the executive, legislative, and judicial branches of the government, and the courts were subject to legislative oversight.

Law in the Soviet Union changed in the early 1990s as a result of reforms initiated by President Mikhail Gorbachev and the breakup of the Soviet Union in 1991. The traditional view of law as an instrument of the state to further the aims of Communist ideology was discarded, and ultimately the Soviet Union itself ceased to exist.

American Indian Law

The American Indian nations in the United States are accorded the status of "domestic dependent nations," and the federal government is committed to operating with them on the basis of government-to-government status.[7] This status as "domestic dependent nations" was first recognized by the U.S. Supreme Court in 1831.[8] The Supreme Court held that our Constitution recognizes Indian sovereignty by classing Indian treaties among the "supreme laws of the land" and establishes Indian affairs as a unique area of federal concern. The Court noted that in the early Indian treaties, the United States had pledged to "protect" Indian nations and that the treaties had established federal trust responsibility in our government-to-government relations with Indian nations. In addition, federal law provides that no obligation established by any treaty lawfully made and ratified prior to March 3, 1871, shall be impaired.[9]

For purposes of determining the status of Indian legal rights, "Indian nation" means any tribe, band, or other group of Indians subject to the jurisdiction of the United States and recognized as possessing powers of self-government. "Powers of self-government" means and includes all governmental powers possessed by an Indian nation—executive, legislative, and judicial—and all offices, bodies, and tribunals by and through which they are executed, including Indian offenses, and means the inherent power of Indian nations, hereby recognized and affirmed, to exercise criminal jurisdiction over all Indians.[10]

Theories of Law

There is no single, widely accepted, comprehensive theory of law and society. The field is complex and polemical. The theories overlap, and theories that are placed under one heading will contain many elements similar to those placed under another heading. The theories discussed in this chapter were grouped as a device to facilitate discussion rather than to reflect any definite status of the theories discussed. In studying theory, we should keep in mind that in modern societies there is a wide gap between what we understand to be right and what is legally required of us. This point will be discussed later in this chapter with the "bad man" example. In addition, the law is often at odds with our personal and subcultural values and morality. For example, it would be against our values to willingly allow a child to starve to death, but in most cases there is no legal duty to save a stranger's child. Two concepts are apparent when looking at the growth of legal theory. First, we cannot adequately study the development of legal theory in the terms of any one moral or ethical view. Second, we must analyze law in a broader context than our own.

In studying law as it develops when a society goes through modernization and social development, two issues are apparent. First, why do changes take place? And second, what are the forces that produce or hinder change in our laws and our legal systems? The answers to these two questions depend to a great extent on our definition of the conceptual basis of law. The two most popular conceptual bases are natural law and positivism. Natural law refers to the concept that there are universal principles that we need to discover and codify into the law—the law is there waiting to be discovered. Positivism is based on the concept that neither law nor the legal system has any natural connection with morality—laws and legal systems are created by humans.

Natural law is considered to be a general body of rules of right conduct and justice common to all mankind. This concept grew from the observation of the operation of the laws of nature and their uniformity. Positive law, on the other hand, consists of regulations formulated by the heads of a country or society. In many cases, natural-law concepts agree with positive laws that have to be enacted by governments. The prohibition against killing, for example, is common to virtually all of mankind, and most nations have enacted laws against it. The antikilling law could be considered as one with both positive and natural law influence.

Natural Law

As noted earlier, the concept of natural law is based on the assumption that, through reason, the nature of individuals can be discovered and that this knowledge will provide the basis for the social and legal ordering of human existence. Jean Dabin stated that natural law "consists in certain principles of right reason, which causes us to know that an action is morally honest or dishonest according to its necessary agreement or disagreement with a rational and sociable nature."[11] The concept of natural law is present in the writings of ancient Greece. For example, Aristotle maintained that natural law has universal validity, is free of passion, and does not depend on whether we accept it or not.[12]

The position that we now accept as natural law had its first extended explication in the writing of Cicero (106–43 B.C.). Cicero was concerned with trying to explain the nature of law in relation to morality. He saw law and morality as one. To him, law was the product of the gods. He contended that law is the highest reason, implanted in nature, which commands what ought to be done and forbids the opposite. Law is intelligence, whose natural function it is to command right conduct and forbid wrongdoing. Accordingly, law was not a product of human action; instead it was the product of God.[13] Cicero also contended that compliance with the moral principles was sufficient for law and that all natural moral requirements are also legal requirements.

The great English legal commentator, William Blackstone (1723–1780), maintained that human laws are but realizations of God's law, the moral laws of nature. Accordingly, rules that look like laws and act like laws, but in fact contradict God's law, are simply not laws at all.[14] Blackstone considered that laws existed in nature and not exclusively in the books labeled "Laws of England." Later in life, Blackstone appeared to be quite willing to recognize a distinction between human laws, laws that were laws even if immoral, and natural laws. Blackstone has traditionally been identified with two of the central positions in natural-law tradition. One position is the idea of morality as a necessary criterion for the existence of valid law. The other is the idea that human law is the realization of higher moral law, such that the higher but unwritten moral law is just as much law as that which happened to be enacted by legislatures or decided by judges. For example, murder would be unlawful even if there was no statute prohibiting it.[15]

SIR WILLIAM BLACKSTONE (1723–1780)

Blackstone's four-volume *Commentaries on the Laws of England* made Sir William Blackstone the best-known of English and American writers on the law. For many years after his death, his books served as textbooks for the teaching of law both in England and in America. Jurists of many countries cite the *Commentaries* as a source for some of their rulings. Although all four volumes of the *Commentaries* appeared in the 1760s, they remain today one of the best general histories of English law.

Blackstone was born in London in 1723. His father died before his birth, and his mother died before he was 12. He was raised by an older brother. He entered Oxford University at age 18. When he first started studying law, he wrote the famous poem "The Lawyer's Farewell to His Muse." He was admitted to the bar in 1746.

At first, Blackstone was not very successful in the practice of law. He returned to Oxford as bursar of a college. His first work on jurisprudence appeared in 1750. At that time, Oxford had no courses on law. In 1758, Blackstone was appointed as Oxford's first professor of common law. His lectures attracted wide attention, and he again entered the practice of law. He was later elected to Parliament. In 1763 he was appointed solicitor general to the queen. He resigned his professorship at Oxford in 1766.

In 1765, the first volume of his *Commentaries* was published. The last volume was published in 1769. The *Commentaries* were an immediate and popular success. Eight editions were printed in his remaining 11 years of life. In the 1770s he was appointed a judge and knighted. Blackstone had nine children. He died February 14, 1780.

Saint Thomas Aquinas's (1225–1274) writings on natural law were more extensive and more sophisticated than those of Cicero and Blackstone. Today, there is a tendency to associate the concept of natural law with Aquinas.

While the concept of natural law does not have a necessary connection with Catholicism or with religion in a formal sense, Aquinas's concept of natural law became the central thesis of Catholic theology. He saw a distinction between higher law and human law and appreciated the distinction between moral soundness and legal validity.

According to Aquinas, law is nothing but an ordinance of reason for the common good, promulgated by him who has the care of the community. That natural law is promulgated by the very fact that God instilled it into individuals' minds so as to be known by the individual. He contended that the first principle in practical reason is the one founded on the nature of the good, i.e., good is that which all things seek after. The first precept of law is based on this principle, and all laws should seek the good and avoid the evil. Every human law has just so much of the nature of law as it is derived from the law of nature. If at any point it departs from the law of nature, it is no longer a law but a perversion of law. Laws framed by individuals are either just or unjust. If they be just, they have the power of binding the conscience from the eternal law from which they are derived. Law may be unjust in two ways. First, a law is unjust when it is contrary to human good. Second, a law is unjust when it is contrary to the divine good. Laws that are contrary to the divine good must in no way be observed because "we should obey God rather than man."[16]

Legal Positivism

Legal positivism has the basic premise that neither laws nor legal systems have any natural or essential connections with morality. Laws and legal systems are posited (put in place) by human beings, thus the name "positivism." A central theme of positivism is that what legal systems ought to be or ought to do is not the same as what legal systems in fact are. They contend that something can be a legal system while still falling far short, morally, of what a legal system ought to be. Accordingly, there is no necessary connection between law and morality. For example, Nazi Germany had a legal system despite the fact that the system contained laws that were immoral. For the most part, positivists analyze law by studying the independent effects of objective social conditions, such as social organization and culture, on legal concepts. They look at changing social conditions as causes for changes in law.

European Pioneer Theorists

Baron de Montesquieu (Charles Louis de Secondat 1689–1755)

When Charles Louis de Secondat was christened in 1689 as the second son of the well-to-do de Secondats, a beggar was chosen from the crowd to be his godfather. His parents did this so that he would always look at the poor as his brothers.[17] His mother died when he was 11. He attended college at Oration in southwestern France. At the age of 24, when his father died, his uncle became his guardian. Not that he needed a guardian, but this was a method to allow his uncle, the Baron de Montesquieu, who was without heir, to pass his land and title to his nephew. When his uncle died, he became the baron.

His most influential work was *The Spirit of Law*, which he completed in 1748. According to him, laws, in their most general signification, are the necessary relations arising from the nature of things. All beings have their laws. That law in general is human reason, inasmuch as it governs all individuals. Montesquieu considered that law was integral to its particular culture. He attacked the natural law's assumptions and contended that laws were the results of societal factors such as customs, physical environment, and antecedents. He argued that law should be considered in relation to its background, its antecedents, and its surroundings. According to him, laws were relative and that there were no good or bad laws.

Herbert Spencer (1820–1903)

Spencer rejected the doctrines of natural law that were popular in 19th-century England. He was strongly influenced by Charles Darwin. According to Spencer, the natural selection and survival of the fittest were the determining factors involved in the evolution of civilization and law. The evolution of society for Spencer was the growing differentiation between individuals in the society and the increasing division of labor. According to Spencer, the only function of government was as that of an overseer who guards the safety of private property and sees that peace is not breached. He argued that society does not need supervision and that maximum freedom of individual action should be promoted by law.[18] To him, any attempts by the government to achieve greater social and economic equality among individuals were ill-advised and unnatural. His laissez-faire doctrines are still present in many political conservative attitudes in the United States.

Sir Henry Sumner Maine (1822–1888)

Sir Henry Sumner Maine founded the English historical school of law. To him, legal history reflected patterns of evolution that recur in different societies and in similar historical circumstances. Maine contended that there was only a limited number of possibilities for building and managing societies, and therefore legal forms reappear in seemingly different garb. He noted that many of the legal rules and legal institutions that were present in Roman feudalism were very similar to those noted in English feudalism. In his classical treatise, *Ancient Law,* Maine contended that the "movement of the progressive societies has hitherto been a movement from status to contract." Status referred to a fixed condition in which the individual is without will and without opportunity. As the societies evolve or progress, they move away from a system of status to a social system based on contracts. To Maine, legal relations were not based on one's birth, but depended on voluntary agreements.[19]

Interrelationship between Society and Law

What is the primary source of law? Is it the will of the people or of those in power? The next three theorists—Karl Marx, Max Weber, and Emile Durkheim—look at these issues. While their approaches are different, all three discussed the essential interrelationships between legal institutions and the social order.

Karl Marx (1818–1883)

Karl Marx was a philosopher, economist, historian, and sociologist. His ideology may have caused more social change than any other person in the modern world. Marx saw law as a form of class rule. Marx stated that every society rests on an economic foundation—the mode of production of commodities. Marx opined that this was true for every society, regardless of its stage of historical development. The mode of production has two essential elements: the physical or technological arrangement of economic activity and the social relations of production. The social relations of production referred to the indispensable human attachments that people must form with one another when engaged in economic activity. He saw the determinant variable as the mode of production and that changes in this variable produce changes in the way in which groups are attached to production technology. His theory of law had three principal assumptions:

1. Law is a product of evolving economic forces.
2. Law is a tool used by the ruling class to maintain its power over the lower classes.
3. In the future (communist society), law as an instrument of social control will disappear.

To Marx, there would be no need for law in the final stages of societal development when societies become stateless.

Max Weber (1864–1920)

Max Weber was a German lawyer and sociologist. Weber is considered by many as the most important historical figure in the development of the sociology of law.[20] He was trained as a lawyer. Both Marx and Weber saw law as an important source of meaning that enables people to interact with others in economic and political life along rational and predictable lines.[21] Both considered the widening scope of political democracy and the inclusion of the working-class interests into electoral politics and lawmaking as basic to changing the rule of law. While Marx considered that the rule of law supported the power of the dominant class in society, Weber looked at the law in relation to the power of the state. Weber viewed the law in its universality and its support for individual freedom.[22]

Weber saw four ideal types of legal systems, which are seldom, if ever, attained in their pure form. He stated that legal procedures are rational or irrational. Rational procedures involve the use of logic and scientific methods to attain specific objectives. Irrational procedures rely on ethical or mystical considerations such as magic or the supernatural. Next, he stated that legal procedures could proceed, rationally or irrationally, with respect to formal or substantive law. Formal law results when legal decisions are based on established rules, regardless of the notion of fairness. Substantive law considers the circumstances of individual cases and the prevailing notion of justice before making any decision in individual cases. Accordingly, his four ideal systems are:

Substantive irrationality: This exists when cases are decided on some religious, ethical, emotional, or political basis rather than by general rules.
Formal irrationality: This exists when rules used are based on supernatural forces. It is irrational because there is a lack of understanding as to why it works and formal because of the strict adherence that is required.
Substantive rationality: This exists when decisions are based on the application of rules from nonlegal sources such as religion, ideology, or science. It is rational, since the rules are derived from specific and accepted sources. It is substantive because there is a concern for justness of outcomes in individual cases.
Formal rationality: This involves the use of consistent, logical rules that are independent of moral, religious, or other normative criteria that are applied equally in all cases.

Weber's typology also identifies three types of administration of justice: Kahdi justice, empirical justice, and rational justice. Kahdi justice is that justice dispensed by the judge of the Islamic Shari'a Court. Empirical justice consists of deciding cases by referring to analogies and relying on and interpreting principles. Rational justice is based on bureaucratic principles. According to Weber, modern societies differ from the past in that modern societies are in pursuit of the rational. He contends that the modern law of the West has become increasingly institutionalized through the bureaucratization of the state.

Emile Durkheim (1858–1917)

Emile Durkheim was a French sociologist whose most important contribution was probably in helping us understand the relationship between law and social solidarity and the evolution of the legal systems.[23] He was a pioneer in the study of law and society. His study of the sociology of law is steeped in positivist methodology. Durkheim sought to examine the social and moral functions of law along with the sources of law in an attempt to highlight the underlying patterns of social connectedness or solidarity.

To Durkheim, law was a measure of the type of solidarity in a society. The term *social solidarity* refers to the persistent and ongoing expectations that people establish with one another within a society. The shared expectations in a primitive society are among persons with similar values, where the expectations are close and personal. As the society becomes more complex, the shared expectations are generally not close personal expectations. For example, you need gas for your car. In today's society, there is a shared expectation with strangers that they will have gas for sale and that you will buy it. If the first station you go to is out of gas, then you will go to the next. In the very primitive society, the family may be depending on you to hunt and bring home food. If you go swimming instead and do not go hunting, the family will have nothing to eat.

According to Durkheim, there are two types of solidarity in a society: mechanical and organic. Simple and homogenous societies are considered as mechanical. In mechanical societies there are similarities of ideas, habits, and attitudes. Most individuals in mechanical societies are almost self-sufficient. Organic solidarity occurs when societies develop and become more complex, heterogeneous, and differentiated by divisions of labor. Durkheim considered law and society as more of a process of development from simple to complex form as the societies become more organic and more differentiated. As this process occurs, the law becomes more independent from its social conditions and more differentiated.

Mechanical societies tend to be repressive, and their law tends to be predominantly penal in nature and regressive. As the societies develop toward organic solidarity, their law tends to move away from regressive and more toward restitutive, with more emphasis on compensation and less on punishment. Contractual law is central to modern societies to regulate the complex relationships that are a part of any organic society.

DURKHEIM ON THE FUNCTION OF CRIME

Durkheim contended that punishment under certain conditions acts as social rituals that provide the "upstanding" members of the society with opportunities to reaffirm and intensify their commitment to shared values and a common identity. He uses an imaginary community of saints to illustrate this point. In the community of saints of exemplary individuals, criminal conduct is unknown. Faults that appear venial to the average person would create a scandal among the exemplary individuals, the same as a crime would in other communities. If, then, the community of saints had the power to judge and punish, it would define these faults as criminal and would treat them as such. To update the parable, we could imagine a society in which murders, rapes, robbery, etc., are eliminated, and the most serious crime remaining was jaywalking. Then the most serious punishment permissible would be imposed for the crime of jaywalking.

From his community-of-saints parable, four important ideas on punishment arise:

- Punishment is more proactive than reactive.
- Ritual punishment and solidarity are functionally linked.
- Punishment is but a reflection of the solidarity needs of the community.
- The behavior being punished may not have any direct harmful consequences for the community.[24]

Bob Roshier disagrees with Durkheim. In his article, "The Function of Crime Myth," he states that to say that crime is functional and hence necessary for a society means that we must always consciously retain a stock of people whom we humiliate, imprison, or at the very least regard as suitable cases for treatment. He states that Durkheim's argument about crime is similar to the dispensation of justice described by Lewis Carroll in *Through the Looking Glass*:

> [The King's Messenger, the Mad Hatter is] in prison now, being punished: and the trial doesn't even begin till next Wednesday and of course the crime comes last of all.[25]

Sociological Jurisprudence Movement

The sociological jurisprudence movement is an attack on legal formalism and rationality. The movement's most active period was from 1910 to 1920. Its leaders were Roscoe Pound, Oliver Wendell Holmes, and Benjamin Cardozo.

The movement predated and set the groundwork for legal realism.[26] After the movement, the appearance of formalism in the law was never the same. Pound and Cardozo are discussed in this section. Holmes will be discussed in the section on legal realism.[27]

Roscoe Pound

Roscoe Pound was a prolific writer who published his final essays when he was in his nineties. For many years he was the dean of Harvard Law School. His writings relied heavily on the philosophies of sociologist Edward Ross and the pragmatist William James. According to Pound, social control requires power—power to influence the behavior of persons through the pressure of their fellow individuals. His notion of social control is reflected in his definition of law as "a highly specialized form of social control, carried on in accordance with the authoritative precepts and applied in a judicial and administrative process." He was more concerned with the results of the law, i.e., how its application affected people than the causes of the development of the legal form.

Pound contended that judges should be given a degree of discretion in individual cases and should move away from mechanical applications of the law. The standards used by judges should concern "equitable application." Formal logic should be merely an instrument used to arrive at a fair decision. Pound contended that the law should act so as to ensure the maximum amount of fulfillment of interests in a society. It should do so by minimizing sacrifices, waste, and useless friction.

Pound traced the stages in the development of law. According to him, the stages started with the primitive forms and advanced toward the "socialization" of law. The goal in the most developed systems should be the maximum fulfillment of wants and desires and that greater weight should be accorded to public and social interests over private interests. He uses the example of the evolution of property rights to show how property-use restrictions have developed in the name of "the public good." For example, at one time, when a person owned land, he or she could use it in any manner he or she desired. Presently, when one owns land, the land is owned subject to use restrictions placed on the property by the government, e.g., only for a single-family residence.

One of Pound's greatest achievements was in reconceptualizing how the law should be understood. Roscoe Pound contended that ideas of what law is for are largely implicit in the concept of what law is.[28] Pound offered conceptions of what constitutes the law. The following list presents his four conceptions of what constitutes the law.

Divinely ordained rules: Law consists of god-given or handed-down rules of conduct.

Recorded traditions of old customs: Under this conception, law is the
traditional or recorded body of precepts in which customs are pre-
served and expressed.

Recorded wisdom of the wise: Law is the recorded wisdom of the wise
men of old who have learned the safe course for human conduct.

Philosophically discovered system of principles: Law may be considered
as a philosophically discovered set of principles that express how
humans ought to conform their conduct.

Pound criticized the English-speaking positivists by stating that the positivists looked at a body of principles and policies and treated them as laws
that are binding on the officials in a society. He attributed this to a lawyer's
natural tendency to associate laws and rules. He stated that English-speaking
lawyers were tricked into this tendency long ago by the fact that English uses
the same word, changing only the article, for "a law" and "the law." Most
other languages use two words, e.g., *loi* and *droit* and *Gesetz* and *Recht*.[29]

Benjamin Nathan Cardozo (1870–1938)

Benjamin Cardozo was born in New York, the son of a Tammany-sponsored
judge on New York's supreme court. His father was charged with political
corruption in the Boss Tweed scandal and resigned from office in disgrace.
His mother died when he was 9 and his father when he was 15. He was raised
by his older sister. Rather than going to public schools, he was tutored at
home by Horatio Alger, who later became famous for writing boys' books
about poor but honest boys who always rose to success and fame. Cardozo
entered Columbia University at the age of 16. Later, as a young lawyer, he was
driven to redeem his family's name that had been disgraced by his father.[30]

In his *The Nature of the Judicial Process*, Cardozo contended that judge-
made law was one of the existing realities of life. In that work, he attempted
to answer the questions: What is it that I do when I decide a case? To what
sources of information do I appeal for guidance? In what proportion do I
permit them to contribute to the results? And, if a precedent is applicable,
when do I refuse to follow it?

He first looked at the source of law used by a judge in making a decision.
He concluded that if the answer is not obvious, then the judge should look
to the common law for the rule that fits the case. According to him, most of
the changes in our legal system have been brought about by judges, and these
modifications are gradual—inch by inch. In his view, the directive forces of
law are philosophy, history, and custom, and the final cause (goal) of law is
the welfare of society.

Legal Realism

The leaders in the legal realism movement were Oliver Wendell Holmes, Karl Llewellyn, and Jerome Frank. The movement, based on pragmatism, was popular from 1920 to 1940. Legal realism viewed law as more of a social science, with sociology, economics, psychology, and philosophy as its guides. To the realists, the laboratory is the real world. As pragmatists, the realists were hostile to formalism, the use of abstractions, and exclusive reliance on strict deductive types of reasoning. According to them, fixed rules and principles should be discarded. Thus, rather than using mechanical reasoning, the judges should be decision makers. Former Chief Justice Charles Evan Hughes, a realist, once stated that the "Constitution is what the judges say it is."

Oliver Wendell Holmes

Oliver Wendell Holmes Jr. (1841–1935) is considered as one of the founders of the legal realism school. Holmes noted that legal realism is based on the concept that judges formulate law by exercising choices as to which laws to use when making legal decisions. Holmes contended that judges make decisions on the bases of their conceptions of justness and then resort to formal legal precedents to support their decisions. Our judges, therefore, should be knowledgeable with not only the law, but also with its historical, social, and economic aspects.

Holmes sought to define "law" as a prediction of what legal officials would do. According to him, a legal duty is nothing but a prediction that if a man does or omits certain things, he will be made to suffer in this or that way by judgment of the court. Holmes used his famous example of a "bad man" to illustrate his concepts. Thus, if you want to know the law and nothing else, you look at it as a bad man would, who cares only for the material consequences that such knowledge enables him to predict, not as a good man, who finds his reasons for conduct in the vague sanctions of conscience.[31] According to Holmes, such a person does not care about the general moral pronouncements and abstract legal doctrines, but only what the courts are in fact likely to do.

McBOYLE V. UNITED STATES

A federal statute was passed in 1919 making it a federal crime to take a stolen vehicle across state lines. The McBoyle case involved a stolen airplane, which was a new form of transportation in 1931 when the case was before the Court. Justice Holmes wrote an opinion that criminal laws must be interpreted very narrowly, and thus he concluded that an airplane was not a vehicle for the purposes of this statute.[32] He concluded that when Congress passed the criminal statute, they intended to include wagons, bicycles, automobiles, and trucks. At that time, most members of Congress did not think of the airplane as a vehicle.

Karl Llewellyn (1893–1962)

Karl Llewellyn, a Columbia law professor, contended that what law officials do about disputes is the law itself. To Llewellyn, rules are the heart of the law, and the arrangement of rules in society in an orderly, coherent system is the business of the legal scholar, while the drawing of a neat solution from a rule to fit the case in hand is the business of the judge and of the advocate.[33] He stated that there is difficulty in framing any concept of law because there are so many things to be included and the things to be included are unbelievably different from each other.

According to Llewellyn, the term *rule* is very ambiguous. It could be prescriptive with what ought to be or what judges ought to do. Or it may be descriptive, e.g., this is what judges actually do in such cases. Or it may be both, what they ought to do and what they do. Llewellyn wrote that there are often respectable legal arguments that can be made on both sides of the same case. A statement by a judge that "this is the rule" usually means "I find this formula of words in authoritative books." Llewellyn argued that a "real rule" and the one that should be used by the judges would be only a prediction of what the courts will do and nothing more. He sees the judge's role as that of a policy maker.

Jerome Frank (1889–1957)

Jerome Frank, an attorney and later federal court judge, berated common-law judges for legislating feebly and timidly and for blindly relying on real or fancied analogies with past cases instead of adapting their decisions to the growing needs of society as revealed by the moral standard of utility.[34] He contended that judges looked for rationalism from legal rules to support the results that they had reached on other grounds. What other grounds do judges use to arrive at proper results? Frank, influenced by psychoanalysis theories, considered the answer to be in the psychological preconceptions and attitudes of the judges. He also stressed what he considered was a judge's "situation sense."[35]

Max Gluckman (1911–1975)

Max Gluckman was a distinguished British anthropologist who pioneered the study of traditional African legal systems. He stressed social conflict and mechanisms for conflict resolution while studying urbanization and social change in colonial Africa. Rather than viewing African societies as closed, stable systems, Gluckman recognized the often chaotic changes in those systems that were caused by colonialism and race conflicts. Despite being interested in conflict and in culturally complex settings, he argued that the social systems could be analyzed as integrated systems.

By stressing the role of conflict in social life and the role of colonialism in modern African societies, Gluckman moved social anthropology in Britain in a Marxist direction. Despite his conflict approach, he never abandoned the more traditional British interest in societies as stable self-regulating systems. He is noted for his use of detailed single-case studies to illustrate general structural principles.

Modern Legal Theorists

John Rawls

John Rawls, a professor of philosophy at Harvard University, examined H. L. A. Hart's principle of fairness. He concluded that we have a moral obligation to obey the rules of a cooperative enterprise. Rawls stated that our moral obligation to obey the law is a special case of the duty of fair play. Rawls contended that obligations differ from duties in that obligations arise out of the consequences of voluntary acts. He used the concept of natural duties to establish a duty to obey all laws. The natural duty is a duty that would be chosen by all rational persons under conditions of impartiality. According to him, the crucial differences between a natural duty and a moral obligation is that the natural duty does not depend on any voluntary act, so it applies equally to the rich and the poor.[36]

Richard Posner

Richard Posner is currently chief judge of the Seventh Circuit Court of Appeals and senior lecturer at the University of Chicago School of Law. Prior to his appointment as an appellate justice in 1981, he was a professor at law school. He has a distinctive stance in that he is a pragmatist in philosophy, economist in methodology, and a Ronald Reagan conservative in politics. Posner defended his pragmatic approach by describing it as an approach that is practical and instrumental rather than essentialist—interested in what works and what is useful rather than in what "really" is. According to him, a pragmatist is not afraid to say that a little forgetting is a good thing. That forgetting emancipates us from the sense of belatedness, which can be paralyzing. And that when applied to law, pragmatism would treat precedent as policy rather than as a duty to follow.[37]

His chief contribution to law was in popularizing the "economic analysis" approach to resolving legal disputes. According to him, law should be designed to ensure that assets and opportunities are in the hands of those who can and would pay most for them. Using this approach, he has argued that mothers should be allowed to auction off their newborn babies[38] and that criminal laws that prohibit rape are just, because "even if the rapist cannot find a consensual substitute ... it does not follow that he values the rape more than the victim disvalues it."[39] He contends that law should aim at achieving the best consequences overall, taking into account not only the community's overall wealth but other desirable consequences as well. Posner has had great influence in American law schools for decades.[40]

Laura Nader

Laura Nader was educated as an anthropologist. In 1960, she was appointed as a professor of anthropology at the University of California. She has written numerous articles on the comparative aspects of law in primitive societies. Nader was interested in how the jurisprudence of advanced civilizations had advanced from the primitive stages and studied the development from an anthropological view.

Laura Nader also researched conflict resolution. She contended that there were three distinct phases or stages in the dispute process: the grievance or preconflict stage, the conflict stage, and the dispute stage. The grievance stage begins when one or more parties perceive that an unjust situation exists. The situation may be real or imaginary. If it is not resolved at the grievance stage, it enters into the conflict stage. At the conflict stage, the situation involves two parties. If it is not solved at the conflict stage, then it enters the dispute stage. At the dispute stage, the situation there is the involvement of a third party who is called on to act as a settlement agent.[41]

Donald Black

Donald Black, a sociologist at Yale University, contends that law is a form of governmental control, and that the quantity of law varies in time and space. It varies across the centuries, decades and years, months and days, even the hours of a day. It also varies across societies, regions, communities, neighborhoods, families, and relationships of every kind. He argues that the more stratification present in a society, the more law it has. Stratification is the vertical aspect of social life. He states that law varies inversely with other social controls and that law is stronger when other social controls are weaker. Black contends that the law varies with rank and increases as it nears the mainstream of culture and decreases as it moves away. The law, according to him, is greater in a direction toward less conventionality than toward more conventionality. Thus, there is less legal control for the more conventional members of a society and more legal control toward those who are less conventional.[42] Black's approach to law exemplifies the positivistic approach noted earlier by Durkheim.

Black is often criticized for his statement that the law is an institution for governmental control. According to his critics, the law is used for more than direct government involvement. For example, people use the law to order their private relations with one another and in many cases to get compensated for physical injuries. In addition, Black is also criticized because he fails to adequately explain some of his terms. For example, he states that "the quantity of law increases with the social complexity," but he fails to explain why the relationship occurs.[43]

Edward Levi

Edward Levi was a professor and later president of the University of Chicago Law School. In his famous work, *An Introduction to Legal Reasoning*,[44] he looked at whether the judiciary should assume the function of lawmaker in spite of, or in conflict with, the enacted law. To answer this question, he looked first at the process of reasoning in the field of case law and in the interpretation of statutes and constitutions. He rejected the concept that the law is a system of known rules and applied by the judges. According to Levi, legal rules are never clear, and if a rule had to be clear before it could be imposed, society would be impossible. He argued that the process of legal reasoning was a three-step process:

1. A similarity is observed between cases.
2. Next, the rule of law inherent in the first case is announced.
3. Then the rule of law adopted in the first case is made applicable to the second case.

Critical Legal Studies

A group of junior faculty members and law students at Yale University began a series of critical legal studies in the late 1960s.[45] The Conference on Critical Legal Studies was organized in 1977, and its annual conferences draw more than 1,000 attendees.

The movement was influenced by Marxist-inspired theorists, and its roots can be traced to the American legal realism movement of the 1920s and 1930s. The legal realists had argued against the traditional concept that the rule of law was supreme. They argued that law was based entirely on the predilections of judges. To support this argument, they pointed out that good lawyers could argue successfully on either side of a given case, and therefore there was nothing about the law that made any judicial decision inevitable. The realists discounted the concept that law was above politics and the economy. They contended that law was not a science and that it was virtually impossible to separate the law from politics, economics, and culture. To them, there was nothing distinctly legal about legal reasoning—that legal reasoning can not operate independently of the personal biases of lawyers and judges. The law consists of many contradictions and, therefore, it is not self-contained models of legal reasoning, as generally considered. Legal decisions are inevitably based on political grounds. Legal realism disappeared in the 1940s, and it was not until the 1970s that the work begun by Holmes, Pound, Cardozo, Frank, and Llewellyn reemerged with the critical legal studies movement. The attack, however, by the critical legal studies movement was much more vehement and expansive in scope.[46]

The critical legal studies movement rejected the concept that law was value free and above political concerns. The critical theorists contend that the law only seems neutral and independent because it reflects the dominant value system of a society and that law only seeks to maintain the status quo. Law to them is a part of the system of power used by the group in power and not a protection against them. Like the Marxist theorists, critical legal studies theorists contend that the law serves to maintain the status quo and thus is actually a part of the system of power used by those in society to maintain their power. Accordingly, law does not protect the weak, but is a weapon against them. The critical legal studies movement's major objective was to develop and gain broader support for new legal doctrines that were more representative of class, gender, and race differences. While the movement did not accomplish its primary goal, it has indicated the extent to which politics influences our legal system.[47]

Feminist Legal Theories

The feminist legal theories are concerned with the influence of gender and gendered conceptions of the law. Many feminists contend that society is patriarchal and dominated by men and is therefore not necessarily hospitable to women. Since law regulates all other societal institutions, the role of gender is particularly crucial in law.[48] Feminists point out that the laws that are obviously about women, such as those involving rape, abortion, sexual harassment, pregnancy, pornography, and child custody, were generally drafted and enacted by men. Originally, feminist legal theory was about women; now it is a general theoretical approach to law. While feminists share a common framework within which debates occur, they disagree too much to have a common set of answers. A common concern of all feminists is: How can the women's situation best be served?

Feminists appear to be equally divided between two broad concepts: (a) women should be treated equally and (b) women should be treated differently from men in order to ensure equality in results. The "equality feminist" contends that women should be treated "just like men." Elimination of employment discrimination based on gender was an early victory for the equality feminists. The "difference feminist" argues that formal similarity of treatment is not enough, because women are different and that equal treatment would reproduce inequality. For example, if women were treated just like men, how could they be given pregnancy benefits?[49] The difference view assumes the existence of "some essential aspect of human nature, something pre-given, innate, biological, and natural that cannot be changed."[50] The difference position is also referred to as the essentialism position.

Many feminists contend that it is not the comparison between men and women that matters, but their relative power to each other. According to Catherine MacKinnon, the task of feminism is to end the subordination of women, not simply to make them equal in an abstract sense.[51]

Critical Race Theory

Critical race theory is mostly concerned with issues involving oppression, difference, and lack of equality. Most scholars trace critical race theory back to a workshop on critical race theory held in Madison, Wisconsin, in 1989. Many of the scholars present at the conference had been previously involved with critical legal studies.[52] Other scholars contend that the 1989 conference merely ratified what had already been in place.

The critical race theorists are a diverse group, speaking about many different areas of the law and with different voices, but with the central theme of fighting oppression. The movement attempts to rectify the wrongs of racism while recognizing that racism is an inherent factor in our present society and that its elimination is impossible. The critical race theorists contend that an ongoing campaign against racism must be conducted to overcome racist oppression. They contend that racism is not only a matter of individual prejudice and everyday practice, but it is also a phenomenon that is deeply embedded within our society and legal institutions. The theorists also believe that they have a duty to eliminate racism through reason and to devote their efforts to separate legal reasoning and legal institutions from their racist roots.

One of the problems with critical race theory is the apparent contradiction between the commitment to racial criticism and the emphasis on racial emancipation. If the language used to describe justice is so infected by racism, what are the objectives of criticism? The theory is also criticized because it lacks a standard methodology and a set of common tenets. Many see the theory as a reformist movement and indistinguishable from traditional civil rights movements.

The basic premise of the critical race theorists is that persons of "color" are being oppressed in the United States. The use of the term *critical* is to acknowledge that there is continuity between critical legal studies and critical race theory. Both are concerned with how the system works to support and maintain a system of oppression. While the critical legal studies advocates generally do not look beyond the law and legal institutions to identify the forces that determine the content of legal rules, the critical race theorists look beyond the law and legal institutions in a search for solutions.

Summary

- Common law is considered as judge-made law because it developed out of decisions made in prior cases that were adopted as precedent. The name *common law* comes from the idea that English medieval law, as administered by the courts of the realm, reflected the "common" customs of the kingdom.
- Whereas civil-law judges resolve disputes by referring to statutory principles arrived at in advance, common-law judges focus more intently on the facts of the particular case to arrive at a fair and equitable result for the litigants.
- The three major nations whose law is based on common law are the United States, Canada, and England.
- The common-law system was originated in England after the Norman Conquest.
- It is used in English-speaking countries except Scotland and South Africa.
- At the time of the Norman Conquest, there was no uniform criminal law in England. Individual courts were dominated by sheriffs who enforced village rules as they saw fit. To reduce the arbitrary aspects of the law, William the Conqueror decreed that all prosecutions should be conducted in the name of the king, a practice that exists today in criminal-law cases where all criminal cases are conducted in the name of the state, people, or commonwealth.
- By the 1600s, the primary law of England was based on the mandatory rules of conduct laid down by the judges. The rules became the common law of England. Prior decisions were accepted as authoritative precepts and were applied to future cases.
- When the English settlers came to America in the 1600s, they brought with them the English common law.
- The legal system in the United States is presently a complex blend of common and statute law.
- One of the basic principles of common law is the doctrine of judicial review. This doctrine provides courts with the authority to review all statutory enactments, judicial decisions of lower courts, and administrative determinations within their jurisdiction. This common-law principle was formally recognized by the U.S. Supreme Court in the famous case of *Marbury v. Madison*.

- As judicial decisions accumulate on a particular kind of dispute, general rules or precedents emerge and become guidelines for judges deciding similar cases in the future. Subsequent cases, however, may reveal new and different facts and considerations, such as changing social or technological conditions.
- In the common-law system, a pyramidal structure of courts exists to define and refine the law. At the base of the pyramid are trial courts. Above the trial courts, layers of appellate courts, composed entirely of judges, exist to adjudicate disputes. These disputes center on whether or not the trial judge applied the correct principles of law.
- The interpretations of law made by appellate courts form the precedents that govern future cases. Furthermore, the importance of a precedent for any given court depends on that court's position in the pyramidal structure; for example, a precedent set by an appellate court has greater force in trial courts than in other similar-level appellate courts.
- If a common-law judge feels that the facts are sufficiently different from prior cases and that there is no binding precedent, then the judge is free to depart from precedent and establish a new rule of decision.
- This new decision sets a new precedent as it is accepted and used by different judges in other cases. In this manner, common law retains a dynamic for change.
- There is no single, widely accepted, comprehensive theory of law and society. The field is complex and polemical. The theories overlap, and theories that are placed under one heading will contain many elements similar to those placed under another heading.
- Natural law is considered to be a general body of rules of right conduct and justice common to all mankind. This concept grew from the observation of the operation of the laws of nature and their uniformity.
- Positive law, on the other hand, consists of regulations formulated by the heads of a country or society. In many cases, natural-law concepts agree with positive laws that have be enacted by governments. The prohibition against killing, for example, is common to virtually all of mankind, and most nations have enacted laws against it. The antikilling law could be considered as one with both positive- and natural-law influence.
- Legal positivism has the basic premise that neither law nor legal systems have any natural or essential connections with morality. Laws and legal systems are posited (put in place) by human beings, thus the name *positivism*. A central theme of positivism is that what legal systems ought to be or ought to do is not the same as what legal systems in fact are.

- A group of junior faculty members and law students at Yale University began a series of critical legal studies in the late 1960s. The movement was influenced by Marxist-inspired theorists, and its roots can be traced to the American legal realism movement of the 1920s and 1930s. The legal realists had argued against the traditional concept that the rule of law was supreme. They argued that law was based entirely on the predilections of judges.
- The critical legal studies movement rejected the concept that law was value free and above political concerns. The critical theorists contend that the law only seems neutral and independent because it reflects the dominant value system of a society and that law only seeks to maintain the status quo. Law to them is a part of the system of power used by the group in power and not a protection against the powerful.
- The feminist legal theories are concerned with the influence of gender and gendered conceptions of the law. Many feminists contend that society is patriarchal and dominated by men and is therefore not necessarily hospitable to women.
- Feminists appear to be equally divided between two broad concepts:(1) women should be treated equally and (2) women should be treated differently from men in order to ensure equality in results. The "equality feminist" contends that women should be treated "just like men." Elimination of employment discrimination based on gender was an early victory for the equality feminists.
- Critical race theory is mostly concerned with issues involving oppression, difference, and lack of equality. Most scholars trace critical race theory back to a workshop on critical race theory held in Madison, Wisconsin, in 1989. Many of the scholars present at the conference had been previously involved with critical legal studies.
- The basic premise of the critical race theorists is that persons of "color" are being oppressed in the United States. The use of the term *critical* is to acknowledge that there is continuity between critical legal studies and critical race theory.

Questions in Review

1. What is the origin of the term *common law*?
2. How does common law differ from civil law?
3. Explain the importance of *Marbury v. Madison*.
4. What did Holmes mean when he stated that "the life of common law has not been logic; it has been experience"?
5. How was the term *civil law* derived?
6. What is the basis of the Soviet legal system?
7. Explain the status of American Indian nations.

8. Explain the difference between natural law and positive law.
9. Explain Weber's four ideal types of legal systems.
10. How did Durkheim explain the development of legal systems?
11. Explain Roscoe Pound's notion of social control.
12. How did the critical legal studies movement start?
13. What are basic concepts of the feminist legal theories?

Endnotes

1. G.F. Cole, S.J. Frankowski, & M.G. Gertz (Eds.). (1981). *Major criminal justice systems* (p. 27). Beverly Hills, CA: Sage.
2. 2 L.Ed.60 (1803).
3. L.M. Friedman. (1997). *American law: In introduction* (Rev. ed., p. 209). New York, NY: Norton.
4. P.K. Byers & S.M. Bourgoin (Eds.). (1998). William Penn. In *Encyclopedia of world biography* (2nd ed.), 17 vols. Gale Research; reproduced in *Biography resource center*. Farmington Hills, MI: Thomson Gale (2007); H. Fantel. (1974). *William Penn: Apostle of dissent* (p. 6). New York, NY: William Morrow.
5. Trial of William Penn as reported in 6 How. St. Trials 951 (1670).

Social Research Methods

3

Chapter Objectives

After reading this chapter you should be able to

- Establish a framework for understanding the relation between law and society through social research
- Explain the relationship between research and policy making
- List and explain the research methods that are used to develop coherent descriptions and explanations about social phenomena
- Discuss the roles sociologists should take when addressing law and societal issues
- Define the concept of *rule of law*

Introduction

Sociological research in America has often focused on areas in which there are significant legal aspects (for example, crime and delinquency). However, there is no one general body of sociological understanding uncritically accepted by everyone. In fact, there are a variety of theoretical perspectives that are simply different ways of perceiving and understanding the social world. Therefore, the distinctive feature of sociology is not so much what is studied but how it is studied and explained.

In this chapter we address several issues relating to scientific inquiry. Our aim is to help students establish a framework for understanding the relation between law and society through social research. Our primary focus is to provide an overview of research methods that are used to develop coherent descriptions and explanations about social phenomena. A secondary emphasis is given to contributions of research to social policy. As such, throughout the chapter, examples are used to demonstrate the relationship between research and policy making. The concluding section raises the issue of differentiating between social and criminal justice.

Fundamentals of Research

Before we discuss some of the various methods that can be applied in researching law in society, it is important to elaborate on a few terms that are found in the process of scientific inquiry. We begin by providing a definition of *research* and discuss the relationship between scientific research and the structure of legal thinking.

Research is defined as a systematic method of inquiry into a phenomenon.[1] The specific feature of a systematic method means that the researcher deliberately conforms to a planned sequence of steps in order to study some phenomenon. Every natural event (phenomenon) is assumed to have a cause that is preceded by a number of conditions that are responsible for it. Consequently, if these causal factors can be distinguished and reinstituted, the event could be duplicated. This assumption in scientific research, which is known as determinism, presumes that a certain level of predictability can be achieved regarding the occurrence of natural events.

Researchers use a standard approach to scientific inquiry that is referred to as the scientific method. The scientific method serves as a tool for developing scientific knowledge and skills. The general structure of the scientific method, which is viewed as necessary for any research study, involves the following elements:

- The gathering of a set of observations from a natural phenomenon
- The formulation of a hypothesis to explain the observations
- The execution of an experiment to test the hypothesis
- The analysis of data from test results
- The reporting of the findings and the generalization of the conclusions

When using scientific inquiry to conduct research relating to law in society, researchers relate the structure of legal thinking to the recurrent types of social interactions on which it is brought to bear. Often the sociological analysis of legal thinking is viewed to be closely associated with logical or philosophical analysis of law, or jurisprudence itself.[2] Vilhelm Aubert notes several characteristics of legal thinking that distinguish it from the kind of thinking applied in the natural sciences. Two of these characteristics are very useful for discussing the relationship between law and science.

1. Scientific approaches tend to emphasize, often to the exclusion of everything else, that aspect of a phenomenon that is general. Judicial opinions, and also legal theory, tend also to stress the unique aspects of the case. Generalizations have a large, but not exclusive, part to play in law. This stems in part from the concern with individual

justice, but it is also related to the need of the judge to avoid falsification of his or her opinions. The normative status of a falsified verdict is very different from the status of a falsified scientific hypothesis. It is the duty of the scientists to risk falsification. It is an equally sacred duty of the judges to take all the care they can to make no proposition that cannot be upheld, and to limit the applicability of their verdicts so as to reduce the likelihood of falsification. The maximal use of empirical data to achieve predictability of other phenomena is the goal of scientists. The minimal likelihood of falsification, if necessary at the cost of generalizability, is the major goal of the judge.[3]

2. Legal thinking is characterized by the absence of probabilism,[4] both with respect to law and with respect to facts. Events have taken place or they have not taken place. A law is either valid or invalid. If factual doubt is very great, the problem is not solved by the assignment of probabilities to alternatives. Rather, it is solved by the introduction of rules about the burden of proof, rules about who shall lose if doubt is of a certain vaguely suggested magnitude. In many cases in which the best available scientific guess is that a person committed a crime, the attitude of the law is that the defendant has not committed the crime because of the operation of the principle *in dubio pro reo*.[4b] Legal thinking is based upon a normative view on truth, that certain kinds of probable truth are more dangerous than others and demand stronger proof. This thought is alien to science.[5]

Methods of Inquiry

In research, one of the critically important decisions to be made is how to go about collecting data. The researcher chooses a method, which is a basic term in research used to describe the gathering of accurate facts (data). The methodology is a general approach to problem solving in various situations. It is the plan or blueprint for a study and includes the who, what, when, where, why, and how of an investigation.

SELECTED RESEARCH TERMINOLOGY

Variables: Concepts that have been operationalized, i.e., the concepts we hold about some phenomenon will be defined and translated into values that can be measured.

Dependent variable: The variable that the researcher is attempting to predict and, by convention, is denoted by the letter Y.

Independent variable: The variable that causes or precedes in time the dependent variable and is usually denoted by the letter X.

Hypothesis: Specific statements about the relationship between two or more variables.

Methodology: The manner in which accurate facts or data are collected when conducting research.

Quantitative research: The researcher tends to gather data in the form of numbers and employs various statistics to explore the relationship between selected variables.

Qualitative research: The researcher tends to gather data in the form of words. The researcher chooses methods that allow for an in-depth inquiry in the hopes of understanding the breadth of the problem under study.

Random assignment: Each element of the population has an equal probability of being assigned to a control and experimental group.

Sampling: A procedure used in research by which a select subunit of a population is studied in order to analyze the entire population.

Measurement: The assignment of labels (usually numbers) to observations and the analysis of the data consists in manipulating or operating on these numbers.

Internal validity: Accuracy within the study itself. (Are we measuring what we think we are measuring?)

External validity: Accuracy in the ability to generalize or infer findings from a study to a larger population.

Reliability: The consistency and stability of the measurement. (If the study were duplicated, would the instrument yield the same answer to the same question upon second testing?)

Several methods can be applied in researching the sociology of law, and often multiple methods are applied in such a study. For example, in a study conducted to better understand the civil and criminal justice system processing of child abuse and neglect cases, Noy Davis and Susan Wells employed a methodology that consisted of four separate studies. The research methods included: (a) a national survey of child protective services, law enforcement, and court personnel in 41 counties; (b) a case study comparison of case processing at two sites; (c) a case study of a site that actively prosecutes cases of child physical abuse; and (d) a prospective case-tracking study of 450 cases at one site.[6] Moreover, some methods allow for direct causal inferences to be made, while others provide less indisputable evidence of causation. Still other methods are not concerned with causal inferences at all. Rather, these methods are interested merely with classifying relations among measures, describing things in terms of a set of characteristics, or discovering those characteristics.

The Experimental Method

The scientific study of the sociology of law is especially useful in three basic types of situations.

1. When exploring the existing state of affairs to gain some insight into the forces and factors that determine social reality
2. When the objective is to describe a relationship between the law and society or vice versa
3. To explain, through sociological research methods, whether legal precepts have attained their intended effects, and whether or not they have also brought about any unexpected and undesirable effects

Data secured by these methods are likely to be more reliable the more quantitative they are (provided that the methods themselves are valid) and the more opportunities there are to apply the experimental method.[7]

Experimental research, also known as the cause-and-effect method and the laboratory method, involves the use of experiments to answer research questions. In experimental research, subjects are randomly assigned to control and experimental groups, and the independent variable can be manipulated. These groups are equivalent except that the experimental group is exposed to the independent variable and the control group is not.

A good illustration of random assignment and variations in administering the treatment can be seen in research conducted by Robert Davis, Madeline Henley, and Barbara Smith on the effects of victim impact statements on sentencing decisions and on victim satisfaction with the criminal justice system. The subjects of this study were individuals who had testified before the grand jury at the New York State Supreme Court between July 1988 and April 1989. The eligible population for inclusion in the study consisted of those who had been victims of robbery, physical assault, attempted homicide, or burglary. A total of 294 victims were randomly assigned to one of three experimental conditions: (a) 104 victims were interviewed, with an impact statement written and immediately distributed to the prosecutor, defense attorney, and judge on the case; (b) 100 victims were interviewed to assess impact, but no statement was written; and (c) 89 victims were assigned to a control condition in which there was no interview or statement. Subsequent interviews evaluated victim's perception of their role in the proceedings and their satisfaction with the outcomes.[8]

Experimental designs allow for exploration, description, and explanation of causal relationships between the existence of law and social phenomena.

For example, let's consider a field experiment designed to assess the effect of various options for police responses to domestic-violence calls. The study was conducted by Lawrence Sherman of the Police Foundation and the Minneapolis Police Department. In the experiment, police systematically varied the use of three approaches when responding to misdemeanor spousal assault calls: (a) ordering the suspect to leave the home for 8 hours, (b) advising the couple to calm down, and (c) arresting the suspect. The researchers found that the third option of arrest and a subsequent night in jail for the offender appeared to produce the best results by cutting the risk of repeat violence against the victim by 50%.[9] The research study was widely publicized and immediately became of interest to state lawmakers. In the 5 years following the study, 10 states enacted laws making spouse assault a separate criminal offense, and over half the states dismantled legislation that prevented police from making an arrest if they did not witness the crime.[10]

It is common to classify research designs into two major groups: experimental and quasi-experimental designs. In experimental designs, subjects are randomly assigned to control and experimental groups, and the independent variable can be manipulated. Quasi-experimental designs may include combinations of these elements but not all of them. Typically, these designs lack the ability to manipulate the independent variable and to randomize subjects. We will first explore the true experimental design and then turn our attention to the quasi-experimental methods.

The Classic Experimental Design

A diagram of the classic experimental design is provided in Table 3.1. The central features of this pretest-posttest control group design are random assignment into experimental and control groups, pretest of both groups O_1 and O_3, treatment to the experimental group only (where X designates the independent variable), and a posttest of both groups O_2 and O_4. The difference between the posttest of the experimental group (d_{eg}) is compared to the difference between the control group (d_{cg}).

To illustrate the application of an experimental design in a social setting, let's suppose that we are interested in studying the cause-and-effect relationship between GRE preparation courses and admission rates to graduate school. Our proposition is that students who take the GRE prep courses score higher on the GRE exam and therefore increase their chances of admittance

Table 3.1   The Classic Experimental Design

	Pretest	Treatment	Posttest	Difference
Experimental group	O_1	X	O_2	$O_{2B}\ O_1 = d_{eg}$
Control group	O_3		O_4	$O_{4B}\ O_3 = d_{cg}$

to graduate school. In the simplest type of experiment, we create two groups that are "equivalent" to each other. Both groups have similar people, who live in similar contexts, have similar backgrounds, and so on. The experiment relies on random assignment of people to groups and administering a pretest to obtain baseline data. One group (the experimental group) gets the GRE preparation course and the other group (the control group) does not. Now, if we observe differences in outcomes (posttest) between these two groups, then the differences must be due to the only thing that differs between them (i.e., that one got the treatment and the other didn't).

Experimental designs are intrusive and difficult to achieve in most social situations. And, because an experiment is intrusive, the researcher is to some extent setting up a factitious situation so that an assessment can be made about the causal relationship with some degree of internal validity, i.e., to rule out the possibility that something other than the treatment caused the outcome. When this occurs, however, it concurrently limits the degree to which the researcher can generalize the results to real contexts outside the controlled experiment. There are two variations of this design that are stronger in this respect: the Solomon four-group design and the posttest-only control group design.

The Solomon Four-Group Design

The Solomon four-group design is an extension of the pretest-posttest control group design. It was named after its developer, R. L. Solomon, who proposed it in 1949 in order to emphasize external validity factors. The Solomon four-group design, presented in Table 3.2, contains the same features as the classic design, plus an additional set of control and experimental groups that are not pretested. Then, a variable is introduced to both experimental groups. The data are analyzed by doing an analysis of variance of the posttest scores between the four groups (i.e., the two experimental groups O_2–O_5 and the two control groups O_{4B} O_6). This design helps determine the effects of pretesting on the groups. This design requires considerably larger samples because of the need for four matched groups.

Table 3.2   The Solomon Four-Group Design

	Pretest	Treatment	Posttest	Difference
Experimental group	O_1	X	O_2	
Control group	O_3		O_4	
Experimental group		X	O_5	
Control group			O_6	
				$O_{2B}\, O_5 = d_{eg}$
				$O_{4B}\, O_6 = d_{cg}$

Table 3.3   Posttest-Only Control-Group Design

	Pretest	Treatment	Posttest	Difference
Experimental group		X	O_1	
Control group			O_2	
				O_1 compared with O_2

The Posttest-Only Control-Group Design

The last of the true experimental designs is the posttest-only control group design. This design is identical to the last two groups of the Solomon four-group design, which are not pretested. The design is diagrammed in Table 3.3.

The samples are randomly divided into two groups, a variable is introduced to one group, and then both groups are posttested to discover the difference, if any, in the two groups as the result of the introduction of the variable. This design is used in those situations where a pretest is not practical. As an illustration, suppose a researcher is examining whether playing violent video games has an effect on aggressive thinking. The researcher selects a sample that is randomly assigned to two groups. One group plays games with very violent content and the other does not. Later, the two groups are interviewed. To assess the effect of the violent games, situation questions are asked and responses are recorded. The responses to the interview in the two groups are compared. A significant difference between the groups will indicate that the violent games may have had an effect on aggressive thinking.

Quasi-Experimental Designs

Quasi-experimental designs attempt to approximate the classic experimental design but typically lack the ability to manipulate the independent variable and to randomly assign it to experimental and control groups. Quasi-experimental designs may be subdivided into the nonrandomized control group pretest-posttest design, the time-series experiment, and the equivalent time-samples design.

Nonrandomized Control Group Pretest-Posttest Design

The nonrandomized control group pretest-posttest design is similar to the true experimental design except the two groups are not equivalent. For example, juveniles released from correctional institutions in Texas where certain types of prerelease counseling is provided are compared to juveniles released from correctional institutions in Kansas where the prerelease counseling is different. Circumstances beyond the control of the researchers prevent the two groups from being equivalent. The lack of equivalent groups may affect the validity of the project.

Time-Series Designs

The time-series experiment involves the taking of evaluations of a group and then introducing a variable into the system. Then, another group of evaluations is made to determine if there is any change in the group. If a substantial change has resulted, the researcher may conclude that the introduction of the variable was the cause of the difference. For example, suppose we were interested in studying the effect of a new law restricting handgun sales on reducing violent crimes. Measures of the violent crime rate would be taken at successive time periods prior to the enactment of the law, and other measurements would be taken after the intervention. This method is sometimes called an interrupted time series because the series of measurements is interrupted by a treatment. It is superior to simple pretest-posttest designs in that multiple measurements show trends and not just a simple analysis of the last point before and the first point after the treatment. The distinction of quality between a time-series design and a before-after design is illustrated by John Monahan and Laurens Walker in their study of the impact of the Community Mental Health Centers Act of 1963.

> In 1963, the year the act was passed, the resident population of state mental hospitals in the United States was approximately 5,000,000. In 1990, it was less than 150,000. These before-after figures have been used to persuade Congress of the effectiveness of the act. When a time-series with more than one measurement before the passage is used, however, the results seem quite different. A time-series shows the population of state mental hospitals to have increased each year from early in the century until 1955, and decreased each year thereafter, with no noticeable acceleration in the rate of decrease in 1963, the year the act was passed. In this light, the most plausible hypothesis is that the factor causing the population decrease began in mid-1950s, and not in mid-1960s. Many now view the introduction of psychotropic medication as the principal method of treating patients, which indeed began in 1955, as the most plausible hypothesis to account for the deinstitutionalization of mental hospitals.[11]

Another example is illustrated by Tomislav Kovandzic's 2001 study on Florida's habitual offender laws. The presented study used a multiple time-series design, pooling annual data for 58 counties in Florida from 1980 to 1998. Substantive findings showed the habitual offender extra prison time and prison population variables suggest that Florida's habitual offender law may have slightly reduced rape, robbery, assault, burglary, larceny, and auto theft. The study suggested that the impacts, although small, were a result of incapacitation as opposed to deterrence. In summary, the results suggested that Florida's habitual offender law was not very effective at reducing crime. The study recommended that the Florida legislature repeal the law and sentence repeat offenders under the state's sentencing guidelines.[12]

Equivalent Time-Samples Design

The equivalent time-samples design is a variety of the control-group time series that attempts to control history in time designs. In this design, the variable is present sometimes and absent at other times, thereby creating an on-again, off-again design. This allows the researcher to study the differences when the variable is present and when the variable is absent. For example, a group of juveniles under study could be introduced to the variable of counseling for 6 months, then counseling withdrawn for 6 months, etc. After a time period of the on-again, off-again counseling, the researcher may be able to notice differences in the juveniles while undergoing counseling compared to when they are not being counseled.

The Observation Method

The field experiment is a research method designed to bring to natural situations some of the precision of the laboratory. The researcher must be in a position to observe changes in behavior of experimental and control groups, so as to be able to evaluate the effects of each of the independent variables.

There is a wide range of research strategies commonly used within field research. One of the best methods of data collection is through participant observation. In this method, the researcher actively participates, for an extended period of time, in the lives of the people and situations under study. This method of research assumes that the researcher will become accepted by the group and therefore be able to acquire detailed information by speaking with the people.[13]

Researchers often adopt the methodology of participant observation when little is known about a phenomenon. By virtue of being actively involved in the situation under observation, the researcher often gains insight and develops interpersonal relationships that are virtually impossible to achieve through any other method. Consider the following excerpt taken from a July 1997 Bureau of Justice Assistance report titled, *Trial Court Performance Standards and Measurement System Implementation Manual.*[14]

> The method described most often for measuring access to justice is observation (sometimes combined with simulation). Observers systematically record what they see and hear. This structured information can then be examined quantitatively as well as qualitatively. These "see, hear, and record" measures range from concrete and objective (Was an observer able to gain entrance to a courtroom?) to subjective (Did activity taking place in a courtroom detract from the dignity of the proceedings?). There are 12 measures of this type.

Although the observations could be carried out by almost anyone, the recommended approach is to use citizen volunteers who are relatively naïve to the legal system and who are unfamiliar with the facilities and "customs" of the courthouse. This results in records of experiences that resemble those of ordinary citizens who have infrequent occasion to do business with the court. Furthermore, the observers chosen should optimally be representative of the jurisdictional community of the court. Representativeness is more important for some measures than others. However, because the same individuals could be asked to obtain data for all the observation measures, it may be helpful to recruit one pool of observers who vary on demographic factors. Observers may be recruited by contacting volunteer organizations, universities, senior citizen groups, and so forth. This "volunteer observer" method has other advantages, notably its relatively low cost. The court must invest staff time to recruit volunteers, orient them to their assignments, and evaluate results. Once the recruitment and orientation are completed, however, the observers may be used to collect data for many measures described throughout the measurement process. Because the observers are relatively few in number, they offer the added advantage of being able to provide court staff with additional information during interviews following their structured assignments. A much richer, qualitative analysis results when explanations, descriptions, and suggestions can be elicited from the observers to augment what is provided on written forms, questionnaires, and checklists.

Types of Participant Observation

Participant observation is distinguishable in terms of the varying degrees in which the researcher interacts with a group of individuals in their natural setting. Typically, there are three ways in which the participant observer functions:

- *Complete observer*: Occurs when the researcher informs others of his or her research activity and simply observes the activities of the group under study. There is no attempt on the part of the researcher to manipulate the environment. The duty of the researcher is to observe and record.
- *Observer as participant*: Has been referred to as the one-visit interview.[15] Although it may not be readily apparent, when a researcher conducts an interview with a respondent, he or she is actually performing the role of participant observer. The researcher observes the respondent's demeanor while dialogue occurs, and as such can gauge the extent to which further inquiry is necessary and possible.
- *Complete participation*: Takes place when the researcher joins in the activities of the group and begins to manipulate the direction of group activity. Often the researcher must disguise himself or herself in order to be accepted into the group, thus allowing for maximum

interaction with the group. Disguised observation is research in which the researcher hides his or her presence or purpose for inter- acting with a group. For example, sociologist Robert Balch went undercover to study the Heaven's Gate UFO cult, which taught that spacecrafts would spirit away its faithful members to the next king- dom. He didn't identify himself as a researcher but rather posed as a new member, sleeping with others in isolated campgrounds and depending on churches for money.[16]

In the process of conducting an observational study, the researcher must maintain a high level of attention and still be able to accurately record the necessary data. The first task in the collection effort involves a descriptive account of the research setting. Basically, the aim is to allow the researcher to describe the setting, the people, and the events that have taken place. It may also be important for the researcher to record initial impressions of each.

There are several common ways to make records of field observations. The choice of which form to use depends on the limitations of the research setting and preferences of the researcher. Some of the more notable recording techniques include field notes, audio- and videotape recording, laptop com- puters, tablets, or smart phones.

The researcher composes field notes while actively observing the research setting. This necessarily means that, where possible, field notes are made of observations on the spot, during the event. This common form of data collection in observational studies consists of writing short phrases, using abbreviations, etc. The primary purpose of field notes is to help the researcher recollect what happened, so that a more detailed document can be produced later. As a routine matter, field notes should be gone through shortly afterwards to add detail and substance. Field notes may not be prac- tical if too many events occur for the researcher to quickly write down observations. If this dilemma occurs, the researcher might instead rely upon audiotape recordings.

The option of using audiotape-recorded observations is very attractive to researchers because it is handy and versatile. Microcassette recorders are relatively inexpensive to purchase and small enough to be carried in a shirt pocket. If necessary, accessories can be purchased to outfit the recorder for hands-free operation. Finally, recorders can be easily concealed if desirable. A vast majority of the population now has access to smart phones with record- ing devices built into them, making this device a very popular form of record- ing. The disadvantage of audiotape recordings is, of course, the possibility of a malfunction in the equipment. If batteries become weak or a moveable part of the device does not function, the data collection effort is jeopardized.

Another observational data-collection technology is videotape record- ing. Portable, handheld smart phones with video capabilities can be used in

a variety of research settings. The greatest advantage of videotaping observations is that it produces a re-creation of events that can be viewed several
times over. The disadvantage, though, is that videotaping may distract the
researcher, thus limiting his or her abilities to record big-picture events. That
is, while the researcher is engrossed with videotaping one event, another
event of equal importance may go undetected by the researcher. Also, as with
audio devices, video equipment is susceptible to malfunction.

Laptop computers can be very effective in recording data in the field.
This is especially true if the researcher possesses good typing skills and is
computer literate. As with the latter two options, equipment failure is always
a possible menace to the data-collection effort. Tablet computers are also
becoming very popular with researchers due to their small size and large
upside of processing capabilities.

As you have no doubt recognized, the four options we have noted are
viable data recording methods only as long as the researcher is involved in
complete observation. If engaged in some form of participation, on-the-spot
recording is often not feasible. In this case, the researcher constructs observation notes as soon as possible after leaving the field.

Simulation Research

Another research strategy commonly used within field research is simulation. In this method, the researcher constructs models of social phenomena.
Sometimes these are qualitative (e.g., subject-oriented models) and sometimes quantitative (e.g., statistical models). A separate type of modeling has
been added to the social scientists' repertoire: models expressed as computer
programs that are run to simulate aspects of the phenomenon under investigation. For instance, little empirical research has been conducted with juries
because of the legal requirements of closed deliberations. Consequently,
mock trials in which jurors respond to simulated case materials have
become a valuable research tool. The mock trial permits both manipulation of important variables and replication of actual cases.[17] In relation to
jury simulations, some researchers have shown a particular interest in how
verdicts are reached by juries. Norman Finkel, a professor of psychology at
Georgetown University, conducted research relating to the tension between
what people say in their capacity as citizens and what they do in their capacity as jurors. His data came from experiments in which people have been
asked to pretend to be jurors and to react to the scenario of a criminal case.[18]
These types of research projects are frequently audiotaped or videotaped and
then analyzed for content.[19] In some areas of social science, the use of computer simulation is well established. For example, microsimulation models
have been used to study the likely impacts of fiscal changes; macroeconomic

models have been used to simulate future economy changes; and simulations have been used to study cognitive patterns of people.

In the recent past, there has been a resurgence of interest in simulation research. Faster and improved computer equipment and software have allowed researchers to build complex simulations more easily. Recent research has shown that computer simulation methods can be an effective tool for the development of theories in addition to prediction. Simulation allows the social scientist to experiment with artificial societies and explore the implications of theories in ways not otherwise possible. Brendan Halpin at the Institute for Social and Economic Research, University of Essex, Colchester, UK, points out:

> A number of important features relevant to simulation in sociology have become apparent. Among these are the benefits of formal statement and manipulation that simulation allows and the way in which simulation work rapidly comes up against (and, to some extent, offers solutions or new approaches to) central problems of sociology such as agency-structure duality and the relationship between macro and micro levels.[20]

The Survey Method

While observational methods of data collection are suitable for investigating a phenomenon that can be directly observed, not all phenomena are accessible to the investigator's direct observation. Therefore, the researcher must collect data by locating people who have experienced a certain phenomenon and asking them to recall specific information about the phenomenon. The researcher engages a sample of individuals presumed to have undergone certain experiences and interviews them concerning these experiences. Their responses constitute the data upon which the research hypotheses are evaluated. Three major methods are used to elicit information from respondents, which are classified by their method of data collection. They are personal interviews, telephone interviews, and self-administered mail surveys.

Selecting the type of survey requires the researcher to first consider issues relating to the population sample, the nature of questioning, availability of data, and resources. Sometimes there is no clear choice of which one is best. This is because each method has its advantages and disadvantages. So, often it comes down to the preference of the researcher. Some researchers are of the opinion that data collected from self-administered mail surveys are riddled with problems of validity and reliability. Others are less concerned with control issues but prefer interviews that enable them to get to very detailed data. Still others rely heavily on mailed surveys to capture large amounts of data in hopes of understanding the research problem under study. Gaining a greater appreciation for each type of survey research requires us to take a closer look at each individual method.

Personal Interviews

Personal interviewing is a dynamic process whereby an interviewer (the researcher) orally solicits responses from persons identified within a sample population (respondents). The interview is viewed as a fairly straightforward method of finding things out, especially if the conversation is clear and fairly to the point.[21]

Three basic terms are used to distinguish between the degree of formality of the interview. They are fully structured interviews, semistructured interviews, and unstructured interviews. The questions, their wording, and their sequence define the extent to which the interview is structured. And, although differences are found in each of these approaches, all of these types of interviewing techniques require that the researcher listen to what is being said and systematically record the responses.

A structured interview is a process in which the researcher develops a predetermined set of questions and asks the respondent for specific replies. The researcher controls the interview and asks all respondents the same questions and in the same order. In addition to questions, structured interviews may involve provocative statements that are intended to prompt an immediate response from the person being interviewed. Again though, the respondent is provided with a list of possible responses in which one is chosen.

Unstructured interviews use open-ended questions to get as much detailed information as possible from the respondent. The unstructured format allows the interviewer the opportunity to probe or ask follow-up questions. And, such interviews are generally easier for the respondent, especially if the information sought is opinion or belief.

Semistructured interviews, then, are surveys that combine both structured and open-ended questions. In the semistructured interview, the researcher possesses great latitude in deciding how the survey will be administered. It relies heavily upon the researcher's ability to perceive how the interview is developing and make changes accordingly. The process is different than the pencil-to-paper structured survey, in that the researcher adjusts the questioning depending upon the respondent's answers. In his 2010 study of Oklahoma district attorneys regarding how they used their prosecutorial discretion and why, Harrison Watts used the semistructured interviews to gain an insight into what factors played a role in the prosecutors determining what crimes to indict.[22]

The choice of a structured, semistructured, or unstructured approach depends on the information desired by the researcher. Sometimes this involves using multiple stages of interviewing. In this technique, the researcher first conducts unstructured interviews to gather preliminary data that will be used to develop and administer semistructured interviews. Findings from this second interview stage are then used to develop a final structured survey. For example, in a study of gang violence, Scott Decker and his fellow researchers interviewed 99 active gang members, representing 29 different gangs in the St. Louis area. They used a semistructured questionnaire to guide the interviews, which had been developed from unstructured interviews conducted before the beginning of the study.[23]

Telephone Interviews

Another way of gathering research data is by telephone. The main attraction of telephone interviewing is that it enables the researcher to gather information rapidly. In comparison to personal interviews, the telephone interview is similar in that it allows for some personal contact between the interviewer and the respondent. One difference, however, is that this method of research allows for large amounts of data to be collected from geographically scattered samples more cheaply than face-to-face interviews. For instances, Barbara Smith and Sharon Elstein used a national telephone survey of 600 prosecutors to study how cases of child physical and sexual abuse are being prosecuted and to examine the outcomes of child sexual abuse cases in criminal courts across the country.[24]

The popularity of the telephone survey method has increased as technological advances in the telephone industry have occurred. Much work has been done to develop random digit dialing (RDD) as a means of providing representative probability samples of all telephone owners. RDD sampling includes both those households listed in telephone directories and those with unlisted, or nonpublished, numbers. An example of how RDD has been used in law and society research is a 1988 study in Ontario, Canada. There, researchers used RDD to select a probability sample of heads of households in order to conduct telephone interviews as a means of assessing experiences with Ontario's civil justice system.[25] As more and more of the population moves toward cell phones and away from land lines, the RDD may need to be reconfigured for cell phone technology.

Computer-assisted personal interviewing (CAPI) is a data-collection technique where researchers use portable computers to enter data directly via a keyboard instead of collecting data on paper questionnaires. Computer-assisted interviewing has been used extensively for telephone surveys and in recent years has been introduced when conducting face-to-face interviews. Tablet computers are very useful in this manner.

Mail Surveys

The most common type of mail survey is the self-administered questionnaire. This method of data collection enables the researcher to survey a large

STRENGTHS AND WEAKNESSES OF SURVEY RESEARCH

	Strengths	Weaknesses
Personal interview	Allows in-depth, free responses	High costs
	Researcher can see respondent's facial expressions, gestures, etc.	Time consuming
	Responses are accurate	Requires skilled interviewers
	Visual presentations are possible	Open to interviewer bias
	High percentage of return	Summarizing data may be more difficult
Telephone interview	Less costly than in-person interviews	Unlisted phone numbers unavailable
	Amount of time to secure data is low	Can be confused with a telemarketing call
	Use of computer technology	Visual presentations not possible
	Verbal comments are easier for most respondents than written ones	Interviewer can bias responses based on verbal cues or voice inflections
Mailed surveys	Inexpensive	Low response rate
	Offer privacy and anonymity	Respondent literacy may be problematic
	Respondent accustomed to the format	Open-ended questions unfeasible
	Interviewer bias is eliminated	Validity of responses
	Data are easier to summarize	No control over who actually completes the survey

Source: Gerald J. Bayens & Cliff Roberson. (2000). *Criminal justice research: Theory and practice*. Incline Village, NV: Copperhouse Publishing.

group of respondents in a minimum amount of time. The advantage of this type of survey is that the questionnaire can be mass mailed, completed, and returned to the researcher in half the time it would take to conduct interviews of only a few respondents. In addition to saving time, the mail survey is an affordable method of gathering information. Typically, only postage costs are necessary to initiate a self-administered mail survey.

While there are clear advantages to mailed surveys, three problems in particular can occur. The first is lack of response. Without follow-up, a mailed survey may unfortunately net only a small percentage return rate in a one-time-only distribution. An illustration of this problem can be seen in the efforts of the Federal Judicial Center, a research, education, and planning agency of the federal judicial system. At the request of the Judicial Conference's Advisory Committee on Bankruptcy Rules, staff of the research division of the Federal Judicial Center developed a questionnaire to help the subcommittee learn the views of various participants in the bankruptcy system concerning the rules and related forms. The center sent a questionnaire to bankruptcy, district, and circuit judges, other bankruptcy court personnel, law professors, and bankruptcy practitioners. A total of 3,145 recipients were sent the questionnaires, which were mailed in January and February of 1995. However, only 23% (720) of those surveyed responded to the seven questions about the nature and extent of their bankruptcy-related work.[26]

Another problem with the mail survey is that while the self-administered questionnaire may have been addressed to a particular person, there are few ways to check on who actually completed the document. The third problem with the self-administered survey is that there is little or no check on the honesty or seriousness of responses.

Historical and Archival Research

When researching the sociology of law, researchers do not always use actual observation, interviewing, or questionnaires as a means of collecting information. Rather, historical and archival data, such as official records, diaries, and newspapers, can be used to reconstruct and analyze phenomena. When using historical documents to extract information, researchers rely upon everyday common-sense knowledge of life in society as well as upon the general knowledge of various subjects related to that under study.[27]

At times, there has been a tendency by some social scientists to view materials that were produced in the past as a mere chronicle of unique events, part myth, allegory, and fiction.[28] More recently, however, historical research has gained much greater acceptance by social scientists who recognize that small, specific events can provide indexes to change. As John Burnham notes, intellectual history may indeed furnish a way into understanding how behavioral, social, or human scientists not only have shared historical forces with the changing social environment, but have interacted with their social, cultural, and intellectual matrix.[29]

Many examples of the use of historical data exist. Lisa Newmark, for example, used official court records to examine client and court outcomes of parental drug testing in child abuse and neglect cases in Washington, DC. In 1987, the family court judges in Washington, DC, began referring abuse and neglect cases for drug testing in order to assist courts and social services in identifying and addressing treatment needs. The overall goal of the court action was to promote child safety as well as family preservation. The research compared a matched sample of 169 drug-involved cases that entered the drug-testing program from a 3-month time period, with a similar group of 159 drug-involved cases from the same period that did not enter drug testing. The findings of the research indicated that drug testing seemed to be a promising tool for courts and social services to use in working with child maltreatment cases in which parents are substance abusers.[30]

The Center for Justice Research and Education at Lamar University (Texas) conducted research for the Florida Governor's Task Force on Domestic and Sexual Violence to construct red flags that might serve as bases to intervene and prevent domestic fatalities. The objective of this research was to break down the various components of domestic cases to determine if combinations of subcomponents are most likely associated with, and therefore predictive of, lethal domestic situations. Primary sources for data included police records, court documents, autopsy reports, and hospital reports. One of the important conclusions drawn from this research was that judges could be made aware of the existence of red flags for domestic fatalities and take them into account when fashioning specific conditions in restraining orders and sentences.[31]

TRIAL LAWYERS ARE A GOOD MODEL FOR HISTORICAL RESEARCHERS

The trial attorney's job is to present enough historical evidence to persuade a jury to accept a hypothesis—either there's sufficient evidence to convict the defendant or there's not. To do this, lawyers do the same things that historians do. They gather and examine evidence, analyze it, synthesize it, and form opinions. They separate fact from fiction, at least from their own point of view, and they try to persuade the jury what's true and what's false. They conduct very sophisticated historical research that uses forensics and other physical and social sciences to support the hypothesis. And, as would a good historian, a good trial attorney can convince people that the obvious isn't always true, and even that people can't always trust their own senses and instincts. An effective trial attorney can persuade jurors to take on a new epistemology and to trust the attorney's interpretation of events. Of course, this is where the power of effective rhetoric pays off. Has anybody here seen the classic Groucho Marx movie *Duck Soup*? Groucho asks, "Who are you gonna believe, me or your own eyes?"

Source: **Michael Mark. (1996). Qualitative aspects of historical research. *Bulletin of the Council for Research in Music Education*, *130*, 38–43.**

In addition to official documents, historical data may also include diary information. Sociologists have taken seriously the idea of using personal documents to construct pictures of social reality, especially when personal interview methods cannot produce reliable data because the events under study are difficult to recall accurately or are easily forgotten. Diaries can be open-ended, allowing respondents to record activities and events in their own words, or they can be highly structured, where all activities are precategorized. An obvious advantage of the free format is that it allows for greater opportunity to recode and analyze the data. But the labor-intensive work required to prepare and make sense of the data may render it unrealistic for projects lacking time and resources, or where the sample is large.[32]

The Case Study

Another method of data collection that can involve historical research is the case study. A case study is defined as an in-depth, multifaceted investigation of a single social phenomenon. It is a method of organizing data for the purpose of analyzing the life of a social unit—a person, a family, a culture group, or even an entire community. By concentrating on a single phenomenon or entity, the researcher aims to uncover the interaction of significant factors characteristic of the phenomenon.

Some of the advantages of the case study method that have been suggested include:

- It permits the grounding of observations and concepts about social action and social structures in natural settings studied at close hand.
- It provides information from a number of sources and over a period of time, thus permitting a more holistic study of complex social networks and of complexes of social action and social meanings.
- It can furnish the dimensions of time and history to the study of social life, thereby enabling the investigator to examine continuity and change in lifeworld patterns.
- It encourages and facilitates, in practice, theoretical innovation and generalization.[33]

Two dominant styles for presenting case study findings are analytic reporting and reflective reporting.[34] The major characteristics of analytic reporting are (a) an objective writing style and (b) information organized into the conventional headings of introduction, literature review, methodology, results, and discussion. Reflective reporting, on the other hand, describes data based on the researcher's intuition and judgment. The researcher attempts to depict a phenomenon by re-creating it contextually.

As an illustration of the use of case studies in law and society research, we consider the NIJ research report titled, *Case Studies in Use of DNA Evidence*. This report provides the results of research pertaining to characteristics of the 28 DNA-exculpatory cases identified during the study. In each of the 28 cases, all of which involved some form of sexual assault, a defendant was convicted of a crime or crimes and serving a sentence of incarceration. While in prison, each defendant obtained, through an attorney, case evidence for DNA testing and consented to a comparison of the evidence-derived DNA to his own DNA sample. In each case, the results showed that there was not a match, and the defendant was ultimately set free.[35]

JUDGE REINSTEIN'S COMMENTS

The following is an excerpt from a commentary by Ronald S. Reinstein, presiding judge, Criminal Department Superior Court of Arizona Maricopa County, about the NIJ research report titled *Case Studies in Use of DNA Evidence*.

This report is an excellent example of the marriage between science and law and of the invaluable resource that DNA evidence has become in the forensic field. When justice can be served in such dramatic fashion by the exoneration of previously adjudged guilty individuals, science demonstrates its practical effect.

Yet the 28 cases cited in the report relate only to individuals released from prison because of DNA testing. Vastly more far-reaching in the long run is the use of DNA typing both to exclude some suspects who otherwise might be charged and to identify many other suspects who might not have been charged but for the DNA typing.

What is frustrating to many who are excited about the possibilities of the use of DNA in the forensics area is the slow pace it is traveling on the road to admissibility. Many jurisdictions do not have sufficient funds to establish their own laboratories or to send to private laboratories items of evidence for typing. Laboratories that perform testing often have backlogs measured in months. Courts, prosecutors, and defense counsel impose a great burden on laboratories' time in the usual discovery battles that occur whenever a new technique arrives on the forensic scene.

It is interesting to observe how quickly some DNA-evidence opponents embrace the science when it benefits certain defendants' interests but how defensive they become when the evidence points toward other defendants. But this is not unique to DNA evidence. It is the responsibility of the court to promote the search for truth. If that search can be assisted by science that can give reliable results, the whole system as well as society benefits.

It is also the responsibility of the court to try to prevent juror confusion caused by lawyers and experts who sometimes seem unable to explain scientific evidence in language the jury understands.

The future should be brighter as the technology improves so that the process of DNA typing will likely become much quicker, less complex, and less expensive. The battle of the experts, it is hoped, will also subside eventually, especially in the confusing area of the statistical meaning of a match.

The conflict between various forensic experts, population geneticists, and statisticians on "the meaning of a match" is a prime example of how science and the law sometimes do not mesh, especially in jurisdictions that follow the Frye test of general acceptance in the scientific community. The numbers being bandied about by various experts are almost beyond comprehension for trial jurors.

It seems logical to allow relevant, reliable, qualitative expert opinion—for example, that the probability of a random match in DNA testing is extremely remote given a reliable multilocus match. Likewise, experts should be able to testify from their experience about whether they are aware of random matches at four or five loci of unrelated individuals, and whether one evidence sample matches another to a reasonable degree of scientific certainty. There is a serious question about whether DNA-match testimony should be treated any differently from that of fingerprints, bite marks, hair and fiber samples, ballistics, shoe prints, and the like.

Restrictions currently imposed in some jurisdictions on the use of DNA evidence unreasonably divest such evidence of its compelling nature. If our justice system's goal is the continuing search for truth, as evidenced by the results of the study described in this report, then a similar argument can be made for the admissibility of relevant and reliable DNA-match testimony in our courts.

Source: **NIJ Research Report Document #161258, June 1996.**

Policy and Evaluation Research

The impact of law and society research is probably most profound in the area of policy research. Since law by its very definition is governmental social control, it is understandable that social scientists are interested in how legislation and litigation influence the lives of citizens in our society. Equally important to researchers is how social events dictate the development of social policies.

In law and society research, policy research is closely aligned with program evaluation and policy analysis. The focus of this type of inquiry is to create an information base of prior successful actions that can be useful when choosing a course of action to remedy problem situations. The ultimate goal is to understand how to best confront a problem that requires an immediate response to some social phenomenon. Consider, for example, prosecutor-led anti-gang programs that have been implemented to target violent, youthful offenders. The Street Terrorism Enforcement and Prevention (STEP) Acts in California, Florida, Georgia, Illinois, and Louisiana provide for sentencing enhancements and civil forfeiture of street gang assets and criminal proceeds.[36] This special legislation enhances the prosecutor's ability to aggressively prosecute gang-related cases. It has been suggested that prosecutors who function in states without similar gang prosecution enhancements could work either to adopt legislation or to amend the existing criminal state statute to add gang offenses.[37] And, in fact, 14 states have undertaken the latter approach by adding sentencing enhancements to their statutes rather than creating new gang offenses.[38]

Evaluation is a method undertaken to effect the development of policy, to fashion the design of social interventions, and to improve the delivery of social programs. The type or scope of the evaluation varies, depending on those issues to be addressed. In one instance, evaluation research is concerned with analyzing the worth of existing laws as they pertain to social programs. Worth in most instances is determined by whether the law has facilitated the intended goals of the social program. Since many of the social programs are publicly funded, value becomes an equally important concern of evaluation research. Value is typically determined by whether the program is operated with economic prudence. On the other hand, evaluation research may be aimed at providing useful information to a variety of decision makers who have a vested interest in the program. Evaluations can be an important tool in improving legislation so that the quality of a program can be improved and the delivery of a social program can be enhanced. Consider the following comments made by Judge Cindy Lederman of the Juvenile Court in Miami-Dade County, Florida.[39]

> Reliance on scientific research is key to realizing the promise of the juvenile court. Decades of research in juvenile and criminal justice, developmental psychology, epidemiology, and other disciplines, including evaluations of promising program interventions, should inform policymaking, decision making, and the development of programs and treatments.
> These factors underscore the need for rigorous program evaluations across the spectrum of child welfare and juvenile justice services to ensure that interventions benefit children in society and do not produce unintended effects that may even increase the risks of delinquent behavior. The juvenile justice

system must be vigilant about the quality of its program, services, and service providers and must work with researchers to design an agenda that will make a positive contribution to the body of evaluation research.

THE DEPENDENCY COURT INTERVENTION PROGRAM FOR FAMILY VIOLENCE

The Dependency Court Intervention Program for Family Violence, a national demonstration project in Miami, Florida, provides an example of interdisciplinary work in jurisprudence. Funded by the Violence Against Women Office, Office of Justice Programs, U.S. Department of Justice, this demonstration project seeks to address the co-occurrence of child maltreatment and family violence in a juvenile setting.[39a] Advocates are provided to battered mothers of dependent children; assessment instruments have been designed to measure the extent and impact of violence on children; and collaboration between the child welfare and domestic violence community has been fostered as the foundation of a communitywide approach to handling child abuse cases in which other forms of family violence are also present.

Because infants and toddlers can tell the court about their development through their actions, an assessment for use with children from 1 to 5 years old has been developed through this program, with assistance from Joy Osofsky, Ph.D., professor of pediatrics and psychiatry at Louisiana State University Medical Center. Parents and dependent children are videotaped in a number of structured and unstructured interactions. The developmental and cognitive functioning of the young child and his or her bonding and attachment with a caregiver are assessed. Preliminary data indicate that, while many of these dependent children are developmentally delayed, the developmental delays often go undetected. The Miami court is now able to reach these children earlier, enhancing their ability to develop in a healthy, age-appropriate manner.

The program is undergoing a rigorous process and outcome evaluation. A quasi-experimental research design is being used to develop data on the needs of children and their families when multiple forms of family violence are present. The demonstration project already has resulted in institutional reform intended to enhance child safety.

Source: **Cindy S. Lederman. (1999). The juvenile court: Putting research to work for prevention.** *Journal of Office of Juvenile Justice and Delinquency Prevention,* **6(2), 27–28.**

There is no special research design or methodology for the collection and analysis of data when conducting evaluation research. Performing a program evaluation is still research and therefore employs research designs similar to other types of research. Two of the more popular methods used to conduct program evaluations are the preexperimental and quasi-experimental designs. Within the preexperimental design, the one-shot case study, which involves a single group that receives the program and then is measured, is possibly the most popular design utilized by evaluators. When quasi-experimental methods are employed, the time-series design, which involves making multiple measures on a single group both before and after the group is exposed to the program, is a common design choice of evaluators. A catalogue of some of the analytic approaches that have been used in evaluation studies is provided by the Bureau of Justice Assistance in the publication *Evaluating Drug Control and System Improvement Projects: Guidelines for Projects Supported by the Bureau of Justice Assistance.*[40]

Differentiating Between Social and Criminal Justice

The judicial discretion of the court, the charging decisions of the prosecution, and the plea-bargaining dealings of the defense are only three examples of the many areas within the justice system that are of constant interest to researchers. However, the implementation of sociological research methods to the evaluation of court processes can be problematic. This is particularly true when the research interest is aimed at the criminal justice system. The reason for this is because the legal system is designed to make determinations about justice on a case-by-case basis. As a result, sociology often operates in the aggregate, focusing on outcome rather than process. Therein lies an important factor when considering the limitations of the sociological approach to the evaluation of court outcomes.

Another factor to consider is the complexity of the justice system. Our system of justice is so complex that the creation of models of the system, ones that can be manipulated to determine effects, is fundamental to our understanding of how the process of justice works and how it should be researched. Consider the following description of the criminal justice system:

> The criminal justice system is an enormous complex of organizations. Subjecting such a system to scientific investigation normally involves making changes in its operations in order to observe the effects directly. Whenever practical, this kind of controlled experimentation is clearly the best kind. But experimentation inside a system is often impractical and even undesirable, not only because the cost could be prohibitive, but

because normal operations are frequently too critical to be disrupted. Instead, the scientist may be able to formulate a mathematical description or model of the system in order to illuminate the relationship among its parts. System analyses involve construction and manipulation of such mathematical models in order to find out how better to organize and operate the real life systems they represent.[41]

The courts are regularly called upon to solve social problems. In fact, there is generally little distinction between social and criminal justice. For example, when alcohol abuse cases involve drunk driving, the criminal court has jurisdiction. We turn to the law to seek the best possible way of dealing with most social issues. We look to the law for the truth to answer many of the problems that occur in society.

On the other hand, there are times when social justice and the law are in conflicting positions. Public opinion, political influences, religious beliefs, and other factors can influence what society will accept as justice. When this occurs, justice and the truth are not viewed as the same.

GUN CONTROL

The following narrative provides a chronicle of the events of the Sandy Hook Elementary School shooting where 20 children and 6 adults were killed. Subsequent to this horrific event, strengthening gun control laws became the focus of major headlines:

- Should public opinion be taken into account when analyzing the applicability of an existing law?
- When social justice issues surface that are in conflict with legal precepts, which should take precedence?
- Should matters of social justice be used for political gain?

Twenty children and six adults were shot and killed at the Sandy Hook Elementary School in Newtown, Connecticut, on December 14, 2012. Before heading to the school, the gunman (20-year-old Adam Lanza) killed his mother, Nancy Lanza, at the home they shared. Lanza took three legal guns from his and his mother's residence and went to the elementary school, where his mother had worked as a substitute teacher. Classes were underway at the school when he arrived. It was reported that earlier in the year, the school principal, Dawn Lafferty Hochsprung, had ordered a new security system installed that required visitors to be visibly identified and buzzed in at the front door. As part of the security system, the school locked its doors each day at 9:30 a.m. On December 14, the door was locked when Lanza arrived. Authorities now know Lanza shot an entrance to gain access into the building. Once inside Lanza used semiautomatic weapons to murder the children and teachers.

On one side of the debate over gun control was an immediate social call for gun restrictions. On the other side was a call for mental health reform and expanded concealed-carry and gun rights. The Second Amendment to the Constitution provides that the citizenry has the right to bear arms. What does this mean exactly? Many question the ability of citizens to carry assault rifles and high-capacity magazines, whereas others claim that the right to bear arms extends to these very items.

The social and criminal justice forces both seek the safety of children and individuals within the United States. The issue that both are faced with is what works with regard to gun violence? The National Rifle Association (NRA) suggested that all schools hire armed security guards to protect our children. In contrast, the Brady Campaign to Prevent Gun Violence, one of the nation's leading gun-control groups, urged the president to look into tougher background checks on gun purchases. This issue is a good example of social and criminal justice both wanting a safer community; however, the ends used to get there are different.

Questions in Review

1. Describe the general structure of the scientific method.
2. What is the difference between quantitative and qualitative research?
3. What are the three classic experimental designs? How do they differ?
4. Why are quasi-experimental methods popular when conducting social research?
5. Participant observation is distinguished in terms of the degree in which the researcher interacts with individuals in their environment. Give an example of a situation in which it would be appropriate for the observer to function as (a) complete observer, (b) observer as participant, and (c) complete participation
6. How do researchers make records of field observations?
7. Develop two semistructured interview questions that could be used to survey citizens' attitudes toward the subject: death row inmates and the court appeals process.

8. What are the advantages and disadvantages of mailed surveys?
9. Are social and criminal justice the same?
10. What lessons can be learned from the Sandy Hook Elementary school shooting?

Key Terms

Scientific method
Methodology
Experimental research
Pretest-posttest control group
Solomon four-group
Posttest-only-control group
Quasi-experimental research
Nonrandomized control group
Historical research
Archival research
Case studies
Evaluation researsh
Participant observation

Simulation research
Survey research
Personal interviews
Telephone interviews
Random digit dialing
Mail surveys
Pretest-posttest design
Time-series experiments
Interrupted time-series design
Equivalent time-sample designs
 policy research
Field experiments

Endnotes

1. G.J. Bayens & C. Roberson. (2000). *Criminal justice research: Theory and practice*. Incline Village, NV: Copperhouse Publishing.
2. V. Aubert. (1973). Researches in the sociology of law. In M. Barkum (Ed.), *Law and the social system*. New York, NY: Lieber-Atherton.
3. V. Aubert. (1973). Researches in the sociology of law. In M. Barkum (Ed.), *Law and the social system*. New York, NY: Lieber-Atherton.
4a. *Probabilism* is defined as the belief that effects will most often occur when certain causes are present, but not in every single case.
4b. The term *in dubio pro reo* means that in a doubtful case, the gentler course is to be pursued.
5. V. Aubert. (1973). Researches in the sociology of law. In M. Barkum (Ed.), *Law and the social system* (pp. 51–52). New York, NY: Lieber-Atherton.
6. N.S. Davis & S.J. Wells. (1996, February). *Justice system processing of child abuse and neglect cases* (Document 173066). Washington, DC: National Institute of Justice.
7. A. Podgorecki. (1974). *Law and society*. Boston, MA: Routledge & Kegan.
8. R. Davis, M. Henley, & B. Smith. (1999). *Victim impact statements: Their effects on court outcomes and victim satisfaction in New York, 1988–1990*. Ann Harbor, MI: Inter-University Consortium for Political and Social Research.

9. L. Sherman & R. Berk. (1984). *Minneapolis domestic violence experiment.* Washington, DC: Police Foundation; L. Sherman & R. Berk. (1984). Specific deterrent effects of arrest for domestic assault. *American Sociological Review, 49*(20), 261–272.

10. L.W. Sherman & E.G. Cohn. (1989). Impact of research on legal policy: The Minneapolis domestic violence experiment. *Law and Society Review, 23*(1), 117–144.

11. J. Monahan & L. Walker. (1990). *Social science in law: Cases and materials* (2nd ed.). Westbury, NY: Foundation Press

12. Tomislav v. Kovandzic. (2001). Impact of Florida's Habitual Offender Law on Crime. Criminology, 39(1), pp. 179–203.

13. R. Bogdan & S.J. Taylor. (1975). *Introduction to qualitative research methods: A phenomenological approach to the social sciences.* New York, NY: Wiley.

14. Bureau of Justice Assistance. (1997). *Trial court performance standards and measurement system implementation manual* (Document 161567). Rockville, MD: National Institute of Justice.

15. F.E. Hagan. (1997). *Research methods in criminal justice and criminology* (4th ed.). Needham Heights, MA: Allyn and Bacon.

16. S. Heller. (1997). A sociologist who went undercover. *The Chronicle of Higher Education, 43*(31), 10.

17. J.H. Davis, R.M. Bray, & R.W. Holt. (1977). The empirical study of decision processes in juries: A critical review. In J.L. Tapp & F.J. Levine (Eds.), *Law, justice, and the individual in society: Psychological and legal issues.* New York, NY: Holt, Rinehart, and Winston.

18. J.Q. Wilson. (1996). Reading jurors' minds. *Commentary, 101*(2), 45–48.

19. J.B. Kessler. (1975). The social psychology of jury deliberations. In R.J. Simon (Ed.), *The jury system in America: A critical overview.* Beverly Hills, CA: Sage Publications.

20. Halpin, B. (August 1999). Simulation in Sociology. American Behavioral Scientist, Vol. 42, No. 10, pp. 1488–1508.

21. G.J. Bayens & C. Roberson. (2000). *Criminal justice research: Theory and practice* (p. 135). Incline Village, NV: Copperhouse Publishing.

22. Watts, Harrison. (Fall, 2011). Exploring the separation of powers doctrine in Oklahoma: A case study of the lack of enforcement of the adultery statute. Professional Issues in Criminal Justice, Vol. 6, No. 3–4 pp. 59–73.

23. S.H. Decker. (1996). Collective and normative features of gang violence. *Justice Quarterly, 13*(2), 243–264.

24. B.E. Smith & S. Goretsky Elstein. (1993, September). *The prosecution of child sexual and physical abuse cases.* Washington, DC: American Bar Associations Center on Children and the Law.

25. W.A. Bogart & N. Vidmar. (1990). Problems and experiences with the Ontario civil justice system: An empirical assessment. In A. Hutchinson (Ed.), *Access to justice: Bridges and barriers.* Toronto, ON, Canada: Carswell.

26. E.C. Wiggins, M. Treadway Johnson, G.A. Mahin, & R.J. Niemic. (1996). *Survey on the federal rule of bankruptcy procedure.* Washington, DC: U.S. Government Document.

27. A.V. Cicourel. (1964). *Method and measurement in sociology.* New York, NY: Macmillan.

28. J.A. Inciardi, A.A. Block, & L.A. Halowell. (1977). *Historical approaches to crime: Research strategies and issues.* Beverly Hills, CA: Sage.

29. J.C. Burnham. (1999). Assessing historical research in the behavioral and social sciences. *Journal of the History of the Behavioral Sciences, 35*(3), 225–226.

30. L.C. Newmark. (1995). *Parental drug testing in child abuse and neglect cases: The Washington, DC, experience.* Washington, DC: National Institute of Justice.

31. B. Johnson, D. Li, & N. Websdale. *Florida mortality review project* (Executive summary). Washington, DC: National Institute of Justice.

32. L. Corti. (1993). Using diaries in social research. *Social Research Update, 1993*(2).

33. A.M. Orum, J.R. Feagin, & G. Sjoberg. (1991). *The case or the case study.* Chapel Hill, NC: University of North Carolina Press.

34. M.D. Gall, W.R. Borg, & J.P. Gall. (1996). *Educational research: An introduction* (6th ed.). White Plains, NY: Longman.

35. E. Connors, T. Lundregan, N. Miller, & T. McEwen. (1996). *Case studies in use of DNA evidence* (Document 161258). Washington, DC: National Institute of Justice.

36. H.P. Gramckow & E. Tompkins. (1999). *Enabling prosecutors to address drug, gang, and youth violence.* Washington, DC: Office of Juvenile Justice and Delinquency.

37. H.P. Gramckow & E. Tompkins. (1999). *Enabling prosecutors to address drug, gang, and youth violence.* Washington, DC: Office of Juvenile Justice and Delinquency.

38. C. Johnson, B. Webster, & E. Connors. (1995). *Prosecuting gangs: A national assessment* (Research in Brief #151785). Washington, DC: Office of Juvenile Justice and Delinquency.

39. C.S. Lederman. (1999). The juvenile court: Putting research to work for prevention. *Journal of Office of Juvenile Justice and Delinquency Prevention, 6*(2), 25.

39a. Lecklitner, G., Malik, N., Aaron, S., and Lederman, C.S. (April 1999). Dependency Court Intervention Program for Family Violence. Child Maltreatment, Vol. 4, No. 2, pp. 175–182.

40. National Institute of Justice. (1992). *Evaluating drug control and system improvement projects: Guidelines for projects supported by the Bureau of Justice Assistance.* Washington, DC: Prepared for the U.S. Department of Justice by Abt Associates.

41. President's Commission on Law Enforcement and Administration of Justice. (1967). *Task force report* (pp. 53–54). Washington, DC: U.S. Government Printing Office.

Legal Structures

4

Chapter Objectives

After studying this chapter, you should be able to

- Describe the relationship between law and society
- Explain the organization of the legal system in the United States
- Discuss how the U.S. legal system functions
- Define and discuss the responsibilities and duties of the key personnel in our legal system
- Explain why the legal system is inherently involved with governmental authority
- Discuss how the laws are enforced
- Explain the legislative process

Introduction

The relationship between law and society is more fully appreciated when we possess a sound understanding about the social organization of law. The legal process is inherently involved with authority and cannot be easily separated from the institutions that execute it. Dynamic associations take place between legislating, interpreting, and enforcing the law. The functioning of law is a process whereby some people render decisions about the law, others are responsible to carry out the law, and all are expected to obey the law.

In this chapter, we are concerned with the organization of the law. We start by identifying and examining the formal structure of the local, state, and federal court systems. Next we focus on the lawmaking function and responsibility of legislative bodies. In the final section, we discuss the enforcement of law and the punishment aspect of our legal structures.

Courts

The judicial system in the United States is comprised of the state courts, created by state constitutions and legislatures, and the federal courts, created by the U.S. Congress under its constitutional powers. In basic terms, a court is "an organ of the government, belonging to the judicial department, whose function is the application of the laws to controversies brought before it."[1] It is the place where judicial proceedings are held by persons who are assembled for the administration of justice; these include the judge, court clerk, court bailiff, court reporter, jurors, and attorneys. Likewise, the phrase "the court" is commonly used to refer to the judge or judges themselves.

The role of the court is to decide the rules of law applicable in a particular case and to settle controversies between parties. The judicial process is carried out by the courts and consists of interpreting the laws and applying them in a just and fair manner to all cases arising in litigation. In general, the courts do not give advisory opinions except when a state constitution authorizes the state supreme court to render an advisory opinion to the legislature with regard to the constitutionality of a statute.

Court Jurisdiction

Court jurisdiction is defined as the authority or power of the court to hear matters of controversy or dispute. Since both state and federal courts exist, initiating the judicial process begins with the decision of which court should take the case. Some courts have exclusive jurisdiction over certain matters (e.g., bankruptcy court) when only one court is empowered by law to hear the case in question. But in some situations, there may be concurrent jurisdiction in which authority coexists between the two or more courts. When this occurs, the plaintiff has a choice of courts in which to initiate litigation. Federal and state statutes govern the nature of the various court jurisdictions.

Readers often get confused over the differences between venue and jurisdiction. Venue refers to the geographical locale where the trial will be held, and jurisdiction refers to the power of a court to act over the parties and the subject matter in dispute.

Court jurisdiction is either original or appellate. A court of original jurisdiction (trial court) has the authority to receive the case when begun, to try the case, and to render a decision based on the presentation of facts and applicability of law. Appellate jurisdiction, which is set by constitution or statute, is the authority to review, overrule, or revise the action of a lower court. The appellate court hears complaints of error committed by an inferior court, whose judgment or decision the appellate court is asked to correct.

The jurisdictions of courts are limited by constitutions or statutes. Small-claims court, for instance, is a court of limited jurisdiction in which the amount in dispute can not exceed a fixed amount. Another example of a court of limited jurisdiction is municipal courts, which have jurisdiction over minor criminal matters, such as ordinance violations and misdemeanor criminal cases. Other examples of courts of limited jurisdiction are juvenile courts, probate courts, and county district courts.

Court Organization

The court system in the United States at both the state and federal levels is hierarchical. At the extreme top of the pyramid are supreme courts or courts of last resort, which are appellate courts. Below the supreme courts are the courts of appeals, which are courts that serve as intermediate appellate courts. Intermediate appellate courts function to hear the initial appeals of trial courts. They may also serve as courts of original jurisdiction when defined by constitution or statute. Trial court is typically the starting point for most court cases. The decisions of trial courts are subject to review by appellate courts.

The State Court System

The judicial power of the state court system is limited by the due process clause of the Fourteenth Amendment of the U.S. Constitution, which states:

> No state shall make or enforce any law which shall abridge the privileges or immunities of citizens of the United States; nor shall any state deprive any person of life, liberty, or property, without due process of law; nor deny to any person within its jurisdiction the equal protection of the laws.[2]

It is in the state courts that most of the legal disputes that surface in the lives of citizens are resolved. Disputes resolved by state courts include traffic and criminal cases as well as civil cases, such as domestic relations, personal injury and property damage, and real estate. Litigants may choose between a jury trial or bench trial. In a bench trial, the judge determines the facts as well as the law. In a jury trial, a jury determines the facts in accordance with the judge's instruction on the law. In a criminal case, then, the jury decides whether the defendant is innocent or guilty. In a civil case, the jury decides whether the defendant is liable to the plaintiff.

In most states, the courts of general jurisdiction are organized into districts, sometimes called circuits, superior courts, or the court of common pleas. Depending on the caseload and geography, the district may embrace from one to many counties and employs from one to many judges and support staff. For example, in Kansas, there are 31 judicial districts. The Third Judicial District covers only one urban county (Shawnee County) and employs 14 district court judges. The Fourth Judicial District covers four rural counties (Anderson, Coffey, Franklin, and Osage Counties) and employs only three district court judges.

State district courts are courts of record. This means that their proceedings and decisions are documented in a written record that is maintained by the clerk of the district court. Records of court decisions and the processes that led to those decisions are extremely important because such records are needed to challenge a decision in an appellate court.

Courts of Limited and Specific Jurisdiction

Some state courts are courts of limited action and have exclusive jurisdiction over specific common-law claims. As an illustration, we refer again to small-claims courts. Small-claims court cases are limited to a monetary amount for damages, such as $5,000 or $10,000, and lawyers are normally prohibited from representing the litigants. Also, no juries and no appeals are permitted. Likewise, traffic courts are courts of limited action. These courts ordinarily handle cases involving citations for traffic violations. While the traffic court is not a court of record, it is sometimes possible to appeal a traffic court's decision, depending on the statute that created the court.

Another example of a court of limited jurisdiction is probate court. The jurisdiction of probate courts is generally restricted to the settlement of estates, wills, and guardianship of minors and legally incompetent persons. In some states, the probate court also has jurisdiction over the adoption of children and other matters such as legal name changes. Appeals from probate court may be taken to either the trial court of general jurisdiction or the intermediate appellate court and are bound by a time limit fixed by statute.

A court of specific jurisdiction is domestic relations court. Domestic relations courts have exclusive jurisdiction over divorce, separation, annulment, support actions, suits involving temporary custody of children, and adoption. In some cases, the functions of the juvenile and family-law courts are combined, and the court has original jurisdiction over all of these matters.

Perhaps the best example of a court of specific jurisdiction is juvenile court. Most states have one or more juvenile courts that handle cases specific to minors under the age of 18 years old. Juvenile courts standing alone ordinarily have exclusive jurisdiction over children in need of care, which includes neglected, dependent, and abused children. Likewise, the juvenile court hears matters that pertain to delinquent acts committed by children.

State Court of Appeals

In the state court system, the next step up from the court of general original jurisdiction is the intermediate appellate court. The purpose of such a court is to relieve the burden on the state court system by lessening the caseload of the supreme court. Procedurally, in all states, a defendant convicted in a criminal case is entitled to one appeal. Likewise, in civil cases, the appellate court must review the verdict upon demand of the party aggrieved in the trial court. Where an intermediate appellate court exists, appeals go directly to that court, with only a few exceptions.[3]

The highest court in a state is usually called the supreme court. A party aggrieved by the decision of the intermediate appellate court can petition the state supreme court to review the case. Such a petition is called a "writ of certiorari." However, the supreme court has the discretion to refuse to review any case. In short, while the intermediate appellate court must review every appeal, the supreme court is not obligated to hear the case. The supreme court in most states is given supervisory control over and appellate jurisdiction from all other courts in the state judicial system, limited only by the state constitution and statutes. In a few states that do not have an intermediate appellate court, appeals are made directly to the supreme appellate court.

Federal Court System

The federal court system is prescribed by Article III of the U.S. Constitution. The jurisdiction of the federal court system consists of: the U.S. Supreme Court, 13 federal courts of appeals, a large number of district courts that serve as courts of general jurisdiction, and a number of specialized courts created by the U.S. Congress under the "necessary and proper clause" of Article I.

U.S. District Courts

The U.S. District Courts are federal trial courts with general federal jurisdiction. Each state has at a minimum one federal district court, while some larger states have several. A total of 92 federal district courts exist, in addition to one court in the District of Columbia and one court in Puerto Rico. There are 649 federal district court judges, the number of which is established by statute. Ordinarily, one judge hears a case, but in certain cases the law either requires or allows a three-judge panel to hear the case.

Each federal district court employs: a U.S. district court clerk, U.S. attorney, U.S. marshal, and one or more U.S. magistrates, bankruptcy judges, probation officers, and court reporters who serve the U.S. district courts. Magistrates are federal judicial officers who serve under the general supervision of the federal district, but who also have some responsibilities as defined in the Federal Magistrate Act of 1979. These responsibilities include the power to conduct some trials, to enter sentences for misdemeanor cases, to conduct hearings, to hear and determine pretrial matters pending before the court, and to provide administrative oversight and mediation for certain types of lawsuits.

The jurisdiction of the federal district courts is set forth in the U.S. Code. Among the types of cases tried are those involving crimes against the United States and cases involving diversity of citizenship (i.e., cases in which a citizen of one state brings a suit against a citizen of another state). Also, these courts of original jurisdiction handle maritime cases, cases involving the enforcement of orders of federal administrative agencies, and civil cases arising under federal statutes or the U.S. Constitution.

The U.S. Congress, under the "necessary and proper" clause of Article I, creates special courts from time to time to deal with particular kinds of cases that are not permanently part of the federal court system. Among these courts are the District of Columbia's local courts, the superior court, and the District of Columbia Court of Appeals. Other courts include the U.S. Court of Appeals for the Armed Forces, which is concerned exclusively with military criminal law, and the territorial courts, which function as district courts for the territories of Guam, the U.S. Virgin Islands, and the Northern Mariana Islands.

U.S. Courts of Appeals

The U.S. courts of appeals were created in 1891 to relieve the U.S. Supreme Court of the task of considering all appeals for cases originally decided by the federal trial courts. They are empowered to review the final decisions of federal district courts, except when direct review by the U.S. Supreme Court is called for by statute. The appeals courts are also empowered to review and enforce orders of many federal administrative agencies. Decisions of the appeals courts are final but subject to discretionary review by the Supreme Court. Each of the 50 states is assigned to one of 11 judicial circuits. There is an additional circuit for the District of Columbia, and another for the Federal Circuit. There are approximately 167 appellate judges, who are appointed by the president, with confirmation from the U.S. Senate, and sit for life. U.S. courts of appeals usually sit in panels of three judges, but may expand to a larger number in certain cases. They are then said to be sitting en banc, with all judges present.

Supreme Court of the United States

The U.S. Supreme Court was created in 1790 in accordance with Article III, Section 1, of the U.S. Constitution. The U.S. Supreme Court consists of the chief justice of the United States and eight associate justices. The president of the United States is empowered to nominate the U.S. Supreme Court justices, and appointments are made with the advice and consent of the Senate.

In Article III, Section 2, the U.S. Constitution defines the original and exclusive jurisdiction of the Supreme Court as (a) all controversies between states and (b) all actions or proceedings against ambassadors or other public ministers of foreign states or their domestic servants, not inconsistent with the law of nations.[4] The court has original but not exclusive jurisdiction over (a) all actions or proceedings brought by ambassadors or other public ministers of foreign states or to which consuls or vice consuls of foreign states are parties, (b) all controversies between the United States and a state, and (c) all actions or proceedings by a state against the citizens of another state or against aliens.

The U.S. Supreme Court only occasionally hears cases in original jurisdiction. Its principal function is as an appellate court, reviewing cases from the U.S. appeals courts, either by writ of certiorari granted to a petitioner who is party to a civil or criminal case or by certification of a question of federal law in a civil or criminal case. Both of these appeals are granted at the Court's discretion. Typically, there is a very limited right of direct appeal from a three-judge district court panel. The majority of U.S. Supreme Court cases are heard by way of the writ for certiorari.

The U.S. Supreme Court may also review, by petition of certiorari, the final judgment of the highest court of a state if: (a) there is a question regarding the validity of a treaty or statute of the United States, (b) the validity of a state statute has been challenged as being unconstitutional or illegal, or (c) a title, right, privilege, or immunity is claimed under the Constitution or treaties or statutes of the United States.

The U.S. Supreme Court convenes annually from the first Monday in October until the end of June. The nine justices sit en banc, and it takes six justices to constitute a quorum. The Supreme Court normally reviews fewer than 200 cases each year. By contrast, it refuses to review nearly 2,000 cases annually; the majority of its decisions consist of denials of certiorari to review decisions of courts of appeals or state supreme courts.

Court Unification Movements

Starting with the state of Illinois in 1964, several states have attempted to reduce expenditure of public monies by unifying their courts at the lower levels. For example, in Illinois, all trial courts were consolidated into one level of courts. A similar situation occurred in California, where many counties unified their municipal and superior courts into one level of courts with general jurisdiction to try all criminal and civil cases. The exception is that family law courts, bankruptcy courts, and other specialty courts were not merged in some states into the single court system. At the same time, there is a movement for the establishment of drug courts to try drug cases and veterans' courts to try vets.

Classifications of Law

Law is viewed in various ways and consequently can be classified differently. Often we think of law in terms of the system in which it operates. Common law, for instance, is a system of jurisprudence that originated in England that is based on written opinions that are binding on future decisions of lower courts in the same jurisdiction. Civil law is a system of legal science that originated under Roman emperor Justinian in the sixth century A.D. and has evolved as a means of regulating private relationships between individuals. In addition to classifying law by systems, other ways in which we think about law include: by source (constitutional, statutory, and case law), by the parties involved (public, private, and administrative law), by substance (civil and criminal law), and by function (substantive and procedural law). Each of these classifications is discussed in the sections that follow.

Common Law and Civil Law Systems

The principal systems of law in the United States are common law and the civil law. In all states except Louisiana (which was originally based on the French civil code), the common law system of England was adopted as the general law of the state, except when a statute explicitly states otherwise. Broad areas of the law, most notably relating to property, contracts, and torts, are traditionally part of the common law. These areas of the law are mostly within the jurisdiction of the states and, as such, state courts are the primary source of common law. Thus, common law is used to fill in gaps. Common law changes over time, and at this time, each state has its own common law on various topics. Federal common law is primarily limited to federal issues that have not been addressed by a statute.

The common-law system is based on precedent and the principle of stare decisis. Although the legislative bodies at the state and federal levels enact written statutes, and sometimes collect portions of those statutes into codes, there is no formal, comprehensive code of common law. Instead, the common law is stated in court decisions, and it is changed or modified by subsequent cases or statutes.

Conversely, the civil law system may be traced back to the Roman law from which most European law systems originated and is a codified system of basic laws set out in codes. In the civil law system, the Code Civil is a general statement of legal principles that is looked to in the interpretation of statutes and cases, and civilian courts do not follow the principle of stare decisis.

Sources of Law: Constitutional, Statutory, and Case Law

Every person who, under color of any statute, ordinance, regulation, custom, or usage, of any State or Territory or the District of Columbia, subjects, or causes to be subjected, any citizen of the United States or other person within the jurisdiction thereof to the deprivation of any rights, privileges, or immunities secured by the Constitution and laws, shall be liable to the party injured in an action at law, suit in equity, or other proper proceeding for redress.[5]

Constitutional Law

Constitutional law is the fundamental law of the land. It contains the principles upon which the government is founded and regulates the divisions of the sovereign powers. It defines basic principles of law that all other laws must follow and delegates authority to various officials and agencies. The source of this law is from people acting in their collective capacity as sovereign in the nation or state in which they live and create constitutions.

The U.S. Constitution is the supreme law in America. No other federal or state law, statute, or case may impose upon its provisions. It is divided into three parts. The first component, Articles I through VII, divides governmental power among the three branches of government (legislative, executive, and judicial) and between the federal and state governments. It also describes the relationships between the states and sets out the means for amending the Constitution.

The second section of the Constitution consists of the first 10 amendments, which are referred to as the Bill of Rights. The first nine amendments provide for and protect individual freedoms. The Fourth Amendment, for example, establishes

the right of the people to be secure in their persons, houses, papers, and effects, against unreasonable searches and seizures, shall not be violated, and no Warrants shall issue, but upon probable cause, supported by Oath or affirmation, and particularly describing the place to be searched, and the persons or things to be seized.[6]

Other similar amendments that have had a profound influence on the criminal justice system include protection from self-incrimination (Fifth Amendment), the right to speedy and public jury trials in criminal cases and jury trials in civil cases (Sixth Amendment), and protection from cruel and unusual punishment (Eighth Amendment).

The third part of the Constitution consists of the amendments that have been added over the past two centuries. These amendments cover a wide range of subjects that reflect social change in America. For example, the Thirteenth Amendment abolished slavery. The Fourteenth Amendment granted the equal protection of the laws and due process of law to all the citizens and residents of the various states. The Fifteenth, Nineteenth, Twenty-fourth, and Twenty-sixth Amendments extended the right to vote.

In addition to the U.S. Constitution, all states have constitutions, which are generally more detailed than the U.S. Constitution. State constitutions often give people within that state more rights than the same language contained in the U.S. Constitution. Moreover, because of the supremacy clause of the U.S. Constitution, no state can give its people fewer rights than those in the U.S. Constitution.

Statutory Law

A primary source of law is statutory law. Statutes are enacted by the legislative branch of government (whether state or federal) to regulate areas within the legislature's jurisdiction. Under the U.S. and state constitutions, statutes are considered the primary source of law in America (i.e., legislatures make the law [statutes] and courts interpret the law [cases]).

Most state statutes are organized by subject matter and published in books referred to as codes. Typically, a state has a civil code, a criminal code, a welfare code, a probate code, a juvenile code, and many other codes dealing with a wide variety of topics. Federal statutes are organized into subject-matter titles within the U.S. Code (e.g., Title 11 for bankruptcy).

There are three classifications of statutes: personal, real, and mixed. Personal statutes pertain to persons and treat property only incidentally. Examples of personal statutes are laws that regard birth, legitimacy, freedom, the fight of instituting suits, incapacity to contract, to make a will, to plead in person, and the like. A personal statute is universal in its operation and is in force everywhere. Conversely, real statutes are those that pertain to property and that do not speak of persons, except in relation to property. The third class of statutes is known as mixed statutes. Mixed statutes are those that concern both persons and property collectively. In this sense, almost all statutes are mixed, there being scarcely any law relative to persons that does not at the same time relate to objects or things.

Each year, legislatures pass both new law and amended law. The exact titles of the session laws (i.e., the collections of statutes passed in each legislative session) vary, as do the titles given to the state law compilations. In Kansas, for example, they are known as Kansas Statutes Annotated; in Michigan, they are called Michigan Compiled Laws; and in North Dakota, they are called the North Dakota Century Code. In the federal system, the U.S. Code arranges federal statutes by subject under 50 titles, with the first 6 dealing with general provisions and the other 44 alphabetically arranged from agriculture to war. The U.S. Code is updated annually, and a new set of bound volumes is published every 6 years.

Case Law

Another source of law is case law, which is law made by the courts. It is known as case law because it derives from judicial decisions in legal cases rather than from written statutes. This necessarily means that judges look for guidance to the decision in a prior case that had similar facts. As courts decide and report their decisions concerning particular suits, these cases become part of the body of law and can be consulted in later cases involving similar problems. Cases are published in reports (such as *United States Reports*) that are produced either by the government or a private publishing firm. Not all cases are published.

Scope of the Law

Laws are often classified according to the scope of the law, i.e., on the parties to whom they apply. We categorize law into two areas according to their scope: private law and public law. Private law exists to govern the relationships between citizens. Disputes typically involve property, contracts, and many other matters. Public law is concerned with regulating the relations of individuals among themselves and with the government. It is also the branch of law that governs the organization and conduct of government itself. Disputes involve the state or its agencies in a direct manner, and usually the state is the party bringing the suit to court. For example, in the criminal law case of *State of California v. John Smith*, the plaintiff is cited as the state.

Administrative Law

Administrative law is the body of law governing administrative agencies (i.e., agencies created by the U.S. Congress or state legislatures, such as the Social Security Administration and state social welfare agencies). Administrative agencies administer law through the creation and enforcement of regulations; most of these regulations provide some type of benefit to applicants. Federal rules and regulations are first published chronologically in the *Federal Register* and then later organized by subject in the Code of Federal Regulations.

Administrative hearings are considered informal, but they serve an important purpose. Usually, an administrative law judge (ALJ) meets with representatives from the agency and the applicant seeking benefits. The applicant may choose whether or not to be represented by an attorney, and many administrative agencies permit paralegal assistance, law students, or law clerks to appear on behalf of applicants. Each side presents its evidence and elicits testimony from its witnesses. The ALJ renders a decision, called an *administrative order*, which may be subject to review by either a higher level within the agency or by a court.

State governments also have administrative agencies that issue rules, regulations, and rulings (i.e., state social welfare agencies). They are typically part of an executive department of the state government. These agencies tend to regulate areas not preempted by federal agencies, but they may also be found in fields subject to both federal and state regulation.

Civil and Criminal Law

In addition to the scope of the law, the type of the dispute allows for further distinctions to be made about cases that come before the court. Generally, court cases are separated into two categories of law: criminal and civil.

Criminal law is imposed for any crime, including an act, omission, or possession under the laws of the United States or a state government that poses a substantial threat of personal injury. Criminal law prescribes both what behaviors in society are unacceptable and what sanctions will be imposed for committing such acts. A criminal action is prosecuted in the name of the federal government ("The United States of America") or the state ("The People of the State"), because criminal behavior is considered to be harming society as a whole. When the prosecutor pursues a criminal case, the intent is to punish the offender. The major categories of crimes are wrongful acts against persons (e.g., homicide, robbery, and assault), against property (e.g., burglary, theft, and arson), and the possession, sale, and manufacturing of drugs.

In a general sense, all other law is civil law (i.e., court proceedings that are not criminal in nature). Civil law deals with acts that inflict injury on a person or a person's rights. Tort suits seek compensation, which is intended primarily to compensate the injured party. This includes lawsuits by private parties as well as those involving governments.

Civil law covers numerous areas, including real estate, domestic relations, partnerships, taxes, contracts, and wills and trusts. In some cases, successful civil litigation can represent a significant turning point for culture in society. For instance, lawsuits filed against major tobacco companies have exposed the dangers of cigarette smoking. Similarly, civil litigation can have an effect on companies that produce certain products. A McDonald's restaurant in Albuquerque, New Mexico, for example, was the target of a lawsuit filed by a patron after she was burned by coffee sold to her.

DIFFERENCES BETWEEN CRIMINAL
AND CIVIL COURT CASES

- In a criminal case, the prosecutor is in charge of the case from beginning to end. The prosecutor may file criminal charges even if the victim doesn't approve or refuses to file criminal charges. Similarly, the prosecutor has the discretion not to file criminal charges despite the victim's desire that criminal charges be filed. This method of beginning the case contrasts with civil cases, where the injured party is the one who initiates legal action.
- In a criminal case, if the defendant is convicted, he or she will be required to pay a fine or be incarcerated, or sometimes both. In a civil case, the party who is held responsible may have to pay money damages or give up property, but the loser does not go to jail or prison.
- In a criminal case, government-paid attorneys represent defendants who want but can't afford legal counsel. Parties in civil cases, on the other hand, usually have to represent themselves or pay for their own lawyers.
- In a criminal case, the prosecutor has to prove a defendant's guilt "beyond a reasonable doubt." In a civil case, the plaintiff has to show only by a "preponderance of the evidence" (i.e., greater than 50%) that the defendant is liable for damages.
- In a criminal case, the defendant is nearly always entitled to a jury trial. A party to a civil action is entitled to a jury trial in some types of cases, but not in others.

Sometimes, the same conduct may violate both criminal and civil laws. A defendant whose actions violate both criminal and civil laws may be criminally prosecuted by the state as well as sued civilly by a victim for monetary damages. For example, in 1995, O.J. Simpson was prosecuted for the murder of Ron Goldman and Nicole Brown Simpson, his former wife. Simpson was acquitted of all criminal charges, but in a separate civil case, the victims' families sued Simpson for "wrongful death." In 1997, a jury of 12 people unanimously decided that Simpson was liable (i.e., responsible) on all eight counts regarding the victims' deaths and ordered to pay compensatory damages of $8.5 million.

Functions: Substantive and Procedural Law

As a final way of classifying law, we want to discuss features of substantive law and procedural law. Substantive law involves the basis for a legal claim. It consists of statutory and case law, thereby establishing the rights and obligations upon which a dispute is based. Procedural law prescribes the rules by which a person can secure his or her substantive rights. Therefore, the rules of procedure exist in accordance with the substantive law that is to be administered.

Although procedural law does not state the law, it outlines the protocol that must be followed in applying the substantive law. Procedural law enables legal counsel to decide what venue is appropriate for the case (i.e., federal or state court). It establishes when a legal action must be filed, what practice will be followed during the litigation, and what evidence can be presented at trial.

BIG BROTHER IS WATCHING

In October 2012, the Atlanta City Council voted to approve the addition of 112 new security cameras, for a total of 762 cameras, to monitor downtown Atlanta. The cameras were part of an effort to address a crime problem that the council felt could threaten Atlanta's tourism and business growth while also intimidating students who attended college downtown. The council noted that students had been victims of countless robberies, burglaries, and assaults. The council failed to address the issue that, by most accounts, crime was down in Atlanta, with fewer than 100 homicides for the fourth year in a row, and major felonies were down 5% that year and 16% since 2009. "This will give us more eyes on the streets so police can respond more readily," said Councilman Michael Julian Bond, who chaired the public safety committee. "Having more eyes is a strong deterrent. Criminals don't want to be seen."[7]

Does this level of surveillance violate our right to privacy when we visit a city?

Participants

The legal process involves the dynamic interaction between four distinct groups of participants. They are litigants, legal counsel, judges, and juries. While we have previously alluded to these groups, the following discussion is intended to present a brief description of the role that each has in the dispute-resolving process of the legal system. Additionally, we discuss the role of the court manager, as it is suggested that such a participant is a necessary component of the justice system.

Litigants

In disputes taken to court, there is a common belief that there will be a winner and a loser. In criminal cases, for instance, when the government brings charges against the defendant, a guilty verdict indicates that the prosecution wins the case. If the defendant is found not guilty, then the government essentially loses the case. In civil matters, the plaintiff files suit against the respondent, which is also the term to designate the person responding to an appeal.

A judgment usually denotes a winner and loser, but where money is involved, it's common for attorney fees and other costs of litigation to eat up whatever award is given to the winning side. And even if there is a substantial judgment, it may be difficult for the plaintiff to collect. Consequently, it's not unusual for a civil case to end up with both sides experiencing large out-of-pocket expenses.

Counsel

Counsel is the term used to describe an attorney who advises and represents a party in a legal proceeding. We generally think the role of counsel is to give advice to another (i.e., what is the prudent thing to do). Counsel also encompasses those attorneys that represent the government in legal actions when some harm has been caused to society.

Prosecutors are lawyers who investigate and try criminal cases. Typically known as a district attorney, state's attorney, or U.S. attorney, these legal officials prosecute criminal defendants in the name of the government. Prosecutors are either public officials acting in their official capacity or private counsel that has been appointed to the role of special prosecutor.

The prosecutor's role is central in processing criminal cases and therefore requires a constant positive relationship with police, judges, and politicians within the jurisdiction in which the judicial system exists. Prosecutors cultivate and maintain good relationships with the police to ensure that criminal law is enforced in accordance with the policies of the prosecutor's office. Prosecutors also maintain a positive relationship with judges in order to influence bail, sentencing, and other judicial decisions that are made during the prosecution of a criminal defendant. Finally, prosecutors rely on elected officials at the local, state, and federal levels to adequately fund criminal justice agencies. Consequently, prosecutors are sensitive to the law enforcement priorities set by politicians who control budgetary decisions.

Defendants who are charged with a crime and face the possibility of being imprisoned undertake a major financial expense to obtain the legal representation of a defense lawyer. In the legal system, people who are indigent qualify for the free or reduced-fee services of a public defender or court-appointed attorney. Criminal defense lawyers perform many functions in the legal system. For example, defense counsel negotiates "plea bargains" with prosecutors, often arranging for reduced charges and lesser sentencing. This occurs as a trade-off for a plea of guilty or nolo contendere, which translates to "no contest" and has the same effect as a plea of guilty, as far as the criminal sentence is concerned.

Occasionally, a criminal defendant decides to represent himself and this "pro se" defense makes sense in some situations. Obviously, the less severe the charged crime, the more reasonable it is for someone to self-represent. For example, a defendant charged with a minor traffic offense or violation of a city ordinance may get by without hiring an attorney. A critical piece of information that someone should consider before deciding whether to hire an attorney is what the punishment is likely to be if they are convicted.

In some civil lawsuits (e.g., small-claims court) that are heard in a formal trial court, appearing on your own behalf is commonplace. However, in most civil court cases, the parties cannot agree on a settlement, thus requiring a civil trial to settle the dispute. In such cases, legal counsel is normally pursued because an attorney provides greater experience and understanding of legal tactics. Civil court processes will be discussed later in the chapter.

Judges

Judges are government officials appointed to decide litigated questions according to law. They serve as the power broker of the judicial process. Impartiality is the first duty of a judge, making certain that no bias exists for or against either of the parties. The judge must also follow and enforce the law, whether good or bad. Judges are bound to declare what the law is and not to make it (i.e., not an arbitrator, but rather a scholar of the law).

Judges are appointed or elected to the bench in a variety of ways. In the federal court system, district judges are nominated by the president of the United States and confirmed by the U.S. Senate as is set forth in Article III of the U.S. Constitution. U.S. district court judges are appointed for lifetime terms in office, provided they exhibit "good behavior" according to Article III of the Constitution. Magistrate judges, who are appointed by the district judges for 8-year terms of office, handle most of the pretrial matters and make recommendations to the district judges regarding the cases referred to them. Also, if all parties to a civil lawsuit so consent, they may request to have their case presided over from beginning to end by a magistrate judge.

This option provides consistency of flow, which is often important to litigants during a civil action.

The chief judge is the administrative head of the court. Every 7 years, a new chief judge is appointed based on seniority. Other criteria considered when appointing the chief judge include: (a) 64 years of age or under; (b) have served for 1 year or more as a district judge; and (c) have not previously served as chief judge.

In the state judicial system, the governor, the governor with confirmation of the senate, or the legislature appoints judges in the state. In many states, judges are chosen by a method that combines appointment and election, which is commonly known as the Missouri Plan. In the initial stage, the governor forms a selection committee that is responsible for collecting and screening applications from individuals seeking appointment to the bench. The committee then recommends a list of three nominees, of which one applicant is chosen by the governor and appointed to the vacant judgeship. After the initial term in office expires, a retention vote is taken during election time. Several states use this selection and retention process, including Alaska, Arizona, Colorado, Iowa, Kansas, Nebraska, Utah, and Wyoming.

Whether in the federal or state court system, almost all judges are lawyers by profession. In addition to needing adequate legal training, good judges are characterized by the following qualities:[8]

- Maintaining neutrality with regard to the parties in litigation
- Being fair-minded
- Being well versed in the law
- Having the ability to think and write in a logical and lucid manner
- Having personal integrity
- Having good physical and mental health
- Possessing good judicial temperament
- Having the ability to handle judicial power sensibly

Juries

Trial by jury is an integral part of our justice system in America. It can be traced back to civil and criminal inquiries conducted under old Anglo-Saxon law in England and translated into a jury of one's peers. The Sixth Amendment of the U.S. Constitution guarantees one's right to a trial by jury, which typically involves a random selection of citizens from within the jurisdiction where the trial is to take place. However, a trial by jury does not always guarantee justice will be served.

For years, the jury system was marked by the appearance of individuals hand selected from certain strata of the population. Discrimination, intentional or not, was often the result. Verdicts reflected the community standards of these strata, and the viewpoints of juries rarely reflected those of the entire community. It was only in 1975 that the U.S. Supreme Court held that women could not be excluded simply because they are women. With the previous measure emphasizing the use of a broadly inclusive list, the advantages of such a list are lost if the selection of names from this list is not random. The American Bar Association's standards call for randomness at each stage of the juror selection process while recognizing that certain practices are nonrandom but nonetheless permissible. Employing these standards eliminates all other nonrandom procedures.[9]

In many states, 12 jurors are required for a criminal trial involving a felony crime. In some states, however, fewer than 12 member jurors are adequate, but a minimum of 6 jurors is always required in any felony trial.[10] For example, Utah and Arizona use eight-person juries, and Florida, Louisiana, Oregon, and Rhode Island use six-person juries.

Grand Juries

A grand jury is a group of citizens convened in a criminal case to determine whether formal charges should be brought against a defendant(s) and whether the case should go to trial. If so, a *true bill* or *indictment* (a formal complaint against the defendant listing the specific criminal charge) is issued. If not, the grand jury dismisses the case by issuing a *no true bill* (also called a *no bill*). That means that the accused is not charged with a crime and therefore is not required to stand trial. The number of members on a grand jury varies in different states, consisting of not less than 12 or more than 24 members who listen to the case.

The Court Administrator

The complex operations of the court system necessitate that a court administrator or manager be an essential part of the judicial system. The court manager's primary role is to oversee the administrative functions of the court, under the direction of the chief judge. Together, they provide an executive component to the court, blending judicial management with the disciplines of business and public administration.[11]

The duties of the court manager vary, depending on the size and location of the court. However, overall the court administrator or manager functions in management areas rather than legal areas. Basic management responsibilities of the court manager include:[12]

> *Personnel management*: Understanding personnel regulations, including the wage and salary systems as well as recruitment, selection, and training of staff

Fiscal management: Preparing annual court budgets; administering accounting, purchasing, payroll, and financial control functions; and guiding the budget through local and state government review processes

Case-flow management: Analyzing and evaluating pending client caseloads as well as preparing and implementing recommendations for effective court calendar management

Automated office management: Assisting the court through analysis, evaluation, and implementation of automated systems, including computers, word processors, telecommunication equipment, microfilm, and microfiche devices and techniques

Jury management: Providing the most efficient and cost-effective way of managing the jury system

Space and equipment management: Planning for physical plant, including assessment of space needs and the purchasing of equipment and supplies

Public education: Acting as a liaison to other agencies, courts and governments, attorneys, and the public to educate and promote the work of the court as a separate but equal branch of government.

Information management: Acting as a clearinghouse for the release of information to the media and the public; providing management information to all departments and branches of government; and collecting and publishing data on pending and completed judicial business and internal functions of the court system

Records management: Developing and managing uniform systems of record storage

Research and advisory services: Identifying problems and recommending procedural and administrative changes to the court

Intergovernmental relations: Acting as a liaison to other government agencies

Secretariat services: Acting as staff for judicial committees

Flow of Litigation in Civil Proceedings

Earlier in this chapter we defined the civil court case. In brief, a civil case arises when an injured party files a case requesting the court to grant damages in the form of a payment of money. In some jurisdictions, if either party in the case requests it, a jury may hear the trial. If neither party requests a jury, the judge hears the case and renders a decision. In civil cases, the party who initiates the action must present a preponderance of the evidence. In other words, the burden of proof is squarely on the plaintiff of the civil suit.

As a formal matter, the plaintiff seeks a favorable judgment by a judge. In practice, however, the judicial process typically does not produce such a result. Instead, most civil cases leave the judicial process after a negotiated settlement between the parties.

The federal and state court systems each have their own rules of procedure that dictate the form and timing of each step in the civil litigation process. To illustrate these incremental steps, we provide a synopsis of civil procedure, which normally consists of: (a) filing the complaint, (b) discovery, (c) pretrial conference, (d) trial and judgment, and (e) conclusion of litigation.

Civil cases are initiated when someone files a complaint. The complaint is a legal document that asserts the facts and legal basis for the claim and requests the desired remedy. In civil cases, the remedy is specified in terms of an amount of money or a specific judicial order directed at the defendant. When the plaintiff files the complaint, the court clerk requires a filing fee to be paid.

Once the complaint has been filed, the defendant is given notice and has a limited time period to respond. This notice is called a summons and is a constitutional due process requirement (i.e., a person being sued has the right to know about the suit and must have adequate time to answer the facts stated in the complaint). Courts typically require a sworn affidavit or a signed registered-mail receipt to show that the person being sued has been served the complaint. This due process is required because if the defendant doesn't respond to the complaint and fails to appear in court, the judge may order in favor of the plaintiff because of default.

In most states, the defendant has 30 to 60 days in which to file an answer to the complaint. The "answer" is a brief response either admitting or denying the statements in the complaint. In addition to stating the factual basis of the defendant's view of why the plaintiff's case is false, the answer also provides opportunity for the defendant to dispute the matter in terms of a legal basis. The defendant also has the opportunity to file a counterclaim by initiating an action against the plaintiff.

If either party wants a jury trial, a request for jury is required at the end of the complaint or answer. Otherwise, the trial will take place before a judge. When a jury trial is requested, the court clerk often requires the payment of an extra fee to cover costs.

The next step in the process involves "discovery," which is simply identifying witnesses and uncovering all the evidence in the case. The purpose of discovery is to learn as much as possible about the issues involved in the civil action. Two discovery methods are commonplace:

Interrogatories: Written requests for information (i.e., set of questions) that requires written answers from the opposing party

Deposition: Oral testimony of witnesses taken outside the courtroom but in the presence of the attorneys for both parties and a court reporter

The next step in the flow of civil litigation is the pretrial conference. After the preliminary work has been completed and the case has been assigned a date for trial, the attorneys may meet with the judge to informally discuss the facts as well as the allegations and rebuttals involved in the lawsuit. At these pretrial conferences, the goal is to exchange information, and sometimes evidence is produced that results in a request to dismiss the litigation without trial. Typically this occurs when certain aspects of the case can be settled by stipulation or agreement between the attorneys with the approval of the judge.

Civil trials take place when the parties cannot agree on a settlement. When legal counsel for either the plaintiff or respondent feels that the civil case is ready for trial, the clerk of the court is notified through the filing of a "notice of trial." The court docket is consulted, and the clerk chooses the next available trial date. The clerk then notifies the parties when and where the trial will be held. In civil cases, the plaintiff's attorney argues the case, and in most jurisdictions the plaintiff's attorney is allowed a rebuttal immediately following the defense's final argument. After the plaintiff has presented evidence, and before the presentation of defense, the defendant may move for a dismissal of the case for failure to state a claim for which relief may be granted.

When a case is heard before a jury, the jury finds in favor of either the plaintiff or respondent. This decision is made based on the facts of the case. In civil cases, judgment is issued in favor of the party judged to have met its burden of proof. The party who receives the favorable judgment is referred to as the "prevailing party." The jury also is called upon to set the amount of damages. In effect, the jury sets the sentence.

Very few civil cases end up before judges or juries. The motives to settle vary from legal to personal reasons. For example, if the evidence gathered during discovery shows that there is no factual issue to be tried, the judge may enter a summary judgment upon motion by one of the parties. Sometimes one of the litigants or legal counsel fails to appear in court or respond to court documents within the time specified. This results in a default judgment. At other times, the parties mutually agree to terminate the suit or the plaintiff may simply discontinue the case. Still other times, the plaintiff and respondent come to an out-of-court resolution. For instance, a Pennsylvania municipality agreed to settle a traffic-stop suit brought by minority drivers who claimed they had been forced to stop because of race-based drug courier profiles.[13] In another case, a class-action lawsuit brought against Honda by dealers alleged that Honda executives conspired to send cars to those willing to pay exorbitant bribes and punished dealers who refused. Under the terms of a settlement approved by a U.S. district court judge, Honda agreed to pay the dealers a total of nearly $330 million. In exchange, the dealers dropped their bribery claims.[14]

The final step in the civil process occurs once the court hands down a judgment. When this happens, the losing party has two basic options. The first option is to simply satisfy the judgment of the court (e.g., monetary damages). If judgment is not fulfilled, the prevailing party may have to take measures to enforce the court's order. The second option is, of course, to appeal the case to a higher court. If the losing party chooses to appeal, no payment is made to the prevailing party. The attorney for the losing party must make an appeal within the time limit prescribed by law or forfeit the right to appeal.

Flow of Criminal Proceedings

When a person breaks a law that is designed to protect society from harm, it is considered a criminal act. Jurisprudence is based on the general understanding that criminal acts cause harm not only to individuals, but also to society as a whole. Therefore, the people within society are responsible for bringing action against those who commit criminal acts. As a matter of practice, public officials who are versed on the law represent the peoples' interests. In America, we know these legal representatives as district attorneys, county attorneys, public prosecutors, or U.S. attorneys.

The prosecution of a criminal act involves the criminal court system. The criminal court has its own rules of procedure that dictate how the prosecution process should take place. Similar to civil cases, the process involves a set of successive actions on the part of the court system. In general, these actions consist of: (a) filing charges, (b) first appearance, (c) preliminary hearing, (d) trial and judgment, and (e) sentencing.

The criminal justice court system is initiated when an individual is charged with a crime. The process of charging an individual for a crime varies. One way in which it occurs is when a citizen files a formal complaint with police. The police report causes the prosecution to review the facts of the complaint to determine if a law has been broken. If so, the prosecutor prepares an affidavit for an arrest warrant. A judge signs a warrant, which is the written authority for police to make an arrest.

Charging someone with a crime also may occur when police make an arrest. Arrests in such cases can be made under the following conditions:

- If a police officer has probable cause to believe that a crime has been committed and that a specific person has committed the crime, that person may be detained under suspicion.
- If a person commits a felony or misdemeanor crime in plain view of a police officer, an arrest can be made without a warrant.

- If a police officer has probable cause to believe that a person has committed a felony crime, even if the crime was not committed in the officer's presence, the officer may arrest the person.

An arrest may be made in a public place, with or without a warrant. But if police wish to arrest a person in a private place, an arrest warrant must be obtained first, unless there are exigent circumstances, such as the possibility that the suspect will flee. Police have a relatively short period of time following an arrest (24 or 48 hours, depending on the state) during which they must either charge the person with a crime or release them.

Once an arrest has occurred, the accused is typically taken to jail. In most criminal court cases, the court establishes a bail amount. Bail is money or property that an accused person puts forth as security (also known as surety) to ensure that they will appear for further criminal proceedings, including the trial and sentencing. Bail may be paid in cash, in the form of a bail bond, or a pledge of property if the court permits this form of security. A bail bond is an agreement with a bail bondsman under which the bondsman puts up bail money in return for a fee. In some cases, however, (e.g., failure to appear cases) there is no bail as the judge requires that the defendant make an immediate appearance in court. Also, if a judge believes that the crime charged is extremely serious, then bail may be denied or set at such a high figure that a defendant may not realistically be able to post bail. In minor offenses, an accused who is well established in the community with a job, a home, and family support may be released on low bail. Occasionally, this includes a signature bond, which is, in effect, no bail at all. The defendant merely signs a bond promising to appear in court. This type of bail is referred to as being released in one's own recognizance (ROR).

The next step in the criminal court process is the arraignment of the accused person. The purpose of this initial court appearance is to ensure that the defendant is aware of the charges that have been brought about by the prosecution and understands the maximum punishment allowed by law, should a conviction occur. The judge also makes inquiry into the ability of the defendant to hire legal counsel for defense. If the defendant is indigent, the court may appoint an attorney. For example, attorney Stephen Jones was appointed by a U.S. district court to serve as the principal defense counsel for Timothy McVeigh when he was charged in the Oklahoma City bombing case in 1995.

The next step in the criminal court process is the preliminary hearing. A preliminary hearing is a formal court process to determine whether there is probable cause for holding the accused for trial. At this hearing, the prosecution presents just enough evidence to the judge to convince him or her that the evidence shows that a crime occurred and that the accused likely committed the crime. The defense attorney may cross-examine any of the prosecution's witnesses and present witnesses on behalf of the defendant. If the judge concludes that probable cause exists, the accused is bound over for trial.

After being formally charged and usually before the start of a trial, a defendant may arrange with the prosecution to enter a guilty plea to a lesser charge (i.e., if the prosecution is willing to charge the defendant with a lesser crime). Plea bargaining includes the prosecutor's agreement to recommend a particular sentence for the charges to which the defendant agrees to plead guilty. The vast majority of criminal cases are settled this way.

If a plea agreement is not reached, the proceedings move toward the trial stage. The U.S. Constitution in the Sixth Amendment guarantees a right to a jury trial in a criminal trial. The defendant, however, may waive this right. If the trial is to be held before a jury, members are selected and sworn in by the court bailiff, court reporter, or other court personnel. A trial jury typically consists of 12 citizens who sit together, listen to the facts of the case, and present their decision (the verdict). In criminal actions, a unanimous vote of the jurors is usually necessary. In a jury trial, the judge rules on points of law and the jury decides questions of fact.

After the jury has been selected, the trial follows standard formats, which consist of the following procedures:

1. An opening statement by the prosecutor
2. An opening statement by the defendant's lawyer
3. Presentation of evidence by the prosecutor
4. Presentation of evidence by the defense
5. Closing arguments by the prosecutor
6. Closing arguments by the defense
7. The judge's charge or instructions to the jury

At the trial, evidence is presented by the prosecutor in the form of witness testimony, documentary evidence, and "demonstrative evidence." Documentary evidence includes such items as police reports, records, and letters. Demonstrative evidence includes all kinds of exhibits, including photographs of the victim of a homicide, or the gun used in committing a robbery. The defendant has the right to present witnesses and other evidence in defense of the charges. The defendant also has the right to "confront" or cross-examine the witnesses brought forward by the prosecution.

Once the submission of evidence has concluded, the judge charges the jury. In this step, the judge instructs the jury with regard to the law relating to the case. While the judge ultimately instructs the jury, each attorney prepares and submits to the judge a set of requested jury instructions. In this way, each attorney can make sure that the judge does not overlook any important point that the attorney wants the jury to take into consideration.

The jury then retires to a private room and considers the case in secrecy. A vote of the jury is taken to arrive at a decision. A jury may find a person not guilty or guilty of all or some of the crimes charged. In some cases, depending upon the evidence presented and the nature of the jury instructions given by the court, a jury may convict a defendant of a lesser offense than originally charged in the indictment. If the jury cannot reach a decision, the judge may order a mistrial. If the defendant is found guilty, the judge has the authority to impose sentence, although in certain jurisdictions the jury determines the sentence. In serious cases, such as capital murder offenses, another hearing might be held to determine the sentence. The sentence is based on specific findings of fact, such as the presence of aggravating or mitigating circumstances, and conclusions of law. The verdict is signed by the judge and recorded so that it may be included in the transcript of the case. If the accused is found guilty, the case is subject to appeal. After acquittal, a criminal defendant cannot be tried again for the same crime (known as double jeopardy). If a mistrial is declared, there must be a new trial with a new jury.

In the final step of the criminal court process, the judge imposes sentencing. There are three basic types of sentencing that pertain to felony convictions: mandatory, indeterminate, and determinate. Mandatory sentencing is law that prescribes a particular sentence for a specific crime, and the judge has no latitude. Indeterminate sentencing allows the judge to establish minimum and maximum time periods of punishment that an offender must serve. For example, an offender may be sentenced to prison for a minimum of 2 years but not more than 5 years. Determinate sentencing is referred to as "truth in sentencing" and requires the judge to confer with a sentencing grid that establishes the type and length of punishment based only on crime severity and criminal history. A small amount of latitude is afforded to the sentencing judge if aggravated or mitigating circumstances exist.

The sentencing process as well as the other steps in the criminal court process is bound by laws that have been enacted by state legislatures or Congress. In the next section we examine this relationship by briefly discussing the principal function of legislative bodies and the process of lawmaking.

Lawmaking

The process of lawmaking is distinguished by the extent to which compromise is incorporated into the political system. While legislators have their own viewpoints about which laws need immediate attention and which do not, citizens who are either proponents or opponents of certain legislation constantly try to influence the work of lawmakers. Considering that this dynamic takes place with each and every legislator, it is no wonder that a legislative session can become besieged with confrontation and confusion.

On a large scale, there are two types of political affiliations that effect lawmaking in America: political parties and interest groups. Political party can be defined as a group of voters, officeholders, and candidates who label themselves as a political party. It is organized around two basic kinds of functions: (a) helping legislative candidates get elected and (b) helping legislators get bills passed through the legislative process. While political parties are not discussed in the U.S. Constitution, today's democratic political system is based on seeing these functions through in order to advance the agendas of certain classes of people in society.

An interest *group* is a formal organization of people who share a common outlook or social circumstance and who band together in the hope of influencing lawmaking. Examples are groups of private companies (e.g., tobacco corporations), unions (e.g., auto workers), tradesmen (e.g., sheet metal workers), professions (e.g., lawyers), government contractors (e.g., construction companies), government bureaus (e.g., public schools), ideologues (e.g., environmentalists), taxpayers, consumers, and the list goes on.

An interest group can use a variety of methods to influence laws. First, it can merely inform legislators of its members' preferences (i.e., proponents or opponents of specific legislation). Second, it may give money or time to help with an election campaign. Third, an interest group may attempt to influence members of the executive branch, who have some lawmaking input.

U.S. Congress

The primary function of the U.S. Congress is the making of laws. Article I, Section 1, of the United States Constitution, provides that:

> All Legislative Powers herein granted shall be vested in a Congress of the United States, which shall consist of a Senate and House of Representatives.

The Senate is composed of 100 members (two from each state, regardless of population) elected by the people in accordance with the Seventeenth Amendment to the U.S. Constitution. A senator must be at least 30 years of age, have been a citizen of the United States for 9 years, and, when elected, be a resident of the state for which the senator is chosen. A senator's term is 6 years, and the terms of both senators from a particular state are arranged so that they do not terminate at the same time.

The House of Representatives is composed of 435 members elected every 2 years from among the 50 states, apportioned to their total populations. A representative must be at least 25 years of age, have been a citizen of the

United States for 7 years, and, when elected, be a resident of the state in which the representative is chosen. If a representative dies or resigns during the term, the governor of the state calls a special election pursuant to state law to choose a successor to serve out the remainder of the term. A resident commissioner from Puerto Rico (elected for a 4-year term) and delegates from American Samoa, the District of Columbia, Guam, and the Virgin Islands complete the composition of the Congress of the United States. Delegates are elected for a term of 2 years.

The resident commissioner and delegates may take part in the floor discussions but have no vote in the full House or in the Committee of the Whole House on the State of the Union. They do, however, vote in the committees to which they are assigned.

Under provisions of the Twentieth Amendment to the U.S. Constitution, Congress must assemble at least once every year, at noon on the third day of January, unless by law they appoint a different day. A Congress lasts for 2 years, commencing in January of the year following the biennial election of members.

The Constitution authorizes each house to determine the rules of its proceedings. Pursuant to that authority, the House of Representatives adopts its rules on the opening day of each Congress. The Senate considers itself a continuing body and operates under continuous standing rules that it amends from time to time. Unlike some other parliamentary bodies, both the Senate and the House of Representatives have equal legislative functions and powers with certain exceptions. For example, the U.S. Constitution provides that only the House of Representatives originate revenue bills. By tradition, the House also originates appropriation bills. As both bodies have equal legislative powers, the designation of one as the "upper" House and the other as the "lower" House is not appropriate.

Preparing and considering legislation is done largely by committees of both houses of the U.S. Congress. There are 16 standing committees in the Senate and 19 in the House of Representatives. In addition, there are select committees in each house as well as various congressional commissions and joint committees composed of members of both houses. Each house may also appoint special investigating committees.

Proceedings of the U.S. Congress are published in the *Congressional Record*, which is issued when Congress is in session. Publication of the *Record* began March 4, 1873; it was the first record of debate officially reported, printed, and published directly by the federal government. The *Daily Digest* of the *Congressional Record*, printed in the back of each issue of the *Record*, summarizes the proceedings of that day in each house and before each of their committees and subcommittees, respectively. The *Digest* also presents the legislative program for each day and, at the end of the week, gives the program for the following week.

Article I, Section 8, of the U.S. Constitution defines the powers of the U.S. Congress. Included are the powers to assess and collect taxes (called the chief power); to regulate commerce (both interstate and foreign); to coin money; to establish post offices and post roads; to establish courts inferior to the Supreme Court; to declare war; and to raise and maintain an army and navy. Congress is further empowered

> To provide for calling forth the Militia to execute the Laws of the Union, suppress Insurrections and repel Invasions [and] To make all Laws which shall be necessary and proper for carrying into Execution the foregoing Powers, and all other Powers vested by this Constitution in the Government of the United States, or in any Department or Officer thereof.[15]

Another power vested in the U.S. Congress is the right to propose amendments to the U.S. Constitution. Should two-thirds of the state legislatures demand changes in the Constitution, it is the duty of Congress to call a constitutional convention. Proposed amendments shall be valid as part of the Constitution when ratified by the legislatures or by conventions of three-fourths of the states, as one or the other mode of ratification may be proposed by Congress.

Under the U.S. Constitution, special powers are granted to both the Senate and House of Representatives. The Senate is assumed certain powers not accorded to the House of Representatives. The Senate approves or disapproves certain presidential appointments by majority vote, and treaties must be concurred in by a two-thirds vote. The House of Representatives is granted the power of originating all bills for the raising of revenue. Both houses of Congress act in impeachment proceedings, which, according to the Constitution, may be instituted against the president, vice president, and all civil officers of the United States.

The House of Representatives has the sole power of impeachment, and the Senate has the sole power to try impeachments. For example, the House of Representatives impeached President Bill Clinton on charges of lying under oath to a federal grand jury and obstructing justice in the Monica Lewinsky case.[16] A subsequent impeachment trial held by the Senate resulted in President Clinton's acquittal. The Senate voted 54–45 to reject the perjury charge and split 50–50 on the obstruction-of-justice allegations. To remove President Clinton from office would have required a two-thirds vote, or 67 total votes.

All bills and joint resolutions must pass both the House of Representatives and the Senate and must be signed by the president, except those proposing a constitutional amendment, in order to become law, or be passed over the president's veto by a two-thirds vote of both houses of Congress. Section 7 of Article I states:

If any Bill shall not be returned by the President within ten Days (Sundays excepted) after it shall have been presented to him, the Same shall be a Law, in like Manner as if he had signed it, unless the Congress by their Adjournment prevent its Return, in which Case it shall not be a Law.[17]

When a bill or joint resolution is introduced in the House, the usual procedure for its enactment into law is as follows:

- It is assigned to the House committee having jurisdiction.
- If favorably considered, it is reported to the House either in its original form or with recommended amendments.
- If the bill or resolution is passed by the House, it is messaged to the Senate and referred to the committee having jurisdiction.
- In the Senate committee, the bill, if favorably considered, may be reported in the form as received from the House or with recommended amendments.
- The approved bill or resolution is reported to the Senate and, if passed by that body, is returned to the House.
- If one body does not accept the amendments to a bill by the other body, a conference committee comprising members of both bodies is usually appointed to effect a compromise.
- When the bill or joint resolution is finally approved by both houses, it is signed by the Speaker and the vice president and is presented to the president.
- Once the president's signature is affixed, the measure becomes a law. If the president vetoes the bill, it cannot become a law unless it is repassed by a two-thirds vote of both houses.

State Legislatures

Most state legislatures convene each year to make law. However, for a bill to become law, it must first survive a sequence of challenges through a system that is rigid and complex. During this process, bills are constantly moving and changing. Occasionally, they flow through the system easily because the bill is supported with little resistance. Most bills, though, never make it completely through the legislative process, especially during the initial year that it has been introduced to the legislative body. In fact, the legislative session is considered successful if one-third of the bills introduced are passed into law.

The following is a brief summary of the legislative process. It provides the mechanics of how a bill is introduced and flows through the system. In this discussion, we have chosen the House of Representatives to illustrate the legislative process; however, a bill can just as readily be introduced on the Senate side.

How a Bill Becomes a Law

States vary on the exact procedures used to enact legislation. In this section, we will discuss generally how a bill becomes a law. There are some variances in the states, but the general procedures are similar.

Introduction of a Bill

Bills that are introduced during a legislative session originate as ideas of one or more legislator. Many times, bills represent the suggested ideas of constituents who request that their ideas be presented during the legislative session. In effect, the legislator "sponsors" the bill for the citizens that live in the jurisdiction that the politician represents. The sponsoring legislator will have his or her legal staff draft a bill that incorporates the idea.

Once the bill has been put in draft form, most legislators then approach other members of that house to obtain cosponsors and try to get as many signatures as possible, although only one signature is required. When signatures have been gathered, the bill is placed in the hopper. Once in the hopper, the bill is a matter of public record and its life officially begins.

Assignment to Committee

Legislation that has been initiated is referred to a committee based on the policy content of the bill. Many of the bills that deal with crime in society, for example, are assigned to the judiciary committee. However, assignment to a committee does not guarantee that the bill will actually be scheduled for a public hearing. This is left to the discretion of the chairperson of the committee. Typically, there are many more bills assigned to a committee than can possibly be heard, and the chairperson's responsibility is to set the priorities for the committee. Bills that have been introduced to solve immediate social problems are given higher priority and receive first consideration to receive a public hearing.

When public hearings are conducted, citizens may attend and address the attending legislators. The legislative members of the committee are assigned according to their level of policy expertise and seniority ranking in the legislature. For example, it would not be uncommon for a house judiciary committee to be composed entirely of lawyers.

Once the proponents and opponents of the bill have had adequate time to make public comment, the legislation can be brought to a vote. Again, however, even though a public hearing has been held, there is no guarantee that the committee chairperson will allow the bill to be taken up by the committee. If a vote is to be taken, however, it occurs in executive session. During executive session, members have their first opportunity to offer amendments to the bill. When this occurs, a substitute bill is created that incorporates the amendments to the original bill.

First, Second, and Third Readings

If the committee members vote to pass the bill out of committee, it may go directly to the house floor for a first reading to all members of the house of representatives. However, if the bill is going to cost money, it may be sent to the house appropriations committee so that a fiscal note can be taken into account for the bill.

Besides a first reading, there are two additional readings of a bill. When a bill is on second reading, any member of the house can again amend it. Once a bill has been through second reading, it automatically moves to the third-reading calendar the next session day. Third reading is strictly for discussion and vote on final passage; no further amendments may be offered. If the bill does pass, it is transferred to the senate.

Senate

When a bill has passed the house of representatives and is transferred to the senate, nearly the same process is duplicated before a bill can be passed into law. The bill is first assigned to the appropriate committee, where public hearings are conducted and a vote taken in executive session. If passed, the subsequent readings take place on the floor by the full senate. If the senate changes the house bill in any way, it must be sent back to the house for concurrence. If the house agrees with the senate amendments, the house again votes and passes the senate version of the bill. In this case, the bill has passed the legislature and is sent on for the approval of the governor.

However, if the house refuses to concur with the senate amendments, the bill is said to be in "dispute," and it is sent to a conference committee.

Conference Committees

Unlike the other legislative processes, the conference committees are not open to the public. They consist of a combination of legislators from both the house of representatives and the senate and are appointed by the speaker of the house and the president of the senate. The committee's task is to amend the language of the bill so that both houses will approval the legislation. Once the bill has been rewritten, the new language in the committee report is brought back to the house and senate for a new vote for final passage. If the bill is approved, it is sent to the final stop in the legislative process, the governor.

Executive Actions

When the bill reaches the president or governor's office, several actions can be taken. The governor or president can choose to veto the entire bill or just veto certain parts of the bill. The executive may choose to support the bill and sign it into law. The president or governor may not support the bill, but allow it to automatically become law by doing nothing. For example, in 1994, a new capital punishment bill that enacted the death penalty was presented by the Kansas State Legislature to then-Governor Joan Finney. Although she personally opposed the death penalty, Governor Finney allowed the law to be ordered by not vetoing the legislation.

Administrative Agencies and Rulemaking

Many local, state, and federal administrative agencies are authorized to make regulations of general applicability that have the effect of law. This means of social control is known as rulemaking and is a principal concern in the study of law and society. The power enabling an agency to adopt a rule requires a specific law to be enacted by government. Generally, this occurs when the legislative body passes a statute that (a) requires enforcing regulations and (b) instructs some agency to make and enforce those rules. Often the same statute will make general rules on a subject, create a commission to promulgate and enforce more specific rules, and indicate how to appeal from any adverse decisions. Then, an agency may adopt only those rules that implement, interpret, or make specific the particular powers and duties granted by the permitting statute.

Beside the power of rulemaking, administrative agencies also have powers in the areas of licensing, issuing orders or advisory opinions, and making decisions about the enforcement of their rules when they are challenged or ignored. While this may seem like too much power to allot individual governmental units, all agency actions are subject to review in the federal courts.

Lobbyists

The term *lobbying* is derived from the early days of the U.S. Congress. Prior to the legislators' meetings being convened and during breaks, people who expected to gain or lose from a particular bill gathered at the lobbies of the buildings in which the two houses of Congress met. Their objective was to informally talk with legislators in an attempt to sway the decision makers. Over time, these impromptu meetings were taken over by professionals who had been hired to perform this service for their clients. These profession-als were given the name "lobbyist," and their activity was called "lobbying." Today, Washington, DC, has thousands of lobbyists; many of them are law-yers and former legislators.

Lobbyists no longer confine their activities to the buildings where legis-lators meet. They visit legislators' offices, invite them to dinner and vacation retreats, and offer to pay them for lectures. There are now large lobbying cor-porations in each state as well as Washington, DC, who offer their services to a variety of different clients.

Governance of Lobbyists

The Lobbying Disclosure Act of 1995 became effective in 1996, repealing the original Federal Regulation of Lobbying Act, enacted in 1946. The new law significantly expanded the registration and reporting requirements for those who seek to affect U.S. government policies or the implementation of federal programs.

While most routine communication with the executive branch does not constitute "lobbying contacts," an individual who repeatedly engages in policy or other advocacy involving either senior executive branch officials or U.S. congressional staff are likely to be a "lobbyist" for purposes of the law. An organization that employs an in-house lobbyist to make lobbying contacts on the organization's behalf is likely to be subject to the Lobbying Disclosure Act's registration and reporting requirements. Also, foreign entities and the U.S. subsidiaries or affiliates of foreign corporations may face special compli-ance issues under this act (in addition to other representation-related statutes). The Lobbying Disclosure Act provides for the imposition of civil fines (up to $50,000) for deliberately failing to comply with the law. Violations must be proven, as in other civil cases, only by a preponderance of the evidence.

The secretary and the clerk are responsible for enforcing the require-ments of the Lobbying Disclosure Act. This office is responsible for ensur-ing the accuracy, completeness, and timeliness of registration and reports. However, some pundits have questioned how aggressively the secretary and the clerk can monitor compliance, given the fact that the U.S. Congress has provided no additional financial resources or personnel with which to carry out the office's new responsibilities under this act.[18]

In most state governments, lobbyists are required to register with the secretary of state's office. However in recent years, several states have estab-lished regulatory agencies to improve the registration process and obtain full disclosure from special interests trying to influence both the legislative and executive branches of state government. For example, in New York, the state commission on regulation of lobbying is empowered to administer and enforce the provisions of the Lobbying Act. The commission is authorized to conduct investigations, administer oaths or affirmations, subpoena witnesses, and require the production of any books or records. The commission also conducts private and public hearings, prepares reports and statements required by the act, and issues advisory opinions. It reports annually to the governor and legislature.

Law Enforcers

Once laws are enacted, government must enforce them, for without some type of enforcement, life would be chaotic, and our social structure would be dismantled to the point of nonexistence. In our society, it is the police who are primarily responsible for the function of law enforcement. This governmental entity collaborates with other agencies within the justice system, attempting to ensure that society complies with established rules, regulations, and the law.

The penal code defines the role of police officials. The courts have ruled time and again that the police are members of an organization empowered by the authority vested in them by society to enforce the laws of the city, county, and state. Besides enforcing laws, police also maintain order and provide helping services to the community. These three functions coexist and oftentimes overlap each other. Consider the following description of the role of a patrolman offered by James Q. Wilson:

> The patrolman's role is defined more by his responsibility for maintaining order than by his responsibility for enforcing the law. By "order" is meant the absence of disorder and by disorder is meant behavior that either disturbs or threatens to disturb the public peace or that involves face-to-face conflict among two or more persons.[19]

Wilson notes that disorderly behavior generally involves infractions of the law, and any intervention by the police is at least under color of the law and in fact might be viewed as an "enforcement" of the law. A judge, examining the matter after the fact, is likely to see the issue wholly in these terms. But the patrolman does not. Though he may use the law to make an arrest, just as often he will do something else, such as tell people to "knock it off," "break it up," or "go home and sober up." According to Wilson, in the policeman's eyes, even an arrest does not always end his involvement in the matter. In some sense, he was involved in settling a dispute; if and how he settled it is important both to the parties involved and to the officer himself. To the patrolman, "enforcing the law" is what he does when there is no dispute— when making an arrest or issuing a summons exhausts his responsibilities.

Local Law Enforcement

Local law enforcement consists of municipal police officers and county sheriff's deputies. Each enforces the criminal code of the state as well as city and county ordinances. Typically the first to respond to crime scenes and traffic accidents, city police officers maintain legal authority within the geographical boundaries of the municipality, while sheriff's deputies are responsible for law enforcement of the larger jurisdiction of the county.

State Law Enforcement

There are many law enforcement agencies that operate within state government. Beside the State Patrol (also referred to many jurisdictions as the State Highway Patrol), other state agencies exist that specialize in certain areas of law enforcement (e.g., alcohol beverage control and wildlife and parks protection). Most states maintain a bureau of investigations to assist local law enforcement with a variety of felony criminal investigations. For example, the Georgia Bureau of Investigations (GBI) is an independent, statewide agency that provides assistance to the state's criminal justice system in the areas of criminal investigations, forensic laboratory services, and computerized criminal justice information. The GBI consists of three divisions (the Investigative Division, the Division of Forensic Sciences, and the Georgia Crime Information Center) and operates in 15 regional offices strategically located throughout the State of Georgia.

The three largest statewide law enforcement agencies are the California Highway Patrol, the Texas Department of Public Safety, and the Pennsylvania State Police. On the other hand, the smallest state law enforcement agencies include the North Dakota Highway Patrol, the Rhode Island State Police, and the South Dakota Highway Patrol.

Federal Law Enforcement

There are over 60 law enforcement agencies at the federal level in the United States.[20] Federal agencies are created by the U.S. Congress under the authority of the necessary and proper clause of Article I, Section 8, of the U.S. Constitution (mentioned earlier in the chapter).

The primary function of federal officers with arrest and firearms authority is criminal investigations of federal law violations. For example, of the 10,389 FBI employees, nearly all were agents, responsible for conducting criminal investigation and enforcement. These federal investigators cover more than 250 federal crimes, including bank fraud, embezzlement, and kidnapping. Since 2001, detecting and preventing terrorist acts has also been a major function of the federal law enforcement agencies, especially those currently under the Department of Homeland Security. Note that federal agents are generally restricted to investigating violations of federal law, and for the most part they have only limited jurisdiction regarding the violations of state statutes.

Punishment

Punishment is the authorized imposition of sanctions aimed at enforcement of legal obligations. It constitutes the core, if not the defining characteristic, of the legal order. The justice model precept requires that unacceptable social behavior that amounts to crime should be punished for the sake of society.

In the United States, crimes are punished according to their seriousness, with greater penalties imposed for more serious crimes. Modes of punishment typically include fines, community supervision, and incarceration. For the crime of murder, the ultimate sanction of death may be imposed in certain states. Moreover, depending on the jurisdiction, the sentencing judge has the power to impose unusual punishments, such as the imposition of the habitual criminal act, which enhances an offender's term of imprisonment.

Penalties for crimes vary greatly from state to state and reflect policy decisions made by courts and legislatures. For example, a state with a significant tourist industry may punish vagrancy very seriously, reflecting the importance of the business of tourism in that state, while another may punish it less severely because it is not of great concern in that state.

When the court issues a sanction, the judge may take into account the convicted person's prior criminal record, age, and other circumstances surrounding the commission of the criminal offense. Sentencing judges may also consider the offender's cooperation with law enforcement authorities.

Sentencing Guidelines

In the federal criminal justice system, sentencing is governed by the United States Sentencing Guidelines (USSG). While federal statutes typically impose maximum and minimum punishments, the USSG sets out factors that federal courts must take into account when deciding the exact sentence to impose. Under the USSG, offenders convicted of crimes are assigned "points" for the presence of certain factors in the commission of those crimes. These factors include:

- The amount of loss to victims
- Whether a weapon was used in the crime
- The age or vulnerability of the victims of the crime

The guidelines also consider the person's prior criminal history, with repeat offenders receiving more "points" in the guidelines, and thus more severe sentences. The guidelines are not considered as restrictions on a judge's authority but, rather, are only considered as advisory in imposing sentences.

Many states have adopted sentencing provisions similar to the federal sentencing guidelines. For example, in 1981, the Washington State Legislature enacted a new sentencing guidelines system to ensure that offenders who committed similar crimes and had similar criminal histories would receive equivalent sentences. Sentences are now determined by the seriousness of the offense and by the criminal record of the offender, a practice that is referred to as "truth in sentencing." Truth-in-sentencing laws require offenders to serve a substantial portion of the prison sentence imposed by the court before being eligible for release. Previous policies that reduced the amount of time an offender served on a sentence, such as good time, earned time, and parole board release, are restricted or eliminated under truth-in-sentencing laws. The definition of truth in sentencing varies among the states, as does the percentage of sentence time required to be served and the crimes covered by the laws. Most states have targeted violent offenders under truth in sentencing.

Correctional Institutions

Most of today's prisons are formally known as correctional institutions. The changing ideologies of punishment that have occurred over the past several decades have altered the prison system. Social change that erupted in the 1960s influenced our penal system, transforming it from the gothic "Big House" to a present-day "human warehouse." Notions of rehabilitation have all but disappeared as the public demands that inmates not be coddled and be made to serve long prison sentences. The result is that the American prison is a highly volatile environment where inmate threats and acts of violence are commonplace.

Until the late 1960s, operating America's jails was left almost entirely in the hands of sheriffs. Little accountability was demanded of those responsible for the care and custody of prisoners. The result too often was that many jails became physical abysses. Staff use of force against inmates was a recognized practice of control, and inmates were locked in solitary confinement in unfurnished cells for extended periods of time for trivial reasons.

During the 1970s, the courts recognized that the U.S. Constitution did indeed extend into the jail, and there was a huge growth in the number of court rulings interpreting the constitutional rights of jail inmates. Additionally, the courts began to impose new duties and liabilities on sheriffs and jail employees.

The impact of court decisions on the American jail was tremendous. Probably no other factor or combination of factors contributed so much to improvement in jail design and conditions in the 20th century. Brutality is now recognized as illegal. Funds for new jails have become available as courts ordered unconstitutional facilities to be improved or closed. The attention of legislatures, citizens, and the media focused on jails as courts declared facility after facility across the nation to be unconstitutional. The accountability that was previously nonexistent was becoming reality. Sheriffs and jail administrators realized that unless practices and conditions improved and conformed to the law, they and their staff would ultimately be held liable. Moreover, America's "keepers of jails" began to strive for professionalism and became innovative in their ideas regarding construction and operation of modern jails. Most notably has been the adoption of the "direct supervision" jail that has flourished in the latter half of the 20th century. Direct supervision is based upon a philosophy that stationing a jail officer within an appropriately designed inmate living area can significantly reduce the rate of serious incidents in the jail.[21]

Community-Based Corrections

Probation is the suspension of a sentence of imprisonment and the imposition of conditions the defendant must meet to satisfy the probation terms.

- A defendant is placed on probation where incarceration is unwarranted and not required by law.
- The conditions of probation ensure that the defendant leads a law-abiding life.

At the end of the probationary period, the defendant is free of the state's supervision. Violating probation terms can result in the revocation of probation and the imposition of the original sentence.

Parole is the conditional release of a prisoner before the expiration of the sentence. Parole is usually granted by a separate state agency, or commission, which considers the applications of prisoners for early release from imprisonment. Typically, parole is granted on certain conditions that must be followed by the paroled offender. Violating these conditions can result in a revocation of parole and reinstatement of the balance of the sentence.

Sex-offender registration laws have been enacted in many states. These statutes require convicted sex offenders to register with local police departments so that various individuals and groups within their communities can be warned of their presence in the community. Typically, convicted sex offenders are classified according to a judgment about the likelihood that they will reoffend and the seriousness of their prior conduct. The classification into which the particular offender falls determines which members of the community receive notice of their presence. So far, these statutes have largely survived court challenges based on arguments that they violate the constitutional rights of the offenders, and their provisions vary from state to state.

Summary

- The relationship between law and society is more fully appreciated when we possess a sound understanding about the social organization of law.
- The legal process is inherently involved with authority and cannot be easily separated from the institutions that execute it.
- Dynamic associations take place between legislating, interpreting, and enforcing the law.
- The functioning of law is a process whereby some people render decisions about the law, others are responsible to carry out the law, and all are expected to obey the law.
- The judicial system in the United States is comprised of the state courts, created by state constitutions and legislatures, and the federal courts, created by the U.S. Congress under its constitutional powers. In basic terms, a court is an organ of the government, belonging to the judicial department, whose function is the application of the laws to controversies brought before it.
- The role of the court is to decide the rules of law applicable in a particular case and to settle controversies between parties.
- The judicial process is carried out by the courts and consists of interpreting the laws and applying them in a just and fair manner to all cases arising in litigation. In general, the courts do not give advisory opinions except when a state constitution authorizes the state supreme court to render an advisory opinion to the legislature with regard to the constitutionality of a statute.
- Court jurisdiction is defined as the authority or power of the court to hear matters of controversy or dispute. Since both state and federal courts exist, initiating the judicial process begins with the decision of which court should take the case. Court jurisdiction is either original or appellate.
- A court of original jurisdiction (trial court) has the authority to receive the case when begun, to try the case, and to render a decision based on the presentation of facts and applicability of law.
- Appellate jurisdiction, which is set by constitution or statute, is the authority to review, overrule, or revise the action of a lower court. The appellate court hears complaints of error committed by an inferior court, whose judgment or decision the appellate court is asked to correct.

- The jurisdictions of courts are limited by constitutions or statutes.
- The court system in the United States at both the state and federal levels is hierarchical. At the extreme top of the pyramid are supreme courts or courts of last resort, which are appellate courts.
- Intermediate appellate courts function to hear the initial appeals of trial courts. They may also serve as courts of original jurisdiction when defined by constitution or statute. Trial court is typically the starting point for most court cases. The decisions of trial courts are subject to review by appellate courts.
- The judicial power of the state court system is limited by the due process clause of the Fourteenth Amendment of the U.S. Constitution.
- It is in the state courts that most of the legal disputes that surface in the lives of citizens are resolved. Disputes resolved by state courts include traffic and criminal cases as well as civil cases, such as domestic relations, personal injury and property damage, and real estate transactions.
- Litigants may choose between a jury trial or bench trial. In a bench trial, the judge determines the facts as well as the law. In a jury trial, a jury determines the facts in accordance with the judge's instruction on the law. In a criminal case, then, the jury decides whether the defendant is innocent or guilty. In a civil case, the jury decides whether the defendant is liable to the plaintiff.
- In the state court system, the next step up from the court of general original jurisdiction is the intermediate appellate court. The purpose of such a court is to relieve the burden on the state court system by lessening the caseload of the supreme court. Procedurally, in all states, a defendant convicted in a criminal case is entitled to one appeal. Likewise, in civil cases, the appellate court must review the verdict upon demand of the party aggrieved in the trial court. Where an intermediate appellate court exists, appeals go directly to that court, with only a few exceptions.
- The highest court in a state is usually called the supreme court. A party aggrieved by the decision of the intermediate appellate court can petition the state supreme court to review the case. Such a petition is called a "writ of certiorari."
- The federal court system is prescribed by Article III of the U.S. Constitution. The jurisdiction of the federal court system consists of: the U.S. Supreme Court, 13 federal courts of appeals, a large number of district courts that serve as courts of general jurisdiction, and a number of specialized courts created by the U.S. Congress under the "necessary and proper clause" of Article I.

- The U.S. district courts are federal trial courts with general federal jurisdiction. Each state has at a minimum one federal district court, while some larger states have several.
- Each federal district court employs: a U.S. district court clerk, U.S. attorney, U.S. marshal, and one or more U.S. magistrates, bankruptcy judges, probation officers, and court reporters who serve the U.S. district courts.
- The jurisdiction of the federal district courts is set forth in the U.S. Code.
- The U.S. Congress, under the necessary and proper clause of Article I, creates special courts from time to time to deal with particular kinds of cases that are not permanently part of the federal court system.
- The U.S. courts of appeals were to relieve the U.S. Supreme Court of the task of considering all appeals for cases originally decided by the federal trial courts. They are empowered to review the final decisions of federal district courts, except when direct review by the U.S. Supreme Court is called for by statute.
- The U.S. Supreme Court was created in 1790 in accordance with Article III, Section 1, of the U.S. Constitution. The U.S. Supreme Court consists of the chief justice of the United States and eight associate justices. The president of the United States is empowered to nominate the U.S. Supreme Court justices, and appointments are made with the advice and consent of the Senate.
- Law is viewed in various ways and consequently can be classified differently. Often we think of law in terms of the system in which it operates. Common law, for instance, is a system of jurisprudence that originated in England that is based on written opinions that are binding on future decisions of lower courts in the same jurisdiction. Civil law is a system of legal science that originated under Roman emperor Justinian in the sixth century A.D. and has evolved as a means of regulating private relationships between individuals.
- The U.S. Constitution is the supreme law in America. No other federal or state law, statute, or case may impose upon its provisions. It is divided into three parts. The first component, Articles I through VII, divides governmental power among the three branches of government (legislative, executive, and judicial) and between the federal and state governments. It also describes the relationships between the states and sets out the means for amending the Constitution.
- A primary source of law is statutory law. Statutes are enacted by the legislative branch of government (whether state or federal) to regulate areas within the legislature's jurisdiction. Under the U.S. and state constitutions, statutes are considered the primary source of law in America (i.e., legislatures make the law [statutes] and courts interpret the law [cases]).

- Laws are often classified according to the scope of the law. That is, on the parties to whom they apply. We categorize law into two areas according to their scope: private law and public law.
- Administrative law is the body of law governing administrative agencies, i.e., agencies created by the U.S. Congress or state legislatures, such as the Social Security Administration and state social welfare agency.
- In disputes taken to court, there is a common belief that there will be a winner and a loser. In criminal cases, for instance, when the government brings charges against the defendant, a guilty verdict indicates that the prosecution wins the case. If the defendant is found not guilty, then the government essentially loses the case. In civil matters, the plaintiff files suit against the respondent, which is also the term to designate the person responding to an appeal.
- The process of lawmaking is distinguished by the extent to which compromise is incorporated into the political system. While legislators have their own viewpoints about which laws need immediate attention and which do not, citizens who are either proponents or opponents of certain legislation constantly try to influence the work of lawmakers. Considering that this dynamic takes place with each and every legislator, it is no wonder that a legislative session can become besieged with confrontation and confusion.
- Once laws are enacted, government must enforce them, for without some type of enforcement, life would be chaotic and our social structure dismantled to the point of nonexistence. In our society, it is the police who are primarily responsible for the function of law enforcement.
- Local law enforcement consists of municipal police officers and county sheriff's deputies. Each enforces the criminal code of the state as well as city and county ordinances. Typically the first to respond to crime scenes and traffic accidents, city police officers maintain legal authority within the geographical boundaries of the municipality, while sheriff's deputies are responsible for law enforcement of the larger jurisdiction of the county.
- Punishment is the authorized imposition of sanctions aimed at enforcement of legal obligations. It constitutes the core, if not the defining characteristic, of the legal order.

Questions in Review

1. What is the difference between original and appellate court jurisdiction?
2. Give two examples of state courts of limited jurisdiction.
3. What is the purpose of a writ of certiorari?

4. Define the original and exclusive jurisdiction of the U.S. Supreme Court.
5. Compare and contrast constitutional, statutory, and case law.
6. In comparison to the other participants in the court system, how important is the court manager? Why?
7. What are the advantages and disadvantages of plea bargaining?
8. How does a bill become law?
9. What are the benefits of community-based corrections programs?

Endnotes

1. *White County v. Givin*, 136 Ind. 562, 36 N.E. 237, (1968).
2. Fourteenth Amendment of the U.S. Constitution.
3. Some appeals (e.g., death penalty conviction) may be taken from trial court decisions directly to the state supreme court.
4. Article III, Section 2, of the U.S. Constitution.
5. 42 U.S.C. Sec.1983 (1988).
6. Fourth Amendment of the U.S. Constitution.
7. E. Suggs. (2012, October 17). Atlanta council votes to spend $2 million for video cameras. *The Atlanta Journal-Constitution*, p. A-1.
8. S. Goldman. (1982). Judicial selection and the qualities that make a "good" judge. *The Annals of the American Academy of Political and Social Science, 462*, 112–124.
9. National Center for State Courts. (1997, July). *Trial court performance standards and measurement system implementation manual* (NCJ 161567). Bureau of Justice Assistance Monographs Series. Washington, DC: Bureau of Justice Assistance.
10. *Ballew v. Georgia*, 435 U.S. 223 (1978).
11. M.D. Hall. (1980). *The court manager: A manual*. Williamsburg, VA: The National Association for Court Management.
12. M.D. Hall. (1980). *The court manager: A manual*. Williamsburg, VA: The National Association for Court Management.
13. Pennsylvania municipality settles to end minority driver lawsuit. (1994, October 25). *Drug Enforcement Report*.
14. Judge OKs huge settlement in bribery suit against Honda. (1998, October 31). *The Detroit News*.
15. Article I, Section 8, of the U.S. Constitution.
16. House Resolution 611, Report No. 105-830.
17. Article I, Section 7, of the U.S. Constitution.
18. J.R. Kraemer & R.C. Westerfeldt. (1997). How to comply with the 1995 lobbying law. *Acquisition Issues, 1997*(Jan./Feb.).
19. J.Q. Wilson. (1968). *Varieties of police behavior*. Cambridge, MA: Harvard University Press.

20. J.A. Conser & G.D. Russell. (2000). *Law enforcement in the United States.* Gaithersburg, MD: Aspen Publishers.

21. G.J. Bayens, J.O. Smykla, & J.J. Williams. (1997). Jail type makes a difference: Evaluating the transition from a traditional to a podular, direct supervision jail across ten years. *American Jails, 11*(2), 32–39.

Social Control

5

Chapter Objectives

After reading this chapter you should be able to

- Identify both formal and informal social controls
- Explain the role of morals and values in our society
- Identify moral reasoning and how that impacts decisions
- Discuss the role of controlling dissent on social control
- Explore the cultural aspects of social control
- Detail the morphology issues involved in social control

Behavior and Social Controls

Social controls are the formal and informal means of enforcing norms. Pretend that you have passed all the exams for this course with an A average. You have successfully completed all the course requirements, but you receive an F as a course grade. When confronted, the professor states that the administration had been pressuring her for awarding too many As. So she selected every fourth student and assigned the selected students failing grades. Unfortunately, you were one of the selected students. Your first statement to the professor is: "You can't do that!" Of course you are correct; the professor cannot do that. There are certain expectations of behavior that the professor is expected to comply with when assigning grades. These expectations of behavior act as social controls on the professor's conduct.

In this chapter, we will examine social controls of behavior. Social controls are methods used by members of a society to maintain order and promote the predictability of behavior. When we think of social controls, generally law is the first social control considered. However, the law is only one of many forms of social control. We will also examine both formal and informal social controls, the role of morals and values, moral reasoning, controlling dissent, cultural aspects, and the morphology issues involved in social control.

Social control may be divided into two distinct processes: (a) internal controls, the internalization of group norms resulting in internal controls, and (b) external controls, controls imposed by external pressures.[1] The internalization of group norms refers to the consequence of the socialization process. During the socialization process we develop rules of behavior for our social group by recognizing what conduct is appropriate, expected, and desirable for given situations. During this process, we acquire a motivation to conform to the norms of our society without the need for external pressures. For example, most of us do not steal—not because of the fear of being caught, but because we were taught that stealing is inappropriate behavior and it is contrary to our moral code. Most people conform to norms because they have been taught that they should conform to them independent of any anticipated reactions of others, i.e., internal controls on our behavior.

Norms make social life possible by making behavior predictable. For example, we count on most persons most of the time to meet the expectations of others. We count on the professor to assign grades based on test scores and what is in the syllabus. The professor expects the students to act in an approved manner during class. Every group within a society, and even human society itself, depends to a great extent on norms to regulate human behavior and to make behavior predictable.[2]

Control through external social pressures includes both positive and negative sanctions. For example, working hard to achieve a promotion is an example of a positive sanction. Getting a speeding ticket for driving too fast is

BEHAVIORAL EXPECTATIONS

Behavioral expectations refers to the idea that each person in interaction with another has certain expectations of the other person as to what might take place. People in society find themselves orienting themselves to each other. I expect that the other person will act predictably, according to the role he or she is occupying in a certain context. On the other hand, once I find myself in a social role, I feel a sense of obligation to conform to it, or at a minimum, a necessity to orient myself to it, even if only to the extent of using it to sensitize myself to what is commonly done. As long as the other person and I mutually orient ourselves in this way, smooth interaction can be assured.[3] Take, for example, an interaction in a college class between the professor and a student when the student asks a question. The student has certain expectations regarding the behavior of the professor. The professor in turn has certain expectations regarding the actions of the student. Suppose the professor states: "That is a good question, but I would prefer to wait until next class to answer it." What are the expectations of the student to this response? How would the rest of the class react if the student demanded an immediate answer to his question?

an example of a negative sanction. Some social controls are formal or official, while others are informal or unofficial. Criminal law is a type of formal control, and public scorn is an informal type of social control. Often the types overlap. Thus, the individual who commits sexual abuse on a child can be subjected to both formal (criminal law) and informal (public condemnation) controls.

Informal Social Controls

Informal social controls consist of techniques whereby individuals accord praise to those who comply with the expectations placed on them and show displeasure with those who do not comply.[4]

Two frequent methods of informal social control are by the use of folkways and mores. Folkways are established norms of common practice such as those that specify modes of dress, language use, and etiquette. William Graham Sumner, in his 1906 book, *Folkways*, describes folkways as customs or habits that have grown up within a social group and are very common among the members of this group. While mores are a type of folkways, not all folkways are considered as important as mores to the society's values. For example, proper table manners are a less strongly held folkway. The violation of the less strongly held folkways produces only a mild reaction, such as surprise or slight scorn.

SOCIAL CONTROL TERMS

culture: The language, beliefs, values, norms, and behaviors of a group or society that are passed from one generation to the next.

ethnocentrism: The use of one's own culture as a measure for judging the ways of other individuals, groups, societies, and cultures. Ethnocentrism generally leads to negative evaluations of others' values, norms, and behaviors.

folkways: Norms that are not strictly enforced.

mores: Norms that are considered as essential to core values.

norms: Expectations of behavior or rules of behavior that have developed from our values.

social control: The formal and informal means of enforcing norms.

subculture: A group whose values and related behavior distinguish its members from the larger culture, i.e., a world within a world.

taboo: A norm that brings revulsion when violated.

values: The standards by which people define what is good or bad, desirable or undesirable, beautiful or ugly.

Sumner is credited with introducing the term *mores*. He defined mores (pronounced MORE-rays) as societal norms that are associated with intense feelings of right or wrong and definite rules of conduct that are not to be violated, for example, incest. Sumner pointed out that mores generally remain unchanged from generation to generation. Any change in mores is usually very gradual. He stated that mores vary from one society to another and that, in most cases, each society believes that its own mores are the most natural and desirable ones. Sumner called this belief ethnocentrism. He stated that ethnocentrism is also defined as the tendency to view one's own group as the center of everything, and all others are scaled and rated with reference to it.

Sociologist Ian Robertson provides us with the following example of the differences between folkways and mores:

> A man who walks down a street wearing no clothes on the upper half of his body is violating a folkway; a man who walks down the street wearing nothing on the lower half of his body is violating one of our most important mores, the requirement that people cover their genitals and buttocks in public.[5]

Robertson also noted that mores and folkways may vary according to your group or status within the same society. For example, the male walking down the street with his upper body uncovered is generally considered as violating a folkway, whereas a female in the same circumstances would probably be violating one of our mores. The mores and folkways of a subculture may vary from those of the general culture. Accordingly, the female walking down the street without any clothes would be acceptable conduct for a subculture that lives in a nudist colony. In addition to folkways and mores, there are taboos. A taboo is a norm so strongly embedded in our culture that the thought of its violation is repulsive. For example, eating human flesh is considered in most cultures as a taboo.

Anthropologist George Murdock attempted to determine if there are any norms that were universals, i.e., norms that are found in all societies. He drew up a list of customs concerning courtship, cooking, family, sex, funerals, games, laws, music, myths, and toilet training. He concluded that while the activities are present in all cultures, there are no universal norms. The norms vary from one culture to another. For example, while no cultures permit generalized incest, it is not a taboo in all cultures. Some cultures allow men to marry their own daughters; with the Burundi of Africa, to remove a certain curse, the sons are required to have sexual relations with their mothers.[6]

Enforcement of Norms

Informal external social controls are techniques by which individuals praise those who comply and condemn those who do not comply. The techniques include praise, ridicule, gossip, reprimands, criticisms, and ostracism. Tom Tyler, in his study on why people obey the law, states that influence by social groups can be instrumental and that social groups reward and punish their members, either by withholding or conferring signs of group status and respect, or more directly by channeling material resources toward or away from particular members. Such variations in rewards and costs are not under the control of public authorities. Tyler also contended that group influence also exerts normative pressure on people, because some individuals look to their social groups for information about appropriate conduct. Such normative influences are similar to the influence of personal morality. Accordingly, people's behavior is strongly affected by the normative climate created by others. He notes that group influence may also exert normative pressure on people, because individuals look to their social group for information about what constitutes appropriate conduct. Tyler's classification of informal social controls splits into two different bases: social relations (friends, family, and peers) and normative values. His social relations classification is similar to the informal external classification generally used, and the normative values classification is likewise similar to the informal internal classification. Tyler contends that concerns about social relations reflect the influence of other people's judgments, whereas normative values reflect a person's own ethical views.

Tyler states that while the social relations aspect of control depends on rewards and punishments, normative influences respond to different factors. Because of normative influences, people focus on the relationship between various kinds of potential behavior and their assessments of what behavior is appropriate. The key feature of normative factors is that the individual voluntarily complies with rules rather than responding to the external situation.[7]

THE KANSAS TURNPIKE

The Kansas Turnpike starts south of Wichita and ends in Kansas City, Kansas. The maximum speed limit on the turnpike is 70 miles per hour. About 70% percent of the traffic drives between 70 to 80 miles per hour. About 10% of the drivers drive in excess of 80 miles per hour. Less than 20% of the traffic drives at or below the posted maximum speed limit. Are the large number of individuals who drive in excess of the maximum speed limit lawless individuals? If not, why then are they willfully violating the law? Why would people, who would not think of stealing and who would point out an error in their favor to a cashier, routinely violate our speed control laws?

Unlike formal controls, there are no official persons to administer the informal controls. As noted by Richard Schwartz, "The two main forms of control may be distinguished: that which is carried out by specialized functionaries who are socially delegated the task of intra-group control (formal), and that which is not so delegated (informal)." He also notes that the two forms of control are in competition, and the likelihood of formal control arising at all in a given sphere is a decreasing function of the effectiveness of informal controls.[8]

Since informal social controls are administered by friends, neighbors, relatives, and other acquaintances, they tend to be more effective in societies that are intimate and in which relations are face to face and less effective in large complex societies. For example, the pressures to conform on the average person are greater in a small town in America than they would be in Los Angeles, Chicago, or New York.

Social Norms and Deviance

One of the problems when studying the behavior of individuals within a society is ascertaining what conduct constitutes deviant behavior. What may be defined as deviant behavior by one group in society may not be considered as deviance in another. Howard S. Becker looked at the relativity of deviance. Becker states: "It is not the act itself, but the reactions to the act, that make something deviant."[9] Thus, people's behaviors must be viewed from the framework of the culture in which the behavior takes place. Becker defines deviance as people who violate rules, as result of which others react negatively to them.

Who decides what constitutes deviant behavior? After pleading "no contest" to charges of taking kickbacks on government contracts, Spiro Agnew, former governor of Maryland and U.S. vice president, stated: "Honesty is different things to different people." In defining deviance, those who embrace functionalism disagree with the conflict theorists. Functionalism takes the pluralistic theory of social control, which posits that the various segments in a pluralistic society, in an attempt to coexist, attain a more or less balanced state, and that the balancing of the tensions produces the whole that we call society. In contrast, the conflict theorists stress that each society is dominated by a particular group whose basic purpose is to maintain control. Thus the purpose of norms is to maintain the status quo so that those in power will remain in power.

Moral Learning

Obedience to social norms to a great extent is based on a person's moral learning, which is a product of his or her socialization. Individual moral codes represent internally consistent principles by which people govern their lives. A significant aspect of moral learning depends on our moral education.

Moral education is instruction focused on questions of right and wrong. Moral education also includes the development of values, the standards by which people judge what is important, worthwhile, and good. Individuals receive moral education from many sources, including their family, church, friends, and teachers—and even television. Schools have always been involved in such education, either intentionally or unintentionally. For example, many stories for young readers include a moral lesson.

During the 1970s, educators in the United States began to develop special teaching methods to help students deal with moral questions. The schools use four methods in moral education: (a) inculcation, (b) values clarification, (c) value analysis, and (d) moral development. Often a combination of these methods is used in an approach called comprehensive moral education.

Inculcation refers to the effort to teach children the values that the teachers believe lead to moral behavior. These values include honesty, compassion, justice, and respect for others. One common method of teaching such standards is to give appropriate praise and punishment. Another method is by setting an example whereby the teachers reflect the desired values in their own behavior.

Values clarification refers to the process of helping students develop their own values and moral standards by teaching them a decision-making process. The learning procedures stress setting goals, choosing thoughtfully from alternatives, and acting on one's own convictions.

Value analysis helps students apply techniques of logic and scientific investigation to matters involving values. The importance of exploring all alternatives, of gathering and evaluating the facts, and of making a logical decision are stressed.

Moral development helps students improve their ability to judge moral questions. The most extensive work on moral development was carried out by Lawrence Kohlberg. He defined six stages of moral development. Stage one is the most basic stage and stage six the most morally developed stage. He considered that stages three and four form the conventional moral orientation, and individuals who have reached stage five or six have developed internalized-principle orientation. These individuals are controlled mainly by their internal controls, whereas the individuals in stage one or two are mainly controlled by external controls. His stages are listed as follows:

1. *Obedience and punishment*: This is the most basic stage and involves a deference to superior power or prestige. At this stage, the orientation is toward avoiding trouble.

2. *Instrumental relativism*: This stage is characterized by naïve notions of reciprocity. Orientation is a primitive form of equalitarianism by attempting to satisfy your own needs by simple negotiation with others.

3. *Personal concordance*: Orientation at this stage is directed toward pleasing others and gaining their approval by conformity to perceived majority values and beliefs.

4. *Law and order*: At this stage, the individual is committed to "doing his or her duty." Orientation is toward being respectful to those with authority.

5. *Social contract*: This stage has a legalistic orientation, with commitments being viewed in contractual terms, and individuals will avoid efforts to break implicit or explicit agreements.

6. *Individual principles*: This stage emphasizes conscience, mutual trust, and respect as the guiding principles for behavior.[10]

If individuals can be classified into these moral stages, then for law as a social control element to be most effective, it would appear that we need to know the stage of moral development of the individuals whose conduct the law is attempting to control. If most of the people in society are at stages one and two, then punishment would appear to be the most effective control mechanism. For individuals in stages five and six, the effect of law as a controlling mechanism would appear to be more limited. Individuals in those higher stages should be more motivated by internalized principles than by rewards and punishments.

There has always been opposition to the teaching of moral education in schools. Many individuals feel that only the family and church should provide such instruction. Others argue that moral education takes class time that should be used for such basic subjects as reading, writing, and mathematics. Proponents of teaching moral education in schools believe that schools in a democratic society must teach such values as hard work, honesty, fairness, cooperation, and tolerance.

Formal Controls

As noted earlier, two key differences between informal and formal controls are that formal controls are administered by specialized functionaries who are socially delegated the task of intragroup control (formal), and they are characterized by explicit established procedures. For example, in a major corporation, the task of firing an employee for misbehavior is often delegated to a personnel officer, and there are explicit established procedures regarding the adverse personnel action.

The law as a formal social control is rarely exercised by use of positive rewards. For example, the good citizen who always obeys the law seldom receives any formal recognition for his or her law-abiding behavior. Likewise, governmental control is most often exercised by the use of or threat of punishment for noncompliance.

Donald Black contends that the "law is stronger where other social controls are weaker" or that the "law varies inversely with other social controls."[11] Black uses rural Mexico as an example. If in one community the family has more social control than in another, Black states that the community with more social control exercised by the family will have fewer marital and family disputes going into courts.

Law as a formal social control mechanism generally takes one of the following forms:

- Criminal law with the use of or threat of sanctions for prohibited conduct
- Administrative law in the context of licensing and inspections
- Tort law by enforcement of duties and standards of conduct
- Contract law in enforcement or threat of enforcement of contractual obligations

Donald Black defines law as "governmental social control."[12] He identifies four specific styles of legal social control: penal, compensatory, therapeutic,

ARE THERE TOO MANY LAWS?

When a social problem becomes apparent, the common solution is to pass a new law. Congress and the state legislatures pass thousands of laws each year. The U.S. Constitution mentions three federal crimes by citizens: treason, piracy, and counterfeiting. Today, there are over 4,500 crimes in federal statutes, according to a 2008 study conducted by John Baker.[13] The new laws are added to the volumes of laws that are already in force. As the number of laws increases, the whole body of law becomes more and more complex and difficult to manage. Everyone is presumed to know the law. In practice, however, how can citizens possibly know the law and how it affects them? Does the enormous number of laws enacted each year indicate that society expects too much of the law? In addition, as the number of laws grows, more and more aspects of life become regulated. And as the new laws interfere in the private affairs of people, they tend to resent them more. In addition, federal laws are different than state laws. In fact, state laws differ from state to state; consequently, if one is traveling, how can they know the laws of the different states they are passing through?

and conciliatory. The penal style is the criminal law model. His compensatory style is somewhat analogous to a civil law model, and the therapeutic style refers to rehabilitation. In the conciliatory style, problems are viewed as conflicts, and the solution of any problem is identified as the resolution. Black contends that any particular conflict in society may have any of the four styles of social control applied to it, but with profound differences as to how problematic situations are conceptualized and handled. As an example, he cites the treatment of labor activists at the turn of the century by way of the penal model rather than one of the other styles. By using the penal model, the conflicts between early labor unions and business were conceptualized and handled differently than they would have been had the conciliatory style been used.

Criminal Law

A crime is defined by California Penal Code, Section 15, as:

> [A]ct committed or omitted in violation of a law forbidding or commanding it, and to which is annexed, upon conviction, either of the following punishments; death, imprisonment, fine, removal from office, or disqualification to hold and enjoy any office of honor, trust, or profit in this State.

The social control of delinquent behavior by the use of criminal law and our criminal justice system is one of the most highly structured social control systems used by society. Criminal law attempts to control individuals by the use of the criminal sentencing process. For example, California Rule of Court 410 states that the general objectives of sentencing include:

1. Protecting society
2. Punishing the defendant
3. Encouraging the defendant to lead a law-abiding life in the future and deterring him or her from future offenses
4. Deterring others from criminal conduct by demonstrating its consequences
5. Preventing the defendant from committing new crimes by isolating him or her for the period of incarceration
6. Securing restitution for the victims of crime
7. Achieving uniformity in sentencing[14]

The rule also states that because, in some instances, the objectives may suggest inconsistent dispositions, the sentencing judge shall consider which objectives are of primary importance in the particular case. The judge should be guided by statutory statements of policy, the criteria in these rules, and the facts and circumstances of the case.

What constitutes a criminal act must be described in a substantive criminal statute that clearly specifies what conduct is prohibited. The government must have legislated the act regarding a crime before the act in question was committed. For example, if I sell my car on Monday to an individual without collecting a sales tax and on Tuesday the state enacts a statute that makes it a crime to sell a car without collecting the sales tax, the state could not prosecute me for the act committed on Monday that is unlawful on Tuesday. The law must exist before the act was committed in order to be a crime.

Next, to qualify as a crime, there must be a criminal penalty designated as punishment for the act. Examine the following section from the Texas Penal Code that describes the crime of public intoxication. First, the section describes precisely what conduct constitutes intoxication. The crime of public intoxication has not been committed until the conduct in question satisfies the requirements of that section. Next, the law assigns a punishment for the crime of public intoxication. Only those punishments authorized by the law may be imposed.

Texas Penal Code, Section 49.02

(a) A person commits an offense if the person appears in a public place while intoxicated to the degree that the person may endanger the person or another.

(b) It is a defense to prosecution under this section that the alcohol or other substance was administered for therapeutic purposes and as a part of the person's professional medical treatment by a licensed physician.

(c) Except as provided by Subsection (e), an offense under this section is a Class C misdemeanor.

(d) An offense under this section is not a lesser included offense under Section 49.04.

(e) An offense under this section committed by a person younger than 21 years of age is punishable in the same manner as if the minor committed an offense to which Section 106.071, Alcoholic Beverage Code, applies.[15]

Laws relating to criminal conduct may be divided into two general areas: substantive and procedural. Substantive criminal law defines crimes and annexes punishments. For example, Section 49.02 shown here is a substantive criminal law. Procedural law sets forth the rules and requirements that must be followed during the investigation, apprehension, and trial of individual defendants. Procedural law is also concerned with carrying out court orders and redress of injuries.

CLIENT CONFIDENTIALITY

Tacoma attorney Douglas Schafer helped bring down a corrupt judge. Instead of getting commended for it, he faced a hearing by the bar association's disciplinary board. Schafer was tipped off about the judge's activities by his client. The case presents a legal quandary: Does a lawyer have a duty to report misconduct, even if it means betraying the client's confidences? Barrie Althoff, the head of the Washington State Bar Association, stated: "While Mr. Schafer's move was beneficial to society, we also believe it violated the Rules of Professional Conduct."

Schafer was tipped off by his client that a lawyer was involved in shady business dealings. Later, when the lawyer was elected to the superior court bench, Schafer found himself in front of the lawyer, who was now a judge. Schafer then informed local, state, and federal officials, despite demands by his client to keep their conversations secret. The state supreme court removed the judge from the bench and suspended the judge's law license.

Schafer contends that lawyers should be guardians of the law, not simply hired guns. Althoff stated that client confidentiality is a fundamental principle of the law and that easing those restrictions would make clients hesitant to speak frankly, undermining a lawyer's ability to offer the best advice.[16] As a member of the grievance committee, how would you vote—to punish or to reward?

Victimless Crimes

The concept of a *victimless crime* is based on the notion that society regards certain acts as morally repugnant and attempts to restrain individuals from committing them. Victimless crimes are differentiated from other crimes in that they are consensual transactions or exchanges. In addition, there is an apparent lack of harm to others. Many people do not consider them as legitimate laws and simply refuse to obey them. For example, illegal betting via the use of football pools exists in almost every large organization during the period shortly before a Super Bowl. Because of the absence of victim complaints and their low visibility, such laws are difficult to enforce.

Roughly one-fourth of all arrests in the United States in the last 10 years have involved the victimless crimes of prostitution, drunkenness, violation of liquor laws, gambling, pornography, and drug abuse violations. Drug abuse crimes are of relatively recent origin. The first serious attempt to regulate drug use in the United States was with the Harrison Act, which was passed in 1914. The legal reaction to drug abuse reached its apex in the 1960s. During the 1960s, the possession of a small amount of marijuana was considered a felony offense in most states. Our severe reaction to drug abuse crimes may have been more of a reaction to the subculture that was heavily involved in the illegal use of drugs, i.e., the hippies. In most states today, the possession of small amounts of marijuana is no longer a felony. Even further, in the 2012 elections, both Washington State and Colorado decriminalized personal possession of marijuana. Drug offenders, however, still comprised about one-third of all persons convicted of a felony in state courts.

It is estimated that 70% of Americans are involved in public gambling. Legal and illegal gambling often exist side by side. What constitutes gambling depends on state law. Every state has statutes that regulate gambling. In many states, certain games of chance are legal and others are not. The federal Congress has attempted to control gambling activities through the exercise of its taxing powers by levying excise and occupational taxes on gambling operations and its ability to control interstate commerce. Most law enforcement researchers agree that criminal law is ineffective in controlling and preventing individuals from engaging in illegal gambling.

The range of sexual conduct regulated by statutes is great and extensive. A common justification for the complete regulation of sexual behavior is to protect the sanctity of the family. There are laws prohibiting adultery in order to restrict sexual relations outside of marriage. There is a complex set of laws and regulations that controls the sale, distribution, and availability of contraceptives, abortions, and artificial insemination. Laws against prostitution have generally been unsuccessful attempts to control private moral behavior through social-control measures. While state laws vary on prostitution, most are considered as discriminatory against women, and there is a tendency to regard only the women involved as offenders and not their clients. There may be 500,000 women engaged in prostitution in the United States.[17]

CRIMINAL OFFENSES: HOW MANY HAVE YOU COMMITTED?

Taking office supplies or using office equipment for personal use
  Up to one year in jail and/or fine
Evading income taxes
  Up to five years in prison and/or fine
Gambling illegally
  Up to six months in jail and/or fine
Illegally copying computer software
  Up to three years in prison and/or fine
Serving alcohol to minors
  Up to one year in jail and/or fine

Committing adultery in states where it is illegal
   Up to one year in jail and/or fine
Importing Cuban cigars
   Up to one year in jail and/or fine
Stealing TV cable signals
   Up to one year in jail and/or fine
Lying on a government job application
   Up to one year in jail and/or fine
Drinking in public
   Up to 30 days in jail and/or fine
Disregarding a jury summons
Up to 6 months in jail and/or fine

Note: Laws and penalties vary among the states.

White-Collar Crimes

The best way to rob a bank is to own it.

A joke that circulated in Washington, DC

White-collar crimes are nonviolent crimes committed for financial gains by means of deception by persons having professional status or specialized skills. Common white-collar crimes include counterfeiting, embezzlement, forgery, fraud, and regulatory offenses. The prosecution of white-collar crime is generally more complicated than that for street crime. The crime is often based on trust between the victim and the offender, and the building of trust expands the time frame of the crime, permitting repeated victimizations of an unsuspecting victim. The extent of white-collar crime has been estimated at over $50 billion per year. Despite its potential for extensive damage, we tend not to regard it with the same fear as we do street crimes. Today, computer-assisted crimes are a major part of white-collar crime.

Civil Commitment

The formal control of deviant behavior is not limited to criminal law. Civil commitment is a noncriminal process that commits individuals, without their consent, to an institution. Civil commitment is based on two legal principles: (a) the right and responsibility of a state to assume guardianship over those who do not have the ability to protect themselves, and (b) the police power of a state to protect society. Every state has some form of civil commitment statutes. The most common are those committing individuals who are a danger to self and others because of mental problems. Most recently, mental illness has been an issue that has arisen out of the mass shootings such as the Sandy Hook Elementary School shooting as well as the Colorado theater shooting. It is estimated that on any given day, there are over 500,000 Americans confined in mental wards. Recently, states have enacted civil commitment statutes for sex offenders. There are criticisms regarding the use of civil commitment. One group of critics contends that civil commitment statutes allow criminals to escape the criminal punishment that they deserve. Another group contends that civil commitment statutes allow for the punishment of individuals who have not been convicted of a crime. Despite the controversy, the use of civil commitment as a form of social control is on the increase.

Administrative Law

Administrative law deals chiefly with (a) the legal powers that are granted to administrative agencies and (b) the rules that the agencies make to carry out their powers. Administrative law centers on the operations of government agencies. It ranks as one of the fastest growing and most complicated branches of the law. Governments at the federal, state, and local levels have established administrative agencies to do the work of government. Administrative agencies deal with matters such as banking, aviation, education, public health, social welfare, labor, commerce, and taxation. Generally, the agencies are established as executive agencies under powers granted by the legislatures.

Tort Law

A tort is a wrong or injury that a person suffers because of someone else's action. The wrong may cause bodily harm; damage a person's property, business, or reputation; or make unauthorized use of a person's property. The individual who suffers harm may sue in civil court the person or persons responsible. Tort law deals with the rights and obligations of individuals where harm has occurred. Tort cases often originate because of an automobile or other type of accident. Other tort cases may occur because of intentional misconduct. The act that causes the harm may result in the actor being civilly liable under tort law concepts and criminally liable under criminal law concepts. For example, I get mad at my neighbor and punch her in the face. She could sue me in civil court for her injuries. The state could also take action against me in criminal court for the assault.

Tort law uses the concept of "duty" to control the conduct of society's members. For example, when you drive an automobile, you have a "duty" to drive safely. If you violate that duty and someone suffers harm, that person can sue you.

Contract Law

Contract law deals with the rights and obligations of parties who enter into contracts. A contract is defined as an agreement between two or more parties that is enforceable by law. Contract law regulates individuals by requiring individuals to abide by contractual obligations or face civil sanctions, generally in the form of monetary damages.

Controlling Dissent

Individual Rights versus Law and Order

In looking at issues involving the need to control dissent, it is necessary to consider the pendulum-like swings that occur in between the public's fear of crime and the concept of individual rights. Most individuals involved in law are oriented toward one or two opposing directions—individual rights or law and order. The law-and-order orientation stresses the need to solve the crime problem. The individual-rights orientation stresses the need to protect an individual's rights and often considers this a greater need than the need to punish offenders. While too great an emphasis on individual rights will restrict law enforcement and allow offenders to escape punishment, arbitrary police practices that may occur under the law-and-order orientation may infringe on constitutional rights.

Civil Disobedience

Civil disobedience is defined as the deliberate and public refusal to obey a law.[18] Many times, civil disobedience is used as a form of protest to attract attention to what the protesters consider as unjust or unconstitutional. The protesters hope that their actions will move others to correct the injustice. In some situations, the individuals involved regard civil disobedience as a matter of individual or moral conviction, and the individuals refuse to obey a law that they believe violates their personal principles.

Unlike acts committed during a riot, rebellion, and other types of violent opposition to law and authority, civil disobedience acts are generally nonviolent. It may also be distinguished from law breaking in general by the fact that individuals who are involved in civil disobedience generally accept willingly their punishment for breaking the law. The Occupy Wall Street movement in New York City spread to other major cities across the country. Protesters refused to leave city property and essentially camped out in parks to protest what they felt was economic injustice.

Throughout history, there has been disagreement over the concept of civil disobedience. Many individuals claim that it is never right to deliberately

ROSA LEE PARKS (1913–1999)

Rosa Parks was born in Tuskegee, Alabama, in 1913. She attended Alabama State Teachers College. She held a variety of jobs, including that of a seamstress. From 1967 to 1988, she worked on the staff of U.S. Congressman John Conyers, Jr.

In 1955, Rosa Parks was arrested for violating a city ordinance that required whites and blacks to sit in separate rows on city buses in Montgomery, Alabama. Front rows of the bus were reserved for whites. Blacks were required to sit in the back rows. She refused to give up her seat in the middle of the bus when a white man wanted to sit in her row. As the results of her actions, she lost her job as a seamstress. Her actions helped bring about the Civil Rights Movement. In 1979, she was awarded the Spingarn Medal for her contributions to the Civil Rights Movement.

Parks's action sparked Montgomery's black leaders to boycott the bus system as a protest against racial segregation. The leaders formed an organization to run the boycott. A local black Baptist minister, Martin Luther King, Jr., was chosen as president. For the next 382 days, thousands of blacks refused to ride Montgomery's buses. Their boycott did not end until the U.S. Supreme Court declared the city ordinance unconstitutional. The success of the boycott encouraged other mass protests for civil rights.[19]

break the law. These individuals contend that defiance of the law will lead to contempt for other laws and that any act of civil disobedience weakens society and may lead to anarchy. Others claim that citizens have a duty to disobey unjust laws, and that such law breaking is one of the best ways of testing the constitutionality of laws.

Historians trace civil disobedience back to when the disciples of Jesus Christ were ordered by the state to stop teaching. They are reported to have stated that they would obey God rather than mortals. St. Thomas Aquinas wrote in the 13th century that people must disobey earthly rulers when the laws of the state disagree with the laws of nature or God. In colonial America, the Quakers refused to pay taxes for military purposes. Prior to the Civil War, abolitionists openly disobeyed the Fugitive Slave Law, which required the return of runaway slaves. Susan B. Anthony was arrested in 1872 for attempting to vote. Henry David Thoreau, in his 1849 essay "On the Duty of Disobedience," declared that people should refuse to obey any law they believe is unjust. Mohandas K. Gandhi led the Indian nonviolence movement to gain independence from British rule, and as a result, India gained independence in 1947. During the Vietnam War, many opponents of the war committed illegal acts in an attempt to change U.S. foreign policy. The illegal acts included refusing to register for the draft, refusing to be inducted into the military services, and refusing to pay taxes.

Freedoms of Speech, Association, and Press

Freedom of speech is the right to speak out publicly or privately. The right covers all forms of expression, including books, newspapers, magazines, radio, television, and motion pictures. Freedom of association is the right to associate freely with others. Freedom of press refers to the right of the press to publish information. None of the freedoms are absolute. As U.S. Supreme Court Justice Oliver Wendell Holmes, Jr., once wrote: "The most stringent protection of free speech would not protect a man in falsely shouting fire in a theatre and causing panic."

Denying individuals the freedoms of speech, association, and press has historically been an effective method of controlling dissent. Most nondemocratic nations deny these freedoms to their people. These nations generally operate under the theory that the government knows best and that the freedoms in question would interfere with the conduct of public affairs. Even democratic nations put various limitations on the freedoms. For example, all nations prohibit certain types of speech that they believe is clearly harmful to the people. Drawing a line, however, between dangerous and permitted speech can be difficult. This was broached by the Supreme Court of the United States in *Snyder v. Phelps*, when members of the Westboro Baptist Church protested at the funeral of a marine who died while on active duty in Iraq. The Court ruled 8–1 in favor of free speech and upheld Westboro's right to picket a military funeral.

Generally, democratic nations place four major restrictions on freedom of speech. First, laws covering libel and slander restrict speech or publications that wrongfully harms a person's reputation. Second, all nations have some forms of laws that forbid actions, speech, or publications that offend public decency involving obscenities or pornography. Third, there are laws that prohibit individuals from spying, treason, or urging violence. Fourth, many laws protect a person's right not to listen to speech that invades their rights, e.g., using loudspeakers on crowded public streets.

Language Morphology Issues

All languages have certain things in common, including a sound pattern, words, and grammatical structure. Grammatical structure is the manner in which certain elements of language are related to others in forming units such as sentences. The two commonly identified aspects of structure are syntax and morphology. Syntax involves relations among elements of a sentence, including the arrangement of words in a particular order. Morphology in one context refers to the patterns of word formation in a particular language, including inflection, derivation, and composition.[20] It also deals with the elements that serve as building blocks for words. The role of morphology varies from language to language. All languages have some sort of word order. In some, however, the word order is more important than in others. For example, Latin allows for more variations in word order than English.

The morphology of a language allows us to build a social trust with the past and the present and, to some extent, the future. It helps build common understandings that are necessary for the establishment of norms and values. It also creates a particular way of thinking and perceiving.

Summary

- Social controls are the formal and informal means of enforcing norms. The law is, however, only one of many forms of social control. We also examined both formal and informal social controls, the role of morals and values, moral reasoning, controlling dissent, cultural aspects, and the language morphology issues involved in social control.
- Social control may be divided into two distinct processes: (a) internal controls—the internalization of group norms resulting in internal controls, and (b) external controls—those imposed by external pressures. The internalization of group norms refers to the consequence of the socialization process. During the socialization process, we develop rules of behavior for our social group by recognizing what conduct is appropriate, expected, and desirable for given situations.
- Norms make social life possible by making behavior predictable. For example, we count on most persons most of the time to meet the expectations of others.
- Control through external social pressures includes both positive and negative sanctions. For example, working hard to achieve a promotion is an example of a positive sanction. Getting a speeding ticket for driving too fast is an example of a negative sanction.
- Criminal law is a type of formal control, and public scorn is an informal type of social control. Often the types overlap.
- Two frequent methods of informal social control are by the use of folkways and mores. Folkways are established norms of common practice, such as those that specify modes of dress, language use,

and etiquette. While mores are a type of folkways, not all folkways are considered as important as mores to the society's values.

- Informal external social controls are techniques by which individuals praise those who comply and condemn those who do not comply. The techniques include praise, ridicule, gossip, reprimands, criticisms, and ostracism.
- Informal social controls are administered by friends, neighbors, relatives, and other acquaintances; they tend to be more effective in societies that are intimate and in which relations are face to face and less effective in large complex societies.
- Obedience to social norms to a great extent is based on a person's moral learning, which is a product of his or her socialization. Individual moral codes represent internally consistent principles by which people govern their lives. A significant aspect of moral learning depends on our moral education.
- Two key differences between informal and formal controls are that formal controls are administered by specialized functionaries who are socially delegated the task of intragroup control (formal), and they are characterized by explicit established procedures.
- The law as a formal social control is rarely exercised by use of positive rewards.

Questions in Review

1. Would you obey a law that you considered to be immoral? Explain your answer.
2. Explain the role of mores and other informal social controls in the orderly process of society.
3. Who determines which informal social controls are binding on us?
4. Who determines which formal social controls are binding on us?
5. Does the average citizen have a right to protest legally enacted statutes that are value neutral?
6. Are there any circumstances in which informal social controls are at odds with formal social controls? If so, which should the citizen obey?

Endnotes

1. M.B. Clinard & R.F. Meier. (1998). *Sociology of deviant behavior* (10th ed.). Fort Worth, TX: Harcourt Brace Jovanovich.
2. J.M. Henslin. (1993). *Sociology: A down-to-earth approach* (pp. 194–195). Boston, MA: Allyn & Bacon.

3. D. Milovanovic. (1994). *A primer in the sociology of law* (2nd ed., p. 122). New York, NY: Harrow and Heston.
4. T. Shibutani. (1961). *Society and personality: An interactionist approach to social psychology* (p. 426). Englewood Cliffs, NJ: Prentice-Hall.
5. I. Robertson. (1987). *Sociology* (3rd ed., p. 62). New York, NY: Worth.
6. J.M. Henslin. (1993). *Sociology: A down-to-earth approach*. Boston, MA: Allyn & Bacon.
7. T. Tyler. (1990). *Why people obey the law*. New Haven, CT: Yale University Press.
8. R.D. Schwartz. (1954). Social factors in the development of legal control: A case study of two Israeli settlements. *Yale Law Journal 63*(4), 471–491.
9. H.S. Becker. (1966). *Outsiders: Studies in the sociology of deviance* (p. 124). New York, NY: Free Press.
10. L. Kohlberg. (1967). Development of moral character and ideology. In L. Hoffman & M. Hoffman (Eds.), *Review of child development research*, Vol. 1. New York, NY: Russell Sage.
11. D. Black. (1967). *The behavior of law* (p. 107). New York, NY: Academic Press.
12. D. Black. (1989). *Sociological justice*. New York, NY: Oxford University Press.
13. J.S. Baker. (2008). Revisiting the explosive growth of federal crimes. *Legal Memorandum, 2008*(26). Retrieved June 29, 2013, from http://www.heritage.org/research/reports/2008/06/revisiting-the-explosive-growth-of-federal-crimes
14. 2013 California Rules of Court. *Rule 4.410. General objectives in sentencing*. Retrieved June 29, 2013, from http://www.courts.ca.gov/cms/rules/index.cfm?title=four&linkid=rule4_410
15. Texas Penal Code, Section 49.02. Retrieved June 29, 2013, from http://www.statutes.legis.state.tx.us/Docs/PE/htm/PE.49.htm
16. As reported in the *Houston Chronicle*, May 27, 2000, p. 14A.
17. R.F. Meirer & G. Geis. (1997). *Victimless crime? Prostitution, drugs, homosexuality, abortion*. Los Angeles, CA: Roxbury.
18. Civil disobedience. (1999). *World book* (Electronic version). Chicago, IL: World Book.
19. D.J. Garrow. (1999). Rosa Lee Parks. *World book* (Electronic version). Chicago, IL: World Book.
20. C.L. Barnhart (Ed.). (1989). Morphology. *American college dictionary*. New York, NY: Random House.

Lawmaking as a Form of Social Control

6

Chapter Objectives

After reading this chapter you should be able to

- Identify the sources of law
- Explain the main difference between formal and informal rulemaking
- Distinguish between proclamations and executive orders
- Discuss the role of administrative lawmaking
- Discuss the role of judicial lawmaking
- Explain how lobbyists and PACs influence legislation

Introduction

Each year in the United States, public officials in local, state, and federal governments contemplate an overabundance of new laws. In their capacity as lawmakers, they enact laws that are fundamentally aimed at promoting the public good. In most cases, this means that lawmakers function to pass those laws that serve to protect our society.

When we consider lawmaking, often our first thought is that of the legislative branch of government. This method of lawmaking involves a process that can be described as cyclical. First, an individual or group of persons in society generates an idea. Next, the idea is forwarded to a political representative, who works to gain support for it and to transform the idea into law. Finally, any outcome legislation is returned back to the society in which it originated.

Throughout the legislative process, there are assorted filters that massage the idea to ensure that any law that is produced will conform to language that is readily identified as legal. Unfortunately, vagueness and verbosity are two common enough characteristics of the language of law, such that the final legislative document often looks very different than the original concept. When this occurs, the rationale for originally introducing the idea gets amended or even completely lost in the shuffle of the legislative process. Consequently, disputes arise with regard to the interpretation of the law or perhaps its application. Here, a second method of lawmaking occurs, as the judiciary may be called upon to translate the law. The best example of this occurrence is the undertakings of the U.S. Supreme Court, the judicial branch of government that is responsible for explaining the U.S. Constitution.

Besides the legislative and judicial lawmakers, some public officials whose responsibility it is to enact laws hold positions in the executive branch of government. On the federal level, for example, executive orders have been used by presidents since the founding of the United States in order to communicate the president's policy preferences to his appointees, Congress, and the public, and to guide agency heads in the exercise of their discretion. (Executive orders are also used by many, if not all, of the governors of the states.) Typically, presidents issue hundreds of executive orders. Over the past four decades, presidents have averaged approximately 60 executive orders annually.

In this chapter we examine the lawmaking responsibilities of each of the three branches of government. After a brief discussion of the nature of lawmaking, we examine legislative lawmaking and consider such concepts as representation, committee work, role orientation, term limits, and congressional investigation. Next we discuss administrative lawmaking by specifically focusing on rulemaking and adjudication. Also, a brief discussion of proclamations and executive orders is provided. In the third part of this chapter, we explore judicial lawmaking by considering the topics of writs and lawmaking by precedents. The final section covers the subject of interest groups and the influence of lobbying efforts and campaign contributions on lawmaking in the United States.

SOURCES OF LAW

The Constitution: The U.S. Constitution is the "supreme law of the land." It provides the fundamental authority by which the U.S. government operates and guarantees the freedom and rights of all U.S. citizens. No laws may contradict any of the Constitution's principles, and no governmental authority in the United States is exempt from complying with it. The federal courts have the sole authority to interpret the Constitution and to evaluate the federal constitutionality of federal or state laws. The Constitution is relatively short, containing only about 4,500 words.

International treaties: When the United States enters into a treaty, it is also considered the supreme law of the land pursuant to the U.S. Constitution, as are federal laws. In the case of a conflict between a treaty and a federal statute, the one that is later in time or more specific will typically control. Treaties to

which the United States are a party may be found in the U.S.
Treaties Service, the Statutes at Large, the Treaties and Other
International Acts series issued by the State Department, as
well as the United Nations Treaty Series. Treaties are often
implemented by federal statutes.

Slip laws: The first official publication of the statute is in the form
generally known as the "slip law." In this form, each law is published separately as an unbound pamphlet. The heading indicates the public or private law number, the date of approval,
and the bill number. The heading of a slip law for a public law
also indicates the U.S. Statutes at Large citation. If the statute
has been passed over the veto of the president, or has become
law without the president's signature because he did not return
it with objections, an appropriate statement is inserted instead
of the usual notation of approval.

 The Office of the Federal Register, National Archives and
Records Administration, prepares the slip laws and provides
marginal editorial notes giving the citations to laws mentioned
in the text and other explanatory details. The marginal notes
also give the U.S. Code classifications, enabling the reader
immediately to determine where the statute will appear in the
code. Each slip law also includes an informative guide to the
legislative history of the law consisting of the committee report
number, the name of the committee in each house, as well as
the date of consideration and passage in each house, with a reference to the *Congressional Record* by volume, year, and date.
A reference to presidential statements relating to the approval
of a bill or the veto of a bill when the veto was overridden and
the bill becomes law is included in the legislative history as a
citation to the Weekly Compilation of Presidential Documents.

 Copies of the slip laws are delivered to the document rooms
of both houses, where they are available to officials and the
public. They may also be obtained by annual subscription or
individual purchase from the Government Printing Office and
are available in electronic form for computer access. Section
113 of Title 1 of the U.S. Code provides that slip laws are competent evidence in all the federal and state courts, tribunals,
and public offices.

Federal Statutes at Large: The U.S. Statutes at Large, prepared
by the Office of the Federal Register, National Archives and
Records Administration, provides a permanent collection of

the laws of each session of Congress in bound volumes. Each volume contains a complete index and a table of contents. From 1956 through 1976, each volume contained a table of earlier laws affected. These tables were cumulated for 1956-1970 and supplemented for 1971-1975 in pamphlet form and discontinued in 1976. From 1963 through 1974, each volume also contained a most useful table showing the legislative history of each law in the volume. This latter table was not included in subsequent volumes because the legislative histories have appeared at the end of each law since 1975. There are also extensive marginal notes referring to laws in earlier volumes and to earlier and later matters in the same volume.

Under the provisions of a statute originally enacted in 1895, these volumes are legal evidence of the laws contained in them and will be accepted as proof of those laws in any court in the United States.

The Statutes at Large are a chronological arrangement of the laws exactly as they have been enacted. There is no attempt to arrange the laws according to their subject matter or to show the present status of an earlier law that has been amended on one or more occasions. The code of laws serves that purpose. An example of a cite to a federal statute is: 42 U.S.C. sec. 9607, which would refer to Title 42, section 9607, of the U.S. Code. Federal statutes may be challenged in federal court.

United States Code: The U.S. Code contains a consolidation and codification of the general and permanent laws of the United States arranged according to subject matter under 50 title headings, in alphabetical order to a large degree. It sets out the current status of the laws, as amended, without repeating all the language of the amendatory acts except where necessary for that purpose. The code is declared to be prima facie evidence of those laws. Its purpose is to present the laws in a concise and usable form without requiring recourse to the many volumes of the Statutes at Large containing the individual amendments.

The code is prepared by the Law Revision Counsel of the House of Representatives. New editions are published every 6 years, and cumulative supplements are published after the conclusion of each regular session of the Congress. The code is also available in electronic form for computer access.

Titles that have been revised and enacted into positive law are legal evidence of the law, and the courts will receive them as proof of those laws. Eventually, all the titles will be revised and enacted into positive law. At that point, they will be updated by direct amendment.

Agency rules and executive orders: Federal administrative bodies issue rules and regulations of a quasi-legislative character; valid federal regulations have the force of law and preempt state laws and rules. Rules and regulations may be issued only under statutory authority granted by Congress. The president also has broad powers to issue executive orders. An executive order is a directive from the president to other officials in the executive branch. Proposed and final rules, executive orders, and other executive branch notices are published daily in the *Federal Register.*

Judicial opinions: The United States is a common-law country. Every U.S. state has a legal system based on the common law, except Louisiana (which relies on the French civil code). Common law has no statutory basis; judges establish common law by applying previous decisions (precedents) to present cases. Although typically affected by statutory authority, broad areas of the law—most notably relating to property, contracts, and torts—are traditionally part of the common law. These areas of the law are mostly within the jurisdiction of the states, and thus state courts are the primary source of common law. Federal common law is relatively narrow in scope, being limited primarily to clearly federal issues that have not been addressed by a statute.

Reported decisions of the U.S. Supreme Court and of most of the state appellate courts can be found in the official reporter of the respective courts. Those decided from at least 1887 to date can also be found in the National Reporter System, a system of unofficial reporters. Decisions of lower state courts are not published officially, but they can usually be found in unofficial reports. When referring to a case, a citation typically includes the name of the case and the volume and pages of the reporter, as well as the date. For example, as follows: *Miranda v. Arizona*, 384 U.S. 436 (1966). Citations to federal courts of appeals are found in volumes abbreviated F., F.2d, or F.3d, and district courts are in volumes abbreviated F. Supp. The decisions of other specialized federal courts, such as claims of bankruptcy decisions, are also reported.

State constitutions and statutes: State constitutions are the supreme law within the state. State statutes must conform to the respective state's constitution. An example of a state statute is Article 16 of chapter 38 of the Kansas Statutes Annotated, which is known as the Kansas juvenile justice code. It reads:

The primary goal of the juvenile justice code is to promote public safety, hold juvenile offenders accountable for such juveniles' behavior and improve the ability of juveniles to live more productively and responsibly in the community. To accomplish this goal, juvenile justice policies developed pursuant to the Kansas juvenile justice code shall be designed to: (a) Protect public safety; (b) recognize that the ultimate solutions to juvenile crime lie in the strengthening of families and educational institutions, the involvement of the community and the implementation of effective prevention and early intervention programs; (c) be community based to the greatest extent possible; (d) be family centered when appropriate; (e) facilitate efficient and effective cooperation, coordination and collaboration among agencies of the local, state and federal government; (f) be outcome based, allowing for the effective and accurate assessment of program performance; (g) be cost-effectively implemented and administered to utilize resources wisely; (h) encourage the recruitment and retention of well-qualified, highly trained professionals to staff all components of the system; (i) appropriately reflect community norms and public priorities; and (j) encourage public and private partnerships to address community risk factors.

Citation: To ensure uniformity in citation styles for all law-related publications or writings, most citations to legal sources in the United States follow the *Uniform System of Citation,* also known as the Bluebook. The Bluebook is updated every few years by a consortium of law schools. Among other things, the Bluebook provides the abbreviations for all state and federal courts, statutory compilations, and administrative rules.

Source: Charles W. Johnson. (1997). ***How our laws are made*** **(22nd ed.). Washington, DC: U.S. Government Printing Office.**

Nature of Lawmaking

Lawmaking is perhaps best understood by exploring some of the perspectives that have been embraced by sociologists and legal scholars. While many views exist with regard to the social need for creating law, our purpose here is to illustrate a few explanations of how law is created when greater emphasis is placed on the lawmaking process as a whole. Consequently, we introduce the relationship between why and how laws are enacted and rejected, by briefly considering three perspectives of lawmaking: the group-influence model, the functionalist view, and the conflict perspective.

Group-Influence Model

The *group-influence model* of lawmaking assumes that the actions of outside forces have a direct effect on decision making. This view of lawmaking focuses on the nature of political persuasion from sources within the lawmaking framework (e.g., party affiliation and constituency). Lawmaking is reasoned to be a necessary function to ensure public order and the protection of members of society from harm. The difficulty with this perspective is that the more powerful the persuasion, the more influence a party or constituent has in deciding what actually constitutes harm and, consequently, what laws are to be enacted.

Functionalist View

Another perspective of lawmaking suggests that social behaviors become acceptable norms when codified into written laws. This *functionalist view* maintains that norms reflect a consensus, a common value system developed through socialization, the process by which individuals learn the culture of their society. Laws then provide a repository of norms, which in turn contribute to the functioning of the social system and are said to develop to meet certain assumed "needs" of the system. This theory of lawmaking is based on the premise that all aspects of a society (e.g., institutions, roles, norms, etc.) serve a purpose and that all are indispensable for the long-term survival of the society. Further, it acknowledges that a supplemental but equally important function of lawmaking is to provide the authority to enforce norms through legal institutions. Any behavior jeopardizing the harmony, stability, equilibrium, and the status quo is considered antisocial and therefore punishable.

The application of the functionalist perspective to lawmaking is derived from a larger theoretical construct in the field of sociology. This approach gained prominence in the works of 19th-century sociologists, particularly those who viewed societies as organisms. The French sociologist Emile Durkheim argued that it was necessary to understand the "needs" of the social organism to which social phenomena correspond. Other writers have used the concept of function to mean the interrelationships of parts within a system, the adaptive aspect of a phenomenon, or its observable consequences.

Conflict Perspective

The *conflict perspective* holds that lawmaking contributes to social, political, and economic control of "have-not" members of society while maintaining the position of the powerful. Laws establish norms that reflect the power of one section of a society over the other sections. Moreover, lawmaking allows for a certain amount of coercion to occur by means of promulgating sanctions to maintain these rules. Laws are thought to originate as a means by which one class or caste dominates or exploits others.

The process of lawmaking and how the justice system operates to protect the rich and powerful is apparent in the following selection from *Law, Order and Power* by William Chambliss and Robert Seidman.

> In America it is frequently argued that to have "freedom" is to have a system which allows one group to make a profit over another. To maintain the existing legal system requires a choice. That choice is between maintaining a legal system that serves to support the existing economic system with its power structure and developing an equitable legal system accompanied by the loss of "personal freedom." But the old question comes back to plague us: freedom for whom? Is the black man who provides such a ready source of cases for the welfare workers, the mental hospitals, and the prisons "free"? Are the slum dwellers who are arrested night after night for "loitering," "drunkenness," or being "suspicious" free? The freedom protected by the system of law is the freedom of those who can afford it. The law serves their interests, but they are not "society"; they are one element of society. They may in some complex societies even be a majority (though this is very rare), but the myth that the law serves the interests of "society" misrepresents the facts.[1]

Legislative Lawmaking

The word *legislation* is derived from the Latin words meaning "law" and "bringing." Originally, the word had more of a religious connotation, in that an act of legislation was an act of a high priest revealing a divine law. Today, we understand legislation to mean a set of social rules that a majority of legislators have declared to be enforceable laws.

It is universally understood that any legislative body maintains as its primary function the business of lawmaking. The chief function of the U.S. Congress, for example, is lawmaking. Moreover, it has been suggested that Congress should carry out that function so that laws are responsive to the views and needs of a majority and should do so in a way that allows the full range of significant views to be heard.[2]

The idea of representation is also a powerful concept with regard to lawmaking. As representatives, lawmakers seek to address the needs of their constituents through the legislative process. Many of the ideas of these constituents find their way into the legislature. Sometimes, appearances are made by average citizens, lobbyists, and in some cases, celebrities such as sports figures and famous actors, who testify about specific legislative needs. Likewise, it is not unusual for a legislator to receive a steady stream of mail from citizens who have a vested interest in a particular piece of legislation. This is especially true with the ease of which electronic mail (email) is sent. Whether proponent or opponent, they constitute the legislator's many and diverse "clientele." Moreover, since reelection to office is so closely tied to taking care of constituents, citizen demands are often translated into legislation, especially those that affect groups of people rather than just one individual. Consider the following excerpt from John Stuart Mill's *Representative Government*, which addresses the legislative duty of representation.

> It is evident that the only government which can fully satisfy all the exigencies of the social state is one in which the whole people participate; that any participation, even in the smallest public function, is useful; that the participation should everywhere be as great as the general degree of improvement of the community will allow; and that nothing less can be ultimately desirable than the admission of all to a share in the sovereign power of the state. But since all cannot, in a community exceeding a single small town, participate personally in any but some very minor portions of the public business, it follows that the ideal type of a perfect government must be representative.[3]

Representation of the people is ever present in the lawmaking process. However, it is only one of many requirements that a senator or representative must consider when maneuvering what has been rightly called the "legislative maze." The role of the legislator in the legislative process requires wearing different hats at different times to get the job done. It requires the ability to develop alternative strategies and tactics in different stages of the legislative process, often in response to a multitude of unexpected and ever-changing circumstances.

Successful lawmaking is often contingent upon its members adhering to a set of game rules. By following such rules, a legislator can expect greater respect by other lawmakers and greater effectiveness in achieving the passage of legislation. Such norms fulfilling these functions include:[4]

Apprenticeship: Early in a member's career, he or she should concentrate on learning the rules of the body, keep a low profile, pay serious attention to committee work, and defer to the senior members of his or her party on major policy issues.

Cordiality: With so many members representing so many diverse interests, and so many diverse and potentially contentious policy issues to be dealt with, a continuing reliance on courtesy to other members is essential to moving policy through the two houses to completion.

Legislative work: Members are expected to spend their time on legislative duties in committee and on the floor and not sacrifice those duties for grandstanding before the media. Members are expected to gain influence by being patient and doing their share of the work, and eventually they will be recognized by their colleagues.

Reciprocity: With each bill required to go through so many stages where different members have influence, it is felt to be imperative that lawmakers put emphasis on helping each other or nothing will move. This requires an approach to legislating that stresses bargaining, logrolling, and compromise.

Specialization: Members are expected to specialize in one or perhaps a few legislative areas, primarily coinciding with subcommittee assignments. In this way, they develop in-depth expertise and can, over time, know their subject so well that other members could respect their views. Given the vast array of topics with which lawmakers have to deal, this fosters a division of labor that makes sure the work is covered.

Seniority: Seniority lends support to the maintenance of smooth working relationships in the legislature by avoiding disruptive and potentially destructive struggles for selecting committee chairs, thus promoting harmony among members. It also provides incentives for members to return to the legislature, specialize on committees, concentrate on doing good committee work, and develop policy specialties. The lawmaking process benefits by having genuine policy experts on hand with whom other members can consult in deliberations and defer in debate.

Legislative Committee Work

Perhaps the most important aspect of legislative duty is the work a lawmaker performs in committee. Committees are miniature legislatures, where bills are introduced, debated, analyzed, and revised before some action is taken. Although one of the chief functions of a committee is to screen out undesirable bills, arbitrary refusal of a committee to report a bill can be remedied by a motion to discharge the committee from further consideration of the bill. If the motion is approved by a majority of members in a respective house, the bill is forwarded to the full house for further consideration.

There are permanent house and senate committees that are commonly referred to as "standing" committees. These standing committees generally contain from 5 to 25 members. As a rule, all standing committee meetings are open to the public. Exceptions to this rule occur but are extremely rare. Most committee business is conducted during the meeting, and action requires the approval of a majority of those appointed and serving on the committee.

In addition to standing committees, there are other types of committees set up by the legislature to achieve certain goals. Special committees, for example, may be created by a house or senate resolution and appointed by the speaker and/or the senate majority leader, and are generally appointed to serve during a specified time period. The number of members assigned to these committees varies according to the specifications of the resolution. For the most part, these committees are used to study and investigate topics of special interest, such as education, technology, etc. Another type of committee is the joint committee, which is commonly established by statute. These committees, like standing committees, are appointed for specific time periods, but membership consists of both senators and representatives.

Role Orientation

The kind of behavior that a lawmaker exhibits while performing the duties of legislative office is predicated on role orientation. Behavior reflects the character of the legislator in terms of how he or she uses authority to make decisions in the legislative process. Four distinctive legislative role orientations that exist in the political power structure are ritualist, tribune, inventor, and broker.[5]

Protocol found within the legislative process has gradually over time become fixed. The modern legislator is expected to master rules of parliamentary procedure and must abide by them throughout the legislative process. Hence the potential exists for the lawmaker to become immersed in assembly rules and routines, rather than in legislative functions within the political system. In other words, parliamentary ritual rather than parliamentary goals absorbs the attention of the legislator. This orientation to the legislative role is referred to as the *ritualist* approach.[6]

A second legislative role orientation is that of *tribune*.[7] The central theme of this orientation is that legislators are chosen by popular election to represent their constituents and therefore gain favor for them. This advocacy role requires the legislator to fight for the popular demands of the people.

Another major orientation, which has been called *inventor*, provides that legislative bodies should be governing bodies, capable of performing policy-making duties.[8] Legislators are expected to be aware of public issues and be capable of determining potential solutions. Through rational deliberation and persuasive argument in debate, alternative solutions to social problems can be explored and result in needed legislation.

The final role orientation that we want to introduce is that of *broker*.[9] As the term suggests, this orientation is one in which the legislator functions as a middleman. The fundamental tasks are to introduce laws that are of interest to constituents, deal with pressure from interest groups, and ensure that legislation will not be detrimental to society as a whole. The legislator is both representative and ambassador and must be adept at compromise, diligence, and conciliation.

Term Limits

Term limits are statutory constraints placed on the number of terms a legislator may serve in office. Proponents of term limits suggest that limitation reduces the potential for incumbents' abuses of power and their obsession with reelection, thus making government more responsive. Some supporters have called for a constitutional amendment similar to the Twenty-Second Amendment, which limits the president's tenure, in order to establish uniform limits. Opponents of term limits cite the benefits of seniority and experience conferred by years in legislative office. They argue that with legislative turnover comes large numbers of newcomers with little or no political experience. Opponents of term limits maintain that such inexperience will hurt voters, as rookie legislators find it hard to navigate the bureaucracy. Moreover, limits force out well-regarded politicians who have formed strong ties with their constituents and erode democracy by taking away voters' rights to choose their representative.

The issue of term limits became particularly important in America during the early 1990s, when the matter squarely focused on members of the U.S. Congress. In *U.S. Term Limits Inc. et al. v. Thornton et al.*, the U.S. Supreme Court ruled in a 5 to 4 decision that states do not have the constitutional authority to regulate the tenure of federal legislators. The case involved an amendment to the Arkansas State Constitution that would have prohibited a candidate from appearing on an election ballot after serving three terms in the House of Representatives and two terms in the Senate. The court ruled that states are prohibited from imposing additional qualifications for holding federal office because the offices are inherent to the Constitution, and thus not in the realm of the Tenth Amendment. The significance of this case is that the only way to limit congressional terms is to amend the Constitution. Despite the Republican majority declaring term limits a priority in their 1994 "Contract With America," the 104th Congress twice failed to muster the two-thirds votes needed for a constitutional amendment. This hot topic has not disappeared from the national agenda. On January 23, 2013, Senator David Vitter (R-LA) introduced an amendment to the U.S. Constitution that would limit the number of terms that a Congress member may serve to three in the House of Representatives and two in the Senate. Interestingly, a poll conducted by the Gallup organization reveals that 75% of Americans say they would vote for a law that would limit the number of terms that members of Congress and the U.S. Senate can serve.[10] This debate does not seem to be going away.

U.S. TERM LIMITS, INC. V. THORNTON, 514 U.S. 779 (1995)

Stevens, J., delivered the opinion of the Court, in which Kennedy, Souter, Ginsburg, and Breyer, JJ., joined. Kennedy, J., filed a concurring opinion. Thomas, J., filed a dissenting opinion, in which Rehnquist, C.J., and O'Connor and Scalia, JJ., joined. [The below case has been edited and abridged.]

Respondent Hill filed this suit in Arkansas state court challenging the constitutionality of §3 of Amendment 73 to the Arkansas Constitution, which prohibits the name of an otherwise eligible candidate for Congress from appearing on the general election ballot if that candidate has already served three terms in the House of Representatives or two terms in the Senate. The trial court held that §3 violated Article I of the Federal Constitution, and the Arkansas Supreme Court affirmed. A plurality of the latter court concluded that the States have no authority "to change, add to, or diminish" the age, citizenship, and residency requirements for congressional service enumerated in the Qualifications Clauses, U. S. Const., Art. I, §2, cl. 2, and Art. I, §3, cl. 3, and rejected the argument that Amendment 73 is constitutional because it is formulated as a ballot access restriction rather than an outright disqualification of congressional incumbents.

Section 3 of Amendment 73 to the Arkansas Constitution violates the Federal Constitution. The power granted to each House of Congress to judge the "Qualifications of its own Members," Art. I, §5, cl. 1, does not include the power to alter or add to the qualifications set forth in the Constitution's text. This Court reaffirms that the constitutional qualifications for congressional service are "fixed," at least in the sense that they may not be supplemented by Congress.

So too, the Constitution prohibits States from imposing congressional qualifications additional to those specifically enumerated in its text. Petitioners' argument that States possess control over qualifications as part of the original powers reserved to them by the Tenth Amendment is rejected for two reasons. First, the power to add qualifications is not within the states' pre-Tenth Amendment "original powers," but is a new right arising from the Constitution itself, and thus is not reserved. Second, even if the states possessed some original power in this area, it must be concluded that the Framers intended the Constitution to be the exclusive source of qualifications for Members of Congress, and that the Framers thereby "divested" States of any power to add qualifications. That this is so is demonstrated by the unanimity among the courts and learned commentators who have considered the issue; by the

Constitution's structure and the text of pertinent constitutional provisions, including Art. I, §2, cl. 1, Art. I, §4, cl. 1, Art. I, §6, and Art. I, §5, cl. 1; by the relevant historical materials, including the records of the Constitutional Convention and the ratification debates, as well as Congress's subsequent experience with state attempts to impose qualifications; and, most importantly, by the fundamental principle of our representative democracy ... that the people should choose whom they please to govern them, *Powell,* 395 U.S., at 547. Permitting individual States to formulate diverse qualifications for their congressional representatives would result in a patchwork that would be inconsistent with the Framers' vision of a uniform National Legislature representing the people of the United States. The fact that, immediately after the adoption of the Constitution, many States imposed term limits and other qualifications on state officers, while only one State imposed such a qualification on Members of Congress, provides further persuasive evidence of a general understanding that the qualifications in the Constitution were unalterable by the States.

A state congressional term limits measure is unconstitutional when it has the likely effect of handicapping a class of candidates and has the sole purpose of creating additional qualifications indirectly. The Court rejects petitioners' argument that Amendment 73 is valid because it merely precludes certain congressional candidates from being certified and having their names appear on the ballot, and allows them to run as write in candidates and serve if elected. Even if petitioners' narrow understanding of qualifications is correct, Amendment 73 must fall because it is an indirect attempt to evade the Qualifications Clauses' requirements and trivializes the basic democratic principles underlying those Clauses. Nor can the Court agree with petitioners' related argument that Amendment 73 is a permissible exercise of state power under the Elections Clause, Art. I, §4, cl. 1, to regulate the "Times, Places and Manner of holding Elections." A necessary consequence of that argument is that Congress itself would have the power under the Elections Clause to "make or alter" a measure such as Amendment 73, a result that is unfathomable under *Powell.* Moreover, petitioners' broad construction is fundamentally inconsistent with the Framers' view of the Elections Clause, which was intended to grant States authority to protect the integrity and regularity of the election process by regulating election *procedures,* see, e.g., *Storer* v. *Brown,* 415 U.S. 724, 730, 733, not to provide them with license to impose substantive qualifications that would exclude classes of candidates from federal office.

> State imposition of term limits for congressional service would impact such a fundamental change in the constitutional framework that it must come through a constitutional amendment properly passed under the procedures set forth in Article V. Absent such an amendment, allowing individual states to craft their own congressional qualifications would erode the structure designed by the Framers to form a "more perfect Union." (The Arkansas Supreme Court's opinion that the amendment was unconstitutional was affirmed [upheld].)

Congressional Investigation

Lawmaking often requires the legislative body to conduct congressional investigations. Congress and its committees have the capacity to convene in order to gather information that is needed to discharge its legislative function. A primary function of the congressional investigation is to hold hearings in which witnesses from executive agencies, private persons, and organizations are called to provide this information.

While there is actually no provision in the U.S. Constitution that specifically grants authority to Congress to conduct investigations, a few U.S. Supreme Court decisions have firmly established the investigatory power of Congress. Two such historical cases are *Watkins v. United States*, 354 U.S. 178 (1957), and *Barenblatt v. United States*, 360 U.S. 109 (1959).

In *Watkins v. United States*, the Court described the breadth of the power of inquiry:

The power of the Congress to conduct investigations is inherent in the legislative process. That power is broad. It encompasses inquiries concerning the administration of existing laws as well as proposed or possibly needed statutes. It includes surveys of defects in our social, economic or political system for the purpose of enabling the Congress to remedy them. It comprehends probes into departments of the federal Government to expose corruption, inefficiency or waste.

...We [U.S. Supreme Court] are mindful of the complexities of modern government and the ample scope that must be left to the Congress as the sole constitutional depository of legislative power. Equally mindful are we of the indispensable function, in the exercise of that power, of congressional investigations. The conclusions we have reached in this case will not prevent the Congress, through its committees, from obtaining any information it needs for the proper fulfillment of its role in our scheme of government. The legislature is free to determine the kinds of data that should be collected.[11]

In *Barenblatt v. United States*, the issue before the Court was whether a subcommittee of the House of Representatives was authorized to compel a witness to provide testimony with regard to his political and religious beliefs without infringing on privileges against self-incrimination as well as First Amendment rights. The Court reaffirmed its position in the Watkins case, finding that House Rule XI, 83d Congress, legitimized the authority of legislative inquiry (i.e., the investigation here involved was related to a valid legislative purpose). The following excerpts from the case provide the essence of the Court's ruling:

> Rule XI has a "persuasive gloss of legislative history" which shows beyond doubt that, in pursuance of its legislative concerns in the domain of "national security," the House of Representatives has clothed the Committee with pervasive authority to investigate.... Where First Amendment rights are asserted to bar governmental interrogation, resolution of the issue always involves a balancing by the courts of the competing private and public interests at stake in the particular circumstances shown.... [T]he balance between individual and the governmental interests here at stake must be struck in favor of the latter.[12]

INVESTIGATING THE PRESIDENT: ARTICLES OF IMPEACHMENT

Three U.S. presidents have faced Articles of Impeachment: Andrew Johnson in 1868, Richard Nixon in 1974, and William Clinton in 1998. In Johnson's and Clinton's cases, the Senate's vote fell short of the necessary two-thirds, while Nixon resigned before the House could vote on the articles.

A glimpse of the impeachment process

1. The House Judiciary Committee deliberates over whether to initiate an impeachment inquiry.
2. The House Judiciary Committee adopts a resolution seeking authority from the entire House of Representatives to conduct an inquiry. Before voting, the House debates and considers the resolution. Approval requires a majority vote.
3. The House Judiciary Committee conducts an impeachment inquiry, possibly through public hearings. At the conclusion of the inquiry, articles of impeachment are prepared. They must be approved by a majority of the committee.
4. The House of Representatives considers and debates the articles of impeachment. A majority vote of the entire House is required to pass each article. Once an article is approved, the

president is, technically speaking, "impeached" (i.e., subject to trial in the Senate).

5. The Senate holds trial on the articles of impeachment approved by the House. The Senate sits as a jury while the chief justice of the Supreme Court presides over the trial.

6. At the conclusion of the trial, the Senate votes on whether to remove the president from office. A two-thirds vote by the members present in the Senate is required for removal.

Andrew Johnson's vetoes of several Reconstruction laws passed by a Republican Congress played a major role in provoking Radical Republican attempts to impeach and remove Johnson from the presidency. Representative Thaddeus Stevens and other Radical Republicans responded to Johnson's opposition by passing laws designed to restrain his power. One of those laws, the Tenure of Office Act, required the president to first obtain the Senate's consent before removing any federal appointees from office. Johnson, however, ignored the law by dismissing Secretary of War Edwin Stanton. Less than a week after Johnson's action, the House voted to impeach Johnson and force the Senate to decide his fate.

A Judiciary committee voted 5 to 4 in favor of impeachment on November 25, 1867. But after a two-day House floor debate in December, Johnson escaped impeachment on a 108 to 57 vote. In January 1868, though, the Senate invoked the Tenure of Office Act and reinstated Stanton as war secretary. Unabated by the impeachment proceedings, Johnson again ousted Stanton in February, in effect daring his enemies in the Congress to continue their vendetta.

The Senate took its first vote in May, which resulted in a tally of 35 to 19, one short of the two-thirds needed for impeachment. After votes on two more impeachment articles also fell short, the Republicans abandoned their effort. Although the attempt to impeach had failed, it did severely affect the political future of Johnson. He served the remaining 10 months of his term but lost the Democratic presidential nomination to New York governor Horatio Seymour. Johnson lost bids for the Senate in 1869 and the House in 1872. Finally, in 1874, Johnson was elected to the Senate. He took the oath in March 1875 but died a few months later.

Richard Nixon found his presidency in a web of political spying and sabotage, bribery, and the illegal use of campaign funds. The disclosure of these activities, and the administration's cover-up resulted in the indictments of some 40 government officials and, ultimately, the resignation of the president.

In June 1972, a burglary occurred at the Democratic national head-quarters in the Watergate apartment complex in Washington, DC. In January 1973, hints of a cover-up emerged at the trial of six men found guilty of the Watergate burglary. With a Senate investigation under way, Nixon announced in April the resignations of his top aides, H.R. Haldeman and John Ehrlichman, and the dismissal of White House counsel John Dean III. Dean was the star witness at televised Senate hearings that exposed both a White House cover-up of Watergate and massive illegalities in Republican fundraising in 1972. The hearings also disclosed that Nixon had routinely audiotaped his office meetings and telephone conversations.

In October 1973, Spiro Agnew resigned as vice president, then pleaded no contest to a negotiated federal charge of evading income taxes on alleged bribes. President Nixon nominated the House minor-ity leader, Rep. Gerald R. Ford, to replace Agnew, and Congress con-firmed Ford as the new vice president in December 1973.

In July, the U.S. Supreme Court ordered Nixon to surrender sub-poenaed tapes that revealed that Nixon had halted an FBI probe of the Watergate burglary six days after it occurred. It was, in effect, an admis-sion of obstruction of justice, and impeachment appeared inevitable.

The House Judiciary Committee by a vote of 27 to 11, with 6 of the committee's 17 Republicans joining all 21 Democrats, referred three impeachment articles to the full membership.

Nixon resigned in August 1974, the first president ever to do so. A month later, President Ford issued an unconditional pardon for any offenses Nixon might have committed as president, thus impeding pos-sible prosecution. President Nixon died in April 1994 in New York City of a massive stroke.

Bill Clinton's impeachment by the House of Representatives, on charges of lying under oath to a federal grand jury and obstructing justice, mes-merized the American public for more than one year. The daily, heavy dose of media coverage/entertainment centered around Independent Counsel Ken Starr's investigation into the details of Clinton's extra-marital affair with White House intern Monica Lewinsky. President Clinton was impeached on two (Articles I and III) of four articles of impeachment. In Article I, which was adopted on a 228 to 206 vote, Clinton was found to have provided false and misleading testimony to a U.S. federal grand jury concerning the details of his relationship with a subordinate government employee. Clinton also gave prior false and misleading testimony in a federal civil rights action brought against him.

In Article III, which was adopted on a 221 to 212 vote, Clinton was accused of obstructing justice by tampering with witnesses and taking other steps to conceal his affair with Lewinsky. He was also accused of concealing evidence that had been subpoenaed in a federal civil rights action brought against him. The Senate acquitted Clinton of the perjury charge on a vote of 55 to 45 and of the obstruction of justice charge on a vote of 50 to 50.

Administrative Lawmaking

Administrative agencies are sometimes referred to as the fourth branch of government, because they engage in lawmaking through rulemaking and adjudication. Rulemaking is the administrative equivalent of the legislative process of enacting statutes. Adjudication, on the other hand, is a process by which an administrative agency issues an order. It is a function that most closely resembles the functions performed by the courts.

The procedures for federal agency rulemaking are governed by the Federal Administrative Procedure Act of 1946 (APA).[13] The Administrative Procedure Act defines *rule* as

[T]he whole or part of an agency statement of general or particular applicability and future effect designed to implement, interpret, or prescribe law or policy or describing the organization, procedure, or practice requirements of an agency and includes the approval or prescription for the future of rates, wages, corporate or financial structures or reorganizations thereof, prices, facilities, appliances, services or allowances therefore or of valuations, costs, or accounting, or practices bearing on any of the foregoing.[14]

There are two types of rulemaking: formal and informal. Formal rulemaking is very time consuming in its procedure and therefore not used as often as informal rulemaking. Section 553(c) of APA provides that for formal rulemaking: "When rules are required by statute to be made on the record after opportunity for an agency hearing, sections 556 and 557 of this title apply." Sections 556 and 557 contain requirements for trial-type hearings, including the right of interested parties to present evidence, conduct cross-examination of witnesses who introduce opposing evidence, and submit rebuttal evidence, and (subject to the possibilities of taking official notice of matters) the rulemaking record is the exclusive basis for the decision.

Informal rulemaking basically exists by default. The APA gives agencies the discretion whether or not to hold oral hearings in informal rulemaking. In an important Supreme Court case, 435 U.S. 519 (1978), the Court emphasized that this discretion was not ordinarily reviewable (i.e., that courts were not free to require additional procedures of agency rulemaking than appear in section 553). However, some specific statutes require that agencies provide an opportunity for oral presentation of data or views or a public hearing, and a few statutes require agencies to provide an opportunity for cross-examination in informal rulemaking. The APA does not specify a minimum period for comment, but a reasonable time must be allowed for comment, with "reasonableness" judged in relation to the particular facts of each rulemaking. Executive Order 12,866 provides that most rulemakings "should include a comment period of not less than 60 days." Individual agency statutes occasionally specify the length of the comment period. As a practical matter, most agencies do provide 60 or more days for complex or controversial rules. Even when a shorter comment period is allowed, the agency may extend the period for comment where a legitimate request for extension has been received. In such a case, of course, notice of the extension is normally published in the *Federal Register*. The *Federal Register* is a government publication used to publish federal rules, orders, and related documents and announcements. The agency must consider the comments and publish the final rule, explaining how it responds to the comments.

Whether rulemaking involves a trial-type hearing (formal) or public-testimony hearing (informal), both types follow a protocol of notice and issuance of its final rules. Section 553 of APA provides that the Notice of Proposed Rulemaking (NPRM) must state the "time, place, and nature" of the public proceedings. Furthermore, the statutory procedure for issuing rules involves a notice of the proposed rule, which is published in the *Federal Register*. Agencies often give additional notice of the rulemaking beyond that provided in the *Federal Register*. General notice may be accomplished through press releases to general, trade, or other specialized publications, and notices to clearinghouse services and loose-leaf reporter services. Specific or "targeted" notices are frequently given to persons and trade associations most likely to be affected by the rule. Advertisements in the media may be used or letters sent directly to concerned individuals or groups. Failure to publish makes a final rule unenforceable against any person not having actual and timely notice of its terms.

The APA requires that the statement of basis and purpose be incorporated in the rule, so the statement of basis and purpose is also subject to the publication requirement. Additionally, in 1996, a new Chapter 8 was added to Title 5 of the U.S. Code establishing a requirement for congressional review of agency rules. Under this process, all federal agencies, including independent regulatory agencies, are required to submit each "rule" to both houses of Congress and to the General Accounting Office (GAO) before it can take effect. For each rule, agencies must submit: (a) a report containing "a concise general state-ment relating to the rule" and the rule's proposed effective date; (b) a copy of any cost-benefit analysis and descriptions of the agency's actions under the Regulatory Flexibility Act and Unfunded Mandates Reform Act; and (c) any other information or statements required by relevant executive orders.

Adjudications are the administrative equivalent of court trials. These pro-ceedings, which are governed by the APA, often involve the issuing, suspend-ing, or revoking of a permit or license. Moreover, adjudication hearings can be required when an employee is being suspended or terminated from gov-ernment employment. Justice Holmes defined adjudications as a process that "investigates, declares and enforces liabilities as they stand on present or past facts and under laws supposed to already exist. That is the purpose and end."[15]

Under the APA, if the statute under which the agency is conducting the program calls for an adjudication (e.g., enforcement action, license applica-tion, etc.) that is "required to be determined on the record after an agency hearing," then the APA procedures apply.[16] Normally, these procedures require an administrative law judge (ALJ) to preside over the hearing and make an initial decision in the case. Although they are not judges under Article III of the Constitution, ALJs are given special status and indepen-dence by the APA. They are selected by the agencies from a special register maintained by the Office of Personnel Management (OPM). The selection process for ALJs is quite rigorous, requiring at a minimum that the ALJ applicant must have at least 7 years of experience in administrative law and/or trial experience as an attorney or a judge. OPM then rates the applicant on a 100-point scale, based on a review of the applicant's experience, a written demonstration, and a panel interview. Agencies then fill vacancies from the top of the register, which prevents agency officers from appointing ALJs they believe will be sympathetic to the agency's point of view in specific cases.[17]

The APA permits the use of other types of adjudicators in certain cases. When not required by statute to be heard under section 554 of the APA, the agency is free to use any employee to preside so long as the due process clause is satisfied. In many cases, the agency head presides over a hearing. Moreover, Congress can specify in other laws that a particular type of adju-dicator be used (e.g., a panel of lawyers, engineers, etc.). As a consequence, there are various major programs where specified non-ALJ adjudicators pre-side over cases that are otherwise similar to APA cases.[18]

The final stage in the adjudication process is the issuance of a decision. If an agency officer makes the initial decision, it is considered final, absent an appeal. On the other hand, if an ALJ conducts a hearing, APA provides that the ALJ shall render either an initial or a recommended decision. Initial decisions are viewed as final, but recommended decisions must be forwarded to the agency for action. Once the decision is made by the agency, the losing party has an opportunity to seek review by the agency head. If no review is sought, the agency head may call the case up "on his own motion." The APA provides that the agency head has "all the powers which it would have in making the initial decision."[19] This broad power to reverse or modify the presiding officer's decision has been tempered by court decisions requiring the agency head to justify such a change, especially where the initial decision was based on witness testimony.[20] Agencies have discretion as to how they structure their appeal process. Some agency heads (usually boards or commissions) hear appeals themselves; others have created special panels or individual positions to hear such appeals.[21]

THE OFFICE OF THE FEDERAL REGISTER

Description: The Office of the Federal Register (OFR) was established in 1935 for the purpose of creating a centrally located system for filing and publishing presidential documents as well as agency regulations and administrative notices. The Federal Register Act (44 U.S.C. Chapter 15) governs the operations of the *Federal Register* publication system. The statute specifically requires that executive orders and presidential proclamations shall be published in the *Federal Register*, except for those that do not have general applicability and legal effect, or those that only affect federal agencies, officers, agents, or employees (44 U.S.C. 1505(a)). In practice, most executive orders are published in the *Federal Register* regardless of subject matter.

Access to presidential documents and federal register information: The *Federal Register* publication system is the product of a unique partnership between the National Archives and Records Administration (NARA) and the Government Printing Office (GPO). The support of these two institutions helps guarantee the public's right to know about the actions of their government. In recent years, the OFR/GPO partnership has developed online editions of every major *Federal Register* publication and posted them on the *GPO Access* service to make it easier for citizens to gain access to essential legal information.

The *Federal Register* is available in an online edition, making new executive orders accessible to the American public on a very timely basis. To help the public sort through the various sources of information, the NARA website (www.archives. gov/index.html) allows direct access to the text of executive orders and other presidential documents. They also provide other information services, such as our historical *Codification of Proclamations and Executive Orders* and an online index of executive orders, which tracks dates of issuance, amendments, revocations, and dates of publication in the *Federal Register.*

The *Federal Register* publication system also depends on its partnership with the Government Depository Library program to ensure that all citizens have equal access to government information. More than 1,350 depository libraries throughout the United States and its Territories provide free public access to *Federal Register* publications in print and online via the *GPO Access* service. *Federal Register* publications are among the most frequently used databases on the *GPO Access* service.

Source: Ray Mosley. (2000). The impact of executive orders on the legislative process: Executive lawmaking? Testimony before the Subcommittee of the Legislative and Budget Process. U.S. Congress.

Proclamations and Executive Orders

The president engages in lawmaking in several different ways. First, as chief executive, he leads the executive branch of government, thereby possessing absolute supervision over the various administrative agencies. This occurs as a result of Congress delegating rule-making authority and emergency powers to the president, cabinet heads, and agency heads, which in effect allows them to legislate. Second, the president has a great deal of authority by virtue of his position under the Constitution (e.g., military commander-in-chief and director of foreign relations). Third, under federal statutes, the president has considerable decision-making power, particularly in matters regarding foreign trade.

The president issues proclamations and executive orders. Proclamations and executive orders have much the same legal effect, but are usually used for different purposes. In general, proclamations are used for ceremonial events (e.g., declaring National Flag Day) or broad policy statements (e.g., Lincoln's Emancipation Proclamation), while executive orders are issued for routine determinations under statutory authority. They are numbered, in separate series, in order of issuance and published in the *Federal Register.*[22]

Although administrative orders are not numbered as proclamations and executive orders, they have much the same effect. They are usually used for particular determinations under foreign trade statutes or to implement foreign policy decisions. Orders are dated only, not numbered; presidential determinations are numbered by year and number (e.g., no. 90-9). They are published in the *Federal Register* and Title 3, CFR.

VETERANS DAY PROCLAMATION: BY THE PRESIDENT OF THE UNITED STATES OF AMERICA

A PROCLAMATION

Whether they fought in Salerno or Samarra, Heartbreak Ridge or Helmand Province, Khe Sanh or the Korengal Valley, our veterans are part of an unbroken chain of men and women who have served our country with honor and distinction. On Veterans Day, we show them our deepest thanks. Their sacrifices have helped secure more than two centuries of American progress, and their legacy affirms that no matter what confronts us or what trials we face, there is no challenge we cannot overcome, and our best days are still ahead.

This year, we marked the 200th anniversary of the War of 1812. We began to commemorate the 50th anniversary of the Vietnam War. We welcomed our veterans back home from Iraq, and we continued to wind down operations in Afghanistan. These milestones remind us that, though much has changed since Americans first took up arms to advance freedom's cause, the spirit that moved our forebears is the same spirit that has defined each generation of our service members. Our men and women in uniform have taught us about strength, duty, devotion, resolve—cornerstones of a commitment to protect and defend that has kept our country safe for over 200 years. In war and in peace, their service has been selfless and their accomplishments have been extraordinary.

Even after our veterans take off the uniform, they never stop serving. Many apply the skills and experience they developed on the battlefield to a life of service here at home. They take on roles in their communities as doctors and police officers, engineers and entrepreneurs, mothers and fathers. As a grateful Nation, it is our task to make that transition possible—to ensure our returning heroes can share in the opportunities they have given so much to defend. The freedoms we cherish endure because of their service and sacrifice, and our country must strive to honor our veterans by fulfilling our responsibilities to them and upholding the sacred trust we share with all who have served.

On days like this, we are called to reflect on immeasurable burdens that have been borne by so few. We pay tribute to our wounded, our missing, our fallen, and their families—men and women who have known the true costs of conflict and deserve our deepest respect, now and forever. We also remember that our commitments to those who have served are commitments we must honor not only on Veterans Day, but every day. As we do so, let us reaffirm our promise that when our troops finish their tours of duty, they come home to an America that gives them the benefits they have earned, the care they deserve, and the fullest opportunity to keep their families strong and our country moving forward.

With respect for and in recognition of the contributions our service members have made to the cause of peace and freedom around the world, the Congress has provided (5 U.S.C. 6103(a)) that November 11 of each year shall be set aside as a legal public holiday to honor our Nation's veterans.

NOW, THEREFORE, I, BARACK OBAMA, President of the United States of America, do hereby proclaim November 11, 2012, as Veterans Day. I encourage all Americans to recognize the valor and sacrifice of our veterans through appropriate public ceremonies and private prayers. I call upon Federal, State, and local officials to display the flag of the United States and to participate in patriotic activities in their communities. I call on all Americans, including civic and fraternal organizations, places of worship, schools, and communities to support this day with commemorative expressions and programs.

IN WITNESS WHEREOF, I have hereunto set my hand this seventh day of November, in the year of our Lord two thousand twelve, and of the Independence of the United States of America the two hundred and thirty-seventh.[23]

BARACK OBAMA

EXECUTIVE ORDER—PREVENTING AND RESPONDING TO VIOLENCE AGAINST WOMEN AND GIRLS GLOBALLY

By the authority vested in me as President by the Constitution and the laws of the United States of America, it is hereby ordered as follows:

Section 1. Policy. (a) Recognizing that gender-based violence undermines not only the safety, dignity, and human rights of the millions of individuals who experience it, but also the public health, economic stability, and security of nations, it is the policy and practice of the executive branch of the United States Government to have a multi-year strategy that will more effectively prevent and respond to gender-based violence globally.

(b) Under the leadership of my Administration, the United States has made gender equality and women's empowerment a core focus of our foreign policy. This focus is reflected in our National Security Strategy, the Presidential Policy Directive on Global Development, and the 2010 U.S. Quadrennial Diplomacy and Development Review. Evidence demonstrates that women's empowerment is critical to building stable, democratic societies; to supporting open and accountable governance; to furthering international peace and security; to growing vibrant market economies; and to addressing pressing health and education challenges.

(c) Preventing and responding to gender-based violence is a cornerstone of my Administration's commitment to advance gender equality and women's empowerment. Such violence significantly hinders the ability of individuals to fully participate in, and contribute to, their communities—economically, politically, and socially. It is a human rights violation or abuse; a public health challenge; and a barrier to civic, social, political, and economic participation. It is associated with adverse health outcomes, limited access to education, increased costs relating to medical and legal services, lost household productivity, and reduced income, and there is evidence it is exacerbated in times of crisis, such as emergencies, natural disasters, and violent conflicts.

(d) The executive branch multi-year strategy for preventing and responding to gender-based violence is set forth in the United States Strategy to Prevent and Respond to Gender-based Violence Globally (Strategy). The Strategy both responds to and expands upon the request in section 7061 of House conference report 112-331 accompanying the Department of State, Foreign Operations, and Related Programs Appropriations Act, 2012 (Division I of Public Law 112-74), for the executive branch to develop a multi-year strategy to prevent and respond to violence against women and girls in countries where it is common.

Sec. 2. Creating an Interagency Working Group. There is established an Interagency Working Group (Working Group) to address gender-based violence, which shall coordinate implementation of the Strategy by the executive departments and agencies that are members of the Working Group (member agencies) in accordance with the priorities set forth in section 3 of this order.

(a) The Working Group shall be co-chaired by the Secretary of State and the Administrator of the United States Agency for International Development (Co-Chairs). In addition to the Co-Chairs, the Working Group shall consist of representatives from:

(i) the Department of the Treasury;

(ii) the Department of Defense;

(iii) the Department of Justice;

(iv) the Department of Labor;

(v) the Department of Health and Human Services;

(vi) the Department of Homeland Security;

(vii) the Office of Management and Budget;

(viii) the National Security Staff;

(ix) the Office of the Vice President;

(x) the Peace Corps;

(xi) the Millennium Challenge Corporation;

(xii) the White House Council on Women and Girls; and

(xiii) other executive departments, agencies, and offices, as designated by the Co-Chairs.

(b) Within 120 days of the date of this order, the Co-Chairs shall convene the first meeting of the Working Group to:

(i) establish benchmarks to implement the Strategy; and

(ii) determine a timetable for periodically reviewing those benchmarks.

(c) Within 18 months of the date of this order, the Working Group shall complete a progress report for submission to the Co-Chairs evaluating the U.S. Government's implementation of the Strategy.

(d) Within 3 years of the date of this order, the Working Group shall complete a final evaluation for submission to the Co-Chairs of the U.S. Government's implementation of the Strategy.

(e) Within 180 days of completing its final evaluation of the Strategy in accordance with subsection (d) of this section, the Working Group shall update or revise the Strategy to take into account the information learned and the progress made during and through the implementation of the Strategy.

(f) The activities of the Working Group shall, consistent with law, take due account of existing interagency bodies and coordination mechanisms and will coordinate with such bodies and mechanisms where appropriate in order to avoid duplication of efforts.

Sec. 3. Strategy to Prevent and Respond to Gender-based Violence Globally. Member agencies shall implement the Strategy to prevent and respond to gender-based violence globally based on the following priorities reflected in the Strategy:

(a) Increasing Coordination of Gender-based Violence Prevention and Response Efforts Among U.S. Government Agencies and with Other Stakeholders.

(i) Member agencies shall draw upon each other's expertise, responsibility, and capacity to provide a comprehensive and multi-faceted approach to issues relating to gender-based violence.

(ii) Member agencies shall deepen engagement and coordination with other governments; international organizations, including multilateral and bilateral actors; the private sector; and civil society organizations, such as representatives of indigenous and marginalized groups, foundations, community-based, faith-based, and regional organizations (including those that serve survivors), labor unions, universities, and research organizations. The Working Group shall consider a range of mechanisms by which these stakeholders may provide input to the U.S. Government on its role in preventing and responding to gender-based violence globally.

(b) Enhancing Integration of Gender-based Violence Prevention and Response Efforts into Existing U.S. Government Work. Member agencies shall more comprehensively integrate gender-based violence prevention and response programming into their foreign policy and foreign assistance efforts. This integration shall also build on current efforts that address gender-based violence, such as the U.S. National Action Plan on Women, Peace, and Security; the Global Health Initiative; the President's Emergency Plan for AIDS Relief; the U.S. Government's work to counter trafficking in persons; and the U.S. Government's humanitarian response efforts. The Working Group shall coordinate these different efforts as they relate to gender-based violence to leverage the most effective programs and to avoid duplication.

(c) Improving Collection, Analysis, and Use of Data and Research to Enhance Gender-based Violence Prevention and Response Efforts. Member agencies shall work to promote ethical and safe research, data collection, and evidence-based analyses relating to different forms of gender-based violence and prevention and response efforts at the country and local level. This work will include the development of a research agenda that assesses agencies' research and data collection capabilities, needs, and gaps; builds upon existing data and research; and is coordinated with the work of other organizations that are prioritizing global gender-based violence research. Member agencies shall prioritize the monitoring and evaluation of gender-based violence prevention and response interventions to determine their effectiveness. Member agencies shall systematically identify and share best practices, lessons learned, and research within and across agencies. Member agencies, as appropriate, shall seek to develop public-private partnerships to support U.S. Government research initiatives and strategic planning efforts.

(d) Enhancing or Expanding U.S. Government Programming that Addresses Gender-based Violence. Consistent with the availability of appropriations, the U.S. Government shall support programming that provides a comprehensive and multi-sector approach to preventing and responding to gender-based violence; shall consider replicating or expanding successful programs; and shall assess the feasibility of a focused, coordinated, comprehensive, and multi-sector approach to gender-based violence in one or more countries.

Sec. 4. General Provisions. (a) Nothing in this order shall be construed to impair or otherwise affect:
(i) the authority granted by law to an executive department, agency, or the head thereof; or
(ii) the functions of the Director of the Office of Management and Budget relating to budgetary, administrative, or legislative proposals.
(b) This order shall be implemented consistent with applicable law and subject to the availability of appropriations.
(c) Independent agencies are strongly encouraged to comply with this order.
(d) This order is not intended to, and does not, create any right or benefit, substantive or procedural, enforceable at law or in equity by any party against the United States, its departments, agencies, or entities, its officers, employees, or agents, or any other person.[24]

BARACK OBAMA

Judicial Lawmaking

Most scholars and jurists recognize that courts perform legislative functions. In general, courts make law by exercising the power of judicial review when contemplating the constitutionality of legislative and executive actions by government. The courts are regularly consulted to decide disputes that arise under the seemingly countless number of new laws and governmental rules that are passed to govern society.

In addition to the Constitution, many federal statutes provide specific standards for judicial review of agency actions under the statute. When a statute provides for review, no other method may be used to establish a court's authority to hear the case, with the exception of cases in which a constitutional issue is raised. Generally, statutes prescribe that legal challenges must be filed in a timely fashion (e.g., 30-, 60-, and 90-day limits) as well as where an action is to be filed. The reviewing court decides all relevant questions of law, interprets statutory provisions, and determines the applica-bility of the agency action. The court has the authority to nullify any agency action, findings, or conclusions the court finds to be arbitrary, capricious, an abuse of discretion, or otherwise not in accordance with law; in excess of statutory jurisdiction, authority, or limitations; or adopted without proce-dures required by law.

The Use of Writs

Another way that judiciary makes law is through the review by writs. A writ is an official court document, signed by a judge or bearing an official court seal, which commands the person to whom it is addressed, to do something specific. That person is typically either a law enforcement official (e.g., a sher-iff who has been instructed to seize property) or a defendant (e.g., a person who is being required to answer charges specified in a legal action). The U.S. Code provides the courts authority to issue various writs to agencies and agency officials. For example, Title 28, section 2241 (d), of the code estab-lished the power to grant a writ of habeas corpus in the following citation:

> Where an application for a writ of habeas corpus is made by a person in cus-tody under the judgment and sentence of a state court of a state which con-tains two or more federal judicial districts, the application may be filed in the district court for the district wherein such person is in custody or in the district court for the district within which the state court was held which con-victed and sentenced him and each of such district courts shall have concur-rent jurisdiction to entertain the application. The district court for the district wherein such an application is filed in the exercise of its discretion and in furtherance of justice may transfer the application to the other district court for hearing and determination.

Another good example of judicial review is the writ of certiorari. *Certiorari* is a Latin word meaning "to be better informed, or to be made cer-tain in regard to." It is also the name given to certain appellate proceedings for reexamination of actions of a trial court or inferior appeals court. The U.S. Supreme Court uses the term *certiorari* in the context of appeals. The U.S. Code under Title 28, section 1254, permits cases in the courts of appeals to be reviewed by the Supreme Court by the following methods:

> By writ of certiorari granted upon the petition of any party to any civil or criminal case, before or after rendition of judgment or decree;
> By certification at any time by a court of appeals of any question of law in any civil or criminal case as to which instructions are desired, and upon such certification the Supreme Court may give binding instructions or require the entire record to be sent up for decision of the entire matter in controversy.

In general, the process begins when someone with a legal claim files a lawsuit in a trial court, such as a U.S. district court, which receives evidence and decides the facts and law. If one of the parties is dissatisfied with a legal decision of the trial court, they can appeal. In the federal system, this appeal usually would be to the U.S. court of appeals, which is required to consider and rule on all properly presented appeals. Since the highest federal court in the United States is the Supreme Court, the party who is dissatisfied with the ruling of the court of appeals can request the Supreme Court to review the decision of the court of appeals. This request is named a "petition for writ of certiorari." The Supreme Court can refuse to take the case. Review on writ of certiorari is not a matter of right, but a judicial discretion. A petition for writ of certiorari is granted only for compelling reasons. In fact, the Court receives thousands of "cert petitions" per year, but more than 90% are denied, and normally without explanation for the denial, other than the terse order, "Petition for writ of certiorari denied." If the court does accept the case, it grants a writ of certiorari.

Lawmaking by Precedents

One of the ways that our judicial system maintains constitutional continuity is through precedents. Judicial precedents derive their force from the doctrine of *stare decisis*, which is Latin for "to stand by that which is decided" (i.e., that the previous decisions of the highest court in the jurisdiction are binding on all other courts in the jurisdiction). *Black's Law Dictionary* defines the doctrine of stare decisis as

> a deliberate or solemn decision of [a] court made after argument on [a] question of law fairly arising in the case, and necessary to its determination, is an authority, or binding precedent in the same court, or in other courts of equal or lower rank in subsequent cases where the very point is again in controversy.[25]

The obvious purpose of the doctrine is to promote stability and permanence in the law[26] and to ensure predictability for those governed by it.[27]

There are actually two types of stare decisis. The best known requires that once a court makes a decision on an issue, lower courts become obligated to follow that precedent. Legal scholars writing in this area call this *vertical stare decisis*.[28] Less commonly noted is stare decisis that applies to courts of equal rank, including the deciding court itself. This is referred to as *horizontal stare decisis*. While vertical stare decisis is virtually absolute, there is currently no such unbending rule obligating courts to adhere to their own prior precedents.[29]

The doctrine of stare decisis is not always to be relied upon, for the courts find it necessary to overrule cases that may have been hastily decided or contrary to principle. However, the task of pursuing an overruling of a precedent decision is an onerous one. The difficulty of doing this is roughly proportional to a number of factors, including the age of the precedent, the nature and extent of public and private reliance on it, and its consistency or inconsistency with other related rules of law.

PROFILES OF THE U.S. SUPREME COURT JUSTICES

John Roberts Jr., chief justice

John Roberts Jr. was born in Buffalo, New York, on January 27, 1955. Roberts's educational training includes an A.B. from Harvard College in 1976 and a J.D. from Harvard Law School in 1979. His judicial appointments include the appointment to the U.S. Court of Appeals for the District of Columbia Circuit in 2003. President George W. Bush nominated him as chief justice of the United States, and he took his seat September 29, 2005.

Antonin Scalia

Antonin Scalia was born in 1936 in Trenton, New Jersey. He studied at Georgetown University, University of Fribourg (Switzerland), and Harvard Law School. After graduation, he was a Sheldon fellow at Harvard before entering private practice in Cleveland, Ohio. In 1967, he became a professor at the University of Virginia. From 1971 to 1977, Scalia served in various government offices as general counsel, Office of Telecommunications Policy; chairman, Administrative Conference of the United States; and Assistant Attorney General, Office of Legal Counsel, U.S. Department of Justice. He later taught at Georgetown, Chicago, and Stanford before being appointed by President Reagan to the U.S. Court of Appeals for the District of Columbia Circuit in 1982. In 1986, Scalia was appointed as a Justice of the U.S. Supreme Court.

Anthony M. Kennedy

Anthony M. Kennedy was born in 1936 in Sacramento, California. His educational training includes Stanford A.B. '58 and Harvard J.D. '61. He was a practicing attorney in Sacramento for 12 years and also served as an adjunct professor at the McGeorge School of Law, University of the Pacific, from 1965 to 1988. Kennedy was appointed to the U.S. Court of Appeals for the Ninth Circuit in 1975. President Ronald Reagan nominated Kennedy to the Supreme Court of the United States on November 30, 1987. The Senate confirmed the appointment on February 3, 1988.

Clarence Thomas

Clarence Thomas was born in 1948 in Pin Point, Georgia. Thomas was educated at Holy Cross College (B.A. 1971) and Yale (J.D. 1974).

Thomas was admitted to the Missouri bar in 1974 and became an assistant attorney general of the state of Missouri the same year. He was an attorney for the Monsanto Company from 1977 to 1979. Thomas was appointed assistant secretary for civil rights in the U.S. Department of Education. In 1982, he was named chairman of the U.S. Equal Employment Opportunity Commission and served in that capacity until 1990. President George H.W. Bush appointed Thomas to the U.S. Court of Appeals for the District of Columbia Circuit in 1990. On July 1, 1991, President Bush nominated Thomas to the Supreme Court of the United States. The Senate confirmed the appointment on October 15, 1991.

Ruth Bader Ginsburg
Ruth Bader Ginsburg was born in Brooklyn, New York, in 1933. She received her undergraduate degree from Cornell University, graduating Phi Beta Kappa in 1954. Ginsburg graduated from Columbia Law School in 1959. Ginsburg joined the faculty at Rutgers School of Law, where she remained for 9 years. In 1972, she was named head of the ACLU's Women's Rights Project. In that same year, Ginsburg left Rutgers to teach at Columbia Law School. Ginsburg was appointed to the U.S. Court of Appeals for the District of Columbia by President Jimmy Carter in 1980. She held this position until 1993, when she was nominated by President Clinton to serve on the Supreme Court. Her appointment was confirmed by the Senate, and she took the oath of office on August 10, 1993.

Stephen Breyer
Stephen G. Breyer was born in San Francisco in 1938. Breyer studied at Stanford, where he graduated in 1959 and then attended Oxford University, graduating in 1961. In 1964, he graduated from Harvard Law School. Breyer clerked for Supreme Court Justice Goldberg in 1964–1965. Two years later he began teaching at Harvard Law. He also taught in Australia and Rome. Breyer has served in several government positions, including: antitrust assistant for the Department of Justice, assistant special prosecutor on the Watergate Special Prosecution Force in 1973, and as both special and chief counsel to the U.S. Senate Judiciary Committee. In 1980, President Carter nominated him to the U.S. Court of Appeals for the First Circuit, where he served as chief judge from 1990 until 1994. In October of 1994, Justice Stephen Breyer was appointed to serve on the U.S. Supreme Court.

Samuel Anthony Alito Jr.
Samuel Alito Jr. was born in Trenton, New Jersey, on April 1, 1950. He graduated from Princeton University's Woodrow Wilson School of Public and International Affairs with a BA in 1972 before attending Yale Law School, where he served as editor of the *Yale Law Journal* and earned a JD in 1975. Alito was commissioned as a second lieutenant in the U.S. Army Signal Corps after his graduation from Princeton and assigned to the U.S. Army Reserve. Following his graduation from Yale Law School in 1975, he served on active duty from September to December 1975 while attending the Officer Basic Course for Signal Corps officers at Fort Gordon, Georgia. The remainder of his time in the army was served in the inactive reserves. He had the rank of captain when he received an honorable discharge in 1980. He was appointed to the U.S. Court of Appeals for the Third Circuit in 1990. President George W. Bush nominated him as an associate justice of the Supreme Court, and he took his seat January 31, 2006.

Sonia Sotomayor
Sonia Sotomayor was born in the Bronx, New York, on June 25, 1954. Her education includes earning the B.A. in 1976 from Princeton University, graduating summa cum laude, and receiving the university's highest academic honor. In 1979, she earned a J.D. from Yale Law School. President George H.W. Bush nominated her to the U.S. District Court, Southern District of New York, and she served in that role from 1992 to 1998. She served as a judge on the U.S. Court of Appeals for the Second Circuit from 1998 to 2009. President Barack Obama nominated her as an associate justice of the Supreme Court on May 26, 2009, and she assumed this role August 8, 2009.

Elena Kagan
Elena Kagan was born in New York, New York, on April 28, 1960. She received an A.B. from Princeton in 1981, an M. Phil. from Oxford in 1983, and a J.D. from Harvard Law School in 1986. After an appointment as a law professor at the University of Chicago Law School and later at Harvard Law School, she served as the dean of Harvard Law School. In 2009, President Obama nominated her as the solicitor general of the United States. After serving in that role for a year, the president nominated her as an associate justice of the Supreme Court on May 10, 2010.

Interest Groups

While there are several ways in which lawmaking may be influenced by interest groups, perhaps the two most influential are (a) influencing the activities of lawmakers by means of lobbying and (b) financing political campaigns. Both methods are used to influence courts, legislative bodies, and executive administrations.

Webster's Dictionary defines the word *lobby* as:

> to conduct activities aimed at influencing public officials and especially members of a legislative body on legislation; to promote or secure the passage of legislation by influencing public officials; to attempt to influence or sway a public official toward a desired action.[30]

Interest groups typically hire a lobbyist to discuss a legislative agenda with a legislator. The primary goal, then, of a lobbyist is to get legislators to introduce or vote for measures favorable to special interests that he or she represents. The fundamental ideology behind lobbying is to provide members of Congress, state houses, and local commissions with the information they need to fully understand the consequences of their legislative decisions to constituents. The right to lobby is protected by the First Amendment of the U.S. Constitution.

To get a sense of lobbying efforts in our nation's capital, we examine excerpts from a report provided by the Center for Responsive Politics, a nonpartisan, nonprofit research group based in Washington, DC. The center reports that in 1998, there were 10,408 registered lobbyists, and total expenditures of the industry were at $1.44 billion. By 2012 the number of lobbyists grew to 12,374, and the total industry expenditures grew to $3.28 billion.[31]

Successful lobbying is often backed up by political clout, which either takes the form of campaign contributions or political pressure from grassroots constituencies. The American Association of Retired Persons (AARP), for example, exerts enormous influence on Capitol Hill through the power of an active membership, even though the organization has no political action committee and its employees make few campaign contributions. Labor unions tend to rely on political action committee and soft money contributions, plus their large memberships, to flex muscle with Congress.

The lobbying industry continues to offer lucrative career opportunities to retiring or defeated members of Congress, as well as prominent congressional staffers and leading executive branch officials. Former lawmakers are especially valuable as lobbyists because they know the process intimately, understand the ins and outs of complex issues they dealt with while serving in Congress, and have personal ties to their former colleagues. In a business where success often depends on having access to decision makers, former members of Congress are more likely to get their telephone calls returned.

Big-name lobbyists can also attract new clients to a firm. Ethics rules that ban former members from lobbying Congress for a year are not difficult to work around. Many former members provide strategic advice to clients, lobby other government agencies, or rely on colleagues in their firms who are not bound by the same restrictions.

Many lawmakers depend on lobbyists as valuable sources of information about complex issues and ideas for legislation. It is not unheard of for lobbyists to draft suggested amendments or bills that sympathetic lawmakers introduce as their own. At the very least, lobbyists are regularly asked for feedback on recommended legislation, sometimes simply to make sure before legislation goes to a vote that the affected parties will not raise any objections.[32]

In the judicial lawmaking process, judges are of course not lobbied in the same fashion as legislators. However, attorneys are in effect lobbyists who have been hired to represent the interest of a party. While the forum and professions involved may be different, the fundamental principle is similar in that the ultimate goal is to influence the decision maker, whether it is a legislator or a judge. The principal method of bringing a party's interest to the attention of the court is though amicus curiae briefs. *Amicus curiae* is a Latin phrase meaning "friend of the court." This legal tenet holds that a party is allowed to provide information (in the form of a legal brief) to a court even though the party is not directly involved in the case at hand.

For example, the National Association of Counsel for Children (NACC) participates in cases of particular importance to the welfare of children by filing *amicus curiae* briefs. In recent years, the NACC has filed briefs in state appellate and supreme courts and in the U.S. Supreme Court. Likewise, the American Civil Liberties Union has been engaged in defense of the Bill of Rights for over 75 years. Many of its efforts have focused on enforcing those portions of the Bill of Rights having to do with administration of the criminal justice system. For example, the ACLU participated as amicus curiae in *Miranda v. Arizona*, 384 U.S. 436 (1966), a U.S. Supreme Court case relegating that a person's right not to be compelled to incriminate himself is essential to the preservation of our accusatorial system of criminal justice. As in 1966, custodial interrogation today remains aimed at inducing a person to confess, and if the Fifth Amendment privilege is to be meaningful, some warning is necessary to ensure that persons subjected to custodial interrogation have in mind their constitutional privilege against self-incrimination.

In general, the effectiveness of interest groups in influencing lawmakers is related to its abilities to finance lobbying efforts. Likewise, when attempting to influence the judicial lawmaking process, it is a reality that interest groups must possess the ability to hire appropriate legal counsel to support court suits. But where money is concerned, perhaps the most publicly criticized spending is that of campaign contributions made to those who are running for office or the bench.

According to Title II of the U.S. Code, the term *contribution* includes:

> any gift, subscription, loan, advance, or deposit of money or anything of value made by any person for the purpose of influencing any election for Federal office; or the payment by any person of compensation for the personal services of another person which are rendered to a political committee without charge for any purpose.[33]

The Federal Election Commission (FEC) is the independent regulatory government agency appointed with directing and applying the federal campaign finance law. The FEC has jurisdiction over the financing of campaigns for the U.S. Senate, the U.S. House, the presidency, and the vice presidency.

Federal campaign finance law covers three broad subjects: public disclosure of funds raised and spent to influence federal elections, the public financing of presidential campaigns, and the restrictions on contributions and expenditures made to influence federal elections.

Source of Funds

There are basically three recognized ways that interest groups provide funding to support campaign efforts of elected officials. They include:

- PACs: Contributions from political action committees
- Individuals: All contributions from individual citizens
- Candidate: Contributions and loans from the candidate to his/her own campaign
- Other: All other revenues collected by the campaign, such as interest from the campaign's bank accounts and loans from outside sources

Political action committee (PAC) is a popular term for a political committee established for the purpose of raising and spending money to elect and defeat candidates. Most PACs represent business, labor, or ideological interests. PACs can give $5,000 to a candidate committee per election (primary, general, or special). They can also give up to $15,000 annually to any national party committee, and $5,000 annually to any other PAC. PACs may receive up to $5,000 from any one individual, PAC, or party committee per calendar year. A PAC must register with the Federal Election Commission (FEC) within 10 days of its formation, providing name and address for the PAC, its treasurer, and any connected organizations. Affiliated PACs are treated as one donor for the purpose of contribution limits.

PACs have been around since 1944, when the Congress of Industrial Organizations (CIO) formed the first one to raise money for the reelection of President Franklin D. Roosevelt. The PAC's money came from voluntary contributions from union members rather than union treasuries, so it did not violate the Smith Connally Act of 1943, which forbade unions from contributing to federal candidates. Although commonly called PACs, federal election law refers to these accounts as "separate segregated funds" because money contributed to a PAC is kept in a bank account separate from the general corporate or union treasury.

PAC contributions and large donations from individuals are the two biggest sources of contributions for most members of Congress. In the 1996 elections, for example, winning U.S. House candidates collected about 39% of their money from PACs, 36% from individual contributions of more than $200, and 19% from small individual contributions. Senators get about 25% of their money from PACs, with large individual contributions accounting for the biggest share of their campaign cash. In 2012, labor PACs alone dispersed $280,429,813 to candidates.[34]

Questions in Review

1. Describe the four role orientations that account for the variety of behavior that a lawmaker may exhibit while performing the duties of legislative office.
2. What are the arguments for and against term limits? What is your personal opinion about term limits? Should there be a federal mandate, or not?
3. What is the main difference between formal and informal rulemaking?
4. What function does the Office of the Federal Register serve?
5. Explain the legal doctrine of stare decisis.
6. Should the lobbying industry be allowed to offer well-paying employment positions to members of Congress and executive branch officials?
7. What is the usefulness of an amicus curiae brief?
8. What is a PAC?
9. In what ways do PAC contributions allow the campaign finance laws to be circumvented?
10. Do you think that there are too many laws in the United States? Provide some reasoning for your response.

Endnotes

1. W. Chambliss & R. Seidman. (1971). *Law, order and power* (p. 503). Reading, MA: Addison-Wesley.

2. B. Sinclair. (1990). Congressional leadership: A review essay and a research agenda. In J.J. Kornacki (Ed.), *Leading Congress*. Washington, DC: Congressional Quarterly Press.

3. Excerpt from John Stuart Mill. (1861). *Representative government*, Chap. 3.

4. Adapted from C.R. Wise. (1991). *The dynamics of legislation: Leadership and policy change in the congressional process*. San Francisco, CA: Jossey-Bass.

5. J.C. Wahylke, H. Eulau, W. Buchanan, & L.C. Ferguson. (1962). *The legislative system: Explorations in legislative behavior*. New York, NY: John Wiley and Sons.

6. J.C. Wahylke, H. Eulau, W. Buchanan, & L.C. Ferguson. (1962). *The legislative system: Explorations in legislative behavior* (p. 247). New York, NY: John Wiley and Sons.

7. J.C. Wahylke, H. Eulau, W. Buchanan, & L.C. Ferguson. (1962). *The legislative system: Explorations in legislative behavior* (p. 247). New York, NY: John Wiley and Sons.

8. J.C. Wahylke, H. Eulau, W. Buchanan, & L.C. Ferguson, (1962). *The legislative system: Explorations in legislative behavior* (p. 248). New York, NY: John Wiley and Sons.

9. J.C. Wahylke, H. Eulau, W. Buchanan, & L.C. Ferguson. (1962). *The legislative system: Explorations in legislative behavior* (p. 248). New York, NY: John Wiley and Sons.

10. *Americans want term limits, end to electoral college.* (2013). Gallup poll. Retrieved June 30, 2013, from http://www.gallup.com/video/160073/americans-term-limits-end-electoral-college.aspx?ref=more

11. *Watkins v. United States*, 354 U.S. 178 (1957), pp. 187–216.

12. *Barenblatt v. United States*, 360 U.S. 109 (1959), pp. 116–129.

13. 5 U.S.C. §§ 551–559, 701–706, 1305, 3105, 3344, 5372, 7521.

14. Section 551 (4) of the Administrative Procedures Act.

15. *Prentis v. Atlantic Coastline Co.*, 221 U.S. 210, 226 (1908).

16. 5 U.S.C. § 554(a).

17. A.T. Sharon & C.B. Pettibone. (1987). Merit selection of federal administrative law judges. *Judicature, 70*(4), 216.

18. W. Robie & M. Morse. (1986). The federal executive branch adjudicator: Alive (and) well outside the Administrative Procedure Act? *Fed. Bar News and J. 33*, 133.

19. 5 U.S.C. § 557(b).

20. See, e.g., *Brock v. L.E. Meyers Co., High Voltage Div.* 818 F.2d 1270, 1277 (6th Cir. 1987).

21. Agency review of administrative law judges' decisions, 66 B.U.L. REV. 1 (1986); ACUS Recommendation 83-3, Agency structure for review of decisions of presiding officers under the Administrative Procedure Act, 1 C.F.R. § 305.83-3 (1988).

22. 44 U.S.C. Sec. 1505.

23. *Presidential proclamation—Veterans Day, 2012.* The White House, Office of the Press Secretary. Retrieved June 30, 2013, from http://www.whitehouse.gov/the-press-office/2012/11/07/presidential-proclamation-veterans-day-2012

24. *Executive order—Preventing and responding to violence against women and girls globally.* The White House, Office of the Press Secretary. Retrieved June 30, 2013, from http://www.whitehouse.gov/the-press-office/2012/08/10/executive-order-preventing-and-responding-violence-against-women-and-gir

25. *Black's Law Dictionary* (6th ed.). (1990). (p. 1406).

26. *State v. Ray*, 130 Wn.2d 673, 677, 926 P.2d 904, 905 (1996).

27. *Keene v. Edie*, 131 Wn.2d 822, 831, 935 P.2d 588, 593 (1997).

28. W. Smith. (1987). Theories of adjudication and the status of stare decisis. In L. Goldstein (Ed.), *Precedent in law* (pp. 81–82). Oxford, England: Clarendon Press.

29. L.C. Marshall. (1989). Let Congress do it: The case for an absolute rule of statutory stare decisis. *Mich. L. Rev., 88,* 177.

30. *Webster's 10th New Collegiate Dictionary.* (1998). Lobby. Springfield, MA: Merriam–Webster.

31. Center for Responsive Politics. (2013). Based on data from the Senate Office of Public Records. Retrieved June 30, 2013, from http://www.opensecrets.org/lobby/index.php

32. A. Shuldiner. (1999). *The bottom line on Washington lobbyists.* Washington, DC: Center for Responsive Politics.

33. Title II, Section 440, of the U.S. Code.

34. Figures taken from the Federal Election Commission.

Dispute Resolution

7

Chapter Objectives

After reading this chapter you should be able to

- Identify the differences between negotiation, arbitration, and mediation
- Explain the steps in dispute resolution
- Discuss the role of arbitration
- Distinguish between various types of alternative dispute resolution (ADR) programs
- Discuss the role of the courts in dispute settlement
- Explain the four general approaches to conflict resolution education for youths

Introduction

Consider the following fact situation: You attend class each class day. You take an active part in class discussions and make As on all your exams, but your final grade for the course is a C. You approach the professor regarding your grade. He states that he does not have time for students who are unhappy with their grades. You tell the professor that you should have gotten an A in the course. He disagrees. A dispute occurs. How is the dispute resolved at your university? What are your options in settling this dispute?

Generally, universities have policies that allow students to complain officially about their grades and to seek redress, i.e., to settle grade disputes. As a general rule, those policies provide several steps that the student should take to resolve his or her complaint. First, the student is generally obligated to discuss the dispute with his or her instructor (negotiation stage). If this discussion does not produce a resolution, the student may present the case to the departmental chair. The chair listens to the student's side and then discusses the dispute with the instructor (mediation stage). If the dispute is not resolved at this point, the student can go to the third stage of the resolution process. At most universities, the departments or schools have standing committees composed of both professors and students to hear students' academic grievances (arbitration stage). If the dispute is not settled at that level, students generally have the right to further appeal the decision to a university-wide committee on academic complaints. It is rare for academic complaints to go beyond this stage. There are a few reported cases, however, where students have resorted to court litigation. In early 2013, a former Lehigh University graduate student's claim of breach of contract and sexual discrimination on the part of the university was rejected by a Pennsylvania judge. The plaintiff was seeking damages in the amount of $1.3 million for lost potential earnings due to a grade that she was issued in a class. That grade essentially made her ineligible to continue in that program.[1]

In this chapter, we examine dispute resolution and its relationship to the law. Dispute resolution is also known as conflict resolution, dispute management, conflict regulation, and dispute processing. For our purposes, we will consider that these terms are interchangeable. That conflicts will arise among members of a complex society is a given fact. Dispute resolution takes many forms. It may result in court-imposed settlements, agreed settlements, informal bargaining, or as the result of alternative dispute resolution (ADR).

Michael Palmer and Simon Roberts contend that disputes are not really settled; they are merely processed or regulated rather than resolved.[2] According to them, third-party intervention through legal or nonlegal means represents the settlement of only the public component of the dispute or conflict and does not alleviate the underlying forces or tensions that created the conflict. Richard Abel contends that the outcome of most conflict resolution is at most only a temporary peace between the parties to the conflict and that the ultimate outcome is more conflicts and disputes.[3] In our grade-dispute scenario discussed at the beginning of this chapter, regardless of the final results, there will probably be feelings of resentment by each of the parties against the other party.

Laura Nader and Harry Todd contend that there are three distinct phases or stages in the disputing process: preconflict or grievance stage, conflict stage, and dispute stage.[4] The preconflict or grievance stage originates when an individual or a group perceives that an unjust situation has developed and considers that there are grounds for resentment or complaint. These grounds may be real or imaginary. The first stage is monadic, since it involves only the one person or party who perceives the injustice. If not resolved at the preconflict stage, the process develops into the conflict stage. At the conflict stage, the aggrieved party communicates his or her resentment or feelings of injustice to the offending party or parties. The conflict stage is dyadic in that it involves the two parties: the offended and the offending parties. If the conflict is not settled at this stage, it progresses to the third stage. At the third stage, the dispute stage, the process is triadic because a third party becomes involved. The third party acts as the settlement agent. Not all three stages are present in every dispute. For example, an aggrieved party may file a lawsuit without confronting the offending party, thereby omitting the second stage. Likewise, at any point in the process, the aggrieved party may discontinue the process or the other party may concede.

Hidden Harmony Myth

According to David Stiebel, when examining dispute resolution, there is the "hidden harmony myth." This myth is based on the common belief that the key to resolving disputes is communications, i.e., "Why don't we talk it out?" or "As long as we are talking, there's hope." Stiebel contends that many of us rely on the myth and accept the assumption that we just need to under-stand each other better. This line of thought assumes that there are no con-flicts, only poor understandings. Unfortunately, in real life, most disputes are based on conflicts of interests, e.g., who owns the property in question or should the employee be fired.[5]

Dispute Categories

Disputes may generally be divided into three important categories: private disputes, public-initiated disputes, and public-defendant disputes. This clas-sification does not include disputes between nations or states. A private dis-pute in one in which there is an absence of any initial participation by public authorities or public intuitions. Two people arguing over the ownership of an animal is an example of a private dispute. Generally, private disputes are processed and managed without the intervention of the government. A pub-lic-initiated dispute is one that occurs when the government seeks to enforce either a conduct norm or attempts to punish someone for violating the norm. The public-defendant dispute is one where the government participates as a defendant in the dispute. For example, an individual challenges the author-ity of the government. Suppose a citizen purchases land with plans to build his or her home on the property. The government denies the permit to build residential property because the land is zoned for commercial use only. The citizen brings court action to require the government to issue the building permit. This is an example of the public-defendant conflict.

Dispute Resolution Methods

As noted previously, disputes are common in all societies. They are also common at all levels, subcultures, etc., within the society. Dispute resolu-tion methods are fairly similar in most societies. The preferred method in each society depends to a large extent on cultural factors and the availability of dispute resolution processes. The two general forms of resolution are (a) by negotiations between the conflicting parties without the intervention of a third party and (b) the adjudicated settlement in which a neutral party decides which of the two parties has the superior claim. In some societies and in some subcultures, direct interpersonal violence is an approved method of resolution. For example, at one time, duels conducted according to specific rules and under a controlled environment were considered as an approved method of resolving certain disputes. Family feuds, such as the feud between the Hatfields of Virginia and the McCoys of Kentucky which started in 1882 and lasted for years, were once used to resolve conflicts between families.

Ridicule and shaming is used in nearly all cultures as a method of pointing out an individual's wrongdoings and to reduce conflict caused by the wrongdoings. In some situations, one or more parties may resort to supernatural agencies. For example, one aggrieved party prays to God for God's intervention to help the other party see the wrongs in his or her actions.

In the colonial towns in New England, the colonists focused on settling disputes through mediation. The colonists had a disdain for the use of legal resolution because this made the disputes public, made people into adversaries, and weakened the community solidarity. The colonists were deeply religious and were bound together in their congregational communities. Their pattern of settling disputes, like other aspects of their lives, was based on their shared commitment to God's word and religious community over individual interests and values. Often, an entire congregation participated in the settlement process. According to Turkel, the pull toward nonlegal dispute settlement was so strong that the colonists used mediation to enforce harmony. When this failed, people who refused to settle their disputes in a spirit of harmony were often forced to leave the community.[6] Turkel uses the example of a dispute that occurred in 1640 in Boston to illustrate his point. In his example, a Mrs. Hibbins had hired a carpenter to do some work on her house. When a dispute arose between her and the carpenter, she proposed that each of them would select a carpenter and that the two selected carpenters would arbitrate the dispute. Mrs. Hibbins then refused to accept the fee set by the two arbitrators. The dispute then went to the First Church of Boston. At the forum of the church, the dispute shifted from the problem of the sum of money due the original carpenter to Mrs. Hibbins's lack of support for community solidarity. The congregation voted to excommunicate her, with the pastor's words:

> I do here, in the name of the whole church and in the name of the Lord Jesus Christ ... pronounce you to be a leprous and unclean person, and I do cast you out and cut you off from the enjoyment of those blessed privileges and ordinance which God hath entrusted his Church withal, which you have abused.

Hierarchy of Types

The process generally moves the dispute resolution through a type of resolution characterized by substantive informal legitimacy to a type characterized by formal legal rationality. The informal and nonlegally rational resolution forms are negotiation and mediation. The formal and legally rational forms are arbitration and litigation.

Negotiation is generally the first step in any dispute resolution. It is conducted by the involved parties or their attorneys. The aim of negotiation is to reach an agreement among the parties without any recommendation or decision by a third party and without adjudication. A negotiated settlement is often predicated on the different resources and power among the parties. For example, you have a dispute with a major corporation. The corporation offers to settle the dispute for less than you feel is just. You may take the settlement not because it is fair, but because you do not have the resources to press the dispute to litigation.

Mediation is like negotiation in that it does not rely on legal rationality to resolve disputes. Mediation attempts to secure an agreement among the conflicting parties. The mediator does not have the power to make and impose decisions on either party. In arbitration, both parties argue their case before a third party. The third party has the power to make a decision. There are two different types of arbitration: one where the parties voluntarily agree to arbitrate future disputes before an arbitration, and the other where the parties agree after a dispute arises to submit to arbitration. In addition, arbitration may either be binding or nonbinding on the parties. When the arbitration is nonbinding, either party may refuse to accept the decision and pursue other dispute resolution methods. Mediation and arbitration are discussed later in this chapter. In examining the types of dispute resolution processes available, it is important to remember that these are analytic distinctions to allow us to see the differences among them. In actual practice, however, the types often blend together, and hybrid processes are the result.

Litigation as a Means of Resolving Disputes

Karl Llewellyn once stated:

> What ... is this law business about? It is about the fact that our society is honeycombed with disputes. Disputes actual and potential, disputes to be settled and disputes to be prevented; both appealing to the law, both making up the business of law.[7]

204 Law and Society: An Introduction

At this point, it should be noted that litigation may only resolve those disputes that have been translated into a legal dispute. To be a legal dispute, the conflict must involve legal rights or property. For example, your next-door neighbor does not like you and has a long-standing grudge against you. His failure to talk to you or to be friendly may be a conflict, but it is not a legal dispute. While the criminal justice system is the most familiar example of law as a means of social control, civil law is generally considered as the vehicle to resolve disputes or conflicts. We are supposed to be a litigious society, i.e., we take our disputes to the courts for resolution. The courts, however, play the role of decision maker in only a small percentage of grievances. According to Lawrence Friedman, only about a third of 1% of all grievances go the whole route.[8] For Friedman, the "real" law of contracts, or landlord-tenant disputes, or auto accidents is not to be learned simply by studying trials and cases. The real law of auto accidents is the law of insurance adjustors and lawyers' negotiations.

The resolution of disputes via the legal system results in the resolution of a specific dispute, but not in the amelioration of broader issues that produced the conflict. In addition, a legal resolution generally does not reduce the tension or antagonism between the parties involved in the dispute.

Many dispute resolution methods are open only to specific groups, e.g., employees and employers with arbitration agreements and college students who have the right to appeal their grades. In theory, the courts are available to all members of society. If there is a wrong that results in a legally recognized injury or loss of property, there should be legal redress available to the injured party.

Donald Black looked at the question of who uses the courts to resolve disputes. According to him, a person is least likely to sue a close kinsman, then a friend, and acquaintance, a neighbor, a fellow townsman, and so on, the likelihood increasing with the relational distance until his world ends. He uses the Arusha tribe of Tanzania as an example. He wrote that disputes between members of the same family line or village are almost always resolved by procedures not involving the government. Only the more distant were likely to go to law.[9] In traditional Japan, fellow members of the village avoid court when the dispute is between members of the same village, but with members of different villages they are more likely to go to court.

Alternative Dispute Resolution

Abraham Lincoln once offered the following piece of advice to law students:

> Discourage litigation. Persuade your neighbors to compromise whenever you can. Point out that how the nominal winner is often the loser–in fees, expenses, and waste of time.[10]

The late Chief Justice Warren Burger once stated: "Our litigation system is too costly, too painful, too inefficient for a truly civilized people."

In recent years, the field of alternative dispute resolution (ADR) has become a growth industry. Now, disputes that in previous years were destined for jury trials or direct settlement negotiations on the day of trial are being resolved through alternative dispute procedures such as mediation, moderated settlement conference, or arbitration. The movement toward ADR is caused by the overcrowded court dockets with long delays in hearing civil cases; very high expenditures in the form of attorney's fees, court costs, and discovery; no assurance of winning in the end or recouping the costs; further estranged relations with the opposing party with whom an ongoing relationship may continue to exist, such as a former spouse; and most important, to avoid the stress, trauma, and sagging spirits of litigation.[11]

Often the settlement will be the result of two or more of those settlement methods. For example, even those disputes settled by agreement of the parties involved do not occur in a vacuum. As noted by Robert Mnookin and Lewis Kornhauser:

> Divorcing parents do not bargain over the division of family wealth and custodial prerogatives in a vacuum; they bargain in the shadow of the law. The legal rules governing alimony, child support, marital property, and custody give each parent certain claims based on what each would get if the case went to trial. In other words, the outcome that the law will impose if no agreement is reached gives each parent certain bargaining chips—an endowment of sorts.[12]

Former Supreme Court Justice Sandra Day O'Connor once stated: "The courts of this country should not be the places where the resolution of disputes begin. They should be the place where the disputes end—after alternative methods of resolving disputes have been considered and tried."[13] Proponents of ADR contend that it relieves the burden on the courts and provides swift justice. Opponents contend that it favors the wealthy; they still have access to the courts, whereas the poor are forced into lesser forums. Another criticism of ADR is that because it is somewhat of an ad hoc system of justice, the resolution outcome may not follow legal norms.

Court-Annexed Arbitration

Every state has adopted some form of ADR. One current trend in ADR is court-annexed arbitration. While courts have had the inherent power to refer cases to arbitration for centuries, it is only recently that it has been used extensively. In many states, the judges have statutory authority to require the parties to submit to nonbinding arbitration. In the typical state statute, the court selects the arbitrator. The arbitrator has the power to conduct a hearing, to administer oaths, and to issue subpoenas. Once the arbitrator has issued an opinion, it is final and binding on all parties unless one of the parties files a motion within 30 days for a trial.

Mediation

Mediation is defined as an attempt to bring about a peaceful settlement or compromise between the disputants through the objective intervention of a neutral party.[14] Mediation involves the use of a neutral third party in a facilitated settlement negotiation. The mediator focuses on the mutual interests of the parties in avoiding a lengthy and costly trial and the risks associated with trials. By definition, this does not obligate the mediator to take a position on the merits of either party's case. During the mediation process, the mediator acts as though each party has a legitimate position, without excessively focusing on the arguments concerning legitimacy.

One of the most famous mediations occurred during the Russo-Japanese War, when President Theodore Roosevelt mediated the dispute between Russia and Japan. In September 1905, at Portsmouth, New Hampshire, as the direct result of Roosevelt's mediation, the Treaty of Portsmouth was signed by Japan and Russia. The disastrous outcome of the war for Russia is considered as one of the causes of the Russian Revolution of 1905. The treaty also established Japan as the first non-European and non-American imperialist nation.[15]

Arbitration

Arbitration is an informally conducted adversary proceedings in which a dispute of law or fact is determined by a neutral arbitrator or panel of arbitrators who issue an award. In binding arbitration, the award can be recorded as a court judgment. Arbitration is generally less time consuming, less expensive, and more informal than a trial. Arbitration may be either binding or nonbinding. In nonbinding arbitration, neither party is required to accept the arbitrator's decision. In binding arbitration—unless the arbitrator violates a law, regulation, or terms of the arbitration agreement—the parties are bound by the arbitrator's decision.

Arbitration was used in the 13th century to settle mercantile disputes in Europe. In the Tudor period in England, mercantile disputes were resolved by the privy council, which consisted of merchant arbitrators. In 1697, the first English arbitration law was established. In 1768, the New York Chamber of Commerce was founded, with one of its stated purposes being the arbitration of disputes among its members. In many countries, arbitration may be compelled by the government as a method of settling disputes between employers and employees. New Zealand has had the statutory authority to compel arbitration involving such disputes since 1904, Canada since 1907, and Italy since 1926. In the United States, the federal government has had the authority to intervene in the case of labor strikes affecting the public welfare under certain provisions of the Taft-Hartley Act of 1947.

At one time, the courts were hostile to the use of arbitration, and any agreements to arbitrate were narrowly interpreted by the courts. That attitude has significantly changed, and the hostility is now a matter of history. In the 1991 amendment to the Civil Rights Act of 1964, Congress created new employee rights and, at the same time, it expressly recognized and encouraged the use of arbitration as a method of determining those rights. That same year, the U.S. Supreme Court decided the *Gilmer v. Interstate/Johnson Lane Corp.* case.[16]

The Gilmer case is credited with beginning the entire practice of using final and binding arbitration for the resolution of employment disputes that are not covered by collective bargaining agreements between employers and unions. The Court held that employers could require employees as a condition of employment to accept compulsory arbitration under the Federal Arbitration Act. The Court said that its intention was to "reverse the long-standing judicial hostility to arbitration agreements ... and to place arbitration agreements on the same footing as other contracts." In 1995, a state court citing the Gilmer case reiterated the policy of state and federal courts of favoring the use of arbitration. The state court stated that the federal policy in favor of enforcing arbitration agreements is so compelling that a court should not deny arbitration "unless it can be said with positive assurance that an arbitration clause is not susceptible of an interpretation which would cover the dispute at issue."[17]

The basis for most arbitration processes involving federal issues is the Federal Arbitration Act (FAA) of 1925.[18] The federal authority to enact the FAA is based on the commerce clause of the federal Constitution. The U.S. Supreme Court in *United States v. Darbury Lumber Co.*[19] held that the commerce clause extended even to intrastate activities that "affect" interstate commerce, and that Congress has the power to make regulations involving intrastate commerce as a means to regulate interstate commerce. For example, the rental of a hotel room in Austin, Texas, to a resident of Texas is an intrastate matter that affects interstate commerce and thus is subject to the FAA. This is because it is a part of the "stream of commerce."

The FAA has been well received by the courts and interpreted expansively by them to support the enforcement of agreements for the arbitration of disputes. In recent years, the U.S. Supreme Court has delivered a string of decisions that favor the use of arbitration in both domestic and international disputes. Every American state has adopted a comprehensive arbitration statute. Most states have adopted the Uniform Arbitration Act (UAA), which is a model statute promulgated by the National Conference of Commissioners on Uniform State Laws. The drafters of the UAA partially tracked the FAA, and most of the provisions are similar. Since the basis for both federal and state arbitration law is statutory, the provisions of the applicable statute must always be considered. In addition, since many arbitration statutes are very general in nature, there remains a common law of arbitration that is based on relevant case law.

Arbitration is based on contract law. The parties have either agreed to settle a present dispute by the use of arbitration or agreed to settle future disputes by resort to arbitration rather than judicial proceedings. For example, the 1925 House of Representative Report on the FAA states:

> Arbitration agreements are purely a matter of contract, and the effect of the bill [FAA] is simply to make the contracting party live up to his agreement. He can no longer refuse to perform his contract when it becomes disadvantageous. An arbitration agreement is placed upon the same footing as other contracts. It is particularly appropriate that this action should be taken at this time when there is so much agitation against the costliness and delays of litigation.

If there is a direct conflict between the FAA and the state law on arbitration and the transaction involves or affects interstate commerce, the FAA preempts the state law, i.e., the issue is decided based on federal law. If the transaction does not involve or affect interstate commerce, then the state law applies. For example, in *Mamlin v. Texas*,[20] there was an employment contract between a New York manufacturer and a Texas sales representative. The contract provided that all disputes under the contract would be settled "under the law of New York," and arbitration was required. The salesman brought suit in a Texas court. The manufacturer sought to compel arbitration of the dispute. At that time, compulsory arbitration was contrary to Texas public policy. The court held that the FAA applied to the dispute, since interstate commerce was involved, and that the FAA permitted the parties to agree that the law of the specified state would govern the contract. Accordingly, the salesman was required to submit to arbitration, and the law of New York was used to settle the dispute.

Arbitration is not without its critics. Lawyers for consumers charge that the details of such contracts—used in a wide variety of transactions, from credit cards to video-rental agreements—are often buried in the contract's small print and deprive buyers of their right to resolve disputes in court. Businesses tend to favor binding arbitration agreements because they can resolve cases quickly and without the uncertainty and expense often involved in jury trials.[21]

EASTERN ASSOCIATED COAL CO. V. UNITED MINE WORKERS

(decided November 27, 2000)

James Smith was a truck driver for Eastern Associated Coal Company and a member of the United Mine Workers labor union. Twice he failed the drug test. Eastern started the process to terminate his employment. The company contended that it had a duty under U.S. Transportation Department regulations to fire him. The union objected. The labor contract between the company and the union contained a binding arbitration agreement. The issue was referred to binding arbitration. The arbitrator held that there was not just cause to fire him. The company appealed the decision of the arbitrator, contending that as a matter of public policy it had a duty to fire a truck driver who had twice tested positive for drug use. U.S. Supreme Court Justice Stephen Breyer, writing the unanimous opinion, said that the arbitrator's rejection of the public duty argument "violates no specific provision of any law or regulation" and upheld the arbitrator's decision.

Query: If you were counsel for the company, would you advise the company to continue to allow the driver to drive company trucks? If he was involved in a fatal accident, would the company be liable for allowing a known drug user to drive one of its units?

Selecting an Arbitrator

The selection of an arbitrator is a crucial decision because of the almost complete finality of the arbitrator's decisions in binding arbitration. The arbitrator generally decides both questions of law and fact and is not typically restricted by the traditional rules of evidence. As noted in *Mantle v. Upper Deck Co.*:[22]

> The standard of review for arbitration awards has been described as "among the narrowest known to the law." The Court may not vacate (reverse) the arbitrator's award based on mere errors in interpretation or application of the law, or mistakes in fact-finding.

Unless required by the arbitration agreement, the arbitrator is usually not required to write a detailed opinion or to support any conclusions with particular facts or law. Accordingly, in most cases, the parties are "stuck" with the arbitrator's decision.

Arbitration panels typically involve either one or three arbitrators. Occasionally there are as many as five. The American Arbitration Association (AAA) generally recommends that only one arbitrator be appointed except in the larger and more complex cases, where panels of three are recommended. The National Association for Dispute Resolution (NADR) rules provide for panels of three arbitrators in all cases.

Often the arbitration agreement will designate a specific arbitrator or require the parties to adhere to a specific process in arbitration selection. Some arbitration agreements provide for the selection of arbitrators according to the rules of the AAA or NADR. Generally in these cases, when a dispute arises and the arbitration clause is invoked, the association will submit a list of possible arbitrators. Each party may strike a specified number of arbitrators off the list. One of the arbitrators remaining is then selected by the association to hear the dispute.

The general qualifications of an arbitrator include:

- Free of bias for or against any of the parties
- Experience within the field or with the ability to grasp any specialized knowledge needed
- Person of integrity and honesty
- Good judgment, analytical ability, and malleability

Conflict Resolution and Delinquency

Will teaching conflict resolution to juveniles reduce delinquency? According to Donni LeBoeuf and Robin V. Delaney-Shabazz, delinquency and youth violence are symptoms of a juvenile's inability to handle conflict constructively.[23] They contend that by teaching young people how to manage conflict, i.e., education in conflict resolution, we can reduce juvenile violence in juvenile facilities, schools, and communities. They also believe that such education can combat chronic truancy. Education in conflict resolution teaches young people the skills needed to engage in creative problem solving. Individuals learn to identify their interests, express their views, and seek mutually acceptable solutions.

There are four general approaches to conflict resolution education for the youths: process curriculum, peer mediation, peaceable classroom, and peaceable school. Most conflict resolution education programs combine elements from these approaches. The processes of conflict resolution are taught as a distinct lesson or course using the *process curriculum* approach, whereby young people are taught to practice principled negotiation as a means of goal achievement. This approach is based on the concept that youths who have practice in negotiations are more successful in discussing disputes and avoiding fights with their peers.

The *peer mediation* approach recognizes the importance of directly involving youth in the mediation process. Accordingly, trained youth mediators work with their peers to find resolutions to conflicts. For example, in a

Las Vegas, Nevada, youth program, peer mediators successfully resolved 86% of the conflicts they mediated, and in the schools covered by the program, there were fewer conflicts and physical fights on the school grounds.

The *peaceable classroom* and *peaceable school* approaches are whole-classroom or school approaches that includes teaching students the foundational abilities, principles, and one or more of the three problem-solving processes of conflict resolution. Conflict resolution education is incorporated into the core subjects of the curriculum and into classroom management strategies. The peaceable school approach is built on peaceable classroom by integrating conflict resolution into the management of the institution, with every member—from crossing guard to classroom teacher—learning and using conflict resolution. Most conflict resolution and peer mediation programs (about 10,000 in all) have been implemented in the elementary, middle, and high schools. There are similar programs in many of our juvenile correctional institutions. In addition, there are over 600 community mediation centers, which are typically based in nonprofit community-based agencies.

International Arbitration and Mediation

International arbitration, i.e., arbitration between two sovereign nations may be a method to prevent wars or to settle wars. As noted by R. Roak Bishop and James D. McCarthy, arbitration is indisputably the king of international dispute resolution.[24] Bishop and McCarthy see at least three reasons for their statement. First, international arbitration awards are easily enforced by treaty obligation through the New York Convention, to which about 100 nations, including the United States, are parties. They also note that the United States is not a party to any treaties that concern the enforcement of a court judgment. Second, arbitration provides a neutral forum that is as free as possible from local bias or prejudice that companies may encounter in an opposing party's national courts. And, finally, arbitration allows for a decision by experts in the subject matter of the dispute and for otherwise tailoring the dispute resolution needs of the parties.

In 1856, the Declaration of Paris expressed the hope that the signatories would use mediation to settle their disputes. At the Second Hague Conference in 1907, the right of friendly powers to offer mediation was recognized. The covenant of the League of Nations stated that the members should submit disputes to mediation. The charter of the United Nations requires its members to submit their disputes to mediation when recommended by the security council. As noted earlier, President Roosevelt was successful as a mediator in the Russo-Japanese War of 1907. In 1966, the Soviet Union mediated the border clashes between India and China. The use of mediation and arbitration is an attempt to prevent disputes from becoming armed conflicts.

Questions in Review

1. What are the differences between negotiation, arbitration, and mediation?
2. What are the steps in dispute resolution?
3. Explain the "hidden harmony myth."
4. Why do only a few disputes go the "whole route"?
5. Why does Friedman claim that the real law of auto accidents is the law of insurance adjusters and lawyers' negotiations?
6. Why is arbitration based on contract law?
7. Explain the various types of ADR programs.
8. What is meant by "court-annexed" arbitration?
9. How are arbitrators generally selected?
10. What are the four general approaches to conflict resolution education for youths?

Endnotes

1. N. Desantis. (2013, February 14). Judge rejects former Lehigh U. student's big lawsuit over grade. *The Chronicle of Higher Education.* Retrieved July 1, 2013, from http://chronicle.com/blogs/ticker/jp/judge-rejects-former-lehigh-u-students-big-lawsuit-over-grade
2. M. Palmer & S. Roberts. (1998). *Dispute processes: ADR and the primary forms of decision making.* London, England: Butterworths.
3. R. Abel. (1973). A comparative theory of dispute intervention in society. *Law & Society Reader, 8*(2), 223.
4. L. Nader, Jr., & H.F. Todd, Jr. (Eds.). (1978). Introduction. In *The disputing process: Law in ten societies* (pp. 14–15). New York, NY: Columbia University Press.
5. D. Stiebel. (1997, May 5). Dispute resolution, *Texas Lawyer.*
6. G. Turkel. (1996). *Law and society: Critical approaches* (p. 38). Boston, MA: Allyn & Bacon.
7. K. Llewellyn. (1960). *The bramble bush* (Reprint, pp. 2–3). Dobbs Ferry, NY: Oceana.
8. L.M. Friedman. (1998). *American law: An introduction* (Rev. ed., p. 91). New York, NY: Norton.
9. D. Black. (1976). *Behavior of law* (p. 43). New York, NY: Academic Press.
10. E.J. Kemp. (1965). *Abraham Lincoln's philosophy of common sense,* Vol. 1 (p. 346). New York, NY: New York Academy of Sciences.
11. J.V. Calvi & S. Coleman. (2000). *American law and legal systems* (4th ed., p. 79). Englewood Cliffs, NJ: Prentice-Hall.
12. R.H. Mnookin & L. Kornhauser. (1979). Beginning in the shadow of the law: The case of divorce. *Yale Law Journal, 88,* 950.

13. J. Roehl & L. Ray. (1987, July). Toward the multi-door courthouse: Dispute reso-
    lution intake and referral. *NIJ Reports SNI, 198,* 2.
14. *American Heritage Dictionary* (4th ed.). (2000).
15. *Columbia Encyclopedia* (6th ed.). (2000).
16. 111 S.Ct. 1647 (1991).
17. *Prudential Securities v. Marshall,* 909 S.W. 2d. 896 (Tex.1995).
18. 9 U.S. Code 1 et. seq.
19. 312 U.S. 100 (1941).
20. 490 S.W. 634 (Tex. Civ. App.–Dallas, 1973).
21. *Wall Street Journal.* (2000, November 29). p. B13.
22. 956 F. Supp. 719, 726 (N.D. Tex. 1997).
23. OJJDP. (1997, March). Fact sheet #55.
24. Mediation special report. (1998, June 29). *Texas Lawyer, 1998,* 2.

Social Change and Law 8

Chapter Objectives

After reading this chapter you should be able to

- Identify organizations that are important to social change in America
- Explain how the 1964 Civil Rights Act has played a role in popular culture in America
- Discuss the role that court decisions have on impacting social change

Introduction

Social change and law reflect the constant interaction between behavior and regulation. Social change refers to reshaping the ways in which people in a society relate to each other with respect to education, employment, religion, and other basic human interaction activities. Law by its very definition presupposes rules made by government to regulate the behavior of people. Thus, the general conception of social change and law is that a dual relationship exists in which the changing social environment causes a response from legislators and judges, and legal changes promote social change.

In this chapter we examine the interplay between social change and law from several views. After a brief discussion of the nature of social change and the law, we examine the unique capacity of the courts to serve as a mechanism for social change. This viewpoint is illustrated in the U.S. Supreme Court case, *Brown v. Board of Education*. Next, we review a list of characteristics found in court decisions that seem to have had more of an impact on social change. We conclude the first part of the chapter by discussing the legitimacy of the law to create social change, the influence of law on public opinion, and the limitations of law to create social change. In the concluding portion of the chapter we discuss the impact of social change on the law by illustrating five social movements that profoundly changed the law in the latter half of the 20h and beginning of the 21st centuries. These include the civil rights movement, the antiwar movement, the women's movement, and the gay rights movement.

Nature of Social Change and Law

There are various conceptions of what constitutes social change. A sound-bite definition might include "the effect of citizen protests" or "the engagement of popular culture." In the broadest sense, social change involves large numbers of people (society) who become engaged in a specific behavior that differs from the usual (change). This definition suggests that social change is a normal and continuous process that occurs when people are faced with unaccustomed situations to which they must respond.

Social change is sometimes an alteration of social life that occurs on a monumental basis. In such cases, social movements (e.g., civil rights) may provide the mechanics for social change. Social life can also be altered not so much by a change in ideology that stimulates action but rather by such things as technological advances (e.g., computers). Lastly, social change may be more a reflection of changes in individual beliefs and attitudes (e.g., aspirations). Thus, social change occurs in diverse ways and at various levels of social life.

Social change may contradict certain fundamental values of people. Consequently, people may accept those changes that are beneficial to them but resist or reject changes that are viewed as nonbeneficial. Law then becomes an essential means to compel such people to engage in long-term support of social change. In this context, law is socially relevant in that change is not simply for the benefit of the individuals themselves, but for some larger purpose such as the development of an entire society.

JEREMY BENTHAM (1748–1832)

English philosopher and social reformer, most noted for theorizing that criminal law had its theoretical basis in utilitarianism. Bentham believed that all actions are right and good when they promote the happiness of the greatest number. He held that laws should be socially useful and not merely reflect the status quo; that people inevitably pursue pleasure and avoid pain; and that the function of law is to award punishment and reward.

Courts as Mechanism for Social Change

When social change is needed but there is little incentive to change, courts have the unique capacity to act where other institutions are politically unwilling or structurally unable to proceed. Former U. S. Supreme Court Justice William J. Brennan opined, "Insulated as they are from political pressures, and charged with the duty of enforcing the Constitution, courts are in the strongest position to insist that unconstitutional conditions be remedied, even at significant financial cost."[1] Moreover, court decisions do not adversely affect the court's ongoing relations with elected officials, interest groups, financial backers, and the like, whose cooperation is required for getting work done, for the simple reason that courts are not structured to need or maintain such ongoing relations. Unlike bureaucracies and large institutions, the parties they deal with vary from case to case.[2]

The role of courts as a mechanism for social change is becoming more obvious in today's society. It is universally understood that courts provide the structural framework in which social change might be possible and can be regulated. And, if asked which court has the greatest capacity to effect social change, undoubtedly most people would reply that the U.S. Supreme Court is most influential. The reason for this notoriety is that the decisions of the U.S. Supreme Court have far-reaching effects by making a national issue out of a local issue.

While there are several U.S. Supreme Court decisions to illustrate this idea, some of the more socially meaningful cases in American history deal with civil rights. The most famous case in which the right to education gave impetus to the civil rights movement of the 1950s and 1960s and hastened the end of segregation in all public facilities was *Brown v. Board of Education.*

In the early 1950s, racial segregation in public schools was the norm across America. Southern schools were segregated under *de jure* segregation; laws specifically prohibited integration. Most Northern schools were segregated too, under *de facto* segregation. For example, 17 states were still segregating their schools; 4 states gave the option of segregation to the school districts; 11 states had no specific laws regarding segregation; and 16 states flatly prohibited it. Segregation existed because, for the most part, segregated neighborhoods provided the students for the local schools and because school districts were sometimes deliberately split up to ensure segregation.[3]

In the fall of 1950, members of the Topeka, Kansas, Chapter of the NAACP (National Association for the Advancement of Colored People) agreed to legally challenge the "separate but equal" doctrine governing public education. Key figures included the chapter president, McKinley Burnett; attorneys Charles Scott, John Scott, Charles Bledsoe, and Elisha Scott; and

NAACP chapter secretary Lucinda Todd. Likewise, their plan involved enlisting the support of fellow NAACP members and personal friends as plaintiffs in what would be a class action suit. A group of 13 parents agreed to participate on behalf of 20 of their children. Each plaintiff was to watch the paper for enrollment dates and take their child to the elementary school for white children that was nearest to their home. Once they attempted enrollment and were denied, they were to report back to the NAACP.

One of the parents, Oliver Brown, was assigned as lead plaintiff, principally because he was the only man among the plaintiffs. His daughter, third-grader Linda Brown, had to walk one mile through a railroad switchyard to get to Monroe elementary school (a school for black children), even though Sumner elementary school (a school for white children) was only a few blocks away. Linda's father had tried to enroll her in the white elementary school, but the principal of the school refused.

On February 28, 1951, the NAACP filed their case as Oliver L. Brown et al. vs. The Board of Education of Topeka (KS). The U.S. District Court for the District of Kansas heard Brown's case on June 25–26, 1951. At the trial, the NAACP argued that segregated schools sent the message to black children that they were inferior to whites; therefore, the schools were inherently unequal. One of the expert witnesses, Dr. Hugh W. Speer, testified that

> if the colored children are denied the experience in school of associating with white children, who represent 90 percent of our national society in which these colored children must live, then the colored child's curriculum is being greatly curtailed. The Topeka curriculum or any school curriculum cannot be equal under segregation.[4]

The board of education's defense was that segregated schools were not necessarily harmful to black children. They argued that the African-American schools were equal in facilities and that teachers were quite competent. The board also argued that, because segregation in Topeka and elsewhere pervaded many other aspects of life, segregated schools simply prepared black children for the segregation they would face during adulthood. The request for an injunction put the court in a difficult decision. On the one hand, the judges agreed with the expert witnesses. In their decision, they wrote, "Segregation of white and colored children in public schools has a detrimental effect upon the colored children....A sense of inferiority affects the motivation of a child to learn."

On the other hand, the precedent of a U.S. Supreme Court case, *Plessy v. Ferguson*, allowed "separate but equal" school systems for blacks and whites, and no Supreme Court ruling had yet overturned *Plessy*. Because of this precedent, the court felt compelled to rule in favor of the board of education.

The NAACP appealed their case to the U.S. Supreme Court on October 1, 1951, and it was combined with other cases that challenged school segregation in Delaware, the District of Columbia, South Carolina, and Virginia. The main issue before the court was focused on whether or not denying education in a specific school simply due to race had violated the Fourteenth Amendment. The Fourteenth Amendment states, in summary, that no person, who is a citizen of the United States, should be denied equal protections under the law or the right to life, liberty, or property. What had to be decided was whether segregation fell under the idea of equal protections.

On May 17, 1954, Chief Justice Earl Warren announced the decision of the unanimous Supreme Court:

> We come then to the question presented: Does segregation of children in public schools solely on the basis of race, even though the physical facilities and other "tangible" factors may be equal, deprive the children of the minority group of equal educational opportunities? We believe that it does ... We conclude that in the field of public education the doctrine of "separate but equal" has no place. Separate educational facilities are inherently unequal. Therefore, we hold that the plaintiffs and others similarly situated for whom the actions have been brought are, by reason of the segregation complained of, deprived of the equal protection of the laws guaranteed by the Fourteenth Amendment.[5]

In effect, the U.S. Supreme Court struck down the "separate but equal" doctrine of *Plessy* for public education, ruled in favor of the plaintiffs, and required the desegregation of schools across America.

This public declaration against segregation in education was only the first step in making the U.S. school system more equal. One year later, the U.S. Supreme Court created procedures under which school boards would desegregate their schools "with all deliberate speed." This decision, although spoken easily, was not implemented easily. School systems that had been segregated since they had begun resisted change. In the most highly publicized and best-remembered confrontation over the implementation of *Brown*, President Eisenhower ordered National Guard troops to help nine black students attend the formerly all-white Central High School in Little Rock, Arkansas. Six years later, state officials were still fighting this ruling. Courts had to order and enforce the segregation ruling time and time again, trying to uphold their decision. In fact, Linda Brown (Thompson) even went to court again in 1979 to sue Topeka for allowing their schools to remain segregated. As a result, attorneys petitioned the federal court to reopen the original *Brown* case to determine if Topeka Public Schools had in fact ever complied with the Court's 1954 ruling.

The case became commonly known as "Brown III." Attorneys Richard Jones, Joseph Johnson, and Charles Scott, Jr. (son of one of the attorneys in the original case) in association with Chris Hansen from the ACLU (American Civil Liberties Union) in New York filed the case, and subsequently the Topeka Public Schools were found to be out of compliance. After several appeals, the U.S. Supreme Court denied Topeka Public Schools' petition to once again hear the *Brown* case. As a result, the school was directed to develop plans for compliance and built several elementary schools to ensure a racially balanced school system. Consequently, in 1999, a federal district court judge ended the court supervision of Topeka Public Schools' desegregation plan and effectively closed the revived *Brown v. Board of Education* case.

TIMELINE OF *BROWN V. TOPEKA BOARD OF EDUCATION*

1896. *Plessy v. Ferguson* establishes the "separate but equal" doctrine, which concluded that segregation does not conflict with the Fourteenth Amendment as long as separate facilities for blacks were "equal" to those of whites.

1951. Attorneys filed court action on behalf of the Rev. Oliver Brown and other black parents in the U.S. District Court in Topeka, Kansas. Rev. Brown's daughter, Linda, wanted to attend Sumner Elementary School, an all-white school, only a few blocks from her home. Instead, the 9-year-old was required to attend Monroe Elementary School, an all-black school, which was 20 blocks from her home. The court, following *Plessy v. Ferguson*, ruled schools attended by black children in Topeka were equal in all respects to those attended by white children. The case was appealed.

1954. The U.S. Supreme Court, in a unanimous opinion written by Chief Justice Earl Warren, ruled that "separate educational facilities are inherently unequal," and the "separate but equal" doctrine had "no place" in public education.

1955. The U.S. Supreme Court's order required the dismantlement "with all deliberate speed" of the separate school systems for black children in the suit, and the case was remanded back to the U.S. district court for implementation.

1955. The district court concluded desegregation had not been accomplished in the Topeka schools, but a good-faith effort had been made. The plan adopted by the Topeka Board of Education was approved as a good-faith beginning to complete desegregation.

1979. Attorney Rich Jones represents Linda Thompson (nee Brown) in the resurrected version of Brown, claiming that the Topeka Unified School District 510 had not followed through on desegregation.

1987. The U.S. district court judge agrees with the school district that it could not control where people live in a neighborhood school system. He noted: "There was no illegal, intentional, systematic or residual separation of races" in Topeka Public Schools. The decision was appealed to the 10th U.S. Circuit Court of Appeals in Denver.

1989. A three-judge panel of the 10th Circuit Court reversed on a 2 to 1 vote, holding that the vestiges of segregation remained with respect to student and staff assignment.

1990. The school district sought review of the court of appeals decision in the U.S. Supreme Court.

1992. The Supreme Court ordered the 10th Circuit to reconsider its decision based on two other recently decided desegregation cases in DeKalb County, Georgia, and Oklahoma City schools.

1993. The school district requested the U.S. Supreme Court to review the case. The U.S. Supreme Court declined.

1994. The district court judge approved the district's desegregation plan, which included geographical boundary changes, a transfer program to enhance racial balance at the receiving school, and the construction of three new schools.

1995. The district court awarded more than $500,000 to plaintiff's attorneys for costs associated with nearly 15 years of litigation. Taxpayers in Topeka, Kansas, approve a bond issue to fund three new elementary schools, two of them magnet schools. The $19.5-million bond issue passes by a margin of more than 2 to 1.

1996. Topeka's three new schools open. Enrollment counts show that integration plans are successful, thereby meeting court standards of racial balance.

1999. Federal district court judge ends court supervision of Topeka Public Schools' desegregation plan and effectively closes the revived Brown v. Board of Education case.

Magnitude of Court Decisions

Court decisions may have a differential effect on social change depending on certain related characteristics. Decisions may have more of a social change impact if:

- The decision clearly and unambiguously delineates the rights and obligations of all persons whose behavior is subject to change as a result of the decision.
- The court decision is self-executing, rather than one that requires an increasing number of other persons to get involved in its implementation.
- The court decision is perceived as authoritative by those at whom it is directed.
- Compliance with the court decision is not dependent on the transfer or reallocation of resources by those opposed to the decision.
- The court provides for the application of sanctions for noncompliance.

Conversely, courts often lend support to social change not so much by executing court decisions, but rather by their inaction. This is particularly true when an appellate court refuses to hear a case, thereby upholding a decision of the lower court. Such inaction favors change by refusing to decide a case in which a lower court decision has gone against forces seeking to preserve the status quo. Similarly, the U.S. Supreme Court makes rulings in which it finds that individual states should be responsible for deciding the magnitude of social change for its citizens. Consider, for example, the attempts of Dr. Jack Kevorkian to provoke the U.S. Supreme Court to decide the issue of euthanasia.

In April 1995, the U.S. Supreme Court rejected Dr. Kevorkian's claim that the Constitution permits doctor-assisted suicides. The justices refused without comment to hear Kevorkian's appeal of a 1994 Michigan Supreme Court ruling that the Constitution contains no right to assist another person's suicide. Kevorkian felt strongly that assisted suicide by medically qualified persons should be an appropriate alternative to life for persons who suffered from intolerable pain and debilitating illness. He vowed to continue to help terminal patients kill themselves.

In September 1998, Kevorkian videotaped the killing of Thomas Youk, a Detroit man who suffered from Lou Gehrig's disease. The homemade tape, which showed Kevorkian administering a lethal injection of potassium chloride, was aired in November 1998 for a national audience by CBS on the popular television show *60 Minutes*. During the show, Kevorkian informed reporter Mike Wallace that he wanted to be charged to force law enforcement authorities to try him again in court and to legally resolve the emotional issue of euthanasia. CBS agreed to turn over the videotape to Michigan prosecutors, and Kevorkian was arrested and charged with first-degree murder.

It took the jury of seven women and five men approximately 13 hours to reach a unanimous guilty verdict. Reportedly, the jurors spent most of their time deliberating not between guilt or innocence, but whether to find Kevorkian guilty of first- or second-degree murder. Kevorkian was convicted of second-degree murder and served his prison sentence until he was paroled for good behavior on June 1, 2007. He served a little over 8 years in prison. Kevorkian died of natural causes in 2011.[6]

Legitimacy of Law to Create Social Change

While social change may be initiated by a number of means, there is a general willingness of people in society to accept law as the legitimate means of creating social change. One reason for this affirmation is that law is a rational approach to alter a specific behavior or practice in society. Nonlegal efforts are often viewed as nonproductive means of achieving social change. This is particularly true when the motivation is to force change, as is frequently the case when demonstrations and riots occur. Another explanation for the legitimacy of law is that it is rooted in the beliefs and values of the people to whom it is supposed to apply. Exercising their moral judgment, their emotions, and their reasoning, people deepen their understanding and shared agreement about legal norms and legal decisions. Consequently, they are committed to legal norms and are willing to obey them.[7] Law in society is also validated as the proper means of obtaining social change because it is inherently authoritative and supported by institutional systems of enforcement and sanctions. Thus, noncompliance of the law initiates different kinds of actions to reinforce accepted modes of behavior.

The legitimacy of law to create social change is reinforced by a belief that the law is fair and just because it is applied equally. The equal protection clause of the Fourteenth Amendment of the U.S. Constitution, for example, prohibits a state from denying any person within its jurisdiction the equal protection of the laws. In other words, the laws of a state must treat an individual in the same manner as others in similar conditions and circumstances. The equal protection clause is not intended to provide "equality" among individuals or classes, but only the "equal application" of the laws. Therefore, the result of a law is not relevant so long as there is no discrimination in its application. By denying the state the ability to discriminate, the equal protection clause of the Constitution is crucial to the protection of civil rights.

Public Opinion

One way in which the law can produce social change is through public opinion. A claim that can be made on behalf of the active role of the courts to produce improvements in society is that court decisions raise the consciousness of citizens about social problems. This heightened awareness sensitizes the public to issues that have social relevance. This then stimulates public opinion, which in effect can have some bearing on the relationship between law and social issues.

Public opinion varies in its support of certain statutes. An illustration of this point is a recent public opinion poll taken by Gallup. This poll pertains to the gun laws in the United States after the school shootings in Newtown, Connecticut. The general public was asked if they thought that gun laws should be stricter. In 2012, 25% felt dissatisfied with current laws and wanted stricter laws. In 2013, that changed to 38%.[8]

Another poll taken by Gallup related to the U.S. Supreme Court's June 2000 ruling that prohibits student-led prayer in school. In *Santa Fe Independent School District v. Jane Doe*, the Court found that prayer does not belong in schools, regardless of who initiates and leads it. The case involved the constitutionality of student-led prayer broadcast over the public address system before high school football games. Telephone interviews of a randomly selected national sample of 1,016 showed that the public disagrees with the Court regarding this issue. When asked about allowing students to say prayers as part of the official program at graduation ceremonies, 83% of Americans favor the idea and just 17% are opposed.[9]

Limitations of Law to Create Social Change

When law is created as an implement of social change, it needs the support of society. Unfortunately, citizens have always been able to find a justification for their resistance to change. In contemporary times, for example, the phrase "make a federal case" has become widely known to mean using a legal action to achieve "something." Far too often, however, the "something" is related to personal agendas rather than the good of society as a whole. Such ideology lends itself to the belief that there are too many laws in society, that many laws have more to do with political correctness rather than jurisprudence, and that survival in today's "litigation-happy" society is predicated on whether one possesses a law degree. Under such thought, the likelihood of supporting social change as a matter of law is quite remote.

Resistance to social change frequently occurs when it conflicts with traditional values, beliefs, and prevailing customs of the society. People are particularly quick to oppose change when it interferes with their habits. Moreover, when it is perceived to deprive the individual of the right to take control over his or her own fate, the level of resistance is elevated. An excellent example of this is the battle between antigun groups and the National Rifle Association (NRA). The motif of antigun activists is to stop unregistered, unlicensed, and unregulated guns. While legislation has been enacted to meet this objective (e.g., the February 1994 Brady Act), many Americans side with pro-firearm lobbying efforts citing Constitutional rights found in the Second Amendment to keep and bear arms. Setting the debate aside, current gun control legislation may realistically have little impact on providing safer streets in communities. Consider these facts from the Bureau of Justice Statistics:[10]

- Despite general support for the idea of stricter gun-control laws, women are more likely to say that the way parents raise their children (38%) is the primary cause of gun violence, rather than the availability of guns (24%).
- According to the National Crime Victimization Survey (NCVS), armed offenders committed 22% of all violent crime incidents, including only 8% by offenders with a firearm.
- Despite the Brady Act, gun homicides involving adult offenders age 25 or older declined from over 10,000 in 1980 to 4,660 in 1999, and increased since then to 5,460 in 2008.

The effectiveness of the law as a compelling force to social change is more or less hindered by a variety of factors. Using our example of gun control legislation, it is clear that the efficacy of such laws is dependent upon its adherence by all people in society. Unfortunately, criminals are more likely to disobey the law because they have no sense of moral obligation. This realization can cause others in society to become noncompliant of the law if only because they feel a need to be armed in order to protect themselves from armed criminals.

Limited economic resources often act as barriers to the social change efforts of law. Burdensome cost associated with social change coupled with the lack of economic resources in a community influence the level of resistance to change. The greater the unequal distribution of wealth, the more likely it is that pockets of society, namely the poor, will resist social change efforts simply because they can't afford it.

Impact of Social Change on Law

Thus far, we have examined the interplay between law and society from the perspective of law creating social change. But what about changes in society that serve as precursors to the creation of law? It stands to reason that increases in social sophistication can effectively cause increases in the promulgation of law. American society over the past two centuries has become larger, more diverse, urbanized, more scientifically and technologically oriented, and industrialized, and thus has exhibited change in all social institutions. And, historically, it has been the totality of social, legal, and political change in the United States that has given rise to changes in the law.

In order to explore the relationship between social change as an implement to law, we briefly examine four connected social movements that served as powerful sources of social change in the United States. They include the civil rights movement, the antiwar movement, the women's movement, and the rights for sexual minorities movement.

Each of these movements has its own rich history that spans many years throughout the 20th century. But setting aside their unique qualities that led to implementing laws in America, it is important to note that these movements coexisted, with the bulk of their efforts occurring within the last four decades. As such, these movements collectively changed American society by challenging the ways that people thought about and behaved toward each other.

The Civil Rights Movement

An estimated 200,000 people attended the August 28, 1963, March on Washington for Jobs and Freedom, urging support for pending civil rights legislation that had been sent by President John F. Kennedy to Congress in June of that year. Highlighting the event was a speech by Dr. Martin Luther King, Jr., in front of the Lincoln Memorial, which has come to be known as "I Have a Dream." King's address captured the idealistic spirit of the demonstration. "I have a dream," he said, "my four little children will one day live in a nation where they will not be judged by the color of their skin but by the content of their character. I have a dream today!"[11]

The 1964 Civil Rights Act banned many forms of discrimination on grounds of race, color, sex, and national origin. Of greatest relevance were Title VI and Title VII of the Act. Title VI reads: "No person in the United States shall, on the grounds of race, color, or national origin, be excluded from participation in, or be denied the benefits of, or be subjected to discrimination under any program or activity receiving Federal financial assistance." Title VII bans discrimination in employment on grounds of race, color, national origin, and sex.

The Antiwar Movement

The antiwar movement focused on America's participation in the Vietnam War. During the 4 years following passage of the August 1964 Tonkin

Gulf resolution, which authorized U.S. military action in Southeast Asia, the American air war intensified and troop levels climbed to over 500,000. Opposition to the war grew as television and press coverage graphically showed the suffering of both civilians and conscripts. In 1965, demonstrations in New York City attracted 25,000 marchers; within 2 years, similar demonstrations drew several hundred thousand participants in Washington, DC, London, and other European capitals. Most of the demonstrations were peaceful, but as the war effort in Vietnam escalated, so too did opposition to the war, to the point that the country was bitterly divided over the American presence in Vietnam.

Many of the antiwar activists were experienced in the principles and methods of nonviolent demonstration because of their involvement in the civil rights movement, which had developed a strong tradition of nonviolent protest. These people believed that the best way to demonstrate their opposition to the use of military force in Vietnam was through peaceful means. However, another faction of people active in revolutionary organizations, possessed the ideologies of militant activists, and frequently organized militant events to protest the Vietnam War. These two ideologies (one of nonviolent demonstration and the other of militant protest) could be found concurrently at rallies, demonstrations, and other antiwar events.

On November 15, 1969, the largest antiwar demonstration took place in Washington, DC. This Moratorium march on Washington was organized by a group called the New Mobilization Committee to End the War in Vietnam, a broad coalition of over 100 antiwar groups. Most of the marchers were young college students, but the event was also well attended by citizens of all ages and from all walks of life, including Vietnam veterans.

The weekend-long antiwar march on Washington included speeches by political and religious leaders and performances by well-known folk singers. An estimated crowd of 300,000 people participated in the event. The events officially ended at about 8 p.m. on Sunday, and many of the marchers, who had come from other areas of the country, boarded their buses and left for home. After nightfall, the scene turned ugly. A group of about 500 militant demonstrators became violent. They began to throw rocks and bottles at windows in government buildings and at the local police. A considerable amount of damage was done to more than 30 store windows. The police responded by firing smoke grenades and tear gas at the demonstrators. Finally, the demonstrators were suppressed, and nearly 100 people were arrested. Other protesters required medical attention, primarily for treatment from the effects of the tear gas.

While the evening violence tarnished the antiwar demonstration, it was considered not to be representative of the general feeling and spirit of the march. The New Mobilization Committee denounced the violence as the work of a "fringe element of radicals" who had no connection with the vast majority of the march's participants. Many of the marchers publicly expressed similar sentiments. And although the weekend was marred by the actions of these militants, the march still played an extremely significant role in the development of American opposition to the Vietnam War. It was later considered by many historians and political analysts to be a turning point at which it was finally made evident that American public opposition to the war was extensive and was a force that needed to be seriously considered by those in the government.

In 1968, President Lyndon Johnson, who was challenged by two antiwar candidates within his own party for the presidential nomination, Senators Eugene McCarthy and Robert Kennedy, chose not to run. The election of President Richard Nixon in 1968 and his reduction in U.S. ground forces did little to dampen the antiwar movement. His decision to invade Cambodia in 1970 led to massive demonstrations on college campuses, most tragically at Kent State University, where four people were killed by members of the Ohio National Guard.[12]

The Women's Movement

Although Abigail Adams pressed for the inclusion of women's emancipation in the U.S. Constitution, the women's movement really dates from 1848, when Elizabeth Cady Stanton, Lucretia Coffin Mott, and others, at Seneca Falls, New York, issued a declaration of independence for women, demanding full legal equality, full educational and commercial opportunity, equal compensation, the right to collect wages, and the right to vote. The women's movement quickly spread and soon extended to Europe. Over the next 100 years, little by little, women's demands for higher education, entrance into trades and professions, married women's rights to property, and the right to vote were conceded.

In the 1960s, the women's movement experienced a rebirth, especially in the United States. The National Organization for Women (NOW), formed in 1966, had over 400 local chapters in only a short few years. NOW, the National Women's Political Caucus, and other groups pressed for such changes as abortion rights, federally supported child-care centers, equal pay for women, the occupational upgrading of women, the removal of all legal and social barriers to education, political influence, and economic power for women. The highest priorities for NOW was the Equal Rights Amendment (ERA).

In October 1971, the House passed by 354 votes to 23 the following version of the ERA: "Equality of rights under the law shall not be denied or abridged by the United States or by any state on account of sex." In March 1972, the Senate passed it by an overwhelming margin of 84 votes to 8.[13]

President Richard Nixon endorsed the ERA, and by early 1973, 30 states had ratified it.[14] But several Supreme Court decisions in the early 1970s clearly showed that the justices were divided on the issue of the ERA. And, after the initial rush to ratification, only three further states ratified in 1974, one in 1975, none in 1976, and in 1977, Indiana became the last state to approve it, leaving the ERA 3 states short of the 38 necessary for ratification. Despite the decision by Congress to extend the ratification deadline from 1979 to 1982, the amendment was never ratified by a sufficient number of states.

The U.S. Supreme Court unwittingly contributed to the failure of the ERA by its *Roe v. Wade* abortion decision. As Hugh Graham notes, "Traditionalist women led by Phyllis Schlafly, and the resulting stalemate ultimately doomed the feminists' congressional triumph of 1972."[15] The defeat of the ERA, like the continuing protest over *Roe* itself, indicated that there were powerful ideological and political limits on the willingness of many Americans to embrace the feminist agenda on sex equality.[16] Changes in statutory laws and court decisions have contributed to a reduction of gender discrimination in the United States. But as many research studies indicate, there is still significant progress needed to remove gender discrimination in society and in business.

Rights for Sexual Minorities

Social change is playing a major role that is impacting the rights of sexual minorities. President Obama announced in 2013 that he had evolved from a position that did not support gay marriage to one that does. Gay marriage has been approved in nine states and the District of Columbia (Connecticut, Iowa, Maine, Maryland, Massachusetts, New Hampshire, New York, Vermont, and Washington). According to a Gallup poll taken in 2013, 54% of Americans say they would vote for a law giving marriage benefits, such as those for insurance, taxes, or Social Security, to spouses of federal employees in same-sex marriages. However, this is not a one-sided debate. There are 31 states that have amended their state constitutions to limit marriage to one man and one woman.

The U.S. Supreme Court will weigh in on this social issue, as the Court will consider arguments in two cases that have the potential to redefine marriage at the national level. The first is California's Proposition 8 ban on same-sex marriage. The second is the constitutionality of the Defense of Marriage Act. This latter case contains a provision that defines marriage as between a man and a woman for the purpose of deciding who can receive a range of federal benefits. The implications of social change on the law are undoubtedly powerful.

Questions in Review

1. Why are organizations such as the NAACP and ACLU important to social change in America?
2. Under what circumstances are court decisions more likely to effect social change?
3. Why is gun control in America such a controversial issue?
4. How has the 1964 Civil Rights Act played a role in popular culture in America?
5. Although the Equal Rights Amendment failed, what contribution to social change did the women's movement play?

Endnotes

1. *Rhodes v. Chapman*, 452 U.S. 337 (1981) p. 359.
2. G.N. Rosenberg. (1991). *The hollow hope: Can courts bring about social change?* Chicago, IL: University of Chicago Press.
3. *Brown v. Board of Education*, 98 F. Supp. 797 (D. Kan. 1951); *Brown v. Board of Education*, 347 U.S. 483 (1954).
4. *Brown v. Board of Education*, 98 F. Supp. 797 (D. Kan. 1951); *Brown v. Board of Education*, 347 U.S. 483 (1954).
5. *Brown v. Board of Education*, 349 U.S. 294 (1955).
6. For more information regarding the Fourteenth Amendment and assisted suicide, see *Washington v. Harold Glucksberg*, 117 S. Ct. 2258, 138 L.Ed. 2d 772 (1997); *Vacco, Attorney General of New York v. Quill*, 117 S. Ct. 2293, 138 L. Ed. 2d. (1997).
7. G. Turkel. (1996). *Law and society: Critical approaches*. Needham Heights, MA: Allyn & Bacon.
8. Gallup Organization. (2013, January 7–10). Princeton, NJ.
9. Gallup Organization. (2000, May 5–7). Princeton, NJ.
10. L.S. Gifford, D.B. Adams, G. Lauver, & M. Bowling. (2000). *Background checks for firearm transfers, 1999* (Bureau of Justice Statistics Report NCJ 180882). Rockville, MD: NCJRS.
11. T. Branch. (1998). *Parting the waters: America in the King years, 1954–1963*. New York, NY: Simon & Schuster.
12. C. DeBenedetti. (1990). *An American ordeal: The anti-war movement of the Vietnam era*. Syracuse, NY: Syracuse University Press.
13. H.D. Graham. (1990). *The civil rights era: Origins and development of national policy: 1960–1972* (pp. 418–419). New York, NY: Oxford University Press.
14. J.J. Mansbridge. (1986). *Why we lost the ERA*. Chicago, IL: University of Chicago Press.
15. H.D. Graham. (1990). *The civil rights era: Origins and development of national policy, 1960–1972* (p. 419). New York, NY: Oxford University Press.
16. R.J. McKeefer. (1993). *Raw judicial power? The Supreme Court and American society*. Manchester, England: Manchester University Press.

Lawyers

9

Chapter Objectives

After reading this chapter you should be able to

- Explain the role of lawyers in our society
- Discuss why society tends to have a love–hate relationship with lawyers
- Discuss the concept that "law is a jealous mistress"
- Explain why law is considered as an adaptive profession
- Discuss the Socratic method of teaching
- Define the duties that an attorney owes to his or her client
- List which decisions that an attorney should make and which decisions that the client should control
- Discuss the concept that a prosecutor's primary duty is not to prosecute
- List the restrictions on attorney advertising

Introduction

If we did not have lawyers, we would not need lawyers.

From the movie *The Murder of Crows*

Once, I decide to take a case, I have only one agenda: I want to win. I will try, by every fair and legal means, to get my client off—without regards to the consequences.

Alan Dershowitz, *The Best Defense*

The law is a jealous mistress.

An anonymous but familiar statement

It is often stated that Americans have a love–hate relationship with lawyers. Lawyers are both cursed and praised. Compare the above three quotes. What do they imply regarding the legal profession? Does the first quote imply that we do not need a legal profession? What does the second quote imply regarding the ethics of the legal profession? Would you agree with Mr. Dershowitz

231

if you were representing someone who had committed a violent crime and you knew that your client was guilty? What does the concept that "law is a jealous mistress" imply about the legal profession?

This chapter examines the legal profession and its role in society. Law is considered as one of the three archetypical "learned" professions, with the Church and medicine being the other two. About 200 years ago, Edmund Burke, an influential British statesman and orator, stated that in "no other country, perhaps, in the world, is the law so general of a study as it is in the United States."[1] Despite the fact that it is so generally studied, it appears that the American people have many misconceptions regarding the legal profession. The authors of this text, one an attorney and former judge and the other a nonlawyer, criminal justice practitioner and educator provide their assessment of the current status of the legal profession.

The Legal Profession

Oliver Wendell Holmes once stated that law embodies the story of a nation's development through many centuries and cannot be dealt with as if it contained only the axioms and corollaries of a book of mathematics. Holmes also stated that in order to know what the law is, we must know what it has been, and what it tends to become.[2] As noted earlier, legal systems were developed as a means of formal control in societies. As legal systems developed, so did the legal profession. As with our legal system, the American legal profession is a hodgepodge of borrowed principles and homegrown theories. It is an adaptable profession and, thus, it changes to meet the needs of times.

The origins of the legal profession have been traced back to the Roman Empire. Roman law allowed individuals to present cases for others. At first, the individuals were trained in rhetoric rather than in the law. Later, Roman "jurists" became popular. Jurists were individuals who were knowledgeable about the law, and they advised individuals about the law. By the time of the Imperial Period, the complexity of Roman law made the legal profession indispensable.

Originally, the word *attorney* implied an agent. During the Middle Ages, attorneys had three basic functions—agent, spokesperson, and consultant. In Rome, they were allowed to appear on behalf of and in place of another person. In France, the attorney could appear with the person, but the person had to also appear. In England, the king's permission was needed to appear in place of another person.

Harold L. Wilensky, in his study of the development of professions, stated that professions passed through the following general stages as they developed into professional status:

- The work becomes a full-time occupation for certain individuals.
- Training schools are established.
- Training schools affiliate with universities.
- Local professional associations are started.
- National professional associations are established.
- Licensing laws are established, giving the profession market control.
- Formal codes of ethics are established.[3]

Looking at the history of the legal system, it is clear that our legal system has developed into a highly professional status along with medicine.

The Legal Profession in the United States

Many individuals contend that we have too many lawyers in the United States. It is often said that we are the most litigious society in history. Our present-day legal system was not developed overnight. It is the result of centuries of evolution. Whereas the legal profession in England makes clear distinctions between those attorneys who are trial lawyers (barristers) and those who are not (solicitors), our legal system lacks these formal distinctions. For the most part, any attorney in the United States may be either a trial or nontrial attorney. In actual practice, most attorneys tend to be generalists. Lawyers who are admitted to practice in one state are not permitted to practice in other states without special permission of the courts of the second state. To practice in a federal court, attorneys must generally be admitted to practice in the state courts and then be admitted to practice in the specific federal court. For example, an attorney who is admitted to practice in California can generally practice in all California state courts, but must be admitted to each federal court before the attorney can practice in that federal court.

Evolution of the Legal Profession in the United States

The legal profession in colonial America was transported from England, but with greater decentralization than existed in England. Prior to the Revolution, the practice of law in colonial America was monopolized by the upper-class merchants and plantation owners' sons. Wealthy merchants and plantation owners tended to send their sons to England to study law.

The power of admission to the practice of law was delegated by the colonial legislators to the courts. The courts then looked to the local bar associations to recommend attorneys for admission. The bar associations became powerful political elites that controlled admission to the legal profession.

Before the Revolution, lawyers were generally unpopular. The Puritans felt that all the laws they needed were contained in the bible. Except for the wealthy, the planters were also opposed to lawyers because of the threat they posed to the planters' political power.

During the American Revolution, most lawyers, being mostly from the upper class, were British sympathizers. After the Revolution, the legal profession became more egalitarian. The English distinction between barristers and attorneys disappeared. The standards of admission were relaxed, and the power of bar associations waned. By 1800, the power of admission to the bar was delegated to the local courts. Accordingly, attorneys were admitted in some courts within their state and not in others. Today, the state bar associations in most states now control admission to the bar.

In the 18th and 19th centuries, neither a college education nor formal legal training was absolutely required for admission to practice. Successful passing of the bar examination was the governing factor. Often the bar examination was oral. The principal method of preparing for the practice of law was by working in the law office of another attorney and "reading" the law. Even today, in some states, an individual may qualify to take the bar examination by "reading" the law.

The first law school was founded in Litchfield, Connecticut. It started out as a specialized law office offering apprentice programs. The course of training was about 14 months and offered no diploma. The training was based on lectures. There was no written material, the theory being that if there were written materials, the students would not need to pay tuition to hear the lectures. William and Mary University established a program in law in 1779. Columbia University started one in 1793 and Harvard in 1816. Today, most formal legal education takes place in universities.

Legal Education

Most lawyers in the United States today have at least a baccalaureate degree in addition to 3 years of law school. Now, our legal education is centered on the universities. The normal educational model for U.S. law schools is for the students to read actual court cases, extract general principles, and then submit to classroom interrogation by law professors. Lectures are rare in law school, with most professors using the Socratic method, wherein a continuous series of challenging questions is put to the students. The students are expected to apply the reasoning and rules of law that they have abstracted from assigned cases to hypothetical scenarios.[4] This procedure is designed to imitate the legal reasoning process of judges.

The Socratic method allows students to think in terms of opposing parties and to consider only those facts that are relevant to the guiding principles of the case. This results in an impersonal analysis of situations and obscures the reality that real cases involve real people with real conflicts. Law professors attempt to instill in their students the ability to sort through the various factual accounts of a conflict and to reduce the event to its barest legal bones, which in turn results in detachment from the parties and their misery. As Professor John T. Noonan once stated,

> Focusing on the rules, [the law professors] instilled in students a sense that the legal system was not the creature of individual caprice or the expression of raw power, but tradition constantly refined by reason.... Their purpose is to increase the sense of responsibility of those who by their thought and action make the system exist.[5]

IS THE PRACTICE OF LAW A CONFIDENCE GAME?

Abraham Blumberg contended that, in many ways, the practice of law, especially in the criminal courts, is a confidence game.[6] Blumberg looked at the fact that over 90% of the convictions in criminal cases were not the product of a combative, trial-by-jury process, but were negotiated, bargained-for pleas of guilty. He held that the high conviction rate without the features of an adversary trial tended to suggest that the "trial" becomes a perfunctory reiteration and validation of the pretrial interrogation and investigation. He also contended that the accused's own lawyer tends to be coopted to become an agent-mediator who helps the accused define his or her situation and restructure his or her perceptions to be concomitant with pleas of guilty. A defense lawyer is considered as "an officer of the court" and is held to a standard of ethical performance and duty to his or her client as well as to the court. According to Blumberg, defense lawyers have close and continuing relations with the prosecutor and the judge, while the accused people come and go in the court system schema. He sees the accused as a secondary figure in the court system and a means to other ends of the courthouse regulars.

Blumberg also recognized that the fees for legal services particularly play into the scenario of a confidence game. With plumbers, doctors, or other experts, there is usually tangible and visible evidence of the value of their services. Since much legal work is intangible, there is often a lack of tangible and visible evidence of the value of the legal work. For example, when the defense counsel negotiates a plea bargain, we never know what bargain the defendant may have received had he or she bargained without an attorney.

DO I NEED AN ATTORNEY?

A few years ago, an automobile insurance company in Florida sent letters to people injured by its automobile policyholders. The letter, entitled "Do I Need an Attorney?" informed the accident victims that it was their decision whether to hire an attorney. The letters generally include statements that:

- Claims are settled faster when no lawyer is involved.
- Lawyers charge a percentage of the recovery plus expenses, but if the victim settles directly with the insurance company, he or she will keep the entire amount.
- Victims can hire a lawyer at a later date if they're not satisfied after negotiating directly with the company. The letter also notes the statute of limitations for filing a claim.
- Some of the letters referred to the accident victims as "customers" of the company, even though they are on the opposite side of a claim against the company.[7]

Why was the insurance company encouraging victims not to hire an attorney?

Do you have any problems with the practice of an insurance company discouraging a victim from seeking legal advice?

Would your answers be different if you were aware of the following facts?

- In a study by the insurance company, it was determined that 66% of the claims with no lawyer involved were processed within 90 days, compared to only 10% with lawyers involved.
- According to the American Trial Lawyers Association, the average settlement in 1996 (industry-wide) with no lawyer present was $3,262, compared to $11,939 when a lawyer handled the case.
- That often in the negotiations between a victim without an attorney and the insurance company, the insurance company encourages the victim to turn over confidential information that may later be used against the victim.
- That the interests of the victims and those of the insurance company are directly opposed. The victim wants to maximize the recovery, and the insurance company wants to minimize it.

The Legal Profession Today

Law is a big business in the United States. Legal work accounts for approximately 2% of the gross national product. About 75% of the attorneys in active practice today are engaged in private practice. Roughly 12% of the attorneys are employed by federal, state, and local government. The remaining lawyers are either in private employment as salaried employees of private companies or are in the small group that comprises the judiciary.

According to a study of California lawyers by the *California Bar Journal*, many attorneys have a pessimistic view of the legal profession. Of the 2,700 attorneys questioned, 63% said that there were too many lawyers in the state, while 67% said that they believe lawyers compromise their professionalism as a result of business and economic pressures. Only 41% felt that attorneys had high ethical standards, and 54% said attorney advertising contributed to this decline in professionalism. Their view of the future was also not very bright. About 64% stated that collegiality and civility would decline, and 43% stated that professionalism would decline. As to the question: Would ethical standards decline? For 31%, the answer was yes.[8]

Lawyers in other states are also unhappy with the present state of the legal profession. For example, one Florida lawyer who makes $700,000 a year stated:

> I'm rapidly approaching that point, in spite of the fact that I have a very lucrative practice. There is so much unethical, sleazy behavior going on that a lot of lawyers are totally exasperated. It's starting to take a mental toll. I don't know how much longer I can stand dealing with these guys.[9]

According to this attorney, some of the problems that currently exist in the legal profession include lax discipline and the practice of delay, diversion, and deception.

Courthouse Work Groups

One of the major organizational goals of trial courts is the efficient disposition of cases assigned to that court. The term *courthouse work group* is used to describe the judges and attorneys who regularly work in a court. The judges and counsel are graduates of the law school system discussed previously. These individuals have similar educational backgrounds, work closely with each other, and most have similar career goals. Harmony within the court systems is promoted by discretion and negotiation within the courthouse work group.

Emotionally involved litigants often have difficulty with the impersonality of their attorney and are frustrated by their advocate's lack of personal involvement in the conflict. Litigants cannot understand how opposing lawyers can talk and laugh together during breaks in the trial. As noted by Calvi and Coleman, individuals not familiar with courthouse proceedings fail to recognize the norms that bind the court personnel. They also point out that courts are permanent organizations where the judge, clerk, court reporter, and bailiff are a fairly static group and that the attorneys work together and oppose each other on a fairly regular basis. According to Calvi and Coleman, the resulting group norms promote the establishment of friendly relations among the courtroom regulars.[10]

Malpractice

Many unhappy clients sue their attorneys. In the medical profession, it is often difficult to obtain a physician who will testify against a fellow physician. This is not the case in the legal profession. Attorneys generally show no reluctance in suing fellow attorneys. The practice has escalated in recent years. All state bar associations have education programs designed to prevent legal malpractice by lawyers. Recent trends in malpractice suits include

- *Failure of the attorney to avoid subjecting the client to the risk of litigation.* As one court noted, the question remains as to whether the defendants, as reasonably prudent attorneys, should have foreseen that the option, as drafted, was likely to result in litigation and whether other attorneys, in similar circumstances, would have taken steps to prevent such a result.
- *Loss of chance to sue.* If the attorney allows the statute of limitations to expire or fails to prevent a default judgment, a client may sue for "loss of chance" to recover on a legal claim.
- *Liability in personal and sexual relationships with clients.* In most states, it is malpractice to have sexual relationships with clients. As one California court stated: "The emotional vulnerability of a client often renders the client dependent upon the lawyer. And that such conduct necessarily falls below the standards of the legal profession."[11]
- *Ethical rules as standards of liability.* While many courts hold that violations of ethical rules may not be relevant in a malpractice suit, there are contrary decisions. For example, an Illinois court held that state ethics rules set the minimum standards of conduct owed to clients.[12]
- *Conflicts of interest.* Attorneys can act in situations that may involve a conflict of interest. For example, a real estate attorney drafts a contract to sell land after advising both parties to the contract as to the legal effects of the document.[13]
- *Liability for loss of evidence.* An Idaho attorney was held negligent for loss of evidence in handling a product liability claim because he allowed the client's car to be destroyed by the insurance company for salvage.[14]

Private Practice

Attorneys in private practice often work 60 hours per week. The private practice of law is highly competitive and rewards workaholism with money and status. One pressure on attorneys in private practice is the request for free legal advice. For example, one Minnesota attorney stated that in addition to doing pro bono work, he gets weekly phone calls from prisoners at a nearby jail as well as people who find his name in the phone book. And then there are his friends and relatives. All of them expect free legal advice. "Pro bono" work is work that attorneys do without expectation of financial reward. For example, the State Bar of Texas encourages all of the attorneys involved in private practice to donate at least 50 hours per year for charity cases, i.e., drafting wills for the elderly who cannot afford an attorney or helping abused spouses get restraining orders. One attorney stated: "People think all lawyers make $250,000 a year. And so they expect you to give them something for free." Note that an attorney who gives free legal advice and leads the person astray may be sued for legal malpractice.

Lawyer Advertising

Prior to 1977, almost all states restricted lawyers from advertising. In *Bates v. State Bar of Arizona*,[15] the U.S. Supreme Court held that attorneys have First Amendment protection, which includes the right to advertise. The Supreme Court held that advertising legal services is not inherently misleading, and while advertising does not provide a complete foundation on which to select an attorney, to deny the consumer one common vehicle (advertising) to obtain relevant information needed for an informed decision was a violation of the First Amendment. The Court held that advertising is a traditional mechanism in a free-market economy for a supplier to inform a potential purchaser of the availability and terms of exchange, and that it may well benefit the administration of justice.

Should Attorneys Be Allowed to Advertise?

The *Bates* case established the right of attorneys to advertise. It did not, however, settle the question as to whether attorneys should be allowed to advertise. Many individuals still feel that advertising is demeaning to the legal profession and should be banned.

The ban on lawyer advertising originated in England as a rule of etiquette and not as a rule of ethics. Early lawyers in Great Britain viewed the law as a form of public service, rather than a means of earning a living, and they looked down on "trade" as unseemly. Eventually, the attitude toward advertising fostered by this view evolved into an aspect of the ethics of the profession. According to Justice Blackmun in the *Bates* case, the belief that layers are somehow "above" trade is an anachronism, and the historical restraint against lawyer advertising has crumbled.

The State Bar of Arizona had argued against permitting attorneys to advertise because it would have an adverse effect on professionalism. The state bar held that

- The key to professionalism was the sense of pride that involvement in the discipline generates and that price advertising would bring about commercialization, which would undermine the attorney's sense of dignity and self-worth.
- The hustle of the marketplace would adversely affect the profession's service orientation and irreparably damage the delicate balance between the lawyer's need to earn and his or her obligation to serve selflessly.
- Advertising would erode the client's trust in his or her attorney.
- If the client perceives that the lawyer is motivated by profit, his or her confidence that the attorney is acting out of commitment to the client's welfare is jeopardized.
- Advertising would tarnish the dignified public image of the attorney.

Another argument presented against attorney advertising is that such advertising is inherently misleading because

1. Such services are so individualized with regard to the content and quality as to prevent informed comparison on the basis of an advertisement
2. The consumer of legal services is unable to determine in advance just what services he or she needs
3. Advertising by attorneys will highlight irrelevant factors and fail to show the relevant factor of skill

Justice Blackmun countered these arguments by agreeing that many services performed by attorneys are indeed unique, and it is doubtful that any attorney would or could advertise fixed prices for services of that type. The only services that lend themselves to advertising are the routine ones: the uncontested divorce, the simple adoption, the uncontested personal bankruptcy, the change of name, and similar types of services.

Regarding the second component of the argument, Blackmun contended that while the client may not know the details involved in performing the specific tasks, he or she is able to identify the services he or she desires at the level of generality to which advertising lends itself. Blackmun also held that the third component was without merit. He stated that while advertising does not provide a complete foundation on which to select an attorney, restricting advertising serves only to restrict the flow of information to the client.

Another argument commonly stated regarding attorney advertising is that it has the undesirable effect of stirring up litigation. The Court stated that while it may produce more litigation, the Court cannot accept the notion that it is always better for a person to suffer a wrong silently than to redress it by legal action. The Supreme Court noted that the middle 70% of our population is not being reached or served adequately by the legal profession, and that advertising may help reach that 70%.

The final argument against attorney advertising is that the economic effects of advertising will increase the overhead costs of the profession, and that these costs then will be passed to consumers in the form of increased fees. In addition, the added cost of practice will create a substantial entry barrier, deterring or preventing young attorneys from penetrating the market while entrenching the position of the bar's established members. The Court noted that in the marketplace, consumers have benefitted from the benefit of price advertising and that retail prices are often dramatically lower than they would be without advertising. It is entirely possible that advertising will serve to reduce, not advance, the cost of legal services to consumers. Regarding the latter portion of that argument, the Court noted that in the absence of advertising, an attorney must rely on his or her contacts with the community to generate a flow of business. In view of the time necessary to develop those contacts, the ban in fact serves to perpetuate the market position of established attorneys.

Advertisement Restrictions

Justice Blackmun stated in the *Bates* decision that, while advertising by attorneys may not be subjected to blanket suppression, advertising by attorneys may be regulated. Advertising that is false, deceptive, or misleading is certainly subject to restraint. Because the public lacks sophistication concerning legal services, misstatements that might be overlooked or deemed unimportant in other advertising may be found quite inappropriate in legal advertising. For example, advertising claims as to the quality of service are not susceptible to measurement or verification and thus are more likely to be misleading. In addition, the requirements of warning or disclaimers or the like may be required to ensure that the consumer is not misled.

The state may place reasonable restrictions on the time, place, and manner of advertising. For example, one New Jersey attorney was disciplined for making false and misleading statements in her newspaper advertisement. She was advertising the advantages of using a "living trust" rather than a will. In her statement, she said that "traditional estate planning was expensive and could tie up property." The bar association's board held that her statements were false, in that probate costs in New Jersey were low, averaging about $74 per case.[16] Attorney A. Frank Johns stated that this form of advertising is not unique. Johns notes:

> The elderly, as target audience, are particularly vulnerable. They're being victimized all the time. These living trust ads, for instance, will crop up in a certain part of the country, then the local bar will discipline someone, and it goes away for a while. But in the meantime, it will crop up somewhere else.[17]

Rosalie Osias, a New York attorney, was criticized for running an ad that included a picture of her lying across a desk stacked with law books, nibbling on a pencil, with her legs in the air. The caption under the picture stated: "Does this law firm have a reputation? You bet it does!!!" Ms. Osias stated that her ads were the only way she could get around the "old-boy" network and attract male clients without playing golf or "taking them to see lap dancers." One of the complaints was that her ads went a long way toward tarnishing the already-sullied reputation of the profession. Others contend that the subjective appeal of an advertisement is something that should be regulated by the lawyer running the ad, not bar associations. From this perspective, bar associations should focus their concern on whether the ad is false and misleading and nothing else.[18]

The first step for an attorney wishing to advertise is to review the rules of his or her state bar association. All state bar associations have restricted the rights of attorney to advertise. The rules vary widely from state to state. In Massachusetts, advertising rules include a ban on dramatizations and testimonials; require a special disclaimer by lawyers who advertise their experience but then refer most of the cases to other lawyers; mandate that solicitations to consumers include a statement warning that selecting a lawyer shouldn't be based solely on an ad; and compel the use of the word *advertising* in large type and red ink on all solicitations. The two states with the strictest rules are Iowa and Florida.[19] About 40 states have adopted the American Bar Association's Model Rules of Professional Conduct in regulating lawyer advertising. The ABA rules are very broad, allowing the media advertising but requiring that the attorney keep a copy of the ad for 2 years and that no false or misleading material be included. As a general rule, advertising may contain the following items:

- A lawyer's name or firm name, address, and telephone number
- The kinds of services the lawyer will undertake
- The basis on which the lawyer's fees are determined, including prices for specific services and payment and credit arrangements
- A lawyer's foreign language ability

- Names of references and, with their consent, names of clients regularly represented
- Other information that might invite the attention of those seeking legal assistance

Solicitation of Clients

Lawyers are generally prohibited from directly contacting individuals and soliciting business. They may, however, send general letters regarding legal rights to victims of crimes or individuals injured in automobile accidents. Several years ago, one of the authors was involved in an automobile accident. The other driver was cited by the police for driving under the influence of drugs and leaving the scene of the accident. Within 2 weeks, the author received 21 letters from different law firms informing him of his right to sue for damages. In a recent commercial airline accident where all the passengers were killed, a nationally known attorney was cited by his bar association because he had "runners" soliciting clients who had lost relatives in the crash.

Fields of Practice

As a general rule, attorneys may not advertise that they are specialists in certain fields unless they have been certified as such by the state bar association. Attorneys may, however, advertise that they handle only domestic cases, etc. They may also advertise that their practice of law is limited to the fields of criminal law, labor law, etc. In addition, they may not imply connections with government agencies or trade associations.

The Internet

Most state bars are attempting to regulate lawyer websites. The general approach taken by the bar associations are that the websites are another form of advertising. The bars restrict client solicitation over the Internet and require advertising disclaimers on infomercials. A few state bars have determined that websites are not subject to advertising regulations because they are requested by a computer user. For example, the Florida bar has said that any contents on a website beyond the home page will be treated as information provided to prospective clients at their request. Thus, Florida law firms are not required to provide the bar association with interior pages of their websites. The State Bar of Texas, however, sees a difference in someone calling a law firm and requesting a brochure or other information provided to prospective clients at their request and a computer user doing a search on a subject and finding a link to a law firm website. Accordingly, the Texas bar wants law firms to file up to 10 pages printed out from a website for approval by an advertising review committee. That committee wants to see the portions of the website that are most likely to raise issues of advertising and solicitations, not the pages that merely list the name of the law firm and its lawyers.[20]

Professional Responsibility

What are the professional responsibilities of an attorney? To understand those duties, we need to look at an attorney's duties to his or her client, the rights of the client, the lawyer's duties to persons other than clients, and conflicts of interest. The American Bar Association has established the *ABA Model Rules of Professional Conduct*. The rules were drafted to encourage states to adopt them. In one form or another, most states have adopted most of the principles and concepts set forth in the model rules. The material for this section is taken from those model rules.

Lawyer's Duties to the Client

The attorney should not undertake a legal matter unless the attorney is competent to handle the matter. The attorney is required to have the necessary legal knowledge and skill; the attorney has the duty to act with thoroughness and to properly prepare for the case (Rule 1.1). There are also the duties to act with reasonable diligence and promptness, without procrastination, as a zealous advocate, and to carry matters through to their conclusion.

Without the consent of the client, an attorney may not reveal information relating to the representation of the client. The only exceptions to this rule of confidentiality are:

- To prevent the client from committing criminal acts that are likely to result in imminent death or substantial bodily harm. For example, a client tells his attorney that he intends to eliminate one of the key witnesses. The attorney has a duty, despite the rule of confidentiality, to disclose this fact to the proper authorities.
- To establish a claim or defense in situations involving a controversy between client and attorney. For example, in one criminal case during jury selection, one of the prospective juror members, a teacher, stated that she would be biased against the defendant because she knew his brother. The defendant then stated to his attorney that he wanted her on the jury because she liked his brother. Neither the defense attorney nor the prosecutor challenged the woman. When the jury, which included the teacher, found the defendant guilty, the defendant filed a grievance with the bar association because his

attorney failed to challenge the teacher. The attorney was allowed to present evidence that, during the secret discussions regarding the discussion with the client during jury selection, the defendant had requested that the teacher not be challenged.

The rule of confidentiality continues after the client-lawyer relationship is over. For example, had O.J. informed his attorneys that he had in fact committed the murder he was charged with, that confidential information could not be disclosed even after O.J. was acquitted.

The rule of confidentiality does not cover physical evidence, but communications about the location of the evidence is protected. In one famous Virginia case, the defendant called his attorney and informed his attorney that he had just robbed a bank. The attorney asked the defendant where the money was that he got from the robbery and the location of the weapon that was used. The defendant stated that he still had both in his possession. The attorney then instructed the defendant to put the money and the gun in a safe deposit box in the local bank under a false identity. Unfortunately, the telephone conversation was overheard by a nosey telephone operator who reported the conversation to the police.

This case has several interesting legal issues involving the rule of confidentiality. First, was the telephone operator bound by the rule of confidentiality? The court said no. Had she worked in the attorney's office, she would have been covered by the rule. Legal assistants, secretaries, etc., are bound by the rule. But third persons who overhear confidential discussions are not bound by the rule and may discuss them with anyone. What about the advice of the attorney regarding the hiding of the evidence? The court said that the attorney did not have a duty to disclose the existence of physical evidence, but that the attorney committed a crime by instructing the defendant to hide the evidence. What if the defendant had walked into the attorney's office and dumped the evidence on the attorney's desk? What should the attorney do in this situation?

The defense has a duty to turn over any evidence in his or her possession, but may refuse to disclose how the counsel gained possession of the evidence.

In civil cases, an attorney has a safekeeping duty for any client's property (nonevidence) that is in his or her possession. Any funds that belong to the client that is in possession of the attorney must be kept in a separate trust fund and cannot be mingled with funds that belong to the attorney. Any funds recovered by an attorney should promptly be delivered to the client. If there is a dispute between the attorney and the client regarding any funds, the disputed funds must be kept separate until the dispute is resolved.

Generally, an attorney may not act as an advocate in cases where the attorney is likely to be a witness. The exceptions to this rule are when the testimony involves an uncontested issue, the testimony relates to the nature and value of legal services rendered, or the disqualification of the attorney would cause a substantial hardship on the client.

Client's Rights

Client's rights issues, not involving property issues, generally involve either the right to be kept informed or the right to make certain decisions. The client's right to be informed includes the prompt response by an attorney to a client's reasonable requests, to explain matters sufficiently to allow client to make an informed decision, and to promptly relay settlement offers. The attorney may, however, delay information when it is likely that the client will react imprudently. For example, when the client is a suicide risk, the attorney may delay telling a client "bad news" until steps may be taken to protect the client.

Often there are disagreements between the attorney and the client over decisions that should be made in legal proceedings. Generally, the client decides the objectives and the attorney decides the means to obtain those objectives. For example, in a criminal case, the defendant has the final decision on whether or not to plead guilty, and the attorney decides on which witnesses to call in defense of the charges. The decision, however, on whether the defendant takes the stand as a witness in his or her behalf belongs to the defendant, not the attorney. In most criminal cases, the defense attorney advises the accused not to take the stand. Often the accused, against the advice of the attorney, takes the stand and the results are disastrous.

The client has the final say regarding decisions involving expenses. The expenses of the suit are normally paid by the attorney and reimbursed by the client. In many cases, the attorney will require the client to deposit funds to cover expenses before they are incurred. The client, not the attorney, has the authority to settle the case. Accordingly, when an offer to settle is made to the attorney, the attorney has a duty to promptly convey that offer to the client. The duty to convey the offer to the client exists even if the attorney knows that the client will refuse it. For example, the prosecutor offers a plea bargain to the defense attorney that is too harsh and that the attorney is positive that her defendant will refuse. Nevertheless, the defense attorney has the duty to promptly convey the offer to the defendant. The decision on whether to take the offer or to settle a civil suit also belongs to the client.

The right of the client to fire an attorney is almost absolute. The client may, however, still owe the attorney reasonable attorney fees. An attorney, once he or she takes a case, has only a limited right to withdraw. Generally, the attorney's withdrawal must be with consent of the client and, if the case is in court, with the consent of the judge. An attorney may, however, withdraw if the client persists in criminal or fraudulent conduct or if the client's objectives are repugnant. The attorney may also withdraw with the consent of the court when the client is unreasonable, or when the client continues to break promises to the attorney after being given a reasonable warning. For example, in one case, Cliff Roberson filed a motion with the court to withdraw from the defense of a murder case. The court permitted the withdrawal despite the fact that the defendant objected to the withdrawal. The reason for the withdrawal was that the defendant had informed his attorney that he intended to commit perjury when he took the stand on his behalf. Roberson could not inform the court that the accused intended to give false testimony. Accordingly, the motion was based on the grounds that "continued representation of the accused by Roberson would violate ethical standards." When such motions are presented, the judges understand the real problem that exists in the case without requiring disclosure of specific facts.

On termination of the attorney-client relationship, the attorney is required to return all unearned fees and property belonging to the client.

Duties to Others

What duties does an attorney owe to the court and third parties? The attorney must exercise candor toward the court and must not make false statements or material facts or misrepresent the law. Other duties of the attorney toward the court or other tribunal include:

- Must disclose material facts when necessary to avoid assisting in criminal or fraudulent acts by the client
- Must not offer evidence that the attorney has reason to believe is false, e.g., perjury
- Must disclose legal authority that is adverse to the client's position
- Must not bring frivolous claims
- Must refrain from ex parte (without the other party being represented) communications with the judge
- Must not illegally influence the judge or jury
- Must not be disruptive in court

In criminal cases, the prosecutor's primary duty is not to convict, but to promote justice. Accordingly, the prosecutor has a duty not to prosecute unless probable cause exists and to disclose to the defense attorney any evidence that is favorable to the defendant. The prosecutor also has a duty not to seek waivers of rights from the accused who are not represented by counsel.

An attorney's duties to third parties include the duty of fairness to opposing party and counsel; not to conceal or destroy evidence; not to encourage a witness to be absent or uncooperative; not to make frivolous discovery requests or fail to comply with reasonable discovery requests; and to respect the rights of third parties. In addition, the attorney is restricted from communicating with another attorney's client without consent or legal authority.

A DILEMMA

You are a criminal attorney. Your client, Robert Garrow, is being tried for murder.

Garrow was an American serial killer who was active in New York in the early 1970s. He was born in upstate New York and grew up in a poor family of farmers. Garrow later said that his parents were severe, violent disciplinarians who regularly physically abused their children with whatever was handy, even bricks. At the age of 15, he was sent to a reform school. He joined the Air Force upon his release, but was court-martialed a year later for stealing money from a superior officer and spent 6 months in a military prison in Florida. He had a long history of sexual dysfunction and committed several acts of bestiality with the farm animals he worked with throughout childhood and adolescence.

During the trial on the murder charge, there is a statewide hunt for three missing teenage girls. While preparing for this murder trial, your client tells you that he murdered the girls and informs you where he buried the bodies. Assume that the information has nothing to do with the murder trial in which you are defending him and that the statement was made to you after you had advised him that his conversations with you were protected by the rules of confidentiality.

Do you report this information to the police?

The attorney informed the police where the bodies were buried, but did not inform the police how he obtained that information. However, there was evidence contained on the bodies that allowed the police to identify the defendant as the offender. The attorney was sanctioned by the state bar association for violating the rule of confidentiality.

Do you agree that the attorney should have been sanctioned for violating the rule of confidentiality?

What purposes does it serve society to uphold the rule in such cases?

Note: For interesting discussions on this case, see: Comment (1975). Legal ethics: Confidentiality and the case of Robert Garrow's lawyers. *Buffalo Law Review, 25,* 211–215.

Conflicts of Interest

Joe and Mark are apprehended shortly after robbing the First National Bank of Chicago. They are arrested and charged with robbery of a federally insured bank. Both want to hire James Sharp as their attorney. Since both are charged with the same crime and the attorney is a long-time friend of both, is there any conflict of interest if Attorney Sharp defends both? Yes. Sharp cannot represent one client if his representation would be directly adverse to one of his other clients. For example, if Joe were to offer to plead guilty and present evidence against Mark in return for a lighter sentence, Sharp's representation of Joe would be adverse to the rights of Mark. Mark, on the other hand, may want to claim that Joe was the ringleader and talked Mark into robbing the bank. Accordingly, in most states in similar situations, Sharp would be allowed to represent only one of the defendants. In some situations, he may be allowed to represent both if both agree and the court approves. This may be accomplished only where the attorney reasonably believes that dual representation would not be adverse to either client.

Attorneys within a law firm are regarded as a single unit; thus if one member of a law firm represents one of the defendants, the court would consider that all members of the firm are representing that defendant. Large law firms go to great lengths to prevent any possible conflicts of interest. In most law firms, before an attorney may take a new client, there must be a check of potential conflicts. As a general rule, attorneys shall not oppose former clients in substantially related matters without the consent of the former client.

Trial Publicity

Attorneys are prohibited from making out-of-court statements that a reasonable person would expect to become public and where there is a substantial likelihood that the statements could materially prejudice the trial proceedings. Attorneys may make the following out-of-court statements:

- Statement regarding the general nature of claim or defense
- Information in a public record
- General scope of an investigation
- Request for public assistance
- Warning of danger if likelihood of harm
- Identity of defendant
- Rebuttal statement to comments made by others to mitigate prejudice

Prohibited Conduct by Attorneys

Attorneys are generally prohibited from entering into business transactions with their clients unless the terms are reasonable and fair, are fully disclosed in writing, the client is given an opportunity to seek advice of independent counsel, and the client consents in writing.

An attorney must not use any information obtained from a client to the disadvantage of the client, except in those cases where the client is suing the attorney. Lawyers are prohibited from preparing wills or trusts that contain gifts to the attorney. Attorneys should not acquire proprietary interest in the subject matter of litigation except for contingency fees or liens to secure the repayment of expenses.

Contingency fees are prohibited in criminal and domestic relations (divorce) cases. Contingency fees are fees accepted by an attorney that are based on a percentage of the recovery in the case. For example, if an attorney accepts a case with a 35% contingency fee, this means that if the attorney wins or settles the matter for the client and the client gets a cash award, the attorney will receive 35% of the award. In most states, expenses are deducted before the attorney calculates his or her fees. If the attorney loses a case with a contingency fee agreement, the attorney does not get paid. Most states require that all contingency fee agreements be in writing.

Future of the Law

Law is a creature of society. Society is rapidly changing, but it shows no signs of going back to the simple habits of the old days. Nor does anybody really expect a Utopia in which government would disappear. Law, legal process, and the legal system are facts of life in the United States. They have a central place, and this is likely to continue. Perhaps the role of law will grow, perhaps not, but it is not about to shrivel or go away.[21]

Many individuals contend that we are too involved with law, litigation, and the legal process. As noted by Friedman, law is a fact of life. Even the simple act of going to college presupposes a vast superstructure of law. Law touches every aspect of our lives. According to Friedman, as long as there is government regulation, there will be a vast superstructure of law, and efforts to cut government involvement have not gotten very far. Conservative governments can only hope to privatize a bit, deregulate a bit, and send some tasks back to the state; for the rest, they can only hope to keep the state from swelling until it bursts like a giant balloon.

One sphere of growth that has attracted much attention is in the area of litigation. Many will contend that we are experiencing a litigation explosion in the United States. For example, judicial review is more common now that it was in the past. Many people believe that the 2000 presidential election was decided not by voters, but by the judicial system. If courts continue to monitor, revise, and oversee what other governmental agencies do, then the courts are encouraging individuals and social groups to bring their demands into courts. Presently, we use litigation to stop the building of dams and bridges and, now, to decide a presidential election. This is a trend that is growing and appears to be unstoppable.

Litigation is not increasing in all areas. Lawsuits in some areas are in fact decreasing. Many scholars contend that the courts are handling fewer cases involving ordinary contract disputes, landlord and tenant disputes, debt collection, and will contests. These staples of the early 20th century legal system have declined due to the expense of litigation and the growth of alternative dispute resolution forums. Laura Nader, in her book on alternatives to litigation, contends that the courts are neglecting "issues that affect the quality of everyday life." According to her, the courts are too involved in big business litigation and fail to look at the issues that would increase the quality of our everyday life.[22]

Courts now intervene in areas and subjects that were once very private. For example, juveniles are now suing their parents. One 12-year-old boy tried to divorce his parents in Florida. While we wonder why the courts need to meddle in private family affairs, there are other areas in which the courts are needed. For example, despite all the talking about downsizing the governments, they continue to grow. The more the government does, the more the need to control it. For the ordinary citizen, there needs to be a method to review government actions or to get the government to listen. In limited situations, the courts are available. As noted by Friedman: "Courts in the United States, for all their faults, give people at least some realistic way to right wrongs done by the government and by private centers of power."[23] Nevertheless, regular courts are often too expensive and formal for the small cases and for day-by-day disputes. Alternative dispute resolution is a growing institution and will probably be used more for those disputes that are not right for formal court proceedings.

Summary

- It is often stated that Americans have a love–hate relationship with lawyers.
- Law is considered as one of the three archetypical "learned" professions, with the Church and medicine being the other two.
- Despite the fact that it is so generally studied, it appears that the American people have many misconceptions regarding the legal profession.

- Oliver Wendell Holmes once stated that law embodies the story of a nation's development through many centuries and cannot be dealt with as if it contained only the axioms and corollaries of a book of mathematics. Holmes also stated that in order to know what the law is, we must know what it has been and what it tends to become.
- The origins of the legal profession have been traced back to the Roman Empire. Roman law allowed individuals to present cases for others. At first, the individuals were trained in rhetoric rather than in the law. Later, Roman "jurists" became popular. Jurists were individuals who were knowledgeable about the law, and they advised individuals about the law. By the time of the Imperial Period, the complexity of Roman law made the legal profession indispensable.
- Originally, the word *attorney* implied an agent. During the Middle Ages, attorneys had three basic functions—agent, spokesperson, and consultant.
- Looking at the history of the legal system, it is clear that our legal system has developed into a highly professional status along with medicine.
- Many individuals contend that, in the United States, we have too many lawyers. It is often said that we are the most litigious society in history.
- Our present-day legal system was not developed overnight. It is the result of centuries of evolution.
- Whereas the legal profession in England makes clear distinctions between those attorneys who are trial lawyers (barristers) and those who are not (solicitors), our legal system lacks these formal distinctions. For the most part, any attorney in the United States may be either a trial or nontrial attorney.
- In actual practice, most attorneys tend to be generalists. Lawyers who are admitted to practice in one state are not permitted to practice in other states without special permission of the courts of the second state.
- To practice in a federal court, attorneys must generally be admitted to practice in the state courts and then be admitted to practice in the specific federal court.
- The legal profession in colonial America was transported from England, but with greater decentralization than existed in England. Prior to the Revolutionary War, the practice of law in colonial America was monopolized by the upper-class merchants and plantation owners' sons.
- The power of admission to the practice of law was delegated by the colonial legislators to the courts. The courts then looked to the local bar associations for recommending attorneys for admission. The bar associations became powerful political elites that controlled admission to the legal profession.

- In the 18th and 19th centuries, neither a college education nor formal legal training was absolutely required for admission to practice. Successful passing of the bar examination was the governing factor. Often the bar examination was oral.

- The principal method of preparing for the practice of law was by working in the law office of another attorney and "reading" the law. Even today in some states, an individual may qualify to take the bar examination by "reading" the law.

- Most lawyers in the United States today have at least a baccalaureate degree in addition to 3 years of law school. Now, our legal education is centered on the universities. The normal educational model for U.S. law schools is for the students to read actual court cases, extract general principles, and then submit to classroom interrogation by law professors.

- Lectures are rare in law school, with most professors using the Socratic method, wherein a continuous series of challenging questions is put to the students. The students are expected to apply the reasoning and rules of law that they have abstracted from assigned cases to hypothetical scenarios. This procedure is designed to imitate the legal reasoning process of judges.

- The Socratic method allows students to think in terms of opposing parties and to consider only those facts that are relevant to the guiding principles of the case. This results in an impersonal analysis of situations and obscures the reality that real cases involve real people with real conflicts.

- Law is a big business in the United States. Legal work accounts for approximately 2% of the gross national product. About 75% of the attorneys in active practice today are engaged in private practice. Roughly 12% of the attorneys are employed by federal, state, and local government. The remaining lawyers are either in private employment as salaried employees of private companies or are in the small group that comprises the judiciary.

- One of the major organizational goals of trial courts is the efficient disposition of cases assigned to that court. The term *courthouse work group* is used to describe the judges and attorneys who regularly work in a court. The judges and counsel are graduates of the law school system discussed previously. These individuals have similar educational backgrounds and work closely with each other, and most have similar career goals. Harmony within the court systems is promoted by discretion and negotiation of the courthouse work group.

- Prior to 1977, almost all states restricted lawyers from advertising. In *Bates v. State Bar of Arizona*, the U.S. Supreme Court held that attorneys have First Amendment protection, which includes the right to advertise. The Supreme Court held that advertising legal services is not inherently misleading, and while advertising does not provide a complete foundation on which to select an attorney, to deny the consumer one common vehicle (advertising) to obtain relevant information needed for an informed decision was a violation of the First Amendment.

- Generally, lawyers are prohibited from directly contacting individuals and soliciting business. They may, however, send general letters regarding legal rights to victims of crimes or individuals injured in automobile accidents.
- As a general rule, attorneys may not advertise that they are specialists in certain fields unless they have been certified as such by the state bar association. Attorneys may, however, advertise that they handle only domestic cases, etc. They may also advertise that their practice of law is limited to the fields of criminal law, labor law, etc. In addition, they may not imply connections with government agencies or trade associations.
- The American Bar Association has established the ABA Model Rules of Professional Conduct. The rules were drafted to encourage states to adopt them. Most states have, in one form or another, adopted most of the principles and concepts set forth in the model rules.
- The attorney must exercise candor toward the court and must not make false statements or material facts or misrepresent the law.
- In criminal cases, the prosecutor's primary duty is not to convict, but to promote justice. Accordingly, the prosecutor has a duty not to prosecute unless probable cause exists and to disclose to the defense attorney any evidence that is favorable to the defendant.
- Law is a creature of society. Many individuals contend that we are too involved with law, litigation, and the legal process.

Questions in Review

1. What is the meaning of the statement "law is a jealous mistress?"
2. Explain why Holmes stated that the story of the development of our legal system may not be explained by axioms and corollaries?
3. Describe the development of a profession as noted by Wilensky.
4. Do we have too many lawyers in the United States? Justify your conclusions.
5. Explain the development of legal education.
6. How does the Socratic method work?
7. Why does Blumberg contend that the practice of law is a confidence game?

8. Do you see any problems with the approach used by the automobile insurance companies in Florida in 1995?
9. Why are many lawyers unhappy working in the legal profession?
10. Should attorneys be allowed to advertise? Justify your conclusions.

Endnotes

1. M.E. Katsh & W. Rose. (2000). The role of law. In *Taking sides: Legal issues* (9th ed., p. xii). New York, NY: Dushkin/McGraw-Hill.
2. O.W. Holmes. (1881). *The common law* (p. 1). Boston, MA: Little, Brown.
3. H.L. Wilensky. (1964). The professionalism of everyone? *American Journal of Sociology, 70*(2), 137–158.
4. J.V. Calvi & S. Coleman. (2000). *American law and legal systems* (4th ed., pp. 36–37). Englewood Cliffs, NJ: Prentice-Hall.
5. J.T. Noonan. (1976). *Persons and masks of the law* (p. xi). New York, NY: Farrar, Straus & Giroux.
6. A.S. Blumberg. The practice of law as confidence game: Organizational cooptation of a profession. *Law & Society Review, 1*(2), 15–40.
7. *Lawyers Weekly USA.* (1997). 97 LWUSA 241.
8. *Lawyers Weekly USA.* (1994). 94 LWUSA 45.
9. *Lawyers Weekly USA.* (1996). 96 LWUSA 2288.
10. J.V. Calvi & S. Coleman. (2000). *American law and legal systems* (4th ed., p. 37). Englewood Cliffs, NJ: Prentice-Hall.
11. *McDaniels v. Gile*, 281 Cal. Rptr. 242 (1991).
12. *Mayol v. Summers*, 558 N.W. 2nd 1176 (1992).
13. *Layton v. Pendleton*, 864 S.W. 2nd 937 (Mo.App. 1993).
14. *Murry v. Farmers Insurance Co.*, 796 P. 2nd 101 (1990).
15. 433 U.S. 350 (1977).
16. *Lawyers Weekly USA.* (1998, December 14). 98 LWUSA 1031.
17. *Lawyers Weekly USA.* (1998, November 30). 98 LWUSA 1013.
18. *Lawyers Weekly USA.* (1995). 95 LWUSA 1059.
19. M.M. Bowden. (2000, May 15). Even tasteless ads rarely violate ethical rules. *Lawyers Weekly USA,* 2000 LWUSA 453.
20. Bar proposes rules to regulate new frontier. (1998, June 22). *Texas Lawyer.*
21. L.M. Friedman. (1998). *American law: An introduction* (Rev. ed., p. 332). New York, NY: Norton.
22. L. Nader. (1980). *No access to law: Alternatives to the American judicial system* (p. 5). Waltham, MA: Academic Press.
23. L.M. Friedman. (1998). *American law: An introduction* (Rev. ed., p. 329). New York, NY: Norton.

Private Life and the Law 10

Chapter Objectives

After completing this chapter, you should be able to

- Explain the relationship between your private life and the law
- Define the right to privacy
- Discuss your rights to privacy as protected by the Constitution
- Discuss the unwritten protections considered as constitutional rights
- Explain how technology issues invade our right to privacy

Introduction

There is a relationship that exists between law, morality, and society. As American society changes, so too has the moral content of law. Throughout history, dominant groups have been able to slip in their views of what is right into the legal code. The effect is a "born again Constitution" bearing different interpretations of the supreme law of the land. The extent of change in moral beliefs and practices more or less necessitates whether legal scholars will decide the public debate of the times. The higher the issue is on the agenda of public debate, the more likely is a legal decision.

For example, the First Amendment right of freedom of speech is designed to protect the expression or publication of one's opinions. This constitutional right is so prized and cherished in American society that the Supreme Court has protected it time and time again. But what of pornography and the present ability of Internet users to send obscene pictures to millions of people on the computer—are those expressions protected under the right of privacy?

Right to Privacy

> The right to be left alone—the most comprehensive of rights, and the right most valued by civilized men. To protect that right, every unjustifiable intrusion by the government upon the privacy of the individual, whatever the means employed, must be deemed a violation of the 4th Amendment.

Justice Louis Brandeis in *Olmstead v. United States* (1928)[1]

The right to privacy is the right to be left alone. While there is no right to privacy explicitly guaranteed in the Constitution, a number of U.S. Supreme Court cases have established law in society that affords protection against many types of intrusions by the government into our private matters and personal lives. In *Katz v. United States*, for example, the Supreme Court ruled that the Fourth Amendment protected individuals' reasonable expectations of privacy and not just property interests.[2]

Interestingly, 21st-century technology has brought forth a number of key Fourth Amendment issues regarding privacy, especially involving private communications, cell phones, and GPS tracking systems. In *Griswold v. Connecticut*, the Court recognized constitutionally protected privacy under the First, Third, Fourth, Fifth, and Ninth Amendments to the U.S. Constitution. A "penumbra" theory for establishing a constitutional right of privacy was reasoned out by Justice Douglas, who delivered the majority's opinion in Griswold:

> [Prior] cases suggest that specific guarantees in the Bill of Rights have penumbras formed by emanations from those guarantees that help give them life and substance.... Various guarantees create zones of privacy. The right of association contained in the penumbra of the First Amendment is one, as we have seen. The Third Amendment in its prohibition against the quartering of soldiers "in any house" in time of peace without the consent of the owner is another facet of that privacy. The Fourth Amendment explicitly affirms the "right of the people to be secure in their persons, houses, papers, and effects, against unreasonable searches and seizures." The Fifth Amendment in its Self-Incrimination clause enables the citizen to create a zone of privacy which government may not force him to surrender to his detriment. The Ninth Amendment provides: "The enumeration in the Constitution, of certain rights, shall not be construed to deny or disparage others retained by the people."[3]

The Supreme Court extended the right to privacy in *Roe v. Wade* by identifying the Fourteenth Amendment as the basis for the right's application. And, in *Whalen v. Roe*, the Court made a comprehensive effort to define the right to privacy, embracing both (a) an "individual interest in avoiding disclosure of personal matters" and (b) an "interest in independence in making certain kinds of important decisions."[4]

Privacy is how we as a society balance the interests of the free flow of information with the rights of individuals. This balance is very delicate and often difficult to maintain. Consequently, various statutes and laws that define privacy protection have been developed.

IN ADDITION TO OUR WRITTEN FEDERAL CONSTITUTION, DOES THE UNITED STATES HAVE AN UNWRITTEN CONSTITUTION?

Yale University professor and noted constitutional scholar Akhil Amar contends that in addition to the written federal constitution, which consists of 8,000+ words, the United States has an unwritten constitution. Amar uses the "right to privacy" concept as one of his arguments to support the contention that there is an unwritten constitution. For example, the First Amendment to the U.S. Constitution only prevents the U.S. Congress from abridging certain freedoms by the phrase "Congress shall not...." The amendment does not expressly restrict state governments from taking such action. He points out that certain key phrases commonly used in discussions on constitutional rights such as the rule of law, right of privacy, separation of powers, and checks and balances are absent from our written constitution.

According to Amar, the Ninth Amendment of the U.S. Constitution recognizes the existence of an unwritten constitution. That amendment provides:

> The enumeration in the Constitution, of certain rights, shall not be construed to deny or disparage others retained by the people.

There are certain rights enumerated in the written constitution. But, as Amar points out, the Ninth Amendment recognizes that there are other rights retained by the people including such rights as the right to privacy.[5]

Privacy Act of 1974

The Privacy Act of 1974 symbolizes congressional affirmation of individuals' fundamental right of privacy and embodies the principal privacy safeguards for personal information by safeguarding against the invasion of privacy through the misuse of records by federal agencies. In general, the act allows a citizen to discover how records are collected, maintained, used, and disseminated by the U.S. government. The act also permits them to gain access to most personal information maintained by federal agencies and to seek correction of any inaccurate, incomplete, untimely, or irrelevant information.[6]

The Privacy Act applies to personal information maintained by agencies in the executive branch of the federal government. The executive branch includes cabinet departments, military departments, government corporations, government-controlled corporations, independent regulatory agencies, and other establishments in the executive branch. The Privacy Act does not generally apply to records maintained by state and local governments or private companies or organizations.

The Privacy Act only grants rights to U.S. citizens and to aliens lawfully admitted for permanent residence. As a result, a nonresident foreign national cannot use the act's provisions. However, a nonresident foreign national may use the Freedom of Information Act (FOIA) to request records about him- or herself.

The Privacy Act governs only records that are maintained in a "system of records." A "record" is defined as personal information about an individual that is maintained by an agency. A record contains individually identifiable information, including but not limited to information about education, financial transactions, medical history, criminal history, or employment history. A "system of records" is a group of records from which information is retrieved by name, social security number, or other identifying symbols assigned to an individual.

The Privacy Act also establishes five requirements that control the record management of federal agencies:

- First, each agency must establish procedures allowing individuals to see and copy records about themselves. An individual may also seek to amend any information that is not accurate, relevant, timely, or complete. The rights to inspect and to correct records are the most important provisions of the Privacy Act.
- Second, each agency must publish notices describing all systems of records. The notices include a complete description of personal data record-keeping policies, practices, and systems. This requirement prevents the maintenance of secret record systems.
- Third, each agency must make reasonable efforts to maintain accurate, relevant, timely, and complete records about individuals.
- Fourth, the act establishes rules governing the use and disclosure of personal information. Agencies are prohibited from maintaining information about how individuals exercise rights guaranteed by the First Amendment to the U.S. Constitution unless maintenance of the information is specifically authorized by statute or by the individual

or relates to an authorized law enforcement activity. The act specifies that information collected for one purpose may not be used for another purpose without notice to or the consent of the subject of the record. The act also requires that each agency keep a record of some disclosures of personal information.

- Fifth, the act provides legal remedies that permit an individual to seek enforcement of the rights granted under the act. In addition, federal employees who fail to comply with the act's provisions may be subjected to criminal penalties.

Freedom of Information Act

The Freedom of Information Act (FOIA) provides individuals with a right to access records that are in the possession of the federal government.[7] The government may withhold information only pursuant to the nine exemptions and three exclusions contained in the act. The exemptions, which essentially protect against the disclosure of information that could harm national security interests, privacy of individuals, functioning of the government, and similar important interests, are as follows:[8]

- Exemption 1: Classified documents
- Exemption 2: Internal personnel rules and practices
- Exemption 3: Information exempt under other laws
- Exemption 4: Confidential business information
- Exemption 5: Internal government communications
- Exemption 6: Personal privacy
- Exemption 7: Law enforcement
- Exemption 8: Financial institutions
- Exemption 9: Geological information

The initial FOIA exemption permits the withholding of properly classified documents. Information may be classified in the interest of national defense or foreign policy. The FOIA provides that, if a document has been properly classified under a presidential executive order, the document can be withheld from disclosure. Classified documents may be requested under the FOIA. An agency can review the document to determine if it still requires protection. In addition, the executive order on security classification establishes a special procedure for requesting the declassification of documents.

The second FOIA exemption covers matters that are related solely to an agency's internal personnel rules and practices. As interpreted by the courts, there are two separate classes of documents that are generally held to fall within this exemption. First, information relating to personnel rules or internal agency practices is exempt if it is a trivial administrative matter of no genuine public interest. A rule governing lunch hours for agency employees is an example. Second, an internal administrative manual can be exempt if disclosure would risk circumvention of law or agency regulations. In order to fall into this category, the material will normally have to regulate internal agency conduct rather than public behavior.

The third exemption incorporates into the FOIA other laws that restrict the availability of information. To qualify under this exemption, a statute must require that matters be withheld from the public in such a manner as to leave no discretion to the agency. Alternatively, the statute must establish particular criteria for withholding or refer to particular types of matters to be withheld. One example of a qualifying statute is the provision of the tax code prohibiting the public disclosure of tax returns and tax return information

The fourth exemption protects from public disclosure two types of information: trade secrets and confidential business information. A trade secret is a commercially valuable plan, formula, process, or device. This is a narrow category of information. An example of a trade secret is the recipe for a commercial food product. The second type of protected data is commercial or financial information obtained from a person where such data is privileged or confidential. The courts have held that data qualifies for withholding if disclosure by the government would be likely to harm the competitive position of the person who submitted the information. Detailed information on a company's marketing plans, profits, or costs can qualify as confidential business information. Information may also be withheld if disclosure would be likely to impair the government's ability to obtain similar information in the future. Only information obtained from a person other than a government agency qualifies under the fourth exemption. A person can be an individual, a partnership, or a corporation. Information that an agency created on its own cannot normally be withheld under this exemption.

The FOIA's fifth exemption applies to internal government documents. An example is a letter from one government department to another about a joint decision that has not yet been made. The purpose of this exemption is to safeguard the deliberative policy-making process of government. The exemption encourages frank discussion of policy matters between agency officials by allowing supporting documents to be withheld from public disclosure. The exemption also protects against premature disclosure of policies before final adoption. While the policy behind the fifth exemption is well accepted, the application of the exemption is complicated. The fifth exemption may be the most difficult FOIA exemption to understand and apply. For example, the exemption protects the policy-making process, but it does not protect purely factual information related to the policy process. Factual information must be disclosed unless it is inextricably intertwined with protected information about an agency decision. Protection for the decision-making process is appropriate only for the period while decisions are being made. Thus, the fifth exemption has been held to distinguish between documents that are predecisional, and therefore may be protected, and those that are postdecisional and therefore not subject to protection. Once a policy is adopted, the public has a greater interest in knowing the basis for the decision. The exemption also incorporates some of the privileges that apply in litigation involving the government. For example, papers prepared by the government's lawyers can be withheld in the same way that papers prepared by private lawyers for clients are not available through discovery in civil litigation.

The sixth exemption covers personnel, medical, and similar files, the disclosure of which would constitute a clearly unwarranted invasion of personal privacy. This exemption protects the privacy interests of individuals by allowing an agency to withhold personal data kept in government files. Only individuals have privacy interests. Corporations and other legal persons have no privacy rights under the sixth exemption. The exemption requires agencies to strike a balance between an individual's privacy interest and the public's right to know. However, since only a clearly unwarranted invasion of privacy is a basis for withholding, there is a perceptible tilt in favor of disclosure in the exemption. Nevertheless, the sixth exemption makes it harder to obtain information about another individual without the consent of that individual.

The seventh exemption allows agencies to withhold law enforcement records in order to protect the law enforcement process from interference. While the exemption was amended in 1986, it still retains six specific subexemptions:

1. Allows the withholding of a law enforcement record that could reasonably be expected to interfere with enforcement proceedings. This exemption protects an active law enforcement investigation from interference through premature disclosure.
2. Allows the withholding of information that would deprive a person of a right to a fair trial or an impartial adjudication
3. Recognizes that individuals have a privacy interest in information maintained in law enforcement files. If the disclosure of information could reasonably be expected to constitute an unwarranted invasion of personal privacy, the information is exempt from disclosure
4. Protects the identity of confidential sources. Information that could reasonably be expected to reveal the identity of a confidential source is exempt. A confidential source can include a state, local, or foreign agency or authority, or a private institution that furnished information on a confidential basis. In addition, the exemption protects information furnished by a confidential source if the data was compiled by a criminal law enforcement authority during a criminal investigation or by an agency conducting a lawful national security intelligence investigation.

5. Protects from disclosure information that would reveal techniques and procedures for law enforcement investigations or prosecutions or that would disclose guidelines for law enforcement investigations or prosecutions if disclosure of the information could reasonably be expected to risk circumvention of the law.

6. Protects law enforcement information that could reasonably be expected to endanger the life or physical safety of any individual.

The eighth exemption protects information that is contained in or related to examination, operating, or condition reports prepared by or for a bank supervisory agency such as the Federal Deposit Insurance Corporation, the Federal Reserve, or similar agencies.

The ninth FOIA exemption covers geological and geophysical information, data, and maps about wells. This exemption is rarely used.

The Right of Publicity

The right of publicity prevents the unauthorized commercial use of an individual name, likeness, or other recognizable aspects of one's persona. It gives a person the exclusive right to license the use of his or her identity for commercial promotion. In the United States, state statutory law largely protects the right of publicity, but only about half the states have explicitly recognized a right of publicity. Of these, many name-protection provisions are part of the right of privacy. In other states, the right of publicity is protected through the law of unfair competition. Tort actions for misappropriation, unlawful endorsement, or unlawful production by the individual, help to protect the right of publicity. Moreover, if a person can establish an aspect of his or her identity as a trademark, federal law may be employed to provide protection. Lastly, the Lanham Act[9] can also provide protection where a person's identity is used to falsely advertise a product. The Lanham Act defines the statutory and common law boundaries to trademarks and service marks. Trademarks are words or symbols used in the advertising of goods and services. The Lanham Act defines the scope of a trademark, the process by which a federal registration can be obtained from the Patent and Trademark Office for a trademark, and penalties for trademark infringement. The law authorizes a trademark owner to file a lawsuit to

- Prevent others from using it in a context where it might confuse consumers
- Recover money damages from someone who used the mark knowing that it was already owned by someone else

The Federal Electronic Communications Privacy Act (ECPA)

In 1986, Congress approved and the president signed the Electronic Communications Privacy Act (ECPA), which establishes the provisions for access, use, disclosure, interception, and privacy protections of wire and electronic communications. Wire communication is defined to include

> any aural transfer made in whole or in part through the use of facilities for the transmission of communications by the aid of wire, cable, or other like connection between the point of origin and the point of reception (including the use of such connection in a switching station).[10]

Electronic communications is defined as

> any transfer of signs, signals, writing, images, sounds, data, or intelligence of any nature transmitted in whole or in part by a wire, radio, electromagnetic, photo electronic or photo optical system that affects interstate or foreign commerce.[11]

In addition to prohibiting unlawful access and certain disclosures of communication contents, the ECPA prevents government entities from requiring disclosure of electronic communications from a provider without proper procedure.

The ECPA prohibits unauthorized accessing of electronically stored email. Specifically, subsection 2701(a) prohibits an entity from obtaining access to, altering, or preventing access to an electronic communication while it is in storage by either (a) intentionally accessing, without authorization, a facility through which electronic communication service is provided or (b) exceeding its authorization in accessing such a facility.

Section 2701 contains three exceptions to the general prohibition:

- Subsection (c)(1) excepts conduct authorized by the provider of the service.
- Subsection (c)(2) exempts conduct authorized by the sender or recipient of the communication.
- Subsection (c)(3) addresses conduct authorized under certain statutory provisions that allow law enforcement authorities to access communications pursuant to process requirements.

Computer Fraud and Abuse Act

In the 1980s, as computers became increasingly central to the conduct of business, computer crimes began to grab the attention of lawmakers. As a result, the Computer Fraud and Abuse Act of 1986 was signed into law in order to clarify definitions of criminal fraud and abuse for federal computer crimes and to remove the legal ambiguities and obstacles to prosecuting these crimes. The act established two new felony offenses for the unauthorized access of "federal interest" computers. One of the felony offenses was established to address the unauthorized access of a federal-interest computer with the intention to commit fraudulent theft. The other felony was established to address "malicious damage," which involves altering information in, or preventing the use of, a federal-interest computer. A malicious damage violation would have to result in a loss to the victim of $1,000 or more, except in cases involving the alteration of medical records. The act also established as a federal misdemeanor trafficking in computer passwords with the intent to commit fraud that affects interstate commerce. This provision was meant to cover the creation, maintenance, and use of "pirate bulletin boards," where confidential computer passwords are revealed. The legislation applied to anyone who

> knowingly and with the intent to defraud, traffics, transfers, or otherwise disposes of, to another, or obtains control of, with intent to transfer or dispose of in any password through which a computer may be accessed without authorization, if such trafficking affects interstate or foreign commerce or such computer is used by or for the Government of the United States.[12]

THE INTERNET WORM

Robert T. Morris was a first-year graduate student in Cornell University's computer science Ph.D. program. Through undergraduate work at Harvard and in various jobs, he had acquired significant computer experience and expertise. When Morris entered Cornell, he was given an account on the computer at the Computer Science Division. This account gave him explicit authorization to use computers at Cornell. Morris engaged in various discussions with fellow graduate students about the security of computer networks and his ability to penetrate them.

Morris began work on a computer program, later known as the Internet worm or virus. The goal of this program was to demonstrate the inadequacies of current security measures on computer networks by exploiting the security defects that Morris had discovered. The tactic he selected was to release of a worm into network computers. Morris designed the program to spread across a national network of computers after being inserted at one computer location connected to the network. Morris released the worm into the Internet, which is a group of national networks that connect university, governmental, and military computers around the country. The network permits communication and transfer of information between computers on the network.

Morris sought to program the Internet worm to spread widely without drawing attention to it. The worm was supposed to occupy little computer operation time and thus not interfere with normal use of the computers. Morris programmed the worm to make it difficult to detect and read, so that other programmers would not be able to kill the worm easily. Morris also wanted to ensure that the worm did not copy itself onto a computer that already had a copy. Multiple copies of the worm on a computer would make the worm easier to detect and would bog down the system and ultimately cause the computer to crash. Therefore, Morris designed the worm to "ask" each computer whether it already had a copy of the worm. If it responded "no," then the worm would copy onto the computer; if it responded "yes," the worm would not duplicate. However, Morris was concerned that other programmers could kill the worm by programming their own computers to falsely respond "yes" to the question. To circumvent this protection, Morris programmed the worm to duplicate itself every seventh time it received a "yes" response. As it turned out, Morris underestimated the number of times a computer would be asked the question, and his one-out-of-seven ratio resulted in far more copying than he had anticipated. The worm was also designed so that it would be killed when a computer was shut down, an event that typically occurs once every week or two. This would have prevented the worm from accumulating on one computer, had Morris correctly estimated the likely rate of reinfection.

Morris identified four ways in which the worm could break into computers on the network:

1. Through a "hole" or "bug" (an error) in SEND MAIL, a computer program that transfers and receives electronic mail on a computer
2. Through a bug in the "finger demon" program, a program that permits a person to obtain limited information about the users of another computer
3. Through the "trusted hosts" feature, which permits a user with certain privileges on one computer to have equivalent privileges on another computer without using a password
4. Through a program of password guessing, whereby various combinations of letters are tried out in rapid sequence in the hope that one will be an authorized user's password, which is entered to permit whatever level of activity that user is authorized to perform.

Morris later released the worm from a computer at the Massachusetts Institute of Technology. MIT was selected to disguise the fact that the worm came from Morris at Cornell. Morris soon discovered that the worm was replicating and reinfecting machines at a much faster rate than he had anticipated. Ultimately, many machines at locations around the country either crashed or became catatonic. When Morris realized what was happening, he contacted a friend at Harvard to discuss a solution. Eventually, they sent an anonymous message from Harvard over the network, instructing programmers how to kill the worm and prevent reinfection. However, because the network route was clogged, this message did not get through until it was too late. Computers were affected at numerous installations, including leading universities, military sites, and medical research facilities. The estimated cost of dealing with the worm at each installation ranged from $200 to more than $53,000. Morris was found guilty, following a jury trial, of violating 18 U.S.C._1030(a)(5)(A). He was sentenced to 3 years of probation, 400 hours of community service, a fine of $10,050, and the costs of his supervision.

Source: **928 F.2d 504 UNITED STATES of America, Appellee, v. Robert Tappan MORRIS, Defendant-Appellant. No. 774, Docket 90-1336. United States Court of Appeals, Second Circuit. Argued Dec. 4, 1990. Decided March 7, 1991.**

TECHNOLOGIES THAT ASSIST INTERNET USERS TO PROTECT THEIR PRIVACY

Encryption: Encryption is a method of scrambling email messages so that they are gibberish to anyone who does not know how to unscramble them. The privacy advantage of encryption is that anything encrypted is virtually inaccessible to anyone other than the designated recipient. Thus, private information may be encrypted and then transmitted, stored, or distributed without fear that outsiders will scrutinize it. There are various encryption programs, anonymous servers, and memory-protection software applications available on the Internet.

Anonymous remailers: Because it is relatively easy to determine the name and email address of anyone who posts messages or sends email, the practice of using anonymous remailing programs has become more common. These programs receive email, strip off all identifying information, and then forward the mail to the appropriate address.

Memory-protection software: Software security programs are now available to help prevent unauthorized access to files on the home personal computer. For example, one program encrypts every directory with a different password so that to access any directory you must log in first. Thus, if an online service provider tries to read any private files, it would be denied access.

STATE AND LOCAL LAW ENFORCEMENT NEEDS TO COMBAT ELECTRONIC CRIME

Former U.S. Attorney General Janet Reno stated,

> Whether it [technology] benefits us or injures us depends almost entirely on the fingers on the keyboard. So while the Information Age holds great promise, it falls in part upon law enforcement to ensure that users of networks do not become victims of New Age crime.

The rapid proliferation of computer systems, telecommunications networks, and other related technologies—upon which virtually everyone relies—presents concomitant widespread vulnerabilities. Increasingly, criminals are abandoning their guns for sophisticated computer-assisted weapons. Recent acts of electronic crime in the United States, such as the $15-million white-collar case dubbed "Operation Derailed" in Atlanta, Georgia, demonstrate the need for increased vigilance by law enforcement. The highly publicized Melissa virus and Solar Sunrise cases further exemplify how reliance on the Internet and electronic correspondence has subsequently increased vulnerability to cybercrime.

The statistics and losses remain staggering, and law enforcement agencies must be able to detect, investigate, and prosecute these cases. A recent report on cybercrime by the Center for Strategic and International Studies (CSIS) says,

> Almost all Fortune 500 corporations have been penetrated electronically by cybercriminals. The Federal Bureau of Investigation (FBI) estimates that electronic crimes are running about $10 billion a year but only 17 percent of the companies who were victimized reported these losses to law enforcement agencies.

In addition, a survey conducted by the Computer Security Institute (CSI) and the FBI of 521 financial institutions, universities, government agencies, and corporations found that 62% reported intrusions.

Of particular concern is the gap between training and technologies available to and used by law enforcement—especially state and local agencies—and the advanced technologies used by persons and groups committing electronic crimes. The National Institute of Justice (NIJ) funded a one-year study to identify, document, and respond to short-falls in state and local law enforcement capabilities and resources for addressing electronic crime. This study built upon a report by the National Cybercrime Training Partnership (NCTP) that sought input from 35 police chiefs across the nation about the status of electronic crime and what training and technical assistance would be of greatest value to them.

Methodology

NIJ designated a management team to oversee the project's day-to-day operations. The team consisted of representatives from the TriData Corporation, the U.S. Tennessee Valley Authority Police, the U.S. Navy Space and Naval Warfare Systems Command, and the U.S. Department of Justice (DOJ). The team held a kickoff meeting to develop the assessment instrument and construct a strategy to implement the study. The assessment instrument, or protocol, was designed by the project management team and reviewed by subject-matter experts, investigators, prosecutors, and training specialists. Groups that contributed to this effort included NCTP members, workshop facilitators, and other subject-matter experts. The protocol was divided into the following sections:

- State and local perspectives on electronic crime
- Profile of electronic crimes and investigation needs
- Legal issues and prosecution
- System vulnerability, critical infrastructure, and cyberterrorism
- Forensic evidence collection and analysis
- Training

The management team, with assistance from five regional offices of NIJ's National Law Enforcement and Corrections Technology Center system and NCTP, selected potential participants. Care was taken to ensure that law enforcement disciplines specifically relevant to electronic crime efforts (such as investigation, search, seizure, forensic examination of electronic media, and unit management) were represented. A total of 126 individuals representing 114 agencies participated in this national inventory. They represented a variety of urban and rural jurisdictions and a broad segment of state and local law enforcement entities, including sheriffs' departments, city police, state bureaus of investigation, crime laboratories, transit police, and regulatory agencies. The agencies and their representatives were selected on the basis of their particular role in combating electronic crime. In addition, researchers interviewed electronic crime experts to gain insight and obtain advice on research design. Researchers also reviewed relevant literature to derive additional background information on tactics, techniques, and technologies currently available.

In the sessions, facilitators asked participants to identify the training, investigative support, and technology capabilities they needed to combat electronic crimes. They were also asked to describe typical offenders and their targets, the most prevalent types of cases, and recently observed trends in electronic crimes. After concluding the workshops, members of the project management team analyzed, documented, and charted the inventory results. They identified significant findings, arrived at general conclusions, and made specific recommendations. During several iterations, the entire management team—along with workshop facilitators and subject-matter experts—reviewed the final report for completeness and accuracy.

Findings

The state and local law enforcement participants in this assessment provided a firsthand perspective of the technology, policies, research, training, and direct assistance required to combat electronic crime. Participants related their experiences with electronic crime and their concerns for the future, thereby providing a wealth of information for government decision makers in both policy and program arenas. The participants identified dozens of needs across the spectrum of electronic crime. These needs were documented, categorized, and evaluated. Ten areas of concern, identified as the "critical ten," dominated the discussions along with commentary on what the future could hold for addressing each need. In addition to these priority needs, two overarching issues emerged: Whether the need is high-end computer forensic training or on-site task force development assistance, progress must be accomplished (a) quickly and (b) in a centralized, coordinated manner.

Why the sense of urgency and the focus on coordination? The window of opportunity for law enforcement to keep pace with electronic crime offenders (let alone get ahead of the problem) is quite short. The capacity of technology used by these offenders is increasing geometrically and at a pace that significantly challenges public-sector resources at the state and local levels. The emphasis on a coordinated approach is both practical and logical, as there is little time and few resources available to address this increasingly significant problem. The greatest impact will be generated if near-term solutions can be crafted and delivered through existing structures that have a broad reach and include most key stakeholders.

The most important aspect of these challenges is the time sensitivity. Unless a national effort is launched in the near term, electronic crimes will outpace the resources of most state and local law enforcement agencies. There is a need to maximize investments in new or expanded tools, training, on-site assistance, and research with regard to electronic crime and cyberterrorism initiatives. During the assessment study, workshop participants determined 10 top-priority needs. They are listed as follows, without reference to priority or ranking:

1. *Public awareness*: A solid information and awareness program is needed to educate the general public, elected and appointed officials, the criminal justice community, and the private sector about the incidence and impact of electronic crimes. With many cases being undetected or unreported, and with the dearth of hard data on electronic crime trends, most individuals are unaware of the extent to which their financial status, businesses, families, or privacy might be affected by electronic crime. Neither are most people aware of how quickly the threat is growing. A multifaceted information and awareness campaign is needed to clearly document and publicize how electronic crimes affect society. Unless the public is made aware of the shift in crime to the whole new arena of the Internet, individuals will continue to be subject to a number of crimes, including fraud, identity theft, child abuse, and denial of services.

2. *Data and reporting*: More comprehensive data are needed to establish a clearer picture of the extent and impact of electronic crime and to monitor trends. In response to the Computer Fraud and Abuse Act, the FBI amended its Uniform Crime Reporting System to address electronic crime. The FBI placed a question within its National Incident Based Reporting System

to document if a criminal offender used a computer in the commission of the crime. However, additional details about the use of computers in crime are needed to fully measure the incidence of electronic crime. Without more data, detailed analysis, or a crime victimization study, it is difficult to track regional or national trends in electronic crime. Hard data are needed both to better understand the era of electronic crime and to communicate it to budget and policy makers as well as to citizens.

3. *Uniform training and certification courses*: Law enforcement officers and forensic scientists need specific levels of training and certification to correctly carry out their respective roles when investigating electronic crimes, collecting and examining evidence, and providing courtroom testimony. This training should reflect state and local priorities. There is a need for both entry-level and advanced training for law enforcement officers and investigators, prosecutors and defense attorneys, probation and parole officers, and judges. First-line officers who secure the initial crime scenes need training on basic forensic evidence recognition and collection techniques. National guidelines should be developed and applied toward a certification program that ensures uniform skill levels. Additionally, prosecutors and judges need awareness training to stay abreast of electronic crime's impact and technology.

4. *Management assistance for on-site electronic crime task forces*: State and local law enforcement agencies need immediate assistance in developing computer investigation units, creating regional computer forensics capabilities, organizing task forces, and establishing programs with private industry. A majority of the agencies represented in this study called for a county (or regional) investigative task force approach to the technically challenging and time-consuming job of investigating crimes involving computers. Agencies are seeking hands-on assistance from experts in electronic crime and in criminal task-force development to enhance their ability to combat electronic crime at all levels. Simply stated, investigative task forces are extremely effective crime-fighting tools. This has been proven with drug and arson task forces. Combining forces among agencies makes it more affordable to acquire the high-tech tools used in analyzing computer evidence and to coordinate strategies and procedures to deal with electronic crime. Direct

assistance in forming electronic-crime task forces is urgently needed for several reasons. Specially trained personnel and dedicated forensic laboratory equipment are often required to examine and retrieve evidence that is necessary for prosecution and contained in a computer's hard drive. Electronic evidence often implicates individuals from jurisdictions where officials' testimony and involvement in case proceedings must be coordinated. Also, for many prosecutors, presenting high-tech evidence in court is challenging, in terms of both ferreting through highly technical terms and making them understandable for a jury.

5. *Updated laws*: Effective, uniform laws and regulations that keep pace with electronic crime need to be promulgated and applied at the federal and state levels. Over the past decade, use of computers and the Internet has grown exponentially, with individuals becoming more dependent on these technologies on a daily basis. As computer use has blossomed, so too has criminal involvement. Deterring and punishing these offenders require a legal structure that will support early detection and successful prosecutions. Examples of emerging trends include the increased reliance of criminals and terrorists on encryption technologies and obvious efforts to cloak the identity and location of offenders. Currently, there is no formal legal mechanism to require that subpoenas generated in one state be enforced in another. There is a practice of cooperation, in which one state attorney general's office voluntarily assists another state authority in either serving an out-of-state subpoena or seeking an in-state court order to enforce the out-of-state subpoena. However, the reliability and consistency of this procedure are not uniform, and the ability to secure enforcement of an out-of-state subpoena on a recalcitrant party is at best questionable. Clearly, the laws defining computer offenses, as well as the legal methods needed to properly investigate current electronic crimes, have lagged behind technological and social changes.

6. *Cooperation with the high-tech industry*: Crime solvers need the industry's full support and cooperation to control electronic crime. Industry support is needed to develop and maintain trusted relationships and cooperative agreements to help sponsor training, join task forces, and share equipment for the examination of electronic evidence. These

cooperative relationships can also encourage the reporting of electronic crime. Many technology firms have their own information security units that, among other responsibilities, detect and investigate electronic crime. Increased cooperation between industry and government provides the best opportunity to control electronic crime and protect the nation's critical infrastructure, which heavily relies upon computer technology.

7. *Special research and publications*: Investigators, forensic laboratory specialists, and prosecutors need a comprehensive directory of electronic crime information, training, and resources to help them combat electronic crime. The federal government, state governments, colleges and universities, trade associations, and private industry are all responding to the need for diverse training in the field of electronic crime. It is critical to communicate the availability of training and professional seminars if these offerings are to be used to their maximum advantage. Many investigators and prosecutors are calling for a clearinghouse of online information and technical guidance on methods, investigative technologies, and research. Examples of specialized technologies include the ability to detect and break encryption, image disks, and index important information. State and local law enforcement agencies also are asking for a clearinghouse of national and state experts and resources. A who's who of electronic crime investigators, unit managers, prosecutors, labs, equipment, expert witnesses, and so forth, would be a well-received guidebook for many practitioners, who frequently note the need for information on how to contact colleagues in other communities. A training directory citing current sources of electronic crime training offerings (print, online, and CD-ROM versions) would be extremely valuable. One such successful nationwide law enforcement network, which supports the dissemination of information on electronic crime, is the FBI's Law Enforcement Online (LEO). However, many law enforcement officers need access to broader information than is contained in LEO, including private-sector specialists and technical data. A multilevel secure network could address this need.

8. *Management and awareness support*: Senior law enforcement managers and elected officials need to become better educated

about the growth and impact of electronic crime on their communities and the need to establish and support dedicated computer crime units. Many participants expressed concern that senior managers do not fully understand the impact of electronic crime and the level of expertise and tools needed to investigate and prepare cases for successful prosecution. It is often the case that managers do not realize the impact of Internet and electronic crime in their jurisdiction or in society in general. Senior management often lacks statistical data on electronic crime, has insufficient funding and personnel resources to create electronic crime units and, in some cases, is unconvinced that electronic crime deserves much attention. The police chiefs and managers who are willing to support an investigative capability for electronic crime often must do so at the expense of other units, or they assign dual investigation responsibilities to personnel.

9. *Investigative and forensic tools*: There is a significant and immediate need for up-to-date technological tools and equipment for state and local law enforcement agencies to conduct electronic crime investigations. Most electronic crime cases cannot be properly investigated and developed without essential cybertools, software, and exposure to higher-end computer technology. Computer systems, software, hardware, intrusion detection tools, decryption technology, and other forensic equipment are expensive and beyond the budgets of most local law enforcement agencies. Even when special equipment is available, it is frequently out of date or incapable of being used for forensic investigations. Insufficient data storage capacity—to properly copy and analyze evidence—is also a common problem.

10. *Structuring a computer crime unit*: As law enforcement agencies begin to address electronic crime, they grapple with how best to structure a computer or electronic crime unit that will adequately investigate crimes involving computers and properly seize and thoroughly analyze electronic evidence. Where does the electronic crime unit belong in the law enforcement agency? Who should be a part of the unit? How should the duties of investigation and the duties of forensic analysis be separated, if at all? The experts are divided over these questions, especially the issue of whether it is better to maintain computer forensics labs with specially trained investigators or

with civilian systems technicians. DOJ would provide a very valuable service to state and local law enforcement agencies if it undertook research to capture the best thinking on the issues confronted when police agencies begin to establish better electronic crime investigation capabilities. The experience of successful existing units should be thoroughly documented along with measures of impact related to different staffing configurations. Results of such research should be widely distributed and used as part of direct technical assistance to state and local agencies.

Conclusion

State and local law enforcement entities will face ever-increasing challenges in investigating and prosecuting Internet and other high-tech crimes. The Internet and high-tech telecommunications have created an environment in which interpersonal and commercial relationships will increasingly involve interstate and international transactions, while state and local authorities remain bound by much narrower jurisdictional limitations.

Critical infrastructure protection is an issue that federal, state, and local law enforcement will have to contend with in the future. Increasingly, critical national functions depend on information networks and are thus susceptible to disruption or security breaches by unauthorized persons. Moreover, it is now possible to attack these infrastructures with far less preparation and expense than in the past. State and local law enforcement agencies are frequently the recipient of threats against critical infrastructure components and, many times, are the first responders to attacks on them.

Addressing these issues and the "critical ten" that emerged from this research must become a high priority. An analysis comparing the key priorities of state and local law enforcement to existing federal training and technology programs should be the next logical step. Both this action and future study are essential if law enforcement is to realistically combat this crime.

Source: **Hollis Stambaugh, David Beaupre, David J. Icove, Richard Baker, Wayne Cassaday, & Wayne P. Williams. (2000).** *State and local law enforcement needs to combat electronic crime.* **NCJ 183451. Washington, DC: National Institute of Justice. Retrieved June 26, 2013, from http://www.nij.gov/pubs-sum/183451.htm**

Abortion

In 1973, in the landmark case of *Roe v. Wade*, the U.S. Supreme Court ruled that the Fourteenth Amendment to the Constitution provided a fundamental right for women to obtain abortions. The Court held that the "right to privacy," established by the Court's precedents in the contraception cases of the 1960s, assured the freedom of a person to abort unless the state had a "compelling interest" in preventing the abortion.

EXCERPT FROM THE 1973 U.S. SUPREME COURT CASE *ROE V. WADE*

Mr. Justice Blackmun delivered the opinion of the Court:

We forthwith acknowledge our awareness of the sensitive and emotional nature of the abortion controversy, of the vigorous opposing views, even among physicians, and of the deep and seemingly absolute convictions that the subject inspires. One's philosophy, one's experiences, one's exposure to the raw edges of human existence, one's religious training, one's attitudes toward life and family and their values, and the moral standards one establishes and seeks to observe, are all likely to influence and to color one's thinking and conclusions about abortion.

In addition, population growth, pollution, poverty, and racial overtones tend to complicate and not to simplify the problem.

Our task, of course, is to resolve the issue by constitutional measurement, free of emotion and of predilection. We seek earnestly to do this, and, because we do, we have inquired into, and in this opinion place some emphasis upon, medical and medical-legal history and what that history reveals about man's attitudes toward the abortion procedure over the centuries....

Jane Roe [an alias], a single woman who was residing in Dallas County, Texas, instituted this federal action in March 1970 against the District Attorney of the county. She sought a declaratory judgment that the Texas criminal abortion statutes were unconstitutional on their face, and an injunction restraining the defendant from enforcing the statutes.

Roe alleged that she was unmarried and pregnant; that she wished to terminate her pregnancy by an abortion "performed by a competent, licensed physician, under safe, clinical conditions"; that she was unable to get a "legal" abortion in Texas because her life did not appear to be threatened by the continuation of her pregnancy; and that she could not afford to travel to another jurisdiction in order to secure a legal abortion under safe conditions. She claimed that the Texas statutes were unconstitutionally vague and that they abridged her right of personal privacy, protected by the First, Fourth, Fifth, Ninth, and Fourteenth Amendments. By an amendment to her complaint, Roe purported to sue "on behalf of herself and all other women" similarly situated....

The principal thrust of appellant's attack on the Texas statutes is that they improperly invade a right, said to be possessed by the pregnant woman, to choose to terminate her pregnancy. Appellant would discover this right in the concept of personal "liberty" embodied in the Fourteenth Amendment's Due Process Clause; or in personal, marital, familial, and sexual privacy said to be protected by the Bill of Rights or its penumbras....

It perhaps is not generally appreciated that the restrictive criminal abortion laws in effect in a majority of States today are of relatively recent vintage. Those laws, generally proscribing abortion or its attempt at any time during pregnancy except when necessary to preserve the pregnant woman's life, are not of ancient or even of common-law origin. Instead, they derive from statutory changes effected, for the most part, in the latter half of the 19th century....

With respect to the State's important and legitimate interest in potential life, the "compelling" point is at viability. This is so because the fetus then presumably has the capability of meaningful life outside the mother's womb. State regulation protective of fetal life after viability thus has both logical and biological justifications. If the State is interested in protecting fetal life after viability, it may go so far as to proscribe abortion during that period, except when it is necessary to preserve the life or health of the mother....

...The statute makes no distinction between abortions performed early in pregnancy and those performed later, and it limits to a single reason, "saving" the mother's life, the legal justification for the procedure. The statute, therefore, cannot survive the constitutional attack made upon it here.

This conclusion makes it unnecessary for us to consider the additional challenge to the Texas statute asserted on grounds of vagueness.

To summarize and to repeat:

1. A state criminal abortion statute of the current Texas type, that excepts from criminality only a life-saving procedure on behalf of the mother, without regard to pregnancy stage and without recognition of the other interests involved, is violative of the Due Process Clause of the Fourteenth Amendment.

(a) For the stage prior to approximately the end of the first trimester, the abortion decision and its effectuation must be left to the medical judgment of the pregnant woman's attending physician.

(b) For the stage subsequent to approximately the end of the first trimester, the State, in promoting its interest in the health of the mother, may, if it chooses, regulate the abortion procedure in ways that are reasonably related to maternal health.

(c) For the stage subsequent to viability, the State in promoting its interest in the potentiality of human life may, if it chooses, regulate, and even proscribe, abortion except where it is necessary, in appropriate medical judgment, for the preservation of the life or health of the mother.

2. The State may define the term "physician," ... to mean only a physician currently licensed by the State, and may proscribe any abortion by a person who is not a physician as so defined....

...The decision leaves the State free to place increasing restrictions on abortion as the period of pregnancy lengthens, so long as those restrictions are tailored to the recognized state interests. The decision vindicates the right of the physician to administer medical treatment according to his professional judgment up to the points where important state interests provide compelling justifications for intervention. Up to those points, the abortion decision in all its aspects is inherently, and primarily, a medical decision, and basic responsibility for it must rest with the physician. If an individual practitioner abuses the privilege of exercising proper medical judgment, the usual remedies, judicial and intra-professional, are available....[13]

Despite a strong pro-life opposition to *Roe v. Wade*, the closest that this decision has ever come to being overturned is in *Planned Parenthood v. Casey*. In its decision, the U.S. Supreme Court by a narrow margin (5 to 4) upheld a 24-hour waiting period, an informed-consent requirement, a parental consent provision for minors, and a record-keeping requirement, while striking down a spousal-notice requirement.[14] By the year 2013, at least 28 states had enacted legislation to restrict the right to abortion. Generally, these restrictions prohibit public funds from being used to perform abortions and regulate the requirements imposed on abortion clinics. Presently, the most restrictive laws on abortion are those in the state of Arkansas.

Pornography

Although there is no widely accepted modern definition of pornography, the common element in all definitions is that the material is sexually explicit. Controversy revolves around whether specific visual presentations are benign or harmful. Moreover, the central question that arises about pornography is whether the materials are artistic or merely obscene. Obscenity is a legal term identifying material that has been judged by the courts to violate specific statutes pertaining to sexually explicit material. The primary issue in statutory law is whether the material violates community standards of acceptability and whether it involves minors.

Since the 1960s, research has been conducted to assess the effects of exposure to sexually explicit material. Primary attention has been paid to commercially produced materials intended to generate sexual arousal and/or activity in adult audiences. Three components have been of principal interest:

- The degree of explicitness
- Whether the material also contains aggression
- Whether it depicts women in demeaning and degrading ways

Whether or not pornography is harmful depends on one's personal views. For those who believe that anything fostering more permissive attitudes toward sexuality or that even viewing others engaging in sexual acts is morally wrong, then exposure to explicit sexual material is clearly unacceptable. Conversely, if one believes that there is nothing wrong with permissive attitudes and being stimulated by explicit materials, then pornography is not harmful. However, there is complete agreement that material involving minors or promoting sexual acts with children is unacceptable.

Pornography and the Internet

Pornography on the Internet is available in different formats, ranging from pictures and short animated movies to sound files and stories. Most of this kind of pornographic content is available to any online user through World Wide Web (WWW) pages. The Internet also makes it possible to discuss sex in chat rooms.

Congress's first attempt to censor pornography came in February 1996 with the passage of the Communications Decency Act (CDA). The CDA imposed broadcast-style content regulations on the open, decentralized Internet and severely restricted the First Amendment rights of all Americans. The CDA prohibited posting "indecent" or "patently offensive" materials in a public forum on the Internet, including web pages, newsgroups, chat rooms, or online discussion lists. However, the Supreme Court ruled that the Internet is entitled to the highest protection under the free speech protections of the First Amendment. In *Reno, Attorney General of the United States, et al., Apellants v. American Civil Liberties Union et al.*, the Court found that the Internet should have the same free speech protection as print. Writing for the Court, Justice John Paul Stevens held that "the CDA places an unacceptably heavy burden on protected speech" and found that all provisions of the CDA are unconstitutional as they apply to "indecent" or "patently offensive" speech. In a separate concurrence, Chief Justice William Rehnquist and Justice Sandra Day O'Connor agreed that the provisions of the CDA are all unconstitutional except in their narrow application to "communications between an adult and one or more minors."[15]

Congress followed with the Child Online Protection Act (COPA), which makes it a crime for anyone, by means of the World Wide Web, to make any communication for commercial purposes that is "harmful to minors," unless the person has restricted access by minors by requiring a credit card number. COPA imposes criminal and civil penalties of up to $50,000 per day for violations. COPA attempts to narrow the focus of the criminal prohibition by using a so-called harmful-to-minors standard. Moreover, COPA establishes a commission to study methods to protect children on the Internet.

Despite the best efforts of Internet activists and the criticisms of civil libertarians, the Child Online Protection Act (COPA) was passed as an amendment to the Internet Tax Freedom Act, an omnibus appropriations bill. Other amendments included provisions for digital signatures, children's privacy, and the Dodd amendment that required ISPs to provide customers with filtering tools.

Questions in Review

1. Describe how the Privacy Act controls the record management of federal agencies.
2. What is the purpose of the Right of Publicity?
3. What is the difference between wire communications and electronic communications?
4. Under the Computer Fraud and Abuse Act, what constitutes malicious damage?
5. Should computer hackers like Robert Morris be severely punished for introducing computer viruses?
6. Should the Child Online Protection Act be repealed as a violation of the First Amendment? Why or why not?

Endnotes

1. 277 U.S. 438 (1928).
2. *Katz v. United States*, 389 U.S. 347 (1967).
3. *Griswold v. Connecticut*, 381 U.S. 479 (1965).
4. *Whalen v. Roe*, 429 U.S. 589 (1977).
5. A. Amar. (2013). *America's unwritten constitution*. New York, NY: Basic Books.
6. A citizen's guide on using the Freedom of Information Act and the Privacy Act of 1974 to request government records. (1977, March 20). House Report 105-37.
7. A citizen's guide on using the Freedom of Information Act and the Privacy Act of 1974 to request government records. (1977, March 20). House Report 105-37.
8. 5 U.S.C. 552 as amended by Pub. L. No. 104-231 110 Stat. 3048.
9. 18 USC, § 1030, PL 99-474.
10. 18 USC, §§ 2510–2522.
11. 18 USC, § 2510(12).
12. 18 USC, § 1030.
13. Roe v. Wade, 410 U.S. 113 (1973).
14. Planned Parenthood v. Casey, 505 U.S. 833 (1992).
15. Reno v. American Civil Liberties Union et al. 117S.Sct. 2329, 138 L.Ed. 2d. 874 (1997).

Crime and Justice Issues

11

Chapter Objectives

After reading this chapter you should be able to

- Identify exceptions to the exclusionary rule
- Explain both the pros and cons of plea bargaining
- Discuss the impact of hate crimes and stalking legislation
- Critically analyze capital punishment from a pro and con position
- Explain the push that has led to prison overcrowding

Introduction

A primary concern of citizens in today's society is crime and justice. Pick up any daily newspaper in the United States and you'll find multiple stories that report crime in the community and what actions by the police, courts, and corrections were taken. We have become a society that knows violence, and many people are more than just a little fearful of being victimized by others. As a whole, the public reaction to crime has been to introduce and pass more laws. In some circumstances, we have taken a second look at existing laws to see if personal rights and privileges have "handcuffed" the criminal justice system that is entrusted with protecting society from wrongdoers.

In this chapter, we examine crime and justice issues facing today's society. While there are many such issues, we have chosen to focus on a few specific matters of law in the areas of citizen rights, victimization, and punishment. We begin by examining the Fourth Amendment protection against unreasonable search and seizure and the exclusionary rule of evidence. Next, we discuss the use of plea bargaining, followed by a general discussion of hate crimes and related laws that deal with such criminal offenses as stalking. In the final portion of the chapter, we take a look at the use of capital punishment and the state of our correctional population in the United States.

285

Exclusionary Rule

The Fourth Amendment to the U.S. Constitution protects "the right of the people to be secure in their persons, houses, papers, and effects, against reasonable searches and seizures." This guarantee protects against actions by the states as well as by the federal government.[1] Generally, the Court has interpreted the Fourth Amendment to mean that before a search or seizure can be effectuated, the police must have probable cause to believe that a crime has been committed and that evidence relevant to the crime will be found at the place to be searched. The exclusionary rule provides that evidence obtained in violation of the Constitution is inadmissible in a criminal trial. The rule excludes all evidence secured by police in violation of recognized constitutional restrictions.

Over the last century, the exclusionary rule has come under fire by critics who suggest some exceptions to the exclusionary should be allowed. Consequently, the U.S. Supreme Court has heard several cases dealing with the issue, and although the exclusionary rule has not been completely discarded, its utilization has been substantially curbed. For example, defendants who themselves were not subjected to illegal searches and seizures may not object to the introduction against themselves of evidence illegally obtained from coconspirators or codefendants.[2] Also, evidence seized through a wrongful search may sometimes be used in the criminal trial if the prosecution can show a sufficient attenuation of the link between police misconduct and obtaining of the evidence.[3]

The most severe curtailment of the rule came in 1984 with the adoption of a "good faith" exception. In *United States v. Leon*,[4] which allows good-faith exceptions to the exclusionary rule, the Court reformulated the test for applying the exclusionary rule and narrowed the scope of Fourth Amendment protection for those arrested for crimes. In this case, police officers received a tip from an informant regarding possible drug dealing among the defendant Leon and others. The officers observed suspicious activities and obtained search warrants. They found incriminating evidence in the searches, but the warrants were later invalidated because the police lacked probable cause and also because the informant was unreliable. Nevertheless, the Court allowed the evidence obtained in the search to be admitted because the police were acting in good faith.

The Court applied a cost–benefit analysis to determine whether the exclusionary rule should be applied. That is, the benefits of deterring unconstitutional police conduct are weighed against the costs of excluding the evidence. The purpose of the rule is to sanction police for overstepping constitutional bounds. In this case, the police were found not to have overstepped their bounds, so the Court concluded that there would be little benefit in applying the rule. The Court found that the costs were much greater. Though the percentage of criminals released was small as a result of its application, the overall number was great. Releasing someone who had broken the law was a cost outweighing any benefit realized in attempting to deter outrageous police conduct.

In 1995, the U.S. Supreme Court further narrowed the application of the exclusionary rule under the Fourth Amendment in *Arizona v. Evans*. The original case involved Isaac Evans, who was pulled over by police for traveling the wrong way on a one-way street. Evans claimed that his license had been suspended, and police ran a records check that showed the suspended license and an outstanding misdemeanor warrant. Police arrested Evans for the outstanding warrant. In the process of the arrest, Evans dropped a marijuana cigarette. Officers then searched Evans's car and found a bag of marijuana under the passenger seat.

An element of the case and the point of major contention by the defendant was that the warrant had been canceled more than 2 weeks before the traffic stop in question. However, the records-checking computer system had not been updated to reflect the changes. In short, Evans had no active warrants for his arrest. At trial, Evans moved to suppress the marijuana evidence, arguing that the exclusionary rule should apply to unconstitutional arrests based on clerical errors, not just cases with errors by police officers.

The trial court threw out the evidence, but the state court of appeals held that because the error was not made by the arresting officer but by a clerical worker, the exclusionary rule would not apply. However, the Arizona Supreme Court reversed this ruling, declaring that there should be no distinction between the police officer and the employees of the court for the purposes of the application of the exclusionary rule. The goal of the exclusionary rule, to prevent police misconduct, should also serve to improve the service of court clerical workers.[5]

The U.S. Supreme Court granted certiorari to determine whether the exclusionary rule requires suppression of evidence seized incident to an arrest resulting from an inaccurate computer record, regardless of whether police personnel or court personnel were responsible for the record's continued presence in the police computer. Judge Rehnquist, writing on behalf of the U.S. Supreme Court majority, said the police officers were unknowingly acting on the errors of court employees who have no stake in criminal proceedings. Any suppression of the evidence would not deter clerical workers from such errors in the future. The Court reversed the decision of the Arizona Supreme Court for the same three reasons it relied upon in *United States v. Leon*. First, the exclusionary rule is designed to deter police misconduct, and no misconduct was found in Evans's case. Second, there is no evidence that court employees are inclined to ignore the Fourth Amendment. Third, there is no evidence that applying the rule will make employees more accurate or deter misconduct. Applying the rule because of a court employee's error would not alter the behavior of the officer making the arrest, because the officer was doing his job. Had the officer not arrested Evans upon notice of the outstanding warrant, the officer would have failed in performing his duty.[6]

Much of the modern debate focuses on whether the constraints placed on police by the exclusionary rule should be lessened even more. Proponents typically support this view by claiming that the exclusionary rule is not grounded in the U.S. Constitution, is not a deterrent to police misconduct, and serves as an obstruction to justice. Those who oppose narrowing the scope of the exclusionary rule argue that to do so would significantly reduce the limitations placed on the government's ability to search the homes and property of citizens. What's more, it would abolish fundamental constitutional protections afforded to citizens and create greater opportunity for police misconduct.

CRIME AND JUSTICE: THE FOURTH, FIFTH, SIXTH, AND EIGHTH AMENDMENTS

The criminal justice system is comprised of police, courts, and corrections. The system functions as a process in which crimes are investigated, charged, prosecuted, and punished. Because the criminal justice system involves actions by the government, citizens enjoy constitutional protections under modern law that stems from both federal and state constitutions. Court rulings typically deal with Fourth, Fifth, Sixth, and Eighth Amendment issues.

Fourth Amendment: Search and Seizure

In the process of investigating a criminal case, police often search for evidence of the crime. The Fourth Amendment to the U.S. Constitution places limits on the government's ability to search the homes and property of citizens. Under the Fourth Amendment, law enforcement officers must have a search warrant, issued upon a showing of probable cause, in order to search a private home or premises without the consent of the occupants. Otherwise, the exclusionary rule applies, and any evidence obtained illegally is inadmissible in a court of law.

There are a few exceptions to the requirement that police obtain a warrant prior to search. At the time of arrest, for example, police may search the individual and the immediate area around the person in a search "incident to an arrest." The exception is necessary to secure the safety of the police officer and the custody of the suspect being arrested. The search also enables the officer to gather the fruits of the crime and prevent the destruction of the evidence. Another exception occurs in circumstances that are viewed as critical and immediate. Certain emergencies that call for immediate action do not allow time to obtain a search warrant; they are exigent circumstances. Police may also search a home or other premises without first obtaining a warrant when the officer in "good faith" believes that:

- A person's life is in danger
- Evidence might be destroyed
- A dangerous suspect may be about to escape

Fifth Amendment: Right to Remain Silent

The Fifth Amendment to the U.S. Constitution provides that no person may be compelled to be a witness against himself or herself. This "right to remain silent" has numerous applications in the law of criminal procedure.

- Under the Fifth Amendment, a person may refuse to answer the questions of law enforcement officers. If a person is called before a grand jury to testify, the person may refuse to answer any questions posing the possibility that they will incriminate themselves. This means that a person can refuse to answer a question requiring them to admit some action constituting a crime or subjecting them to criminal prosecution. Prosecutors may give such individuals immunity from prosecution in order to compel them to testify despite their Fifth Amendment right.
- The Fifth Amendment also means that criminal defendants cannot be called as witnesses at their own trials without their consent.

Lastly, under the Fifth Amendment, a person may not be tried twice for the same crime. The principle of law known as "double jeopardy" means that if a person is found not guilty of a crime, they cannot be tried again for the same crime. However, a person who is found not guilty of a crime under state law may, under certain circumstances, be tried for the same conduct under federal law. Likewise, conduct constituting a crime may amount to a negligent or intentional injury of another person. It is not considered being put "in jeopardy" for a person to be sued under the civil law. Because the proof requirement in a criminal case is higher (proof beyond a reasonable doubt) than in a civil case ("preponderance of the evidence"), an injured person can seek damages for that injury under the civil law of torts. The suit can be made regardless of whether the defendant has been found not guilty of a crime based on the same set of facts (as was the case with O. J. Simpson).

Sixth Amendment: Right to Counsel

The Sixth Amendment to the U.S. Constitution guarantees the right to legal counsel at all significant stages of a criminal proceeding. The right to legal counsel is considered so important that there is an associated right given to persons who are indigent and unable to pay for legal counsel to have counsel appointed and paid for by the government. The Sixth Amendment right to counsel has been extended to

- The interrogation phases of an investigation
- The trial
- Sentencing proceedings
- At least an initial appeal of any conviction

Likewise, the Sixth Amendment guarantees the right to a public trial by jury. Under common law, a criminal defendant is entitled to a public trial by jury in cases of felonies and in cases of misdemeanors where the term of imprisonment may exceed 1 year. Under current constitutional law principles, a jury trial is required where the term of imprisonment may exceed 6 months. Individual states may provide for a jury trial in a broader class of criminal cases. Moreover, the Sixth Amendment states that "the accused shall enjoy the right to a speedy ... trial." This provision is interpreted as meaning that the trial should take place as soon as possible without depriving the parties of a reasonable period of time for preparation. The purposes of this right are:

- To protect an accused from prolonged detention in jail prior to trial
- To prevent long delays that could impair the defense of an accused person through the loss of evidence
- To prevent or minimize public suspicion and anxiety connected with an accused who is yet untried

Eighth Amendment: Cruel and Unusual Punishment

The Eighth Amendment prohibits the infliction of cruel and unusual punishment. Lack of uniformity by the courts in interpreting this constitutional requirement has caused confusion concerning what punishment is prohibited. The Supreme Court ruling in *Trop v. Dulles*, 356 U.S. 86 (1958), asserted that the meaning of the Eighth Amendment must be drawn from "the evolving standards of decency that mark the progress of a maturing society." Several years later, in *Furman v. Georgia*, 408 U.S. 238 (1972), the Court ruled that the imposition and carrying out of the death penalty under those circumstances constituted cruel and usual punishment. However, it reversed itself 4 years later in *Gregg v. Georgia*, 428 U.S. 153 (1976), when in effect the Court lifted the ban on executions in the United States.

Plea Bargaining

In the United States, very few criminal cases are determined by trial. In fact, approximately 90% of cases are decided by guilty pleas.[7] The prosecutor and defense engage in plea bargaining to reach an agreement that spares the state the cost of a trial in exchange for some leniency to the defendant. Typically, the leniency involves a reduced charge or reduced sentence for a guilty plea.

Plea bargaining may be explicit or implicit. Explicit bargaining involves overt negotiations between two or more parties in the case (defense counsel, judge, prosecutor) that results in an agreement on the terms under which the defendant will plead guilty. Implicit bargaining means that the defendant simply understands that a more severe sentence is likely to be imposed if the case goes to trial.

Plea bargaining allows the defendant to avoid a trial and the possibility of a verdict that may result in a more severe sentence by agreeing to plead guilty to a lesser offense. Victims are often most distressed at the perceived ability of the defendant to "get off easy" by bargaining with the prosecutor to lower the offenses of which they may actually be guilty. Many victims and advocates rightfully consider victim participation in the plea negotiation process as essential to providing victims with a voice in the system.

Several states have passed laws that dramatically impact plea bargaining. For example, the "three-strikes legislation" has greatly reduced plea bargaining rates. Likewise, various mandatory sentences have reduced the capacity for plea negotiations. For example, New York's tough drug control laws and Massachusetts's gun control legislation prescribe mandatory incarceration of violators. However, limited plea bargaining has its own consequences in the sense that such laws clog the court system. As more and more defendants opt for trials, court capacities diminish and court costs rise. In order to free crowded court calendars, civil cases are pushed back beyond the point of tolerance of citizens seeking justice. Evaluations of the impact of this type of legislation have shown invariably that it tends to be subverted by practitioners whenever they perceive that injustice would result:

> Prosecutors refuse to press for conviction, juries refuse to convict, and judges refuse to sentence people under these provisions. Hundreds of imaginative ways are found at every level of the criminal justice system (including the police) to circumvent the intent of such laws.[8]

Hate Crimes

In 2011, there were 6,222 hate crime incidents reported to the FBI involving 7,254 hate crime offenses. The 2011 statistics reflected the following number of crime offenses by bias motivation:

- 3,465 were motivated by racial bias
- 1,318 were motivated by religious bias
- 891 were motivated by ethnicity/national origin bias
- 1,508 were motivated by sexual orientation bias
- 58 were motivated by disability bias
- 14 were motivated by multiple biases

In the United States, all of the states, with the exception of Arkansas, Georgia, Indiana, South Carolina, and Wyoming,[9] have passed some form of hate crime statute. These laws have come in a variety of forms, including

- Outlawing vandalism against religious institutions, such as churches and synagogues
- Outlawing intimidation of individuals
- Allowing for civil actions against perpetrators of hate crimes
- Holding parents liable for the actions of their children
- Requiring states to compile statistics on hate crimes

In addition, some states have gone further by enacting statutes that "enhance" criminal penalties for hate-motivated crimes.

On the federal level, several efforts have resulted in legislation to control hate crimes. Of particular importance are the Hate Crimes Statistics Act, the Hate Crimes Sentencing Enhancement Act, and the Church Arsons Prevention Act.

The Hate Crimes Statistics Act, which originally became law in 1990, was reauthorized in the 104th Congress. This law calls for states and localities to voluntarily report all hate crimes to the FBI. Under the Hate Crime Statistics Act, the attorney general collects data on the number of crimes committed each year that are motivated by "prejudice based on race, religion, sexual orientation, or ethnicity." The attorney general has directed the Federal Bureau of Investigation's Uniform Crime Reporting Program to collect the data and produce annual reports.

Meanwhile, the FBI has trained almost 3,700 staff members from almost 1,200 state, local, and federal law enforcement agencies on how to prevent, prosecute, and deal with the aftermath of hate crimes. In these training programs, the FBI works with the Justice Department's Community Relations Service (CRS). Created by the 1964 Civil Rights Act, CRS is the only federal agency whose most important purpose is to help communities cope with disputes among different racial, religious, and ethnic groups. CRS professionals have helped with Hate Crime Statistics Act training sessions for hundreds of law enforcement officials from police agencies around the country.

The Hate Crimes Sentencing Enhancement Act, which was part of the Violent Crime Control and Law Enforcement Act of 1994, provides for tougher sentencing when it is proven beyond a doubt that the crime committed was a hate crime. Because federal law enforcement agencies do not yet have jurisdiction over anti-gay hate crimes, this law can only be used against hate crimes based on sexual orientation when the offense occurs on federal property, such as a national park.

Likewise, Congress passed the Violence Against Women Act, a comprehensive federal response to the national problem of violence against women. This legislative package included $1.6 billion in funding for improved law enforcement and prosecution programs, victims services such as domestic violence shelters and rape crisis centers, and education and research programs. It also included new domestic violence offenses as well as changes in immigration law and other legal forms. Most significantly, it includes a civil rights remedy—a provision allowing a woman to sue in federal or state court for an act of gender-motivated violence that rises to the level of a felony.[10] The Violence Against Women Act was reenacted in 2013 and included additional protections for gay individuals and individuals living on Indian reservations.

In the aftermath of the rash of fires at black churches, and with the strong support of the Leadership Conference on Civil Rights, Congress passed and President Clinton signed into law the Church Arsons Prevention Act of 1996. The law enhances federal jurisdiction over and increases the federal penalties for the destruction of houses of worship. Congress and the Clinton administration provided $12 million for a federal investigation of the church fires. In addition, the act gives a continuing mandate to the Hate Crime Statistics Act.

The Hate Crimes Prevention Act (HCPA) undertook amending Section 245 of Title 18 U.S.C., one of the primary statutes to combat racial and religious bias-motivated violence. The current statute, which was enacted in 1968, prohibits intentional interference, by force or threat of force, with the enjoyment of a federal right or benefit (e.g., voting, going to school, etc.) on the basis of race, color, religion, or national origin. Government must prove both that the crime occurred because of a person's membership in a protected group (e.g., race, religion, etc.) and because he or she was engaging in a federally protected activity.

IN SUPPORT OF THE HATE CRIMES PROTECTION ACT: THE CASES OF JAMES BYRD AND MATHEW SHEPARD

On June 7, 1998, in Jasper, Texas, 49-year-old James Byrd, Jr., was the victim of a hate crime, targeted simply because he was black. Byrd was savagely beaten, then shackled by his ankles with a 24-foot logging chain to a pickup truck and dragged for three miles. His body, minus his head, neck and an arm, was dumped between a black church and cemetery, where it was found a few hours after daylight.

Police arrested Lawrence Russell Brewer, 31, Shawn Allen Berry, 23, and John William King, 23, for the crime of first-degree murder. FBI investigators disclosed that the suspects had ties to white-supremacist groups and that two had tattoos of the Aryan Brotherhood, a racist prison gang. One carried a lighter engraved with an emblem of the Ku Klux Klan. All three men were tried and found guilty. Brewer and King received the death penalty and will be executed by lethal injection. Berry will serve the rest of his life in prison.

Between the night of October 6 and the early morning of October 7, 1998, in southern Wyoming, Matthew Shepard was brutally attacked and tied to a fence simply because he was gay. Shepard met Russell Henderson and Aaron McKinney, who told him they were gay. Henderson and McKinney drove Shepard to a remote area, where they severely beat him and then left the 21-year-old University of Wyoming student to die in near-freezing temperatures. Five days after the beating, he died from his injuries in a Colorado hospital.

Russell Henderson, 21, and Aaron McKinney, 21, were charged with first-degree murder, aggravated robbery, and kidnapping. Henderson decided to plead guilty to the charges of felony murder and kidnapping, with robbery as the underlying motive. He was subsequently sentenced to two consecutive life sentences. A jury in Laramie, Wyoming, found Aaron McKinney guilty of felony murder, kidnapping, and aggravated robbery and sentenced him also to two life sentences. Chasity Pasley, the girlfriend of Russell Henderson, was sentenced to 15 to 24 months in jail for her attempted cover-up of her boyfriend's role in Matthew Shepard's murder.

CRIMES AGAINST DISABLED PERSONS

The victimization of individuals with disabilities was largely over-looked on the national level prior to passage of the Americans with Disabilities Act (ADA) of 1990 (42 U.S.C. 12101). The ADA provided a new framework for governmental and nonprofit agencies responding to individuals with disabilities. Since its implementation, the Department of Justice and other federal agencies have initiated a variety of efforts to provide information to state and local criminal and juvenile justice agencies and victim-assistance programs on the intent and require-ments of the act. Several milestones that illustrate the victim-service field's growing awareness and concern about addressing the needs of victims with disabilities are noted as follows:

- In 1990, the National Organization for Victim Assistance (NOVA) first helped to bring awareness to the many obstacles faced by disabled victims seeking services with its publication entitled *Responding to Disabled Victims of Crime* in 1990.
- In 1992, the National Resource Center on Child Sexual Abuse (NRCCSA) published a comprehensive series of articles, writ-ten by research and practitioner experts, on the sexual abuse of children with disabilities. In addition, the Center's annual National Symposium on Child Sexual Abuse regularly features a training track on child victims with disabilities.
- In 1993, with support from the Office for Victims of Crime, the National Center for Victims of Crime (NCVC) developed a training curriculum entitled *Differently Abled Victims of Crime* that provides extensive information on how to provide special-ized services and information to disabled crime victims.
- In 1993, the National Center on Child Abuse and Neglect (NCCAN) released findings from a comprehensive national study entitled *A Report on the Maltreatment of Children with Disabilities*. The study focused on maltreated children who had physical, intellectual, or emotional disabilities. It found a significant correlation between maltreated children and abuse and offered key recommendations for responding to abused children with disabilities.
- After the passage of the Americans with Disabilities Act in 1990, the National Institute of Justice (NIJ), within the U.S. Department of Justice, launched an initiative to examine the implications of the ADA for criminal justice agencies at the

state and local levels. In 1993, NIJ published *The Americans with Disabilities Act and Criminal Justice: An Overview* as a bulletin in its *Research in Action* publication series.

- In 1994, Dick Sobsey's books, *Violence and Abuse in the Lives of People with Disabilities: The End of Silent Acceptance* and *Violence and Disability: An Annotated Bibliography*, were published. The texts extensively review literature on violence and abuse toward individuals with disabilities and provide guidance for prevention of abuse and victimization. Although much of the material focuses on individuals with developmental disabilities and abuse in institutions, the books give new weight to the overall issue of victims with disabilities.

- In 1997, the Victims of Crime Committee of the Criminal Justice Task Force for People with Developmental Disabilities in Sacramento, California, issued its report outlining evidence of the high rates of violent and criminal victimization of people with developmental and other substantial disabilities (including mental retardation; autism; cerebral palsy; epilepsy; traumatic brain injury; severe major mental disorders; degenerative brain disease such as Alzheimer's, Parkinson's, and Huntington's; permanent damage from stroke; organic brain damage; and others). These high rates of victimization, coupled with underreporting of the crimes and low rates of prosecution and conviction, led the committee to develop 59 recommendations to improve the reporting, investigation, and prosecution of such crimes. In addition, the group called for multidisciplinary teams to provide victim support and numerous measures to prevent abuse and victimization by service providers. Finally, the committee recommended that the Bureau of Justice Statistics include information on victims with developmental and other substantial disabilities in its Crime Victimization Survey. Members of the committee, including Daniel Sorensen, chair, and Joan Petersilia, presented the recommendations to the California legislature and to members of Congress.

- On October 27, 1998, the president signed the Crime Victims with Disabilities Act of 1998, which represents the first effort to systematically gather information on the extent of the problem of victimization of individuals with disabilities. This legislation directed the attorney general to conduct a study on crimes against individuals with developmental disabilities within 18 months. In addition, the Bureau of Justice Statistics had to include statistics on the nature of crimes against individuals with developmental disabilities and victim characteristics in its annual National Crime Victimization Survey beginning in 2000. The legislation was sponsored by Senator Mike DeWine (OH), a former prosecutor, and represents an unprecedented level of attention to an often overlooked crime victim group.

Adapted from: **Jane Sigmon & Christine Edmunds. (2000). Victimization of individuals with disabilities. In A. Seymour, M. Murray, J. Sigmon, C. Edmunds, M. Gaboury, et al. (Eds.).** *National victim assistance academy 2000* **(chapter 15). Washington, DC: National institute of Justice.**

Stalking

Stalking first garnered widespread public concern when a popular young actress named Rebecca Schaeffer was shot to death in 1989 by an obsessed fan who had stalked her for 2 years. High-profile cases of celebrities being stalked have raised the public's awareness of this crime. Television and radio talk shows and the mass market print media all ran stories about stalking, its potentially deadly consequences, the terrifying helplessness victims experienced, and celebrities who had been stalked.[11] But the majority of stalking victims are ordinary people, mostly women, who are being pursued and threatened by someone with whom they have had a prior relationship.

Researchers estimated that approximately 1 million women and 400,000 men are stalked each year in the United States. About half of all female stalking victims reported their victimization to police, and about 25% obtained a restraining order. Assailants violated 80% of all restraining orders. About 24% of female victims who reported stalking to the police, as compared to 19% of male victims, said their cases were prosecuted. Of the cases in which criminal charges were filed, 54% resulted in a conviction. About 63% of convictions resulted in jail time.[12]

Although stalking is a gender-neutral crime, women are the primary victims and men the primary perpetrators. Data from the National Violence Against Women Survey (NVAW) suggest that 78% of stalking victims are women; 22% are men. By comparison, 94% of stalkers identified by female victims and 60% identified by male victims were male. Young adults were stalkers' primary targets: 52% of victims were 18 to 29 years old when the stalking began, and 22% were 30 to 39. On average, victims were 28 years old when the stalking started. Most victims knew their stalkers: 77% of female victims and 64% of male victims knew their stalker. Current or former husbands and former dates or boyfriends stalked 38% and 14% of female victims, respectively. Overall, 59% of female victims compared with 30% of male victims were stalked by intimate partners or former intimate partners. Previous reports indicate that the stalking of a woman by an intimate or a former intimate partner typically occurs after she attempts to leave the relationship. The NVAW survey found that 21% of victims who were stalked by intimate partners said it occurred before the relationship ended, 43% said afterward, and 36% said both before and afterward.[13]

Interstate Stalking Punishment and Prevention Act of 1996

In 1996, Congress enacted a law prohibiting interstate stalking and stalking on federal property. This federal legislation, the Interstate Stalking Punishment and Prevention Act of 1996, contains several provisions of law, including:[14]

- Interstate domestic violence (Title 18 U.S. Code 2261)
  Crossing a state line: A person who travels across a state line or enters or leaves Indian country with the intent to injure, harass, or intimidate that person's spouse or intimate partner, and who, in the course of or as a result of such travel, intentionally commits a crime of violence and thereby causes bodily injury to such spouse or intimate partner shall be punished.
  Causing the crossing of a state line: A person who causes a spouse or intimate partner to cross a state line or to enter or leave Indian country by force, coercion, duress, or fraud and, in the course or as a result of that conduct, intentionally commits a crime of violence and thereby causes bodily injury to the person's spouse or intimate partner shall be punished.
- Interstate stalking (Title 18 U.S. Code 2261A)
  Whoever travels across a state line or within the special maritime and territorial jurisdiction of the United States with the intent to injure or harass another person, and in the course of, or as a result of, such travel places that person in reasonable fear of the death of, or serious bodily injury to, that person or a member of that person's immediate family shall be punished.
- Interstate violation of protection order (Title 18 U.S. Code 2262)
  Crossing a state line: A person who travels across a state line or enters or leaves Indian country with the intent to engage in conduct that
  1. Violates the portion of a protection order that involves protection against credible threats of violence, repeated harassment, or bodily injury to the person or persons for whom the protection order was issued shall be punished.

2. Would violate this subparagraph if the conduct occurred in the jurisdiction in which the order was issued, and subsequently engages in such conduct, shall be punished.

Causing the crossing of a state line: A person who causes a spouse or intimate partner to cross a state line or to enter or leave Indian country by force, coercion, duress, or fraud, and, in the course or as a result of that conduct, intentionally commits an act that injures the person's spouse or intimate partner in violation of a valid protection order issued by a state shall be punished.

Punishment

A person who violates these sections shall be both fined and imprisoned

- For life or any term of years if death of the victim results
- For not more than 20 years if permanent disfigurement or life-threatening bodily injury to the victim results
- For not more than 10 years if serious bodily injury to the victim results or if the offender uses a dangerous weapon during the offense
- For not more than 5 years in any other case

State Anti-Stalking Legislation

All 50 states and the District of Columbia have some form of anti-stalking law. Most state statutes define stalking as a crime involving "the willful, malicious, and repeated following or harassing of another person."[15] Generally, anti-stalking laws can be classified into three different categories based on the punishment. They include

- Statutes that make stalking a misdemeanor offense
- Statutes that distinguish between first-time and chronic offending, with penalties ranging from misdemeanor to felony offenses, respectively
- Statutes that make all stalking a felony offense

VICTIMOLOGY

Andrew Karmen, who wrote a comprehensive text on victimology entitled *Crime Victims: An Introduction to Victimology*, broadly defined *victimology* as

the scientific study of victimization, including the relationships between victims and offenders, the interactions between victims and the criminal justice system—that is, the police and courts, and corrections officials—and the connections between victims and other societal groups and institutions, such as the media, businesses, and social movements.

The scientific study of victimology can be traced back to the 1940s and 1950s. Until then, the primary focus of research and academic analysis in the field of criminology was on criminal perpetrators and criminal acts, rather than on victims. Two criminologists, Mendelsohn and Von Hentig, began to study the other half of the offender/victim dyad: the victim. They are now considered the "fathers of the study of victimology."

In their efforts to understand crime, these new "victimologists" began to study the behaviors and vulnerabilities of victims, such as the resistance of rape victims and the characteristics of the types of people who were victims of crime, especially murder victims.

In the course of his legal practice, Mendelsohn interviewed his clients to obtain information about the crime and the victim. He viewed the victim as one factor among many in the criminal case. His analysis of information about victims led him to theorize that victims had an "unconscious aptitude for being victimized." Von Hentig studied crime and victims in the 1940s, and Steven Shaffer later published *The Criminal and His Victim*. Their analysis of murder focused on the types of people who were most likely to be victims of homicide. The most likely type of victim Von Hentig identified is the "depressive type," who was seen as an easy target, careless and unsuspecting. The "greedy type" was seen as easily duped because his or her motivation for easy gain lowers his or her natural tendency to be suspicious. The "wanton type" is particularly vulnerable to stresses that occur at a given period of time in the life cycle, such as juvenile victims. Von Hentig's last type was the "tormentor," the victim of attack from the target of his abuse, such as the battered woman.

Von Hentig's work provided the foundation for analysis of victim-proneness that is still evident in the literature today. Wolfgang's research followed this lead and later theorized that "many victim-precipitated homicides were, in fact, caused by the unconscious desire of the victims to commit suicide."

Viewed from the perspective of criminology, victimology initially devoted much of its energy to the study of how the victims contribute—knowingly or unknowingly—to their own victimization, and potential ways they may share responsibility with offenders for specific crimes.

The negative effects of "victim blaming" have been a key tenet in the fight to improve the treatment of crime victims. Research into ways in which victims "contribute" to their own victimization was (and continues to be) viewed by victims and victim advocates as both unacceptable and destructive.

As crime victim services and rights have expanded throughout the last two decades, practitioners and public-policy makers have looked to research to provide a more scientific foundation for service design and delivery. More recent avenues of studies in victimology have included

- How various components of the criminal justice system treat victims
- The impact of victimization
- The effectiveness of certain interventions with crime victims

Extensive qualitative and quantitative research about the nature and scope of crime victim services has been conducted and published. Studies about the effectiveness of interventions with crime victims have also been done. In addition, the debate about the scope and focus of victimology is evolving and is illustrated in the sharply contrasting topics of research that are found in a variety of victimology journals.

Adapted from: **J.N. Burnley, C. Edmunds, M.T. Gaboury, & A. Seymour (Eds.). (1998). Theoretical perspectives of victimology and critical research. In *1998 National Victim Assistance Academy* (chapter 3). Washington, DC: National Institute of Justice.**

Capital Punishment

Throughout the history of mankind, people have been put to death for committing certain types of transgressions against society. The Code of Hammurabi (1750 B.C.) used the death penalty as a means of retaliation against those who committed crimes. "An eye for an eye" is a common quotation used to depict the retaliatory nature of this doctrine of punishment. In the seventh century B.C., the Draconian Code of Athens made death the prescribed penalty for every crime committed. Later, in the fifth century B.C., the Roman Law of the Twelve Tablets codified the death penalty. A death sentence was carried out in cruel fashion involving such methods as being buried alive, beheading, crucifixion, hanging, and stoning to death. The most infamous execution in history occurred approximately 33 A.D., with the crucifixion of Jesus Christ.

Law reform regulating the use of the death penalty began to emerge in Europe in the 19th century. For example, between 1832 and 1837, Britain did away with many capital offenses. By the end of the 20th century, more and more European countries had abolished capital punishment. Today, only a few European countries retain the death penalty.

The Death Penalty in America

Capital punishment was first used in America in 1622, when a thief named Daniel Frank was put to death in Virginia.[16] Most of the early colonies were very strict in their use of the death penalty. Under the capital punishment laws of New England, which were enacted between 1636 and 1647, the death penalty was imposed for such crimes as adultery, bestiality, blasphemy, man-stealing, murder, rape, rebellion, sodomy, and witchcraft.[17] In 1665, the New York colony instituted the so-called Duke's Laws, which dictated that death was the proper punishment for denial of the true God, premeditated murder, killing someone who had no weapon of defense, killing by lying in wait or by poisoning, sodomy, buggery, kidnapping, perjury in a capital trial, traitorous denial of the king's rights or raising arms to resist his authority, conspiracy to invade towns or forts in the colony, and striking one's mother or father.[18] By 1776, most of the colonies had roughly comparable death statutes, and the method of execution was hanging.

The first tangible reforms to capital punishment in America occurred in the mid-1800s, as two progressive ideologies about punishment began to converge. First, it became apparent that executions were becoming more of a public spectacle for amusement rather than an event to deter crime. Public hangings encouraged merchants to sell alcohol to citizens who were on hand to celebrate the execution. The melee that often ensued because of drunkenness caused total disruption of the justice process. As a result, many states enacted laws providing private hangings. Rhode Island (1833), Pennsylvania (1834), New York (1835), Massachusetts (1835), and New Jersey (1835) all abolished public hangings. By 1849, 15 states were holding private hangings.[19]

The second progressive force that reformed the use of capital punishment was the advent of the prison system in America. In 1790, the Philadelphia Society established the first penitentiary at the Walnut Street Jail. This institution served as the model for what became known as the Pennsylvania system, thus setting the stage for using incarceration as a form of punishment. The Auburn or New York system of incarceration emerged next in the United States. This method of imprisonment, which involved the use of corporal punishment and hard labor, was adopted by many states as a clear alternative to reliance on capital punishment.

As new ideas about punishment began to take hold along with the building of more prisons, the 20th century saw a constant decline in the number of executions in America. Between 1930 and 1967, 3,859 persons were put to death by state and federal authorities. The years 1935 and 1936 were peak years, with approximately 200 executions each year. An average of 128 persons were executed annually during the 1940s, 72 during the 1950s, and 19 during the 1960s.[20] This decline in executions led many to believe that, like the European countries, the United States would ultimately cease to apply the death penalty either by law or de facto through lack of use.[21] However, this has not been the case. After the U.S. Supreme Court reaffirmed the constitutionality of capital punishment in *Gregg v. Georgia*, 428 U.S. 153 (1976), executions resumed. Since this landmark case, over 700 persons have been executed in the United States, most occurring in the southern states.

Starting in 2010, there was a decrease in the number of persons executed by the states each year. It appears that public support for capital punishment is decreasing, and the states have reduced its use for financial reasons.

Imprisonment

The U.S. prison population has quadrupled in the past 30 years. In 1980, the total prison population was 320,000. At year end 2011, 1,598,780 were incarcerated in federal and state prisons. The people behind bars were held as follows:[22]

- 1,598,780 in state and federal prisons
- 18,394 in territorial prisons

Between 2010 and 2011, the imprisonment rate or the number of sentenced prisoners divided by the U.S. resident population times 100,000 actually declined from 500 to 492 per 100,000 U.S. residents. About 61% of the sentenced prison population in 2011 was age 39 or younger. About 1 in every 11 black males in their late 20s was serving a sentence of a year or more in a state or federal prison. The imprisonment rates indicate that about 0.5% of all white males, more than 3.0% of all black males, and 1.2% of all Hispanic males were imprisoned in 2011. Between 6.6% and 7.5% of all black males ages 25 to 39 were imprisoned in 2011, which were the highest imprisonment rates among the measured sex, race, Hispanic origin, and age groups.

The percentage of all prisoners housed in private prison facilities increased slightly in 2011 from 7.9% to 8.2% of state and federal inmates. Texas (18,603 inmates) and Florida (11,827 inmates) had the highest number of inmates in private prisons.[23] The high rate of incarcerating prisoners has become a major concern with state budgets already seriously lacking funding throughout the country.

What major factors have contributed to increased correctional populations? Some scholars suggest that changes in sentencing and parole policies and practices are the principal cause of increased numbers of people in prison. One clear example is the effect of drug sentencing policies that mandate the incarceration of drug manufacturers and dealers. Changes in parole policies have also increased prison populations by means of reduced tolerance for parole violators, increased rates of revocation and readmission to prison, and the abolition of parole in some jurisdictions.[24]

Private Prisons

The use of private firms to operate correctional institutions has steadily grown in the United States since the mid-1980s. An annual survey of private adult facilities has shown an increase from about 3,000 prisoners in 1987 to more than 84,000 state inmates and 27,000 federal inmates in 2006. In fact, 7% of the 1.5 million prisoners in the United States are held in privately operated prisons.[25]

In 2000, private corporations ran approximately 6% of all U.S. jails and prisons. This equates to the management of roughly 112,000 inmates. Correctional Corporation of America (CCA) is the leading private correctional corporation, with 52% of the private prison market. CCA was founded in 1983 and manages approximately 68,000 adult and juvenile inmates in 75 facilities under contract or under development and ownership of 45 facilities in the United States, Puerto Rico, and United Kingdom. The next largest private prison organization is Florida-based Wackenhut Corrections Corporation, which holds about 27% share of the private correctional market. As many as 20 other private firms are involved in what has been frequently called "prison for profit."[26]

The movement toward privatizing corrections is not supported by all. Opponents argue that cost reductions to taxpayers can only be achieved by lowering the standard of care and treatment of prisoners. Inhumane treatment of prisoners in profit-making institutions has been known to happen. For example, the state of Missouri entered into a 3-year, $6-million contract for services with Capital Correctional Resources Inc., a private jail-management company. Between 1995 and 1997, more than 2,000 prisoners were transported to Brazoria County Detention Center in Angleton, Texas. In 1997, a videotape of a shakedown surfaced, which showed that prisoners were beaten by guards, shocked with stun guns, and bitten by dogs. Consequently, the prisoners filed several state and federal lawsuits. A judgment was rendered in a class-action suit, and the inmates were awarded $1.1 million. Another $800,000 was granted for attorneys' fees as well as $300,000 to cover costs for the litigation.

Questions in Review

1. What is the good-faith exception to the exclusionary rule?
2. What are the pros and cons of plea bargaining?
3. What difficulties arise when laws in society specify crimes against certain people?

4. Are laws against stalking sufficient in today's society?
5. Why are you for or against capital punishment in America?
6. Should changes in the law be made to reduce prison crowding?

Endnotes

1. *Mapp v. Ohio*, 367 U.S. 643 (1961).
2. *Rakas v. Illinois*, 439 U.S. 128 (1978); *Rawlings v. Kentucky*, 448 U.S. 98 (1980).
3. *New York v. Harris*, 495 U.S. 14 (1990).
4. *U.S. v. Leon*, 468 U.S. 897 (1984).
5. 177 Ariz. 201, 866 P. 2d 869.
6. *Arizona v. Evans* (93-1660), 514 U.S. 1 (1995).
7. Statistics from the U.S. Sentencing Commission.
8. E.E. Flynn. (1976, May). Turning judges into robots. *The Forensic Quarterly*, 50(2): 143–149.
9. A. Smith & C. Foley. (2010, September). *State statutes governing hate crimes*. Washington, DC: Congressional Research Service.
10. 42 U.S.C. 13981 (1996).
11. Domestic violence, stalking, and antistalking legislation: An annual report to Congress under the Violence Against Women Act. (2013, March).
12. National Institute of Justice. (1997, November). *The crime of stalking: How big is the problem?* Washington, DC: Author.
13. P. Tjaden & N. Thoennes. (2000). *Extent, nature, and consequences of intimate partner violence: Findings from the national violence against women survey* (NCJ 181867). Washington, DC: U.S. Department of Justice.
14. The Interstate Stalking Punishment and Prevention Act of 1996 (18 U.S.C. § 2261A, 2261, 2262).
15. M. Puente. (1992, July 21). Legislators tackling the terror of stalking. *USA Today*, p. 49.
16. H.A. Bedau. (1982). *The death penalty in America*. New York, NY: Oxford University Press.
17. H.A. Bedau. (1982). *The death penalty in America*. New York, NY: Oxford University Press.
18. H.A. Bedau. (1982). *The death penalty in America*. New York, NY: Oxford University Press.
19. P.E. Mackey. (1976). *Voices against death: American opposition to capital punishment, 1787–1975*. New York: Burt Franklin & Co., Inc., 1976.
20. U.S. Department of Justice. (1997, December). Bulletin. Washington, DC: Bureau of Justice Statistics.
21. F. Zimring & G. Hawkins. (1986). *Capital punishment and the American agenda*. New York, NY: Cambridge University Press.
22. Bureau of Justice Statistics. (2012, December). Correctional surveys: National probation data survey, national prisoner statistics, survey of jails, and the national parole data survey. In *Prisoners in 2011* (NCJ 239808). Washington, DC: Author.

23. A. Beck. (2000, August). *Prisoners in 1999* (NCJ 183476). Washington, DC: U.S. Department of Justice, Bureau of Justice Statistics.
24. J. Petersilia. (1999). Parole and prisoner re-entry in the United States. In M. Tonry & J. Petersilia (Eds.), *Prisons*, Vol. 26 of M. Tonry (Ed.), *Crime and justice: A review of research*. Chicago, IL: University of Chicago Press.
25. W.J. Sabol, T.D. Minton, & P.M. Harrison. (2007). *Prison and jail inmates at midyear 2006*. Washington, DC: U.S. Department of Justice, Bureau of Justice Statistics.
26. G. Gaes. (2008, March). Cost, performance studies look at prison privatization. *National Institute of Justice Journal, 2008*(259). Retrieved July 2, 2013, from http://www.nij.gov/journals/259/prison-privatization.htm

Labor Issues and the Law

12

Chapter Objectives

After reading this chapter you should be able to

- Explain the key legal issues in the relationship between employees and employers
- Define the current government labor policies
- Provide a brief history of the labor movement in the United States
- Explain the functions of the National Labor Relations Board
- Discuss the requirements of the Labor-Management Reporting and Disclosure Act of 1959
- Define the concept of federal preemption
- Discuss employers' and employees' rights
- Explain the Fair Labor Standards Act
- Discuss the rules regarding employee discrimination and workers' compensation

Introduction

Probably in no other area of society does law dictate the relationships between individuals and between companies and individuals than in the area of labor law. The majority of Americans are employed by a business or governmental organization. Labor law has a profound effect on all. It is a mirror reflection of our society.

Prior to the Industrial Revolution, most individuals lived on a farm or in a small community. Bosses knew their employees by name. The Industrial Revolution profoundly altered this relationship. Bosses no longer knew their workers personally and therefore felt little responsibility for them. Most employees were "at will" employees, meaning that they could be fired without notice and without cause. The lives of most employees were grim. Our courts and legislatures gradually realized that employees lacked the ability to bargain with employers on an even basis and that governmental regulation was needed. As a result of government intervention, the relationships between employers and employees are now extensively regulated by the law. The law

307

sets minimum wages that employers must pay, provides extensive rules and regulations that the employers must follow, and gives workers many rights and privileges that were not present in the early years of our country. Labor law affects every member of our society.

NEW YORK STATE EMPLOYMENT LAWS KNOWN AS LABOR STANDARDS

The regulatory agency in the state of New York that oversees labor law is the Division of Labor Standards.[1] The Division of Labor Standards enforces the New York State labor laws that govern

- Minimum wage
- Hours of work
- Child labor
- Payment of wages and wage supplements
- Industrial homework
- Apparel industry registration
- Registration of professional employer organizations
- Farm labor

The division also enforces the Employment Agency Law outside New York City. This law falls under Article 11 of the General Business Law.

- Wage and hour law
- Payment of tips received by credit card and cash
- Child labor
- Apparel industry
- Farm labor
- Licenses, permits, certifications, and registrations
- Professional employer organizations
- Mandatory overtime for nurses

Governmental Labor Policies

As industrialization spread across America during the 19th century, factory workers found that employment conditions became unbearable and that their wages were inadequate. Workers, many of whom were women and children, worked 60 to 70 hours per week and oftentimes more. For many, these hours were spent standing alongside assembly lines in suffocating, dimly lit factories, performing monotonous yet dangerous work with heavy machinery. Other workers labored over solitary tasks and were paid piece-meal. Conditions in the coal mines were equally oppressive. Because of these intolerable conditions, workers attempted to band together into associations and unions in order to press for higher pay and better working conditions. Most state courts, who were favorable to the manufacturers and mine owners, regarded these coordinated efforts by workers as criminal conspiracies.

In 1842, the Massachusetts Supreme Court was the first state high court to reject the use of criminal law to prevent worker organizations. The court ruled that workers could join together for legitimate economic goals and that their actions would become illegal only if they used illegal means to achieve the goals.[2] As other state courts followed the lead of the Massachusetts court, employers and mine owners then turned to civil lawsuits to curtail union activities

In 1890, the Sherman Act was passed by the U.S. Congress. The Sherman Act outlawed monopolies and other combinations of actions that tended to restrain trade. The courts, being generally unfriendly to workers, relied on the act to issue antistrike orders by declaring that strikes and labor associations illegally restrained trade.

During the Great Depression, which started in 1929, public sympathy shifted to the workers. Legislatures reacting to public opinion began to take steps to protect the rights of workers. Accordingly, the Norris-LaGuardia Act was passed in 1932. This act prohibited federal courts from issuing injunctions in nonviolent labor disputes. No longer could employers and mine owners obtain an injunction by merely claiming that the union was planning or conducting a strike. Congress, in declaring that workers should be permitted to organize unions and to use their collective power to achieve legitimate economic ends, established a national policy of promoting collective bargaining between employers and employees. This policy, which still prevails today, led to explosive growth in labor union membership in the 1940s. The term *collective bargaining*, when used in situations involving labor issues, refers to negotiations between an employer and a group of employees, in most cases a union, to form a work contract between the employer and the group of employees.

National Labor Relations Act

Perhaps the most important piece of labor legislation passed by the U.S. Congress was the Wagner Act, which is also known as the National Labor Relations Act (NLRA) of 1935. The stated goal of the NLRA was establishment and maintenance of industrial peace in order to preserve the flow of commerce. The act protected the rights of workers to form unions and encouraged management and unions to bargain collectively and productively. The cornerstone of the act is Section 7, which guarantees employees the right to organize and join unions, to bargain collectively through representatives of their own choosing, and to engage in concerted activities.

Section 8 established the concept of an unfair labor practice (ULP). That section made it an ULP for an employer to

- Interfere with union organizing efforts
- Dominate or interfere with any union
- Discriminate against a union member
- Refuse to bargain collectively with a union

The NLRA also established the National Labor Relations Board (NLRB). The purpose of the NLRB was to administer and interpret the NLRA and to adjudicate labor cases. The board has five members appointed by the president and approved by the Senate. The Board makes final agency decisions about representation and ULP cases. The NLRB has two primary tasks:

- *Representation*: The board decides whether a particular union is entitled to represent a group of employees.
- *Adjudication*: The board adjudicates claims by either workers or employers that the other side has committed an unfair labor practice. The board, however, does not have any enforcement power. If it appears that the losing party is not accepting a board's ruling, the board must appeal to the U.S. Court of Appeals to obtain a court order to enforce its order.

After the passage of the NLRA and throughout the 1930s and 1940s, the unions grew in size and power. Strikes and work stoppages became common. Employers complained of union abuse. Congress responded by adopting the Taft-Hartley Act, also known as the Labor-Management Relations Act of 1947. This act was designed to curb union abuses. It amended the NLRA to outlaw certain union acts and to make those selected acts as unfair labor practices. Thus, it became a ULP for a union to

- Interfere with employees who are exercising their labor rights under Section 7 of the NLRA
- Encourage an employer to discriminate against a particular employee because of a union dispute with the employee
- Refuse to bargain collectively with an employer
- Engage in an illegal strike or boycott, particularly secondary boycotts.

In a continuing move to prevent union abuses, Congress also passed the Labor-Management Reporting and Disclosure Act of 1959. That act requires financial disclosures by union leaders and guarantees union members free speech and fair elections.

Present State of Labor Unions

Labor unions reached their high point in membership in the late 1940s and early 1950s. At that time, about 30% of the workforce belonged to a union. Today that percentage is less than 15%. Many employers now contend that unions are no longer needed in modern America. Union supporters contend that while the pay of CEOs has soared, the wages of the average worker, in real dollars, have fallen since the 1970s.

Federal Preemption

All states have some form of labor statutes, most of which are patterned after the federal statutes. There are three general types of state labor relations statutes. One type is under state antitrust statutes, and it bans or limits union activities in those areas not covered by federal statutes. Another type sets up comprehensive labor relations frameworks similar to the NLRA for those employment cases not covered by federal statutes. Another type of state statutes covers only a narrow range of activities. An example of the latter type is where several states have enacted a statute that bans picketing and boycotting entirely in those areas not covered by federal labor law statutes. In situations that are involved in interstate commerce or that affect interstate commerce, the federal law applies. In situations not covered by federal law, states labor statutes then apply. The doctrine of "preemption" provides that states have no jurisdiction to regulate issues or practices that are governed by federal law. Preemption clearly applies in labor issues that involve interstate commerce, i.e., commerce that flows across state lines. Since most of the federal labor statutes are very comprehensive and indicate a desire by the federal government to govern labor issues and establish uniform policies, and because most involve interstate commerce, in most cases federal law applies.

Exclusivity

Under Section 9 of the NLRA, a validly recognized union is the exclusive representative of all employees in a bargaining unit. The key issues under Section 9 are

- Which organization is the validly recognized union
- What constitutes the bargaining unit

Once a union is selected as the recognized union, only that union has the right to bargain on behalf of the employees in a designated unit. The union must bargain for all employees within the unit, even those who are not union members.

Generally, a union's efforts to become the recognized union involve the following pattern: a campaign, obtaining authorization cards, recognition, petition, and finally election. The campaign starts when union organizers talk with employees and interest them in forming a union. Union organizers then obtain authorization cards from employees. The authorization cards state that the particular workers who signed the cards authorize the union to be their exclusive bargaining agent. After the union obtains authorization cards from a sizeable number of the employees, the union may ask the employer to recognize it as the exclusive representative for the bargaining unit. If the employer refuses to recognize the union voluntarily, the union may then petition the NLRB for an election. If the union has authorization cards from 30% or more of the employees, the regional office of the NLRB will normally order an election. The election will be supervised by the NLRB. If the union obtains more than 50% of the workers' votes at the election, then it will be designated by the NLRB as the recognized union for that bargaining unit.

Often the question of what constitutes a bargaining unit is complex. To be a bargaining unit, the employees must share a community of interest. For example, attorneys and janitors would not be in the same bargaining unit. Nor would truck drivers and payroll clerks be considered to share a community of interest. Generally, security guards cannot be of the same bargaining unit as other employees because the security guards are required to protect company property, which includes preventing other employees from stealing from the company. Confidential employees and managers may not be in the same bargaining unit as other employees. Confidential employees are employees who work so closely with executives of the company that it would be unfair to allow them to participate in a union with other employees. For example, the personal secretary to the CEO would be considered as a confidential employee.

Once the NLRB has excluded managerial and confidential employees, the board then looks at various criteria to determine which employees should be considered as one bargaining unit. To be a bargaining unit, there must be a "community of interest" among the employees. The criteria used to determine if there is a community of interest include the following:

- Are the employees roughly equal in pay and benefits, and the methods of computing both? For example, employees paid on a commission would not normally be grouped with employees who are paid hourly wages.
- Do the employees have similar total hours per week and type of work?
- Are similar skills and training required by the employees?
- Is there a previous bargaining history of the employees?

**DO GRADUATE STUDENTS HAVE THE RIGHT
TO ORGANIZE A LABOR UNION?**

The University of Illinois graduate students attempted to organize a
labor union. A state labor relations board said that the graduate students did not have the right to form a labor union. An Illinois Court of
Appeals for the First District overruled the board's decision. The court
said that the board had wrongly qualified students' jobs as teaching
assistants and research assistants as "financial aid." The court held that
the proper test to determine if the students should be excluded from
organizing is whether or not the students' jobs are so closely related to
their own academic roles that collective bargaining would be detrimental to the educational process.[3]

Employers and Employee Rights

The NLRA guarantees employees the right to talk among themselves about
forming a union, to hand out union literature, and to join a union. Employees
may urge other employees to sign authorization cards or join the union.

The employer may restrict organizing discussions if the discussions
interfere with discipline or production. For example, a worker has no right to
leave his or her assigned duties during working hours to discuss union activities with other employees. An employer may tell employees why it thinks that
union membership would not be beneficial to the employees. The employer's
efforts must be limited to explanation and advocacy. While the employer
may vigorously present anti-union views to its employees, the employer may
not use threats or promise of benefits to defeat a union organizing effort. For
example, it would be an ULP for an employer to promise a pay raise if the
union organizing efforts are voted down.

Bargaining Subjects

The general goal of collective bargaining is to obtain a labor contract between
the employer and the union containing benefits for the employees. The labor
contract is also known as a collective bargaining agreement. A frequent
question is what issues are employers required to bargain with the union
about. First, almost any issues can be the subject of collecting bargaining, but
employers are only required to bargain on mandatory issues. Generally, the
mandatory issues are wages, benefits, work rules, working hours, and conditions of employment. Nonmandatory issues include product design, advertising, sales, financing, corporate organization, and location of employment

facilities. Employers are not required to bargain over the issue of closing a plant, but may be required to bargain with the union on the effects of the closing. In one case, the Boeing Company of Seattle started subcontracting out its work. The union contended that this was a mandatory bargaining issue. The court held that while Boeing had a right to increase its subcontracting, that the issue was subject to mandatory bargaining.[4]

The union and the employer generally will seek to insert in the collective bargaining agreement clauses that make their positions more secure. For example, the employer may insist on a "no strike" agreement in the contract. This means that during the course of the labor contract that the union will not strike. In return, the union usually insists on a "no lockout" clause, which means that the employer will not prevent union members from working during a labor dispute. No strike/no lockout clauses are legal.

"Hot cargo clauses" are illegal and may not be the subject of bargaining. A hot cargo clause is one where the employer agrees not to do business with a specific company. For example, if the union is having problems with one company, the union may not bargain with other companies not to conduct business with the company involved in the dispute.

While both the union and the employer have a right and a duty to bargain in good faith and with an open mind, they are not obligated to reach an agreement. As long as both sides make a reasonable effort to reach an agreement, they have complied with the requirements to bargain. If the employer rejects a union demand for financial reasons, the employer must allow the union to inspect its books.

When it is clear that an agreement cannot be reached, a "bargaining to impasse" results. Once an impasse results, then the employer may implement new policies or change wages, hours, or terms of employment. The employer in implementing the new terms may only implement terms that were proposed during the collective bargaining. For example, Major League Baseball's agreement with the major league baseball players expired in December 1993. The players and owners bargained throughout the first eight months of 1994 and failed to reach an agreement. In August 1994, the players struck, thus ending the season. The owners and the union continued to bargain until December 1994, at which time the owners unilaterally imposed a salary cap and changed the aspects of "free agency." In 1995, a federal court ruled that the owners had violated the NLRA by imposing new rules concerning mandatory subjects. The owners were then required to restore the original contract and the players returned to the playing field.[5] Later, a collective bargaining agreement was reached between the owners and the players.

Most collective bargaining agreements have provisions for the enforcement of the terms of the agreement. In most cases, the employer or the union must enforce the agreement through the grievance-arbitration process. Once an arbitrator issues a ruling, the ruling may then be enforced in a court action. The courts will generally refuse to enforce an arbitrator's award only when it is contrary to public policy.

Right-to-Work Laws and Unions

The NLRA prohibits unions from bargaining for a closed shop. A closed union shop is one where the employer must hire only union members. The NLRA provides that states may prohibit certain union security agreements that are otherwise valid under federal law. Union security agreements that may be prohibited by state law include those agreements known as union or agency agreements. In most states, the union and the employer may agree on "union" or "agency" shops. A union shop is one where membership in the union is required. In a union shop, the employer retains the right to hire anyone, but all new hires must then join the union. Generally, the new employee has a period of time, about 30 days, before union membership is required. If the new employee objects to union membership for personal, religious, or political reasons, the employee is not required to join the union, but must pay dues. An agency shop is one where the new employee is not required to join the union, but he or she must pay union dues. Some states, especially in the South, have right-to-work laws, which means that union and agency shops are illegal.

MICHIGAN'S RIGHT-TO-WORK LAW

What right-to-work laws really are about is giving you the right to work for less money.

President Obama in a public speech at the Daimler Detroit Diesel plant in Redford, Michigan, on December 10, 2012

The term *right to work* (RTW) is a misnomer. RTW does not regulate the right of a person to seek and accept gainful employment. RTW laws prohibit a labor union and employer from negotiating union security clauses. Union security clauses are contract provisions that address the collection of union dues. In non-RTW states, such as Michigan, the parties are free to negotiate a range of union security options. Unions typically prefer "union shop" terms that require every person benefiting from union representation to pay union dues. Supporters of right-to-work laws contend that RTW helps attract more businesses to a state.

On December 11, 2012, Michigan enacted its right-to-work laws for both private sector and public sector employers. The laws make it unlawful to require an employee to become a union member or to pay union dues or fees as a condition of employment. Michigan, which at one time was considered as the birthplace of the modern labor movement, has become a so-called right-to-work state. It was in Flint, Michigan, where workers sat down in a General Motors plant in the late 1930s and emboldened the industrial labor movement that many individuals claim gave birth to the American middle class. The state was also the birthplace of the United Auto Workers. As of January 2013, 23 states had right-to-work laws on the books, along with some other states—mostly in the Northeast—where such laws were being considered by state legislatures.

SHOULD PUBLIC EMPLOYEES HAVE A RIGHT TO COLLECTIVE BARGAINING?

Wisconsin may not be a right-to-work state, but a controversial 2011 Wisconsin law (Act 10) severely restricted the power of state public-sector unions and led to a failed attempt to recall Governor Scott Walker. (Note: Act 10 does not apply to "public safety employees."[6])

Act 10, as the state law is known, denies state public workers the right to collectively bargain on all issues except base wages, bans employers from automatically deducting union dues from workers' paychecks, and makes it tough to recertify a union. Mary Bell, president of the Wisconsin Education Association Counsel (WEAC), stated: "Wisconsin educators are extremely disappointed with the appeals court ruling. Act 10 is a ploy to eliminate workers' rights to have a voice through their union—political payback for citizens who didn't endorse the governor." The WEAC was one of the plaintiffs in this case. Governor Walker disagreed and stated: "[The] court ruling is a victory for Wisconsin taxpayers. The provisions contained in Act 10, which have been upheld in federal court, were vital in balancing Wisconsin's $3.6 billion budget deficit without increasing taxes, without massive public employee layoffs, and without cuts to programs like Medicaid."[7]

Should state employees have the right to collectively bargain about their working conditions?

Concerted Action

Concerted action is a phrase that refers to tactics that union members take in unison in order to obtain a bargaining advantage. Many types of concerted actions are illegal. The two most common concerted actions are strikes and picketing. The NLRA guarantees employees the right to peacefully strike subject to some limitations. For example, a union may not violate a valid no-strike clause. It is permissible for a union, absent a no-strike clause, to call a strike to put economic pressure on an employer to engage in collective bargaining. In most states, public employees are prohibited from striking.

There is no protection for violent strikes. Unless prohibited by contract, the union may use partial strikes to exert pressure on an employer. A partial strike is where the union strikes part of the company or for certain periods of time. A partial strike may be very disruptive to an employer.

Generally, the employer has the right to hire replacement workers during a strike involving economic issues, e.g., wages, benefits, and working hours. And after the strike is settled, the employer generally has no duty to lay off the replacement worker in order to provide a position for a returning striker. After an economic strike, an employer who hires workers back may not discriminate against the workers who participated in the strike. If the strike is caused by an ULP by the employer, the employer is required to rehire the worker and may be required to dismiss the replacement worker.

Unions may generally picket the employer's work site as long as the picketing is peaceful. A secondary boycott is illegal. A secondary boycott is a picket line establish against a company that does business with the employer involved in the labor dispute. For example, the union is involved in a labor dispute with a shoe company. It is illegal for the union to picket a trucking company that has a contract with the shoe company.

A *lockout* refers to the situation where management locks the workers off from their jobs. Generally, a defensive lockout is legal. For example, the company locks out the employees during a labor dispute because the company has reason to believe that the union members, when admitted to the job site, will conduct a sit-down strike. An offensive lockout is generally illegal unless the parties have reached an impasse in the collective bargaining.

Union Affairs

When a union is selected as the exclusive bargaining power for a group of employees, the union has a duty to treat each employee fairly. The duty of fair representation requires that a union represent all members fairly, impartially, and in good faith. The union may not favor some employees over others. In addition, a union may not discriminate against a member based on race, sex, national origin, religion, etc. A union may discipline a member for violation of valid union rules, such as engaging in an illegal strike or sit-down. The union may not discipline a member for criticizing union officials, for protected speech, or for attempting to replace union leadership through valid elections.

Fair Labor Standards Act

The Fair Labor Standards Act (FLSA), enacted in 1938, regulates wages and restricts child labor. The act requires time-and-a-half pay for nonexempt employees who work more than 40 hours per week. The act does not limit the number of hours that adult employees can be forced to work, only that those hours worked in excess of 40 hours per week must be paid overtime pay.

The wage provisions of the act do not apply to "exempt employees," i.e., managerial, administrative, or professional employees. Employers are free to require exempt employees to work more than 40 hours per week without having to pay time-and-a-half. For example, most law firms work their new associate attorneys far longer than 40 hours per week without any additional pay.

The FLSA prohibits "excessive child labor." Most states have extensive statutes that regulate the hours and types of labor that children under 16 may be worked. Generally, children under the age of 14 may be employed only in agriculture and entertainment. Children under 16 years of age are generally permitted to work only limited hours and only during nonschool time. Children are also generally restricted from working in hazardous jobs.

The Supreme Court has stated that state employees are not covered by the FLSA. The Court held that if a state has not waived its immunity, it cannot be sued in federal court unless there is (a) an express statement of intent by Congress and (b) a valid exercise of power under the Fourteenth Amendment. Congress cannot revoke states' immunity when the statute is based on the Commerce Clause.[8] The act was passed under the authority granted Congress by the Commerce Clause and thus is subject to the restrictions of the Eleventh Amendment.

THE TRIANGLE SHIRTWAIST FIRE, MARCH 25, 1911

At 4:45 p.m. on that Saturday afternoon, the workday was over for about 275 girls who worked for the Triangle Shirtwaist Company in lower Manhattan, City of New York. The young girls worked on the 8th, 9th, and 10th floors making $6 a week assembling women's tailored shirts. As the girls were gathering their belongings and putting on their coats, someone yelled "Fire!" The fire quickly raced out of control. The foreman and male tailors attempted to douse it with water buckets. The 275 girls panicked in desperation and attempted to take the two passenger elevators and the stairways at one end of the loft. Unfortunately, the doors to the stairways opened in rather than out, and the crush of young women at the door slammed them shut. In addition, the doors to the stairways on the 9th floor were locked. The elevator operators of the two elevators brought the elevators to the 8th floor, and the girls tried frantically to get on. The elevators held only 10. The cars made several trips to bring a few havoc-stricken passengers down to street level. Finally, the girls on the 8th floor were able to open the doors at the stairways, and many raced to safety down the stairs, many with clothes almost completely burned from their bodies. Many girls tried to jump to safety. The firemen held blankets and attempted to catch them. Most were unsuccessful.

People on the street noticed the fire. They then saw what they assumed were bolts of cloth flying out the windows. One bystander remarked that Isaac Harris, the owner, was trying to save his best material. As the objects hit the ground, the crowd realized that it was not bolts of cloth, but bodies that were hitting the ground.

When Fire Engine Company 72 arrived (from 6 blocks away), they had trouble maneuvering their hose wagon because of the bodies lying in the street. A total of 146 young girls died in the fire. Most of the casualties were found on the 9th floor, and a considerable portion of those who had jumped also came from the 9th floor. Firemen later found 25 charred bodies on top of the elevator cars and 19 dead bodies melted against the locked doors on the 9th floor.

The origin of the fire is in question. Many think that it was started by one of the male tailors who was smoking and threw his cigarette onto the clutter-filled floor. The owners, Isaac Harris and Max Blanck, were acquitted of any wrongdoing, specifically regarding whether the doors on the west side were locked or not. Twenty-three families sued Harris and Blanck. The families recovered $75 each. As a result of the fire, the New York legislature created a commission headed by Senator Robert F. Wagner, Alfred E. Smith, and Samuel Gompers to investigate the conditions in the city's sweatshops. The investigation resulted in the present labor laws protecting factory workers in health, disability, and fire prevention. Now all factory doors are required to open outward, no doors are to be locked during working hours, and if there are more than 25 employees, sprinkler systems must be installed. The building still stands and is now part of New York University.[9]

Discrimination

The primary basis of present-day legislation on employment discrimination is Title VII of the Civil Rights Act of 1964, as amended by later statutes. As a general rule, an employer may not discriminate against employees because of sex, race, national origin, color, or religion. In addition, there are also restrictions on discrimination based on age if the employee is 40 years of age or older. The first employment discrimination statute passed by the U.S. Congress was the Equal Pay Act of 1963. That act required that women receive equal pay based on equal or similar duty assignments. A year later, in 1964, the Civil Rights Act was passed. Both statutes were based on the Commerce Clause of the Constitution and therefore do not apply to situations not involving or affecting interstate commerce. All states, however, have their own equal employment opportunity laws to protect employees in those limited situations not covered by federal law. The Americans with Disabilities Act was passed in 1990. That act prohibits discrimination against individuals with disabilities.

Equal Employment Opportunity Commission

The Civil Rights Act of 1964 established the Equal Employment Opportunity Commission (EEOC). Its basic purpose is to administer and enforce Title VII of the Civil Rights Act. The commission is composed of five members, not more than three of whom may be from the same political party. Any employee who feels that he or she has been illegally discriminated against may file a complaint with a local office of the EEOC. The local office generally will conduct an investigation and make a recommendation as to whether relief is needed. The EEOC may file a suit or may give the employee a "right to sue" letter so that the employee may file a court action. There is also a general counsel who is responsible for the conduct of all litigation involving discrimination issues.

Pregnancy

The U.S. Supreme Court, in *General Electric Co. v. Gilbert*,[10] decided that discrimination based on the fact of pregnancy was not included under the protection against sexual bias. Now, however, firing a woman who is pregnant may be a form of sexual discrimination under the Pregnancy Discrimination Act of 1978. Even requiring a pregnant woman to take a leave of absence in the last 2 months of her pregnancy may be a form of sexual discrimination, since the physical strain of the pregnancy varies from woman to woman and with the type of employment involved. Establishing definite time periods when a pregnant woman must take a leave of absence is frowned on by the courts. The general rule is to allow the woman and her doctor to decide when during the course of pregnancy it would be best for her to stop working and when it would be safe for her return to work. The act requires employers to treat pregnancy and medical problems related to illnesses on an equal basis with all other medical conditions.

Age Discrimination

The 1967 Age Discrimination Act is the basic protection that employees over the age of 40 years have against discrimination based on their age. The act also protects workers against mandatory retirement in most occupations. An employer may not force an employee to retire before the employee reaches 70 years of age except in cases based on safety considerations and in the case of certain executives who will receive more than a set amount in retirement. Except for the fact that, in some cases, an employee may be forced to retire, employees over the age of 70 are still protected against employment discrimination because of their age.

Reverse Discrimination

The Civil Rights Act protects not only minority groups, but all groups in the protected categories from illegal employment discrimination. For example, in the *McDonald v. Santa Fe Trail Transportation* case,[11] three employees—one black and two white—were accused of stealing merchandise from a shipment. The employer fired the two white employees and not the black employee. The Court found that, since all three were equally involved, firing the white employees and not the black employee was discriminatory toward the discharged white employees. Presently, there is an issue over whether affirmative action programs should be permitted. Affirmative action programs are designed to give minorities a preference based on the concept of affirmative action to make up for past discrimination. One affirmative action issue that has not been finally decided by the courts is whether admission programs in institutions of higher education may consider race in any manner in deciding which students to admit.

EMPLOYEES' EMAIL

Laurie Restuccia and Neil LoRe worked for Burk Technologies, a Boston-area electronics manufacturer. They thought that their email at the company was private. Each had their own passwords to get into the system, and the company never warned them that their emails could be monitored. They did not know that the company maintained a backup system that allowed the company to retrieve messages that employees thought were deleted. A supervisor using a supervisor's password accessed their email and discovered an extensive collection of movie reviews, travel plans, artwork, and office gossip. The personal email between the two employees totaled 40 full pages over a 4-month period. The company fired both employees.

The two employees sued the company for a violation of their right of privacy. After a 2-week jury trial, the jury ruled that any privacy interest the employees may have had was outweighed by the company's interest in monitoring their productivity. One point stressed by the company in defense of the suit was that unlike regular mail, which is transmitted directly from person to person, email involved a middleman, the employer's computer network. The company contended that sending an email isn't like sending a letter in a sealed envelope; it is more like posting a note on someone's desk in plain view.[12]

Workers' Compensation

Workers' compensation plans are designed to ensure that workers receive payment for injuries incurred at work. All states have some form of workers' compensation statutes. Prior to workers' compensation, if an employee was injured on the job, he or she was required to sue the employer to get any recovery. If the worker was at fault in any manner, generally the worker could not recover. Workers' compensation is a form of insurance to protect both employers and employees. Generally, employers are protected because of the protections against being sued for an employee's injuries. Employees are protected in that if they are injured in a work-related incident, they receive medical repayments and a percentage of their wages during the period of recovery. The payments received by a worker under the workers' compensation programs will be less than would generally be received in an award by court, but the worker trades that for the certainty of recovery. The payments are funded either by the employer buying private insurance or by a special tax imposed on employers.

CAN A WORKER DEMAND THAT A COWORKER BE PRESENT AT A DISCIPLINARY MEETING?

The NLRB has ruled that workers can demand that a coworker be present at a disciplinary meeting and that the coworker does not need to be a union member. Accordingly, an employer who fires or disciplines an employee for refusing to meet alone may be guilty of an unfair labor practice and may be required to reinstate an employee with back pay. The case involved two employees at an epilepsy foundation who were involved with a project about teenagers with epilepsy. One of the employees wrote a memo stating that their supervisor was no longer needed on the project. The executive director told one of the employees that she wanted to meet with him and the supervisor. The employee requested the presence of another worker, stating that he felt intimidated by the supervisor. The director refused the request and fired the employee.[13]

Questions in Review

1. When do employees have the right to strike?
2. Explain the meaning of an impasse.
3. Explain the effects of the Industrial Revolutions on labor law.
4. What effect did the Sherman Act have on the rights of employees to organize?
5. What facts support the statement that the NLRA was the most important piece of labor legislation passed by the federal government?
6. What is the present national labor policy regarding the right to collective bargaining?
7. What constitutes collective bargaining?
8. What are the purposes and functions of the NLRB?
9. What are the purposes and functions of the EEOC?
10. Explain the concept of federal preemption.

Endnotes

1. New York State Department of Labor. (n.d.). *Employment laws known as labor standards*. Retrieved July 2, 2013, from http://www.labor.state.ny.us/workerprotection/laborstandards/labor_standards.shtm
2. *Commonwealth v. Hunt*, 45 Mass.111 (1842).
3. *Lawyers Weekly USA*. (2000, August 7). 2000 LWUSA 701.
4. Boeing strike is over outside work. (1995, October 14). *New York Times*, p. 7.
5. *Silverman v. Major League Baseball Player Relations Committee*, 1995 U.S. App. LEXIS 8163 (2d Cir. 1995).
6. *Wisconsin Education Association Council et al. v. Walker et al.*, 7th U.S. Circuit Court of Appeals, Nos. 12-1854, 12-2011, and 12-2058 (decided January 21, 2013).
7. J. Beck. (2013, January 21). *7th Circuit upholds constitutionality of controversial Wisconsin union law*. Retrieved July 2, 2013, from http://www.insidecounsel.com/2013/01/21/7th-circuit-upholds-constitutionality-of-controver
8. *Seminole Tribe of Florida v. Florida*, 517 U.S. 44 (1996), and *Alden v. Maine*, No. 98-436, June 23, 1999, as reported in *Lawyers Weekly USA*, 9916003.
9. P. Rosa. (n.d.). *The Triangle Shirtwaist fire*. Retrieved July 2, 2013, from www.historybuff.com/library/refshirtwaist.html

10. 429 U.S. 125 (1976)
11. 427 U.S. 273 (1976)
12. *Lawyers Weekly USA*. (2000, February 21). 2000 LWUSA 176.
13. *Lawyers Weekly USA*. (2000, August 7). 2000 LWUSA 689.

Index

A

Arbitrators, selecting, 209–210
Abortion, 10, 278. *See also Roe v. Wade*
Adams, Abigail, 228
Adams, John, 33
Administrative law, 25, 103–104, 151
    executive orders; *see* Executive orders
    formal, 177
    informal, 177, 178
    overview, 177
    proclamations, 181, 182–183
Administrative orders, 104
Affirmative action, 321
Age discrimination, 321
Agnew, Spiro, 142
Alger, Horatio, 50
Alito, Jr., Samuel Anthony, 192
Alternative dispute resolution (ADR), 200,
    204–205
Amar, Akhil, 259
American Civil Liberties Union (ACLU),
    219
American Indian law, 39–40
American Revolution, 32
Americans with Disabilities Act (ADA), 27,
    295
Anonymous remailers, 268–269
Anthony, Susan B., 153
Antiwar movement, 226–228
Appellate courts, 132, 163
Aquinas, Thomas, 42–43
Arbitration, 203, 205–206, 206–208. *See*
    also International arbitration
Association, freedom of, 154
Aubert, Vilhelm, 3
Austin, John, 4, 5

B

Baby M. case, 9
Barenblatt v. United States, 174
Becker, Howard S., 142
Behavior, social, 1

expectations, 138
predictability, 138
social controls, relationship between,
    138
Bentham, Jeremy, 216
Big Brother, 106
Bills, path to law, 122–124
Bishop, R. Roak, 211
Black, Donald, 6, 54–55, 145, 204
Blackstone, William, 41, 42
Bledsoe, Charles, 217
Blumberg, Abraham, 235
Bolshevik Revolution, 38
Bond, Julian, 106
Brady Campaign to Prevent Gun Violence,
    89
Brennan, William J, 217
Breyer, Stephen, 191
Brown III, 219
Brown v. Board of Education, 15, 215, 218,
    220–221
Brown, Oliver, 218
Burden of proof, 65
Burger, Warren, 205
Burnett, McKinley, 217
Bush, George H.W., 191
Bush, George W., 190, 192
Byrd, James, 294

C

Capital punishment. *See* Death penalty
Cardozo, Benjamin, 6–7, 24, 48, 50, 56
Carroll, Lewis, 48
Carter, Jimmy, 191
Case law, 27, 103
Catholics in early America, 34
Cause-and-effect method, 67
Centers for Disease Control and Prevention,
    27
Chambliss, William, 19
Child abuse and neglect, 66
Church Arsons Prevention Act, 293

Citations, 164
Civil commitment, 150–151
Civil disobedience, 152–154
Civil law system, 12, 13, 104, 105
    depositions, 112–113
    historical roots of, 100
    interrogatories, 112
    proceedings, flow of litigation, 111–114
    spread of, 35–36
    statutory principles of, 58
Civil Rights Act, 226
Civil rights movement, 226
Civil War, 143
Clinton, Bill, 174, 176–177, 191, 293
Code, U.S., 102, 162–163, 178, 195
Collective bargaining, 313–315
Common law system, 15
    basis of, 100
    Canada, 31
    consequences of, 37
    England, 31
    historical development, 31, 34, 36–37
    overview, 31
    principles of, 58
    U.S., 31
    usage, 31
Communism, 39. See also Socialist law
Community Mental Health Centers Act, 71
Community-based corrections, 130–131
Community-of-saints parable, 48
Computer Fraud and Abuse Act, 265–266
Conduct, rules of, 24
Confidentiality, client, 148
Conflict paradigm, 19
Conflict resolution, 7
    delinquency, use in; see under
        Delinquency
Congress, U.S., 118–121, 127
    function of, 166
Congressional Record, 119
Consensus paradigm, 18–19
Constitution, U.S., 98, 99, 101, 102, 109, 118,
        119, 120, 129, 132, 170, 223
    law, as source of, 160
Constitutional law, 13–14, 101–102
Constitutional rights, 152
Contract law, 152
Corpus Juris Civilis (Body of Civil Law), 36
Correctional institutions, 129–130
    prison population, 303–304
    private prisons, 304–305
Corrections, community-based, 130–131

Counsel, right to, 290
Counsel, role in legal process, 107–108
Court administrators, 110–111
Court system
    appellate, 94
    federal courts, 94, 97–99
    jurisdiction, 94–95, 96
    limited and specific jurisdiction, 96
    overview, 94
    small-claims court, 95
    state court of appeal, 96–97
    state courts, 94, 95–96
    Supreme Court, U.S.; see Supreme
        Court, U.S.
    U.S. courts of appeals, 98
    U.S. district courts, 97–98
    unification movements, 99
Courthouse work groups, 237–238
Crime Victims with Disabilities Act,
        296–297
Crime, victimless. See Victimless crime
Criminal justice, 87
Criminal law system, 12–13, 104, 105
    defining crime, 146
    objectives, 146
    proceedings, flow of, 114–117
Critical legal studies movement, 60
Critical race theory, 57–58, 60
Cruel and unusual punishment, 290–291
Cultural insanity defense, 10
Culture, definition of, 139
Cultures, professional, 3
Customs, 24

D

Davis, Noy, 66
De Montesquieu, Baron, 43–44
De Secondat, Charles Louis, 43–44
Death penalty, 10
    decline in use, 302–303
    history of use, 302–303
    overview, 301
Declaration of Paris, 211
Defense of Marriage Act, 229
Delinquency, 145
    conflict resolution for, 210–211
    peer mediation, use of; see Peer
        mediation
Dependency Court Intervention Program
        for Family Violence, 86
Dependent variables, 65

Depositions, 112–113
Depression, Great, 309
Dershowitz, Alan, 231
Deviance, 142
Disabled persons, crimes against, 295–297
Discrimination, 319–320, 321
Dispute resolution, 7
    adjudicated settlement, 202
    alternative; *see* Alternative dispute
        resolution (ADR)
    arbitration; *see* Arbitration
    hierarchy of resolution types, 203
    mediation; *see* Mediation
    private, 201
    process, 200–201
    third-party intervention, 202
DNA testing, 83–84
Double jeopardy, 289
Durkheim, Emile, 47, 48
Dworkin, R. M., 5, 24

E

*Eastern Associated Coal Co. v. United Mine
        Workers,* 209
Ehrlick, Eugen, 20
Eighth Amendment, 290–291
Eisenhower, Dwight D., 219
Electronic Communications Privacy Act
        (ECPA), 265
Electronic crime. *See also* Worm, Internet
    growth in, 269, 270
    importance of combatting, 271–277
    methodology, 270–271
Empirical justice, 46
Employment Agency Law, 308
Encryption, 268
Equal Employment Opportunity
        Commission, 320
Equal Rights Amendment (ERA), 228–229
Equivalent time-samples design, 72
Ethnocentrism, 139, 140
Euthanasia, 222–223
Exclusionary rule, 286–288
Executive orders, 13, 181, 183–187
Experimental designs
    classic, 68–69
    overview, 67–68
    posttest-only control-group design;
        see Posttest-only control-group
        design
    quasi-experimental designs, 70, 71–72

Solomon four-group designs; *see*
        Solomon four-group designs
Experimental method, 67–68
External validity, 66
Extradition, 22

F

Fair Labor Standards Act (FLSA), 318
Family feuds, 202
Federal Administrative Procedure Act of
        1946 (APA), 177, 178, 179
Federal Elections Commission (FEC), 195
Feminism, 56, 60
Feminist legal theories, 56–57, 60
Fifth Amendment, 258, 289–290
First Amendment, 257, 258, 259
Folkways, 139
Formal irrationality, 46
Formal rationality, 46
Fourteenth Amendment, 223
Fourth Amendment, 258, 286, 288
Frank, Jerome, 52, 56
Freedom of Information Act (FOIA),
        261–264
Friedman, Lawrence M., 19, 22, 23, 250
Furman v. Georgia, 291

G

Gamble, Blaine, case of, 10
Gambling, 149
Gandhi, Mohandas K., 153–154
Gay marriage, 10
Gay rights. *See* Sexual minorities movement
General Accounting Office (GAO), 178
General Business Law, 308
Gilley, Bruce, 21
Gilmer v. Interstate/Johnson Lane Corp., 207
Ginsberg, Ruth Bader, 191
Gluckman, Max, 52–53
Goldman, Ronald, 13, 105
Gompers, Samuel, 319
Graham, Hugh, 229
Grand jury, 110
Gregg v. Georgia, 291
Griswold v. Connecticut, 258
Group-influence model, 165
Gun control, 88–89

H

Hadith, 38
Halpin, Brendan, 76
Hansen, Chris, 220
Hate crimes, 292–294
Hate Crimes Prevention Act (HCPA), 293, 294
Hatfields and McCoys, 202
Henderson, Russell, 294
Henley, Madeline, 67
Hidden harmony myth, 201
Hochsprung, Dawn Lafferty, 88
Holmes, Oliver Wendell, 34, 48, 51, 232
Homeland Security, Department of, 128
Horn, Michael S., 21
Humanity, crimes against, 21–22
Hume, David, 20
Hypothesis, 66

I

Impeachment, articles of, 174–176
Inculation, 143
Independent variables, 66
Individual rights, 152
Industrial Revolution, 307
Internal Revenue Service, 11
Internal validity, 66
International arbitration, 211–212
International law, 22
Interrogatories, 112
Interstate Stalking Punishment and
    Prevention Act, 298–299
Islam, 15, 38
Islamic legal systems, 15, 25
    principles, 38
    sanctions for violations, 38

J

Jefferson, Thomas, 32
Jesus Christ, 153, 301
Jews, in early America, 34
Johnson, Andrew, 174, 175
Johnson, Lyndon, 228
Judges, role in legal process, 108–109
Jury, grand. See Grand jury
Jury, trial by, 37, 109–110
Justice system. See also Court system
    administration of, 46
    complexity of, 87

criminal; see Criminal justice
    social, 87, 88
Justinian Code, 36
Juvenile justice code, 164

K

Kagan, Elena, 192
Kahdi justice, 46
Katz v. United States, 258
Kennedy, John F., 226
Kennedy, Robert, 228
Kennedy. Anthony M., 190
Kent State University shootings, 228
Kevorkian, Jack, 222, 223
King, Jr., Martin Luther, 226
Kohlberg, Lawrence, 143
Koran, 38
Kornhauser, Lewis, 205
Kovandzic, Tomislav, 71

L

Labor law. See also Collective bargaining
    concerted actions, 316–317
    government policies, 308–309
    labor standards, 308
    National Labor Relations Act (NLRA),
        309–311, 315, 316
    overview, 307–308
    unions, labor; see Unions, labor
Laboratory method, 67
Lanza, Adam, 88
Lanza, Nancy, 88
Law. See also Law and society; Lawmaking;
        Legal rules; Legal systems
    constitutional; see Constitutional law
    defining, 4–7, 23
    development, stages of, 49
    morality, relationship between; see
        Morality and the law
    norms, study of, 3
    paradox of, 2
    Pound's conceptions of, 49–50
    pressures on, outside, 10
    science, relationship between, 64–65
    social needs, relationship between, 2
    sociology of, 2, 3
    win or lose nature of, 4
Law and society. See also Lawmaking
    description of, 2
    norms, 2

problems of, 22
theories of; *see specific theories and*
    theorists
Law enforcement, federal, 127–128
Law enforcement, local, 127
Law enforcement, state, 127
Law schools, 234–235
Law, rule of, 20–22
Lawmaking, 117–118
    conflict perspective, 166
    functionalist view, 165
    group-influence model, 165
    judicial, 187–188
    legislative; *see* Legislative lawmaking
    precedent, by, 189–190
Lawyers
    advertising, 239–241, 241–243
    advocate role, 4
    American view of, 231–232
    clients, duties to, 244–246
    conflicts of interest, 238, 239
    courthouse work groups, 237–238
    development of profession, 232–233
    ethical standards, 238, 239, 250
    fields of practice, 243
    hiring, 236
    history of profession in the United
        States, 232–233
    Internet use by, 243–244
    malpractice, 238
    origin of profession, 232
    others, duties to, 247–248
    private practice, 239
    rights of the client, 246–247
    solicitation of clients, 243
    trial publicity, 239
Legal positivism, 43, 59
Legal realism, 51
Legal rules. *See also* Law; Legal systems
    civil laws; *see* Civil law system
    common law system; *see* Common law
        system
    criminal laws; *see* Criminal law system
    procedural, 12
    socialist law; *see* Socialist law
    substantive, 12
Legal systems. *See also* Lawmaking; Legal
        rules
    civil laws; *see* Civil law system
    common law; *see* Common law system
    defining, 23
    dysfunctional aspects of, 9–10

enforcement, 8
Islamic legal systems; *see* Islamic legal
    systems
role of, 7–9
social engineering aspect of, 7–8
status quo, perpetuation of, 9
Legislative lawmaking, 15
    committee work, 168–169
    defining, 166
    overview, 166–167
    representation, 167
    role orientation, 169–170
Letelies, Orlando, 22
Levi, Edward, 55
Lewinsky, Monica, 176
Lincoln, Abraham, 204
Litigants, role in legal process, 107
Llewellyn, Karl, 52, 56, 203
Lobbying Disclosure Act, 125
Lobbyists, 124–126, 160

M

Maine, Henry Summer, 44–45
Man, rule of, 20
Mantle v. Upper Deck Co., 209
Marbury v. Madison, 32, 33–34, 58
Marshall, John, 32, 33
Marx, Karl, 45
Marxism, 8, 53, 55, 56
McBoyle v. United States, 51
McCarthy, Eugene, 228
McCarthy, James D., 211
McKinney, Aaron, 294
Mead, William, 34
Measurement, 66
Mechanical societies, 47
Mediation, 202–203, 206
Melloan, George, 21
Memory-protection software, 269
Mental illness, 151
Methodology, 66
Mills, John Stuart, 167
Miranda rights, 14
Miranda v. Arizona, 14
Moffitt, Ronni Karpen, 22
Moral education, 142–143
Moral order, 11
Moral stages, 144
Morality and the law, 11, 12
Mores, 139
Morphology, language, 154–155

Morris, Robert T., 266, 267, 268
Mott, Lucretia Coffin, 228
Murdock, George, 140

N

Nader, Laura, 54, 200
Napoleon, Code of, 36, 37
National Association for the Advancement
    of Colored People (NAACP),
    217–218
National Center on Child Abuse and
    Neglect (NCCAN), 295
National Conference of Commissioners on
    Uniform State Laws, 208
National Labor Relations Act (NLRA),
    309–311, 315, 316
National Organization for Women (NOW),
    228
National Rifle Association (NRA), 10, 89
National Violence Against Women Survey
    (NVAW), 297–298
Natural law, 41–42, 59
New York Convention, 211
Newmark, Lisa, 80
Ninth Amendment, 258
Nixon, Richard, 174, 175–176, 229
Noonan, John T., 235
Norman Conquest, 32, 58
Norms, 138, 139, 140–141, 142, 167
Norris-LaGuardia Act, 309

O

O'Connor, Sandra Day, 205
Obama, Barack, 183, 187, 192, 229, 315
Observation method, 72–73
Occupational Safety and Health Act, 14
Office of Personnel Management (OPM),
    179
Opinions, judicial, 163
Organic societies, 47

P

Palmer, Michael, 200
Parks, Rosa, 153
Parson, Talcott, 19
Participant observation, 73–75
Pasley, Chasity, 294
Peaceable classroom, 211
Peaceable school, 211

Peer mediation, 210–211
Penal code, 35
Penn, William, 34–35
Pinochet, Augusto, 21
Planned Parenthood v. Casey, 280
Plea agreements, 116
Plea bargaining, 291–292
Plessy v. Ferguson, 218, 219
Police Foundation, 68
Policy research, 84–86
Political action committees (PACs),
    195–196
Pornography and the law, 257, 281–282
Positive law, 59
Posner, Richard, 53–54
Positivism, legal, 43, 59
Posttest-only control-group design, 70
Pound, Roscoe, 5, 18, 23, 48, 49–50
Pregnancy discrimination, 320
Pregnancy Discrimination Act, 320
Press, freedom of the, 154
Privacy Act of 1974, 259–261
Privacy, right to, 258–259
Private laws, 25
Private prisons, 304–305. *See also*
    Correctional institutions
Probabilism, 65
Procedural law, 106
Proclamations, 181
Property rights, 24
Proposition 8, 229
Prostitution, 149
Protestants in early America, 34
Publicity, right of, 264
Pulpit Freedom say, 11
Punishment
    changing ideologies regarding, 129
    Durkheim's theories on, 48

Q

Quakers, 34, 35, 153
Qualitative research, 66
Quantitative research, 66
Quinney, Richard, 19

R

Ragan, Ronald, 190
Random assignment, 66
Rational justice
Rawls, John, 53

Realism, legal, 51
Reasonable doubt, 13, 105
Regina v. Dudley and Stephens, 16–18
Reinstein, Ronald S., 83–84
Reliability, 66
Remailers, anonymous, 268–269
Reno, Janet, 269
Representatives, U.S. House of, 118–119, 120
Research. *See also* Survey methods
    archival, 80–81, 82
    experimental designs; *see* Experimental designs
    historical, 80–81, 82
    policy research; *see* Policy research
    scientific method; *see* Scientific method
Reverse discrimination, 321
Right to remain silent, 289–290
Right-to-work laws, 315
Roberts, Jr. John, 190
Roberts, Simon, 200
Robertson, Ian, 140
Roe v. Wade, 229, 258–259, 278–280
Roosevelt, Franklin D., 196
Roshier, Bob, 48
Rousseau, Jean Jacques, 20
Rules, 52

S

Sampling, 66
Sandy Hook Elementary School Shooting, 88–89, 151
Santa Fe Independent School District v. Jane Doe, 224
Scalia, Antonin, 190
Schaeffer, Rebecca, 297
Schafer, Douglas, 148
Schlafly, Phyllis, 229
School prayer, 224
Schur, Edwin, 4
Science and law, relationship between, 64–65
Scientific inquiry, 64
Scientific method, 64
Scott, Charles, 217
Scott, Elisha, 217
Scott, John, 217
Search and seizure, 288–289
Segregation, 218, 219
Self-government, 40
Self-recrimination, 258

Sentencing guidelines, 128–129
Sentencing objectives, 146
Separate but equal, 15, 219, 220
Sexual conduct, 149
Sexual minorities movement, 226, 229–230
Shari'a Court, 46
Shepard, Mathew, 294
Sherman, Lawrence, 68
Simpson, Nicole Brown, 13, 105
Simpson, O.J., 13, 105
Simulation research, 75–76
Sixth Amendment, 109, 290
Slip laws, 161
Smith, Alfred E., 319
Smith, Barbara, 67
Social change
    courts as mechanism for, 217–218, 222–223, 223–224
    defining, 216
    law, relationship between, 224–225225–226
    limitations of law as implement of, 224–225
    public opinion, role of, 224
Social controls, 23
    defining, 137, 139
    external, 137, 143–144
    formal, 142, 144–145
    informal, 139, 142
    internal, 137, 138
    sanctions, use of, 138–139
    social pressures, use of, 138–139
Social engineering, 7–8, 24
Social phenomena, models of, 75
Social rituals, 48
Social solidarity, 47
Socialist law, 15, 25, 38–39
Society, defining, 4
Sociological jurisprudence movement, 48–49
Sociology
    law, of, 22
    norms, study of, 3
Solitary confinement, 129
Solomon four-group designs, 69
Sotomayor, Sonia, 192
Speech, freedom of, 154
Spencer, Herbert, 44
Stalin, Joseph, 39
Stalking, 297–298, 298–299
Stanton, Elizabeth Cady, 228

Starr, Ken, 176
State legislatures, 121–122
Statutes at Large, U.S., 161–162
Statutory law, 25, 27, 102
Street Terrorism Enforcement and
        Prevention (STEP) Acts, 85
Subculture, 139
Substantive irrationality, 46
Substantive law, 106
Substantive rationality, 46
Sumner, Graham, 139, 140
Sunna, 38
Supreme Court, U.S., 14, 15, 32, 33, *See also*
        specific cases
    appointments to, 98
    creation, 98
    jurisdiction, 99
    social change through, 217–218,
        222–223
    writs, 33
Survey methods
    mail surveys, 78–80
    overview, 76–77
    personal interviews, 77–78
    telephone interviews, 78

T

Taboo, 139, 140
Taft-Hartley Act, 207
Term limits, 170
Third Amendment, 258
Thomas, Clarence, 190–191
Thoreau, Henry David, 153
Time-series design, 71
Todd, Harry, 200
Todd, Lucinda, 218
Tort law, 151
Treaties, international, 160–161
Trevino, Javier, 22
Trial by jury, 37
Trial lawyers, 81
Trial, speedy, 290
Triangle Shirtwaist Fire, 318–319
Tribune, 169
Trop v. Dulles, 291
Truth, in law, 3
Twentieth Amendment, 119
Tyler, Tom, 141

U

U.S. Term Limits, Inc., v. Thornton, 514 U.S.
        799, 171–173
Uniform Arbitration Act (UAA), 207
Unions, labor
    concerted actions, 316–317
    exclusivity, 311–312
    federal preemption, 311
    rights to, 313
United States Sentencing Guidelines
        (USSG), 128
United States v. Darbury Lumber Co., 207
United States v. Leon, 286
Unwritten constitution, 259

V

Vagrancy laws, 19
Values, 139
Values clarification, 143
Variables, 65
Veterans Day, 182–183
Victimless crime, 148–149
Victimology, 299–301
Vietnam War, 154, 226, 227, 228
Vitter, David, 170

W

Wagner, Robert F., 319
Wallace, Mike, 222
Warren, Earl, 219
Watergate, 176, 191
Watkins v. United States, 173
Weber, Max, 5, 23, 46–47
Wells, Susan, 66
White-collar crimes, 150
Wilensky, Harold L., 232
William the Conqueror, 58
Wills and trusts, 37–38
Wilson, James Q., 126
Women's movement, 228–229
Worker's compensation, 322
Worm, Internet, 266–268
Writs, 188–189

Y

Youk, Thomas, 222